This book comprises papers examining the latest developments in economic theory given at the Sixth World Congress of the Econometric Society in Barcelona in August 1990. This is the latest in a series of collections which cover the most active fields in economic theory over a five-year period. With papers from the world's leading specialists, this book gives the reader a unique survey of the most recent advances in economic theory.

Econometric Society Monographs No. 20

Advances in economic theory
Sixth World Congress
Volume I

Econometric Society Monographs

The Econometric Society is an international society for the advancement of economic theory in relation to statistics and mathematics. The Econometric Society Monograph Series is designed to promote the publication of original research contributions of high quality in mathematical economics and theoretical and applied econometrics.

Other titles in the series:
Werner Hildenbrand, Editor *Advances in economic theory*
Werner Hildenbrand, Editor *Advances in econometrics*
G. S. Maddala *Limited-dependent and qualitative variables in econometrics*
Gerard Debreu *Mathematical economics*
Jean-Michel Grandmont *Money and value*
Franklin M. Fisher *Disequilibrium foundations of equilibrium economics*
Bezalel Peleg *Game theoretic analysis of voting in committees*
Roger Bowden and Darrell Turkington *Instrumental variables*
Andreu Mas-Colell *The theory of general economic equilibrium*
James J. Heckman and Burton Singer *Longitudinal analysis of labour market data*
Cheng Hsiao *Analysis of panel data*
Truman F. Bewley, Editor *Advances in economic theory – Fifth World Congress*
Truman F. Bewley, Editor *Advances in econometrics – Fifth World Congress* (Volume I)
Truman F. Bewley, Editor *Advances in econometrics – Fifth World Congress* (Volume II)
Hervé Moulin *Axioms of cooperative decision making*
L. G. Godfrey *Misspecification tests in econometrics*
Tony Lancaster *The econometric analysis of transition data*
Wolfgang Härdle *Applied nonparametric regression*
Alvin E. Roth and Marilda A. Oliveira Sotomayor *Two-sided matching*
Jean-Jacques Laffont, Editor *Advances in economic theory – Sixth World Congress* (Volume 1)
Jean-Jacques Laffont, Editor *Advances in economic theory – Sixth World Congress* (Volume 2)
Christopher A. Sims, Editor *Advances in econometrics – Sixth World Congress* (Volume 1)
Christopher A. Sims, Editor *Advances in econometrics – Sixth World Congress* (Volume 2)
Halbert White *Estimation, inference and specification analysis*

Advances in economic theory Sixth World Congress

Volume I

Edited by

JEAN-JACQUES LAFFONT
Universite des Sciences Sociales de Toulouse

CAMBRIDGE UNIVERSITY PRESS
Cambridge, New York, Melbourne, Madrid, Cape Town, Singapore, São Paulo

Cambridge University Press
The Edinburgh Building, Cambridge CB2 2RU, UK

Published in the United States of America by Cambridge University Press, New York

www.cambridge.org
Information on this title: www.cambridge.org/0521416663

First published 1992
First paperback edition 1995

A catalogue record for this publication is available from the British Library

Library of Congress Cataloguing in Publication data

Econometric Society. World Congress (6th: 1990: Barcelona, Spain)
Advances in economic theory: Sixth World Congress / edited by
Jean-Jacques Laffont.
p. cm. – (Econometric Society monographs: no. 20)
ISBN 0 521 41666 3
1. Economics – Congresses. I. Laffont, Jean-Jacques, 1947–
II. Title. III. Series.
HB21.E23 1992
330'.01'5195 – dc20 91–26036 CIP

ISBN-10 0-521-41666-3 hardback
ISBN-10 0-521-48459-6 paperback

Transferred to digital printing 2005

Contents

List of contributors *page* ix

Editor's preface x

Chapter 1 Foundations of game theory 1

Kenneth G. Binmore

Chapter 2 Refinements of Nash equilibrium 32

Eric van Damme

Discussion of "Foundations of game theory," Kenneth G. Binmore, and "Refinements of Nash Equilibrium," Eric van Damme 76

Eddie Dekel

Chapter 3 Explaining cooperation and commitment in repeated games 89

Drew Fudenberg

Chapter 4 Repeated games: cooperation and rationality 132

David G. Pearce

Comments on the interpretation of repeated games theory 175

Ariel Rubinstein

Chapter 5 Implementation, contracts, and renegotiation in environments with complete information 182

John Moore

Chapter 6 Implementation in Bayesian equilibrium: the multiple equilibrium problem in mechanism design 283

Thomas R. Palfrey

Implementation theory: discussion 324

Mathias Dewatripont

Contributors

Kenneth G. Binmore
University College, London

Eric van Damme
Center for Economic Research, Tillburg University

Eddie Dekel
University of California at Berkeley

Drew Fudenberg
Massachusetts Institute of Technology

David G. Pearce
Yale University

Ariel Rubinstein
Tel Aviv University

John Moore
London School of Economics

Thomas R. Palfrey
California Institute of Technology

Mathias Dewatripont
Université Libre de Bruxelles

Editor's preface

This book, *Advances in economic theory – Sixth World Congress* contains invited papers as well as discussions presented at symposia of the Sixth World Congress of the Econometric Society in Barcelona, Spain, August 1990. The topics, the speakers and the discussants were chosen by the Program Committee. The purpose of symposia was to survey important recent developments in economic theory. An accompanying volume in econometrics is edited by Christopher Sims. All manuscripts were received by the end of February 1991.

Jean-Jacques Laffont

Chairman of the Program
Committee for Economic Theory
of the Sixth World Congress
of the Econometric Society.

CHAPTER 1

Foundations of game theory

Kenneth G. Binmore

1 ANTEDILUVIA

Writing on the foundations of game theory is a Herculean task. I don't know which of the labors of Hercules provides the most apt metaphor. It is tempting to cite the Augean stables, which housed three thousand oxen but had not been cleaned for thirty years, but this would imply too harsh a judgment. The nine-headed Hydra, which grew two heads for each that was struck off, would do very well for a piece on refinements of Nash equilibrium, but this task has fallen to Eric van Damme (1990). I shall therefore settle for the wrestling match with the giant Antaeus, although I fear his feet are so firmly entrenched that it would truly take a Hercules to move them.

In brief, I believe the foundations of game theory to be a mess. Much of what we say in defending what we do does not hang together properly. Even when something coherent is on offer, it is hard to find two game theorists who are able to agree on whether it is right. This does not mean that the models game theorists have developed are worthless. As Aumann (1985) put it, while lecturing in Finland:

> the ordinary laws of economic activity apply to our fields as well. The world will not long support us on our say-so alone. We must be doing something right, otherwise we wouldn't find ourselves in this beautiful place today.

I am not sure that I share Aumann's confidence in the laws of economic activity, but I agree that "we must be doing something right," and that it would be folly to abandon the insights that game theory has brought to economics on the grounds that foundational issues remain unresolved. After all, people formulated correct and useful theorems in mathematics long before proper logical foundations for the subject were developed. Why should the same not be true of game theory?

My own view is that the attempt by traditional game theory to treat situations in which it is "common knowledge that the players are perfectly rational" axiomatically à la Bourbaki has got about as far as it can go. A definition-axiom-proof-theorem format closes the mind, the aim being to shut out irrelevancies. But we have perhaps bolted the stable door before the horse has arrived.

The early days of modern mathematical analysis offer an apt analogy. Mathematicians like Euler discovered many wonderful results without agonizing over precisely what real numbers are, or what it means for a series to converge. Sometimes a little agonizing would have been appropriate because sometimes their neglect of foundational issues led them into error. However, their wrong results are now remembered only in history books. Later mathematicians, like Dedekind or Weierstrass, put analysis on a proper basis by showing how real numbers can be constructed from the rationals, and how sentences containing the word "infinity" can often be translated into carefully worded statements in which only finite magnitudes occur. Their approach was therefore *reductionist* or *constructive*. Only later, after their innovations had been thoroughly absorbed by the mathematical community, did coherent *axiomatic* treatments of the concepts become possible.

As regards game theory, too many of our wonderful results are wrong for foundational issues to remain neglected. Nor has the game theory community made the conceptual advances that would tell us what a satisfactory axiomatic foundation for game theory would look like. Perhaps the time has come to embrace the reductionist methodology of Dedekind or Weierstrass wholeheartedly and to stop seeking intellectual short-cuts that are unlikely to be found.

The difficulties ought not to be underestimated. A properly founded game theory would have answers to questions like: What is the self? What do we have in common with others? What does it mean to know something? How do we learn? How should we learn? Right now we do not even know to what extent such questions are meaningful. But genuine progress is unlikely if we continue to regard the problem of scientific induction or the problem of personal identity as difficulties best left to philosophers. Game theorists cannot afford to take the same attitude to such questions as cyclists do to keeping their balance. Cyclists do not need to ask how they sustain their equilibria because they seldom find themselves upended in the ditch at the side of the road. But game theorists are not so fortunate.

For game theory to become a reliable tool, we have to explore the fundamental issues until we know at least what we do not need to know. We can then perhaps agree on methods for evading the issues that are not central to our concerns.

2 AUMANN'S ARK

Herbert Simon (1976) draws a distinction between *substantive rationality* and *procedural rationality*. He comments that economists confine their attention almost exclusively to the former, and psychologists to the latter. It is therefore not surprising that most of what has been written on the foundations of game theory has treated rationality from the substantive viewpoint. This abstracts away the question of *how* rational players reach their conclusions and seeks instead to characterize axiomatically *what* the conclusions must be directly.

The cornerstone of this substantive approach is Bayesian decision theory. Naive Bayesians believe that rationality endows its adherents with the capacity to pluck prior probability assessments from the air. This makes it possible for them to ask, along with Kadane and Larkey (1982), whether there is any point to game theory at all. Why do players not simply maximize expected utility, and, if this behavior is not in equilibrium: so what?

Such a view neglects that what players believe must depend on what they know. In game theory, the players know things about the other players, and this knowledge matters. Only comparatively recently have formal attempts been made to explain how such knowledge manifests itself in the beliefs players hold about the strategic choices to be made by their counterparts in the game. Aumann (1987), Bernheim (1984), Brandenburger and Dekel (1987a, 1987b), Pearce (1984), Reny (1985), Tan and Werlang (1984) are some of the pioneers in this area.

The most conservative of these approaches is Bernheim and Pearce's notion of "rationalizaility." The only restriction placed on beliefs is that it is common knowledge that the players are Bayesian optimizers: that they behave as though maximizing expected utility with respect to a subjective probability distribution. In two-player games, it is an easy consequence of a suitably strong version of Von Neumann's minimax theorem that a strategy is a best reply to something if and only if it is not strongly dominated. "Rationalizability" for such games therefore reduces to the iterated deletion of strongly dominated strategies. Does it therefore follow that game theory is helpless with a game like *Dodo* (figure 1.1) in which no strategies are strongly dominated?

This question will be used as a pretext for some preliminary remarks about knowledge. Something is *common knowledge* if everybody knows it, everybody knows that everybody knows it, and so on. The idea was introduced in this form by Lewis (1969), but Aumann (1976) deserves the major credit for formulating the notion in an operationally useful manner. In a game of complete (or symmetric) information, the rules of the game are assumed to be common knowledge among the players. (Harsanyi's theory of games of incomplete information proceeds by reducing such objects to games of complete information, and so a foundational discussion can confine itself to the latter.) To this must be added what the players know about each other. As regards "rationalizability," one round of deleting strongly dominated strategies is justified by the fact that both players are Bayesian optimizers. Two rounds are justified if both players know this. Three rounds are justified if both know that both know it, and so on.

The rules of the game subsume the payoffs that the players get at each outcome of the game. Orthodox theory holds that such Von Neumann and Morgenstern utilities have no objective reality. They are constructs deduced from an individual's primitive preferences over lotteries along with the subjective probabilities that are taken to describe the individual's beliefs. To sustain the conclusion that nothing can be said about a game beyond the fact that a "rationalizable" strategy will be played, one needs an explanation of how it comes about that the player's utilities are commonly known, but *nothing whatever* is known about their beliefs (beyond those that describe chance moves explicitly modeled in the game).

Aumann's (1987) approach leads to a notion he calls *subjective correlated equilibrium.* (The word "subjective" is intended as a reminder that the players need not have the same prior, although no such examples will be considered here.) Brandenburger and Dekel (1987b) have shown that a payoff pair is sustainable as a subjective correlated equilibrium if and only if it is rationalizable. A study of Aumann's theory will therefore help in locating what is missing from the notion of rationalizability.

The idea of a correlated equilibrium is usually illustrated using the game *Chicken* as in Binmore and Brandenburger (1990). However, it is traditional for authors who write on foundational issues only to propose questions which any fool can answer. Consider, therefore, the game *Dodo* shown on the left of figure 1.1.

	left	*right*
top	2, 2	0, 0
bottom	0, 0	1, 1

	LEFT	RIGHT	
TOP	$\frac{1}{6}$	$\frac{1}{6}$	0
BOTTOM	$\frac{1}{6}$	0	$\frac{1}{6}$
	0	$\frac{1^*}{6}$	$\frac{1^\dagger}{6}$

Figure 1.1 The game Dodo

A random variable chooses one of the cells in the 3×3 matrix given on the right of figure 1.1 with the indicated probabilities. Player I learns only whether the chosen cell is on the TOP row or in one of the two BOTTOM rows. Player II similarly learns that either LEFT or RIGHT has occurred. The players treat their information as an instruction on how to play *Dodo*. For example, if player II learns RIGHT, then she plays *right*. If both believe that the other will play this way, then both will be optimizing by following their instructions. For example, player II optimizes by playing *right* after observing RIGHT because $0 \times \frac{1}{6} + 1 \times \frac{1}{2} > 2 \times \frac{1}{6} + 0 \times \frac{1}{2}$.

The backdrop for the full story is a space Ω representing the players' entire universe of discourse. Each state $\omega \in \Omega$ represents a "possible world." It is important for Aumann that such a state ω be *all-inclusive*. It must specify every relevant detail of the possible world it describes, including how players behave, and what they know or believe in that world. Aumann (1989b) explains that game-theoretic considerations within such a framework are neither normative nor descriptive, but *analytic*. They cannot be normative, because people just "do what they do." To advise the players, the analyst would need to be part of the world in which they dwell: but he is not.

Since this is a Bayesian story, both players have prior probability distributions defined on Ω. (Mertens and Zamir (1985) address some of the technical difficulties that arise in such assertions. Vassilakis and Zamir (1990) develop the theory further.) A state $\omega \in \Omega$ now occurs. Player I observes that event $P_1(\omega)$ and player II observes $P_2(\omega)$. Suppose that player I uses action $b_1(\omega)$ in state ω and player II uses action $b_2(\omega)$. For the analyst to be able to characterize this behavior as Bayesian rational, it is necessary that, for all possible deviations d_1 and d_2:

$$\begin{aligned} \mathscr{E}\{u_1(b_1, b_2) | P_1(\omega)\} &\geq \mathscr{E}\{u_1(d_1, b_2) | P_1(\omega)\} \\ \mathscr{E}\{u_2(b_1, b_2) | P_2(\omega)\} &\geq \mathscr{E}\{u_2(b_1, d_2) | P_2(\omega)\} \end{aligned} \tag{1.1}$$

where $\mathscr{E}\{u_i(s) | E\}$ is player i's expected utility conditional on the observation of E given that the strategy pair s is used.

Now consider the implications of some hypotheses about the rationality and knowledge of the players. Suppose that the players' behavior can be characterized as Bayesian rational in every possible world. Then (2.1) holds for all $\omega \in \Omega$. Suppose also that the players know what they are doing in every possible world. Then, for example, if RIGHT is the subset of Ω in which $b_2(\omega) = right$, then it must be the case that $P_2(\omega) \subseteq \text{RIGHT}$ whenever $b_2(\omega) = right$. Moreover, if P_2 partitions Ω, then it follows that P_2 partitions RIGHT. Thus, (2.1) implies that, for all deviations d_2:

$$\mathscr{E}\{u_2(b_1, b_2) | \text{RIGHT}\} \geq \mathscr{E}\{u_2(b_1, d_2) | \text{RIGHT}\}.$$

Of course, three similar inequalities with LEFT, TOP, and BOTTOM respectively replacing RIGHT also hold. It is this conclusion that Aumann (1987) uses to justify his claim that correlated equilibrium expresses Bayesian rationality in a game-theoretic setting.

Aumann (1989b) does not regard this conclusion as expressing the intuitive ideas behind the original definitions of equilibrium notions. He observes that these are *local* in character since they involve "conscious choices of the players based on their information" and it is "meaningless to speak of a player's information 'in general', without referring to a specific state." The *global* conditions in the preceding discussion were that players are Bayesian rational and that they know what they are doing in *every* state.

To pursue this point, suppose that the players become better informed than in the previous story. Player II now learns, not only whether LEFT or RIGHT has occurred, but the precise column in which the selected cell lies. Player I learns the cell's row. Notice that, if event $*$ occurs, player II will *not* be Bayesian rational. She should choose *left* if she believes that player I is equally likely to play *top* or *bottom*. However, if event † occurs, both players are Bayesian rational. Not only this, they know the action the other player is fated to take. The analyst may then observe that each is optimizing in full knowledge of the choice made by the other. Aumann's purpose in describing this example is to deny that the notion of Nash equilibrium requires common knowledge of Bayesian rationality. In this framework, it is enough that each player knows the choice of the other and each is, in fact, Bayesian rational. In the current example, although a Nash equilibrium is played if event † occurs, player I ascribes probability $\frac{1}{2}$ to event $*$ in which player II is not Bayesian rational. For further insight into this issue, see Aumann and Brandenburger (1990).

I do not fully understand what it means to speak of a player's prior when he may not be Bayesian rational. Attention in what follows will therefore be restricted to Aumann's global formulation. Even then, his assumption of the existence of priors may not seem entirely Kosher to a really orthodox Bayesian. Nau and McCardle (1990) address this question using de Finetti's "coherence" criterion for rationality: namely, that opportunities for making a Dutch book should not be offered to outside observers, who could thereby use the players as a "money pump."

They distinguish three levels at which the players may be vulnerable to a Dutch bookie, and argue that:

1 No player should use a strategy that exposes the player to a Dutch book.
2 No player should use a strategy that would expose the player to a Dutch book after strategies are deleted at the first or at the current level.
3 The players as a group should not use joint strategies that expose the group to a Dutch book.

Nau and McCardle show that, after the deletion of all strategies at levels one and two, a strategy that remains must be part of a subjective correlated equilibrium. (The close connection between their levels one and two and the requirements for rationalizability will be evident.) The use of the level three requirement leads to the same conclusion but with the rider that the correlated equilibrium is one in which the players have a *common prior*. (One cannot deduce such a conclusion from theorems about the impossibility of rational individuals "agreeing to disagree." Such theorems *begin* with a common prior and deduce that a posterior distribution must be common if appropriate information is common knowledge.) Traditionally, the assumption that players have a common prior has been defended by appealing to a philosophical principle that Aumann calls the *Harsanyi doctrine*. Loosely speaking, it says that, if rational players are envisaged as being in identical situations prior to their receiving any private information, then they must necessarily have the same beliefs, because every influence that could make them different has been abstracted away.

Does the result of Nau and McCardle make an appeal to the Harsanyi doctrine unnecessary within Aumann's framework? If states are really to be seen as all-inclusive descriptions of different possible worlds, then the status of the Dutch bookie comes into question. Is he outside the universe of discourse? If so, why does his Dutch book matter? More fundamentally, why does Aumann insist on all-inclusive states? What is bought by this insistence?

An important purchase is that Aumann is then able to argue that the fundamental structure of the model *must* be common knowledge among the players. This includes the players' information partitions and their priors. A later section reviews how he sees this as involving no self-reference difficulties. For the moment, however, an informal discussion of why the priors must be common knowledge will be offered.

Suppose that player j were to learn that a particular state ω had occurred, but continued to entertain two different possibilities for the subjective probability assigned by another player to an event E. Then the state ω would not be an *all-inclusive* description of the world. Thus everybody must know what everybody's beliefs would be in all states of world. Similarly, everybody must know that everybody knows, and so on. Assuming Bayesian consistency across different states, everybody's prior must be common knowledge (although this does not imply that the priors themselves are common).

Common knowledge of such matters as priors and information partitions matters if one cares whether the players in Aumann's story who "just do what they do" would indeed be prepared to ratify the action fate had decreed for them, if they were to be gifted with the power of "conscious choice." In order for player I to ratify b_1 in (2.1), he would need to ratify that player II would ratify b_2. Thus player II would need to ratify that player I would ratify that she will ratify b_2, and so on. Such an infinite regression of ratifications of ratifications is clearly meaningful provided that information partitions, priors, and the players' Bayesian rationality are common knowledge.

The next section follows Aumann into the realms of epistemic logic to explore further his contention that such matters can be taken for granted in his framework. However, a pause for breath will allow time for a moment of reflection. Aumann explicitly denies his players "conscious choice." The ratification story above has been grafted onto his structure (although he doubtless has such a story very much in mind). But, for the graft to take, there are at least two small but troublesome details that ought not to be overlooked.

The inequalities (2.1) were defended from the point of view of the analyst. The analyst takes a godlike stance and compares two universes: one in which player i is fated to play $b_i(\omega)$ in state ω, and one in which player i is fated to play $d_i(\omega)$. The two universes, however, are otherwise identical. But a player who is seeking to ratify the choice he finds himself disposed to make lives in a given universe. He must compare two states in the *same* universe. Part of his information about what state actually obtains is the strategy in the game he finds himself disposed to make. If he were disposed to play d_i rather than b_i, he would therefore have different information. Does this therefore not mean that, from his point of view, the $P_i(\omega)$ on the left of (2.1) should not be the same as that on the right?

Shin (1988) makes a similar point. Recognition that this is a possible issue raises the question of whether what I now find myself thinking can be useful evidence in guessing what someone else may be thinking. This is, of course, a primrose path much trodden by those who want to demonstrate that cooperation is rational in the one-shot *Prisoner's Dilemma*.

There are philosophers, inspired by the so-called Newcomb paradox, who teeter on the edge of this fallacy by toying with a methodological tool they call "causal decision theory." See, for example, Harper (1988). They are mentioned chiefly to draw attention to ways of thinking which are not expressible within Aumann's scheme. My own view is that a more radical rethinking than they propose is necessary if the issue of "conscious choice" is to be faced squarely. This would involve actively modeling the players as computing machines so that the process by means of which they reach decisions can be studied formally. Newcomb's paradox evaporates in such a framework (like the barber in a town who shaves everyone who does not shave himself).

However, the point that seems to me most relevant is one I have argued elsewhere (1987c). It seems harmless to assume that a player will always know what he is doing. But there is a sense in which this is *impossible* for a computing machine programmed to ratify its own decisions. This denial of the obvious will perhaps seem more plausible after the next section.

3 NOAH'S KNOWLEDGE

Although Aumann (1989a) is followed here for the sake of consistency, he is not an originator in this area. In mentioning Hintikka (1962), Halpern (1986), Bacharach (1985, 1987a, 1987b), Gilboa (1990), Kaneko (1987), Kaneko and Nagashima (1987), Samet (1988) and Shin (1990), justice is not done to many other authors. Walliser (1987) surveys a wide range of papers in the field.

In (1989a), Aumann's aim is to be very explicit about precisely what a state ω is. This requires being very formal about the notion of knowing something. This section confines its attention to some of the high spots in the case of one player to be called Noah.

The objects of knowledge are to be formulas. Primitive sentences like, "I had two eggs for breakfast today" are represented by primitive letter symbols like a or b. From these, more complicated sentences can be constructed using the usual logical connectives. Certain sentences like $A \vee \sim A$ (read as "A or (not A)") are said to be tautologous because they must be true whatever A may be. (If this is not a familiar notion, skip to the next section!)

To proceed further, it is necessary to venture into the realm of *modal logic*, for which some useful references are Konyndyk (1986) and Hughes and Cresswell (1985). Figure 1.2 reproduces the specifications for (S5) and (G) from Boolos (1979). These are two of many modal logics that have been studied. Aside from the rules of inference and axioms schemes listed, it is to be understood that all the tautologies of regular logic are to be counted as axioms also. Items under a horizontal line in figure 1.2 represent deductions that can be made from items above the line. For example (S5:2) is the standard logical principle *modus ponens* that says that B can be deduced from A and $A \Rightarrow B$. The modal operator $\Box$ is read as "necessitation" in abstract accounts. It comes with a companion $\Diamond = \sim\Box\sim$ read as "possibility."

(S5:1)	$\Box(A\Rightarrow B)\Rightarrow(\Box A\Rightarrow\Box B)$	(G:1)	$\Box(A\Rightarrow B\Rightarrow(\Box A\Rightarrow\Box B)$
(S5:2)	$\dfrac{A\Rightarrow B \quad A}{B}$ (S5:3) $\dfrac{A}{\Box A}$	(G:2)	$\dfrac{A\Rightarrow B \quad A}{B}$ (G:3) $\dfrac{A}{\Box A}$
(S5:4)	$\Box A\Rightarrow A$	(G:4)	$\Box(\Box A\Rightarrow A)\Rightarrow\Box A$
(S5:5)	$\Box A\Rightarrow\Box\Box A$		
(S5:6)	$\sim\Box A\Rightarrow\Box\sim\Box A$		

Figure 1.2 The model logics (S5) and (G).

In game theory, it is orthodox to make assumptions about the properties of knowledge that are equivalent to using (S5) with $\Box$ interpreted as a knowledge operator. Aumann (1989a) does so explicitly. To signal this interpretation, $\Box$ is written as k while (S5) is being assumed.

One should think of (S5) as being a set of principles for extending the collection of tautologies. For example, (S5:3) says that, if A is a tautology, then kA is a tautology. Thus it must be true that Noah knows anything that must be true.

What is a state ω? In this setting, it is a list of formulas. The list includes all tautologies in (S5). However, if only tautologies were included in the list, the specification of a state would provide no information of any substance. A state ω must therefore list formulas f that are *not* tautologies. It might include, for example, a letter y that represents, "You ate two eggs for breakfast this morning." For logical coherence, $\sim f$ is excluded from the list when f is included, and g is included whenever f and $f \Rightarrow g$ are included. Finally, Aumann insists that states be all-inclusive. This translates into the requirement that, for *every* formula f, either f or $\sim f$ is in the list that constitutes a state ω.

Notice that, although *modus ponens* is permitted in constructing such a list, one certainly may not always use the other rule of inference of (S5). In some possible worlds, y and $\sim ky$ will be in the list, because people do not always know what others ate for breakfast.

The formulae in the list ω that begin with k are those that Noah knows in state ω. Denote the sublist of all such formulas by $\kappa(\omega)$. Aumann defines an *information set* by:

$$I(\omega) = \{\zeta : \kappa(\zeta) = \kappa(\omega)\}.$$

It is the set of states that Aumann's analyst cannot distinguish from ω, once ω has occurred, if he restricts himself to making use only of what Noah knows. If ω has occurred, $I(\omega)$ is the set of states that are *possible* given Noah's knowledge.

The definition of an information set given above guarantees that information sets partition Ω. It is therefore important to note that one would not wish to use the definition except when (S5) is being assumed. In general, a more primitive definition is appropriate. A state ζ should be deemed possible, given Noah's knowledge, if and only if it includes all formulas in $\kappa(\omega)$ after their initial k has been deleted. This reduces to Aumann's definition when (S5) is assumed. To be more precise, items (S5:4) thru (S5:6) translate to (I:2) thru (I:4) in figure 1.3, when expressed in terms of information sets. (It is not a mistake that (I:3) is a consequence of (I:4).) Note, in particular, that (I:4) says that I *partitions* the universe Ω.

Binmore and Brandenburger (1990) and Geanakoplos (1988) are

	(K:0) $K\Omega=\Omega$	
	(K:1) $K(E\cap F)=KE\cap KF$	
(I:2) $\omega\in I(\omega)$	(K:2) $KE\subseteq E$	(knowledge)
(I:3) $\zeta\in I(\omega)\Rightarrow I(\zeta)\subseteq I(\omega)$	(K:3) $KE\subseteq K^2E$	(transparency)
(I:4) $\zeta\in I(\omega)\Rightarrow I(\zeta)=I(\omega)$	(K:4) $\sim KE\subseteq K(\sim KE)$	(wisdom)

Figure 1.3 Alternative characterization of the orthodox knowledge assumptions

user-friendly accounts that explain the relation that holds between properties of information sets and the set-theoretic knowledge operator K defined by $KE=\{\omega:I(\omega)\subseteq E\}$. (In words, KE is the set of states in which Aumann's analyst can deduce from the player's knowledge that the event E has occurred.) Briefly, the conditions (K:0) thru (K:N) are equivalent to (I:2) thru (I:N) for $N=2$, 3 or 4.

Bacharach (1985) calls the last three of the conditions for the set-theoretic knowledge operator K, the axioms of *knowledge*, *transparency*, and *wisdom* respectively. Their very close connection with the concluding three principles of (S5) will be evident. Debate among game theorists about what assumptions about knowledge make sense has mostly centered on the axiom of wisdom. The reservations that many feel about this assumption are expressed at some length in Binmore and Brandenburger (1990). Such reservations have led to some interesting attempts to see how far it is possible to go without (K:4). See, for example, Samet (1987), Geanakoplos (1988) and Brandenburger, Dekel, and Geanakoplos (1989). However, the temptation to chase this particular rabbit must be resisted because Aumann beckons us on. There is, in any case, an equally bright-eyed quarry awaiting our attention later on.

Aumann (1989a) is, of course, interested in common knowledge and so needs two different knowledge operators, k_1 and k_2, in a two-player game. At the current level of abstraction, this is a complication that can be accommodated without difficulty. Continuing the line of inquiry of the preceding section, the question is whether information partitions and such matters can properly be regarded as being common knowledge among players. (See Kaneko, 1987 or Gilboa, 1990). Among other motives, Aumann (1989a, p. 17) wishes to make it clear that the self-reference implied by answering such questions in the affirmative is harmless.

Aumann (1989a, p. 24) uses quotes in saying that the answer to whether a player "knows" the information partitions is an unqualified "yes." The quotes appear because this is an example of what he calls "dictionary" knowledge as opposed to "real" knowledge. He does not assert the existence of a formula in the list $\kappa(\omega)$ that refers explicitly to information partitions. Before it would be possible to do so, it would be necessary to explain how to code statements about information partitions as formulas. If

I understand it, the claim is rather that a player's "real" knowledge, which is all that is operationally significant, is *as though* the player were equipped with the "dictionary" knowledge. In a sense, the "real" knowledge *incorporates* the "dictionary knowledge."

For example, consider, as a piece of "dictionary" knowledge, the assertion that it is "common knowledge" that all players reason logically. In the case of only one player, this is reflected in the fact that $\kappa(\omega)$, the player's "real" knowledge, necessarily includes all formulae of the form $k^n t$, where t is a tautology (S5:3 and S5:5).

Aumann's epistemology lays to rest some of the concerns that critics have expressed. However, it does not address the "conscious choice" question raised in the preceding section. Here the issue arises if it is asked *how* players come to know things. Mathematicians, for example, come to know that theorems are true by proving them. But (S5) is definitely not a sound set of principles for "knowability" if this is to be understood as provability in (Peano) arithmetic. In fact, the modal logic (G) characterizes the "provable principles of provability" in this context (Boolos, 1979; Solovay, 1976).

To focus on this point, imagine that Noah is replaced by a computing machine called NOAH. NOAH has an *algorithm* to add new facts to the old facts that she finds in her memory banks. Binmore and Shin (1990) give the (not very profound) reasons why one should prefer the necessitation operator $\Box$ of (G) to that of (S5) in characterizing what is knowable to such a machine (see also Shin, 1987; Artemov 1990). However, one does not lose (S5:5). This is a theorem of (G), and so it remains "common knowledge that players reason logically." The loss of (G5:6) may be attended with some relief. But the appearance of (G:4) makes it impossible to append the principle (S5:4) consistently to the principles of (G). We are in trouble with the principle: *what I know is true*. Neither (K:2) nor (I:2) can now be claimed as tautologies.

It may help to be more concrete. A Turing machine may be thought of as a program for a regular computer written on the assumption that no limitations of storage space need be observed. Suppose that, for each *all-inclusive* state ω, possibility questions are resolved by a Turing machine $S = S(\omega)$ that sometimes answers NO to questions that begin: *Is it possible that*... ? Unless the answer is NO, possibility is conceded. (Timing issues are neglected.)

Consider a specific question concerning the Turing machine N. Let the computer code for this question be $[N]$. Let $[M]$ be the computer code for the question: *Is it possible that M will answer* NO *to* $[M]$? Finally, let T be a Turing machine that outputs $[x]$ when its input is $[x]$. Then the program $R = ST$, that consists of first operating T and then operating S, responds to $[M]$ as S responds to $[M]$.

Suppose that R responds to $[R]$ with NO. Then S reports that it is *impossible that* R responds to $[R]$ with NO. If what I know is true, it must therefore be that R never responds to $[R]$ with NO. But, if we as observers know this, why don't we replace S with a better program: one that accurately reflects our knowledge? Either our algorithm for determining what is possible is "incomplete" in that it allows as possible events that we know to be false, or it is "inconsistent" in that it rejects as impossible events we know to be true.

The relevant limitation on algorithmic knowledge appears as (G:4). It is called Löb's theorem in proof theory, where it is shown to be equivalent to Gödel's second incompleteness theorem.

The mention of Gödel focuses attention on the self-reference involved in asking how R responds to $[R]$. Binmore (1987a), Anderlini (1988), and Canning (1988) offer successively more elaborate exploitations of Gödel's self-reference construction to matters that are more directly relevant for game theory than what can be numbered among the tautologies available to an algorithmic player.

In this literature, the players are modeled as Turing machines who exchange their Gödel numbers before the game is played. The Gödel number of a Turing machine embodies an exhaustive description of the design of the machine. This step ensures that it is "common knowledge" how the players "reason." Given a game prefixed by such an exchange of Gödel numbers, call a machine *rational* against a set H of machines, if it always recommends a best reply to whatever is recommended by an opponent in H. (It is necessary to bear in mind that Turing machines may compute for ever. An opponent may therefore make no recommendation at all. No restriction is placed on the behavior of a rational machine in playing such an opponent.) Let $O(H)$ denote the set of machines rational against H. If T denotes the set of all Turing machines, define $T^0 = T$ and $T^n = O(T^{n-1})$ $(n = 1, 2, \ldots)$. These sets are not empty. Canning (1988) defines a game to be *solvable* for a given set S of machines if there exists a machine in S that never fails to make a recommendation and which is rational against machines in S. He then shows that no game without dominating strategies is solvable for $S = T^n$ $(n = 0, 1, 2, \ldots)$. One might ask whether this unpalatable conclusion can be evaded by restricting attention to "self-rational" sets satisfying $S = O(S)$. The limiting value of T^n as $n \to \infty$, if meaningful, suggests itself as a possible candidate for such a self-rational set. However, Canning (1988) shows that there are no self-rational sets.

An easy consequence is that there is no algorithm that can decide whether or not a machine is in the set T^1 of all machines that are rational against all opponents. (The set T^1 is not recursive.) Thus, as Anderlini (1988) observes, a Turing machine can know the Gödel number of an opponent without knowing whether the opponent is "rational." Indeed, a Turing machine can know its own Gödel number without knowing that it is itself "rational." Such conclusions are no more paradoxical than the claim that one can know the code of a computer program without knowing what the consequences of its use would be under all possible circumstances.

It is tempting to brush aside such difficulties on the grounds that what is knowable for NOAH is irrelevant to what Noah may know or do. Penrose (1989) bravely puts the case for this unfashionable proposition. Perhaps the flashes of insight with which some mathematicians are gifted are indeed inexplicable if Penrose is wrong, and perhaps we do need to look to quantum phenomena to understand their creative abilities. My own feeling, however, is that such speculative thinking is best put to one side until more mundane hypotheses have definitely been shown to be inadequate.

4 MOUNT ARARAT

If it is argued that all this epistemology is just so much counting of angels on the end of a pin, then I have to agree. If it is further argued that Aumann's framework is coherent, then I agree with this also. It is therefore admitted that Aumann's ark is seaworthy. So why not climb aboard for the ride? Who cares if the ark is clinker-built, so long as it will float?

The answer is that there is no reason to care provided that one does not wish to go beyond Mount Ararat, where the ark is *already* beached. That is to say, Aumann's system works well in providing foundations for that part of game theory *as-it-is* which holds together fairly coherently. Where it does not work so well is in dealing with those problems that have reduced game theory as-it-is to a state of confusion and disarray: namely, the problems of equilibrium selection and equilibrium refinement.

Partly, its failure in dealing with these issues is healthy because some of game theory as-it-is takes for granted ideas that ought not to be taken for granted. The following example has sequential equilibrium as its target. The game *Horse* of figure 1.4 is a modified version of a game used by Selten (1975) to motivate trembling-hand perfect equilibria, and by Kreps and Wilson (1982b) to motivate sequential equilibria. The doubled edges indicate the two Nash equilibria in pure strategies. The equilibrium *aar* is sequential, but *dal* is not. Conventional wisdom therefore calls for the rejection of *dal* on the grounds that it advocates an "irrational" choice for player II at a node that is not reached in equilibrium.

But consider the following possible background story. A conference of game theorists decides whether to recommend *aar* or *dal*. Potential players of *Horse* do not directly observe the conference decision, but they have common knowledge of a common prior about what this will be. This prior

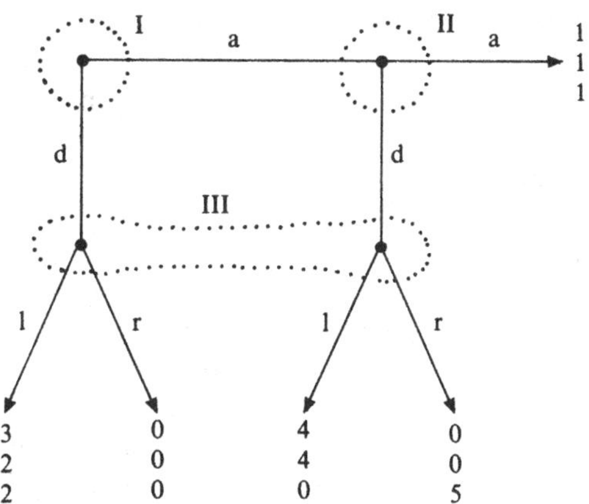

Figure 1.4 The game Horse

is updated by each potential player after he receives a notification of the conference decision in the mail. The updating takes account of the fact that a tiny fraction of recipients will be mailed the wrong notification. Consider now a player II who is mailed the notification *dal*. She therefore does not anticipate being called upon to make a decision. But suppose she is required to do so. She attributes this to player I's having been mailed the notification *aar*. Being a good Bayesian, she updates her beliefs about the notification received by player III. If her updated probability that player III's notification is *dal* does not exceed $\frac{1}{4}$, it is *not* irrational for player II to choose *a*.

The technical details that make a slightly more complicated version of this story work are given in Binmore (1987c). It is its moral that will be emphasized here. In fact, unlike conventional fables, the story has at least three morals. The rest of this section is loosely structured by considering some of their implications in the reverse order to which they are listed below.

The first moral concerns "possible worlds." The story does not defend the retention of *dal* in all possible worlds. Indeed, the retention of *dal* in some possible worlds is defensible only because it is rejected in other possible worlds. The second moral concerns "correlated trembles" (see Myerson, 1986). What a player learns about how another thinks by observing her play is *not* irrelevant to the predictions he makes about how opponents will play in the future. The third moral is that it cannot be taken for granted that the question of how an equilibrium should be *defined* can be separated from how an equilibrium is *selected*.

The example demonstrates that all of these points can be made without leaving Mount Ararat. But I do not see how the questions they raise can be seriously addressed unless attempts are made to dig deeper foundations for game theory. Perhaps there is some elegant way forward that finesses the all-too-evident difficulties. If not, Harsanyi and Selten (1988) have proposed one possible approach. In Binmore (1987c), I point to an even stonier path.

Harsanyi and Selten (1988) have been much criticized for proposing a theory of equilibrium selection that is said to be complicated and arbitrary. Neither criticism makes much sense to me. Nothing would seem to guarantee that a good theory will be simple, and those who aspire to a unique theory of "perfect rationality," devoid of arbitrary or culturally determined elements, are simply baying at the moon. Harsanyi and Selten seem more deserving of congratulation than criticism in that they face up to urgent tasks that are usually shirked. In particular, equilibrium selection is not a problem that can be left for someone else to clear up the morning after. It will be an intrinsic part of any decent theory. Nor do Harsanyi and Selten neglect the fact that progress on such issues cannot be made without a theory of some kind of *procedure* (or algorithm) that rational players use in reaching their supposedly rational conclusions. This is not to endorse Harsanyi and Selten's "tracing procedure," nor Skyrms (1990) "deliberative procedure": still less my own essays in this direction. Insofar as these take Bayesian ideas for granted, they are necessarily suspect when procedural rationality is under discussion, since one cannot expect a player to achieve a consistent set of beliefs until *after* he has finished thinking (Binmore, 1987). Finally, their recognition of the tension that exists between what they call payoff dominance and risk dominance deserves more attention than it receives. (Payoff dominance is the same as Pareto dominance.)

An aside that arises from this last point will provide a point of contact between this lecture and that of Erik van Damme (1990). The selection of the equilibrium (*top*, *left*) in the game *Dodo* of figure 1.1 may seem unproblematical. But, suppose that x is added to each of player I's payoffs in the bottom row and to each of player II's payoffs in the right column. This does not affect the best reply correspondences, and hence it is sometimes maintained that the essential structure of the game is unchanged, and therefore presumably that (*top*, *left*) should still be selected. This invariance is reflected in the fact that (*top*, *left*) risk dominates (*bottom*, *right*) whatever x may be, and also the fact that the Carlsson/van Damme technique always picks (*top*, *left*). But the (*bottom*, *right*) payoff dominates (*top*, *left*) when $x>1$.

Harsanyi and Selten (1988, p. 88) give priority to payoff dominance over risk dominance on intuitive grounds. But, as we have seen, others have different intuitions. Clearly something more than intuition is called for even in as simple a game as *Dodo*. My own view is that progress on this, as on most issues, is unlikely unless attempts to model the reasoning processes of the players explicitly are made. Aumann and Sorin (1989) use finite automata for this purpose in looking at *Dodo*-like games in a repeated context. Anderlini (1990) uses Turing machines in the one-shot case. "Metaplayers" each choose a Turing machine to play *Dodo* on their behalf. But, before the machines play they exchange their Gödel numbers. The strategy a machine uses is therefore a function of the opponent it faces. With subsidiary assumptions (that are not innocent), Anderlini (1990) shows that the only equilibrium available to the metaplayers in their machine-selection game is the payoff dominant equilibrium in *Dodo*.

So much for equilibrium selection: next comes the subject of correlated trembles. It would be nice to be able to say that we should be looking for a game theory that is a synthesis in which the thesis is the theory of Harsanyi and Selten and the antithesis is that of Kohlberg and Mertens (1986). Harsanyi and Selten are nearer bedrock in many respects. They do not, for example, take for granted some unformalized pre-play "cheap talk" session (Kohlberg, 1989; Farrell, forthcoming). However, Harsanyi and Selten's approach leaves no room for the forwards induction arguments of Kohlberg and Mertens, although such arguments are often intuitively very compelling, even without a cheap talk justification. In the Harsanyi and Selten theory, a deviation from equilibrium is simply a mistake which conveys no information about the deviant's future intentions. One reservation about seeking a synthesis of the two theories is that, if forwards induction arguments are taken as seriously as perhaps they should be, then they call into question the principle of *backwards induction* which is fundamental to both approaches. I plan to say little on this subject since the role of *Chicken Licken* is not flattering to the ego and, in any case, the subject of refinements of equilibrium lies outside my strict terms of reference. On the refinement program, let me only say that the chaos in which it is currently engulfed would seem enough, in itself, to justify a weather eye being kept on the sky.

Not even the successive deletion of dominated strategies in the finitely repeated *Prisoners' Dilemma* is safe. It is well-recognized that some sort of paradox is involved when this (and such country cousins as Selten's (1978) *Chain-Store* game or Rosenthal's (1981) *Centipede* game) are analyzed according to orthodox principles. See, for example, Kreps and Wilson (1982a), Reny (1985), Basu (1985), Binmore (1987b), Bonnano (1989), Gilboa (1990), Bichierri (1988, 1989), Petit and Sugden (1989), among numerous others.

In brief, traditional game theoretic analyses begin with the hypothesis that it is "common knowledge that the players are perfectly rational." What this means is less than clear, as the preceding sections indicate. However, whatever it means, the hypothesis certainly cannot still be maintained after one or more of the players has been observed to play irrationally. The traditional method of dealing with this difficulty is to ignore it. Although players may have behaved stupidly in the past, it is always assumed that they will be clever in the future. This is not an incoherent way of proceeding. For example, if stupid behavior genuinely can be attributed to many independent trembling-hand errors, then the traditional approach makes perfectly good sense. Blume, Brandenburger, and Dekel (1989a, 1989b) provide a very general framework within which this traditional approach can be formalized. But the elbow-jogging explanation will seldom be a realistic explanation when real people play. People who behave stupidly usually do so because they are stupid. When playing against such people, one can learn from their deviations from rationality in the past what their deviations from rationality are likely to be in the future. As Kohlberg and Mertens stress, and as is realized explicitly in the models in which Turing machines exchange Gödel numbers, one can also make deductions about what a clever player expects to happen later in the game from his earlier actions. But is a given deviant very clever or just plain stupid? To answer such a question one needs more information than traditional game theorists usually allow themselves. To pluck yet again the single string on this minstrel's harp, what is lacking is some model, however primitive, of how people reason.

One can, incidentally, not only learn from an opponent's past play about what she may do in the future, one may also learn things about what is to be expected from third parties. As Harsanyi (1977) explains, the fact that we share a common biological and cultural history means that we are not free-standing independent entities. In particular, my trembles now will be correlated, not only with my trembles in the past, but also with the trembles of others: hence Aumann's emphasis on the notion of a *correlated* equilibrium.

This brings us to the question of "possible worlds." Game theory cannot escape counterfactuals. It is *necessary* to consider the consequences of a rational player behaving irrationally. In making this point, Selten and Leopold (1982) quote Lewis' (1976) opening sentence in his book on counterfactuals. "If kangaroos had no tails, they would topple over." They suggest that, to make sense of such a statement, a computer model of a kangaroo is required. This must be rich enough in structure to allow the tail to be removed by a variation of its parameters. One can then examine the construct so obtained to check whether its center of gravity lies above its base or not.

Varying the parameters of the kangaroo introduces a tremble. Such a tremble creates a possible world in which kangaroos have no tails. Within this world, the stability of tailless kangaroos makes sense. But there are *many* possible worlds in which kangaroos have no tails. In some of these worlds, pigs can fly. Lewis (1976) tells us to look at "closest" possible worlds to our own. Traditional game theory takes this to mean worlds created by independent trembling-hand errors. And there is indeed a sense in which such possible worlds are "closest" to an idealized world inhabited by rational super-beings. But this will only sometimes be a useful interpretation of "closest."

Although we may strive to be rational, and perhaps occasionally succeed in behaving as a super-being would behave, nevertheless our mistakes, *if we were to make them*, would not be the mistakes a super-being would make. They would be the mistakes that a human striving to be rational would make. To know what such mistakes are likely to be, it is necessary to know something about how people think and learn. To be more precise, it is necessary to be informed about the libration that generates the equilibrium – the *process* by means of which equilibrium is achieved. If deviations occur, the explanation of first resort should be that something has gone wrong in this process.

Of course, to study trembles based on such considerations is bound to be difficult. But one does not get to heaven by following the path of least resistance: only the straight and narrow path leads to salvation.

5 REINVENTING THE ARK?

Game theory is about the behavior of idealized people in idealized circumstances. This allows Aumann (1985) to say that game theory is not to be judged by whether it is "true" or "false." He prefers to compare game theory with...

> a filing system in an office operation, or to some kind of complex computer program. We do not refer to such a system as being "true" or "false"; rather, we talk about whether it works or not...

Here Aumann is disingenuous. What does it *mean* that something "works" or "works well"? Surely, to hark back to the quotation of section 1, more is involved than "our say-so alone." But, if objective criteria are to be applied, then the fact that the system "works" presumably means that it embodies some "truth" about the way things are. There therefore seems no good reason for placing game theory in some special category from which the normal criteria of scientific inquiry are excluded.

But, since Aumann thinks that the filing system metaphor also applies to science as a whole, perhaps he is only saying that people are often naive about what the normal criteria of scientific inquiry are. As he observes, cosmology, meteorology, and evolution are not studied according to the simplistic paradigms of straight physics, in which predictions are tested directly with laboratory experiments. Nevertheless, such disciplines are deemed to be scientific because their practitioners do not simply accept or reject an idea because it tickles their intuition. In scientific disciplines, ideas are subjected to serious critical examination. They may not always be subject to refutation by laboratory experiments, but their coherence can always be tested by *thought experiments* in the style popularized by Einstein.

Is game theory a scientific discipline in this sense? Its semi-mathematical character makes it amenable to such an approach, but those who condemn game theory as pseudo-scientific or metaphysical are certainly not left short of ammunition. The literature on signaling games, for example, draws all kinds of contradictory conclusions from hypotheses said to be "reasonable" or "plausible." But, if someone claims that it is reasonable for Mary to believe X if John does Y, we are entitled to ask: why is it reasonable? What thought processes led Mary to this conclusion? What is Mary's history of experience that she should reason this way?

To put the same point more generally, if something more is to be offered in defense of the choice of a particular equilibrium concept beyond the suggestion that it is intuitively pleasing, then we need to be told something about the equilibriating process, or *libration*, by means of which the equilibrium is envisaged as being achieved. We need such information, not only to determine the circumstances under which the concept is intended to be applicable, but also so that attempts can be made to construct formal models as examples of the libration in question. The investigation of such formal models then provides a thought experiment with which the theory may be tested. Milgrom and Roberts (1990), for example, offer insight into the circumstances under which adaptive learning models lead to convergence on a correlated equilibrium or to a rationalizable outcome. Kalai and Lehrer (1990) study circumstances under which fully rational learning leads to Nash equilibrium. Fudenberg and Kreps (1988) and Samuelson (1990) show that quite natural assumptions can lead to outcomes that fit no pre-existing equilibrium paradigms. In different papers, Selten (1983, 1988) considers very different librations and obtains results that reflect these differences. Other papers include Blume and Easley (1990), Brock, Marimon, Rust, and Sargent (1988), Canning (1987), Crawford (1988), Jordan (1989, 1990), Linhart, Radner, and Schotter (1989), and Stanford (1990).

However, none of this denies the aptness of Aumann's metaphor of an office filing system. On the contrary, one of the virtues of the reductionist approach advocated here is that its use *compels* that attempts be made to classify solution concepts according to the environments in which it makes sense to apply them. It is perhaps daunting to contemplate the possibility of riding out the flood, not in one cosy ark, but in a whole armada of arks, but this is what is being suggested.

Von Clausewitz's (1976) classic *On War* observes that, to plan a campaign, it is necessary to be informed about the theater of operations and the armies. In game-theoretic terms, this may be translated as saying that the strategies chosen will depend on the game being played and on the nature of the players playing it. As emphasized in the preceding section, it is not enough to say what the game and the players are in one particular idealized world. It is necessary to have a rich enough view of the environment from which the game and its players have been abstracted to be able also to say what they *would be* in "nearby" possible worlds. This makes it necessary to classify equilibrium concepts by the environment to which they apply even when the aim is only to examine idealized worlds in which there is supposedly "common knowledge of perfect rationality."

I do not believe this view is controversial in so far as the environment is interpreted as referring only to the physical circumstances in which the game is played – its *theater of operations*. This is perhaps because our technical prowess is adequate, in principle, to deal with trembles that alter the rules of the game (including the players' preferences and their beliefs about formal chance moves). Fudenberg, Kreps, and Levine (1988) show what is possible in this direction. The view becomes controversial only when the environment is interpreted so as to include the players' mental processes – Von Clausewitz's *armies*. (Here the players' mental processes are to be understood as including the players' pre-play memories.) But, insofar as what is being proposed is controversial, it should be noted that it only carries the approach pioneered by Kreps and Wilson (1982a) and the notorious "gang of four" (1982) to its logical conclusion. My own view is that the interesting part of a game-theoretic classification table will be that in which trembles in the physical environment appear only as epiphenomena. Perhaps this view is wrong, but it explains why I concentrate on this part of the classification table in what follows.

Modeling the players' thinking processes carries us into the area of *bounded rationality*. As observed above, I believe that the problems of bounded rationality can never be entirely evaded, no matter how idealized the players, unless realism is to be abandoned altogether. As Meggido (1986) puts it, the evasions necessary to avoid bounded rationality require that players can "even decide undecidable problems." As I hope sections 2 and 3 make clear, things that matter are swept under the carpet when the fact that players make "conscious choices" is abstracted away (see also Lipman, 1989). Perhaps what is swept away does not matter so very much when only simultaneous-move games are considered, but it certainly does matter in games which allow signaling opportunities of some sort to arise.

How is bounded rationality studied? Following a suggestion of Aumann (who else?), Neyman (1986), Rubinstein (1986), and Abreu and Rubinstein (1988) envisage metaplayers like those considered earlier. As before, the metaplayers choose a computing machine to play a game on their behalf. However, in this literature, attention is not directed at machines with no upper bounds on their storage capacity. The metaplayers are therefore not allowed to choose any Turing machine. Their choice is restricted to *finite automata* (Meggido and Wigderson (1986) are an exception). These may be thought of as machines with an upper bound on how much information they can remember. Usually, the game that they play is repeated. Often it is some version of the repeated *Prisoners' Dilemma*, and the aim is to provide a "non-cooperative justification for cooperative behavior."

An obvious and much repeated criticism is that the automaton-selection game that the metaplayers are asked to solve is more complicated than the original game. My own view is that this criticism misses the point of the most interesting interpretation of this literature. One need not regard the metaplayers as being more than a metaphor for an evolutionary process that selects the computing machine that actually plays. Some preliminary explorations of this view are Fudenberg and Maskin (1990) and Binmore and Samuelson (1990).

However, there are many possible evolutionary processes: biological, social, and economic. Different outcomes must be expected to arise from different processes. In particular, economists have yet properly to take on board the fact that the study of biological processes popularized by Maynard Smith (1982) is not necessarily relevant to the socio-economic processes that shape most economic behavior. Boyd and Richerson (1985) make this point very forcefully with a number of thought-provoking models. Following Dawkins (1976), one may think about socio-economic processes in terms of behavior-determining "memes" (norms, ideas, rules-of-thumb) which are replicated from head to head by imitation or education. (Such a meme would be identified with the computing machine chosen by a metaplayer rather than with the economic agent whose head it infests.) Of course, as in biology, the mechanics of the replication process will be usually be overwhelmingly important in determining what the process converges to.

These are deep issues to which it is not possible to do justice in such a piece as this, even if I felt competent to do so. Fortunately, Selten (1989) has recently discussed many of the relevant issues in the form of a dialog between proponents of various research strategies. I differ from him only in being less critical of "armchair reasoning." He is obviously right to criticize those who believe that it is possible to distil wisdom from the air in thinking about evolutionary questions. Theorizing in a vacuum is seldom profitable. But it does not follow, as he puts it, that it is idle to speculate about the evolution of unicorns until unicorns have been found in nature. One needs to know what various types of evolution *might* generate in order to know what to look for in designing experiments or examining empirical data. In particular, there is an important role for the study of computer simulated evolutionary processes in which many factors that matter in the real world are artificially controlled or suppressed altogether. The fact that the mythical "possible worlds" investigated in such studies may not be close to the actual world is less important than the fact that they provide a means of testing the relative importance of different parameters in determining the route that various evolutionary processes may take. Only when we know what is likely to matter, can we hope to construct theories that are adequately simple and precise to be usable. This is not to deny the importance of data from the real world. However, as the astronomer Eddington observed, one is unwise to put overmuch confidence in observational results until they are confirmed by theory!

A second important classification problem concerns the manner in which the complexity of the finite automata to be admitted is constrained. It is not obvious how complexity should be measured (see, for example, Abreu and Rubinstein, 1988; Banks and Sundaram, 1989; Ben-Porath, 1986; Gilboa, 1988; Kalai, 1990; Kalai and Stanford, 1989; Lehrer, 1988; Meggido and Wigderson, 1986; Neyman, 1986; Rubinstein, 1987; Stearns, 1989, among numerous others). Although it is generally acknowledged that counting the number of states in a finite automaton is at best a rough and ready measure, this is what is usually done.

Most work follows Neyman (1986) in positing a fixed, exogenously determined upper bound on the number of states a finite automaton can have. Cooperation can then emerge as equilibrium behavior in the finitely repeated *Prisoners' Dilemma* even when the number of repetitions is small compared with the bound imposed on the allowable number of states. However, it is important that, for such results, the bound is *active* in equilibrium. The equilibrium machines use so much of their capacity in keeping track of what their opponent is doing that they have no capacity left for even simple tasks like counting the number of times that the *Prisoners' Dilemma* has been repeated so far. The resulting situation therefore resembles the indefinitely repeated *Prisoners' Dilemma* for which cooperation in equilibrium is unproblematic.

Neyman forbids a metaplayer to use an automaton beyond a certain level of complexity, although the metaplayer would certainly wish to breach this constraint if he were able to do so. Abreu and Rubinstein (1988) consider a situation that is more familiar to economists. In their model, extra complexity can be seen as being available at a cost. The methodology requires that complexity appear explicitly, along with game payoffs, in a metaplayer's preference relation. Thus the level of complexity becomes *endogenous.* The players could use more complex machines than those selected in equilibrium, but they choose not to do so. Aumann (1989b) classifies such a model as lying outside the area of bounded rationality. I would prefer to say that the Neyman model is one in which rationality is *uniformly* bounded.

With surprisingly mild assumptions, Abreu and Rubinstein (1988) are able to shrink the folk theorem's set of Nash equilibria in a repeated game quite sharply. Their results are particularly neat when game payoffs are ranked lexicographically above an aversion to complexity. By looking at suitable defined evolutionary stable strategies, rather than Nash equilibria, Binmore and Samuelson (1990) eliminate all but the equilibria that yield a utilitarian outcome. Their result is to be contrasted with a similar conclusion of Fudenberg and Maskin (1990) which also uses complexity considerations, but not within the framework of Abreu and Rubinstein. The trembles in the former are in the design of a machine (its thinking processes). Fudenberg and Maskin (1990) have conventional trembling-hand errors.

So far this chapter has concentrated on two extremes of what is a continuous spectrum. The early part of the paper was concerned with what I have called *eductive* librations elsewhere (Binmore, 1987a). If the players are to be modeled as computing machines in an eductive context, they are highly complex machines who get to equilibrium by thinking their way there. Game theory is traditionally eductive in its outlook. At the other extreme are the *evolutive* librations we have just been considering. Here the players are modeled as very simple stimulus-response machines who get to equilibrium as a consequence of less successful machines being displaced by their more successful brethren. The two extremes are studied because the central part of the spectrum is tough to handle. Nevertheless, it is this part of the spectrum that is clearly of most interest for applications.

There is work that seeks to gain insight into the central part of the spectrum. Boyd and Richerson (1985), Fudenberg and Kreps (1988), Milgrom and Roberts (1990), and Selten (1988) have already been mentioned. In such work, attempts are made to bypass theories of how and why a player comes to be as he is: instead, the plausibility of models of learning studied is evaluated using appeals to our powers of introspection. A prime difficulty is that we know very little about how people think and learn. Introspection curiously provides little guidance in such matters. Psychologists offer various theories, together with greater or lesser quantities of evidence in their support, but those theories that are formalizable strike most game theorists as being too mechanical to reflect the way people really think in game-like situations. Any theory that offers no role for looking ahead and anticipating the actions of others is clearly inadequate for game-theoretic purposes. In constructing models, one therefore works largely in the dark. My feeling is that the time is past when experimental work in this area can be left to psychologists. They wear different blinders to economists that focus their attention on different matters and lead them to construct different research agenda. If learning models are to be properly informed by empirical data, I suspect economists will need to free themselves of their traditional prejudices by running experiments of their own.

What of computer science and progress in artificial intelligence? Can this not be brought into harness? The literature on neural networks sounds particularly attractive. See, for example, Arbib (1985, 1987). However, it is the work of Holland and his collaborators on classifier systems that has received more attention from economists (Holland, 1975; Goldberg, 1989). Both approaches offer complex systems capable of sophisticated learning in a suitable environment. Can one not run computer simulations in which the players are modeled as such a system and then gain insight from observing the behavior that evolves? Personally, I am sceptical about such a methodology. There is no doubt that a Holland classifier system can generate good algorithms quickly for problems that might otherwise be intractable. But, even if a study of the algorithm were to result in its being possible to characterize the way it works in terms of some easily appreciated heuristics, what reason would one have to argue from the appearance of such heuristics in the simulation to the presence of such heuristics in the way real people think? We have few grounds, if any, to think that the Holland methodology reflects much of what goes on in real people's brains. Even the neural network approach is doubtful on this score. Neurophysiologists are at best lukewarm in assessing its verisimilitude. When it comes to gaining insight into how people think, the artificial intelligence route suffers from the same basic problem as the analytical route: we are unlikely to get anything significant out unless the assumptions we feed in bear some relation to the way things actually are. This is not to say that I advocate abandoning such lines of inquiry. Perhaps the games that will be of interest to game theorists of the future will be computerized markets and the players they need to study will be the descendants of today's computerized learning systems. But, right now, games are played by people.

6 POSTEFFLUVIA

Only a few words will be said in summary. This chapter began by reviewing current orthodoxy. It was argued that this provides a solid basis for much of the literature on simultaneous-move games. But when things become more complicated, the framework is stretched to breaking point. The difficulties with the modal logic (S5) discussed in section 3 are symptomatic of a more serious malaise for which no obvious palliatives are available when games with a dynamic structure need to be analyzed.

To deal with such difficulties, it is necessary to model the way players think. Such models must be sufficiently rich that one can predict how the players *would* think if they lived in "possible worlds" close to, but not identical, with the worlds in which the analysis is conducted. Such a view makes the study of bounded rationality central to any new advances.

Progress on bounded rationality is not out of reach. The recent literature on finite automata leaves room for optimism. Indeed, the study of the manner in which finite automata may be selected by evolutionary processes seems an exciting prospect for future work. But, we shall have to put aside the goal of one single unified game theory. Instead, it will be necessary to classify the environments to which game theoretic ideas are to be applied much more closely than is attempted at present. Different environments may call for different game theories, some of which may not resemble anything we have now very closely.

References

Abreu, D. and A. Rubinstein (1988), "The structure of Nash Equilibrium in Repeated Games with Finite Automata," *Econometrica*, 56:1259–82.

Anderlini, L. (1988), *Some Notes on Church's Thesis and the Theory of Games*, Cambridge Economic Theory Discussion Paper.

(1990), "Communication, Computability and Common Interest Games," Working Paper, St. John's College, Cambridge.

Arbib, M. (1985), *In Search of the Person*, Amherst: University of Massachusetts Press.

(1987), *Brains, Machines and Mathematics*, Berlin: Springer-Verlag.

Artemov, S. (1990), "Kolmogorov's Logic of Problems and a Provability Interpretation of Intuitionistic Logic," in R. Parikh (ed.), *Theoretical Aspects of Reasoning About Knowledge*, San Mateo, CA: Morgan Kaufmann.

Aumann, R. (1976), "Agreeing to Disagree," *The Annals of Statistics*, 4:1236–9.

(1985), "What is Game Theory Trying to Accomplish?" in K. Arrow and S. Honkapohja (eds.), *Frontiers of Economics*, Oxford: Basil Blackwell, pp. 28–88.

(1987), "Correlated Equilibrium as an Expression of Baysesian Rationality," *Econometrica*, 55:1–18.

(1989a), "Interactive Epistemology," Working Paper, Cowles Foundation, Yale University.

(1989b), "Irrationality in Game Theory," Working Paper, Hebrew University.

Aumann, R. and A. Brandenburger (1990), "Epistemic Conditions for Nash Equilibrium," Working Paper, Harvard Business School.

Aumann, R. and S. Sorin (1989), "Cooperation and Bounded Recall," *Games and Economic Behavior*, 1:5–39.

Bacharach, M. (1985), "Some Extensions to a Claim of Aumann in an Axiomatic Model of Knowledge," *Journal of Economic Theory*, 37:167–90.

(1987a), "A Theory of Rational Decision in Games," *Erkerntnis*, 27:17–55.

(1987b), "When Do We have Information Partitions?" Working Paper, Oxford University.

Banks, J. and R. Sundaram (1989), "Repeated Games, Finite Automata and Complexity," Working Paper No. 183, University of Rochester.

Basu, K. (1985), "Strategic Irrationality in Games," Working Paper, Institute of Advanced Study, Princeton University.

Ben-Porath, E. (1986), "Repeated games with finite automata," Working Paper, Hebrew University.

Bernheim, D. (1984), "Rationalizable Strategic Behavior," *Econometrica*, 52:1007–28.

Bicchieri, C. (1988), "Common Knowledge and Backwards Induction: a Solution to the Paradox," in M. Vardi (ed.), *Theoretical Aspects of Reasoning About Knowledge*, Los Altos: Morgan Kaufmann.

(1989), "Strategic Behavior and Counterfactuals," *Erkerntnis*, 30:69–85.

Binmore, K. (1987a), "Modeling Rational Players, I and II," *Economics and Philosophy*, 3 and 4:179–214 and 9–55.

(1987b), "Modeling Rational Players, I," *Economics and Philosophy*, 3:9–55.

(1987c), "Modeling Rational Players, II," *Economics and Philosophy*, 4:179–214.

Binmore, K. and A. Brandenburger (1990), "Common Knowledge and Game Theory," in K. Binmore (ed.), *Essays on the Foundations of Game Theory*, Oxford: Basil Blackwell.

Binmore, K. and H. Shin (1990), "Algorithmic Knowledge and Game Theory," University of Michigan Discussion Paper.

Binmore, K. and L. Samuelson (1990), "Evolutionary Stability in Repeated Games Played by Finite Automata," University of Michigan Discussion Paper.

Blume, L., A. Brandenburger, and E. Dekel (1989a), "Equilibrium Refinements and Lexicographic Probabilities," Working Paper, Harvard Business School.

(1989b), "Lexicographic Probabilities and Choice Under Uncertainty," Working Paper, Harvard Business School.

Blume, L. and D. Easley (1990), "Bayesian Learning in Repeated Games: an Example of Non-Convergence to Nash Equilibrium," Working Paper, Cornell University.

Bonnano, G. (1988), "A Set-Theoretic Approach to Noncooperative Games, I and II," Working Paper No. 330, UC Davis.

Boolos, G. (1979), *The Unprobability of Consistency*, Cambridge University Press.

Boyd, R. and P. Richerson (1985), *Culture and the Evolutionary Process*, Chicago: University of Chicago Press.

Brandenburger, A. and E. Dekel (1987a), "Common Knowledge with Probability 1," *Journal of Mathematical Economics*, 16:237–45.

(1987b), "Rationalizability and Correlated Equilibria," *Econometrica*, 55: 1391–402.

Brandenburger, A., E. Dekel, and J. Geanakoplos (1989), "Correlated Equilibrium with Generalized Information Structures," Harvard Business School Discussion Paper.

Brock, W., R. Marimon, J. Rust, and T. Sargent (1988), "Informationally Decentralized Learning Algorithms for Finite-Player, Finite-Action Games of Incomplete Information," Working paper, University of Wisconsin.

Canning, D. (1987), "Convergence to Equilibrium in a Sequence of Games with Learning," European University Institute Working Paper.

(1988), "Rationality and Game Theory when Players are Turing Machines," London School of Economics ST/ICERD Discussion Paper 88/183.

Crawford, V. (1988), "Learning and Mixed Strategy Equilibria in Evolutionary Games," Working Paper, University of California at San Diego.

Dawkins, R. (1976), *The Selfish Gene*, Oxford University Press.

Farrell, J. (forthcoming), "Meaning and Credibility in Cheap-Talk Games," in M. Demster (ed.), *Mathematical Models in Economics*, Oxford University Press.

Fudenberg, D. and D. Kreps (1988), "Learning, Experimentation and Equilibrium in Games," Working Paper, MIT.

Fudenberg, D., D. Kreps, and D. Levine (1988), "On the Robustness of Equilibrium Refinements," *Journal of Economic Theory*, 44:354–80.

Fudenberg, D. and E. Maskin (1990), "Evolution and Cooperation in Noisy Repeated Games," *American Economic Review*, 80.

Geanakoplos, J. (1988), "Common Knowledge without Partitions, with an Application to Speculation," Cowles Foundation Discussion Paper No. 914, Yale University.

Gilboa, I. (1988), "The Complexity of Computing Best-Response Automata in Repeated Games," *Journal of Economic Theory*, 45:343–53.

(1990), "A note on the Consistency of Game Theory," in R. Parikh (ed.), *Reasoning About Knowledge*, San Mateo, CA: Morgan Kaufmann.

Goldberg, A. (1989), *Genetic Algorithms in Search, Optimization and Machine Learning*, Addison-Wesley.

Halpern, J. (ed.) (1986), *Theoretical Aspects of Reasoning about Knowledge*, Los Altos: Morgan Kaufmann.

Harper, W. (1988), "Causal Decision Theory and Game Theory," in W. Harper and B. Skyrms (eds.), *Causation in Decision, Belief Change, and Statistics*, Dordrecht: Kluwer.

Harsanyi, J. (1977), *Rational Behavior and Bargaining. Equilibrium in Games and Social Situations*. Cambridge University Press.

Harsanyi, J. and R. Selten (1988), *A General Theory of Equilibrium Selection in Games*, Cambridge, MA: MIT Press.

Hintikka, J. (1962), *Knowledge and Belief*, Ithaca: Cornell University Press.

Holland, J. (1975), *Adaptation in Natural and Artificial Systems*, University of Michigan Press, Ann Arbor.

Hughes, G. and M. Cresswell (1985), *An Introduction to Modal Logic*, Methuen.

Jordan, J. (1989), "Bayesian Learning in Normal-Form Games," forthcoming in *Games and Economic Behavior*.

(1990), "The Exponential Rate of Learning in Repeated Games," Working Paper, University of Minnesota.

Kadane, J. and P. Larkey (1982), "Subjective Probability and the Theory of Games," *Management Science*, 28:113–20.

Kalai, E. (1990), "Bounded Rationality and Strategic Complexity in Repeated Games," in *Game Theory and Applications*, Academic Press.

Kalai, E. and E. Lehrer (1990), "Rational Learning Leads to Nash Equilibrium," Northwestern University Discussion Paper 895.

Kalai, E. and W. Stanford (1989), "Finite Rationality and Interpersonal Complexity in Repeated Games," *Econometrica*, 56 (2):397–410.

Kaneko, M. (1982), "Structural Common Knowledge and Factual Common Knowledge," Working Paper, RUEE, 87–27.

Kaneko, M. and T. Nagashima (1988), "Players' Deductions and Deductive Knowledge and Common Knowledge as Theories," Virginia Polytechnic Institute Discussion Paper E88–02–01.

(1990), "Game Logic, I and II," Virginia Polytechnic Institute Discussion Paper EPO-3–1 and 2.

Kohlberg, E. (1989), "Refinements of Nash Equilibria: The Main Ideas," Working Paper 89–073, Harvard Business School.

Kohlberg, E. and J. Mertens (1986), "On the Strategic Stability of Equilibria," *Econometrica*, 54:1003–37.

Konyndyk, K. (1986), *Introduction to Modal Logic*. University of Notre Dame, South Bend.

Kreps, D., P. Milgrom, J. Roberts, and R. Wilson (1982), "Rational Cooperation in the Finitely Repeated Prisoners' Dilemma," *Journal of Economic Theory*, 27:245–52.

Kreps, D. and R. Wilson (1982a), "Reputation and Imperfect Information," *Journal of Economic Theory*, 27:253–79.

(1982b), "Sequential Equilibria," *Econometrica*, 50:863–94.

Lehrer, E. (1988), "Repeated Games with Stationary Bounded Recall Strategies," *Journal of Economic Theory*, 46:130–44.

Lewis, D. (1969), *Conventions: A Philosophical Study*. Cambridge, MA: Harvard University Press.

(1976), *Counterfactuals*. Oxford: Basil Blackwell.

Linhart, P., R. Radner, and A. Schotter (1989), "Behavior and Efficiency in the Sealed-Bid Mechanism," Working Paper, New York University.

Lipman, B. (1989), "How to Decide How to Decide How to ... 1989," Working Paper, Carnegie Mellon University.

Maynard Smith, J. (1982), *Evolution and the Theory of Games*. Cambridge University Press.

Meggido, N. (1986), "Remarks on Bounded Rationality, IBM Research Paper RJ5270.

Meggido, N. and A. Wigderson (1986), "On Play by Means of Computing Machines," in J. Halpern (ed.), *Theoretical Aspects of Reasoning about Knowledge*, Los Altos: Morgan Kaufmann.

Mertens, J. F. and S. Zamir (1985), "Formulation of Bayesian Analysis for Games with Incomplete Information," *International Journal of Game Theory*, 14:1–29.

Milgrom, P. and J. Roberts (1990), "Adaptive and Sophisticated Learning in Repeated Normal Form Games," Working Paper, Stanford University.

Myerson, R. (1986), "Multistage Games with Communication," *Econometrica*, 54:323–58.

Nau, R. and K. McCardle (1990), "Coherent Behavior in Noncooperative Games," *Journal of Economic Theory*, 50:424–44.

Neyman, A. (1986), "Bounded Complexity Justifies Cooperation in the Finitely Repeated Prisoners' Dilemma," *Economic Letters*, 19:277–9.

Pearce, D. (1984), "Rationalizable Strategic Behavior and the Problem of Perfection," *Econometrica*, 52:1029–50.

Penrose, R. (1989), *The Emperor's New Mind*. Oxford University Press.

Pettit, P. and R. Sugden (1989), "The Backwards Induction Paradox," Working Paper, University of East Anglia.

Reny, P. (1985), "Rationality, Common Knowledge, and the Theory of Games," Working Paper, University of Western Ontario.

Rosenthal, R. (1981), "Games of Perfect Information, Predatory Pricing, and Chain-store Paradox," *Journal of Economic Theory*, 25:92–100.

Rubinstein, A. (1986), "Finite Automata Play the Repeated Prisoners' Dilemma," *Journal of Economic Theory*, 39:83–96.

(1987), "The Complexity of Strategies and the Resolution of Conflict: an Introduction," in Bryant and Portes (eds.) *Global Macroeconomics: Policy Conflict and Cooperation*, New York: Macmillan Press, pp. 17–32.

Samet, D. (1987), *Ignoring Ignorance and Agreeing to Disagree*. Technical Report M.E.D.S Discussion Paper No. 749, KGSM, Northwestern University. Forthcoming in *Journal of Economic Theory*.

Samuelson, L. (1990), "Evolutionary Foundations of Solution Concepts for Finite, Two-Player, Normal-Form Games," Working Paper, State University of Pennsylvania.

Selten, R. (1975), "Reexamination of the Perfectness Concept for Equilibrium Points in Extensive-Games," *International Journal of Game Theory*, 4:25–55.

(1978), "The Chain-Store Paradox," *Theory and Decision*, 9:127–59.

(1983), "Evolutionary Stability in Extensive 2-Person Games," Working Papers 121 and 122, Bielefeld.

(1988), "Anticipatory Learning in Two-Person Games," Working Paper B-93, Friedrich-Wilhelms-Universität Bonn.

(1989), *Evolution, Learning and Economic Behavior*. Kellogg Graduate School, Northwestern University. Nancy L. Schwarz Memorial Lecture.

Selten, R. and U. Leopold (1982), "Subjunctive Conditionals in Decision Theory and Game Theory," in Stegmuller/Balzer/Spohn (eds.), *Studies in Economics*, Berlin: Springer-Verlag, *Philosophy of Economics*, vol. 2.

Shin, H. (1987), *Logical Structure of Common Knowledge, I and II*. Nuffield College, Oxford.

(1988), "A Comment on Aumann's Definition of Bayes-Rationality," Working Paper, Nuffield College.

Simon, H. (1976), "From Substantive to Procedural Rationality," in S. Latsis (ed.), *Method and Appraisal in Economics*, Cambridge University Press.

Skyrms, B. (1990), "Dynamic Models of Deliberation and the Theory of Games," in R. Parikh (ed.), *Reasoning About Knowledge*, San Mateo, CA: Morgan Kaufman.

Solovay, R. (1976), "Provability Interpretation of Modal Logic," *Israel Journal of Mathematics*, 25:287–304.

Stearns, R. (1989), "Memory-Bounded, Game-Playing Computing Machines," Working Paper, SUNY at Albany.

Tan, T. and S. Werlang (1984), "The Bayesian Foundations of Rationalizable Strategic Behavior and Nash Equilibrium Behavior," *Journal of Economic Theory*, 45:370–91.

Van Damme, E. (1990), "Refinements of Equilibrium," Paper delivered at Barcelona World Congress.

Vassilakis, S. and S. Zamir (1990), "Common Beliefs and Common Knowledge", University of Pittsburgh Working Paper 259.

Von Clauswitz, C. (1976), *On War*. Princeton: Princeton University Press (first published 1832).

Stanford, W. (1990), "Pre-Stable Strategies in Discounted Duopoly Games," forthcoming in *Games and Economic Behavior*.

Walliser, B. (1990), "Epistemic Logic and Game Theory," Technical Report, ENPC-CERAS Discussion Paper.

CHAPTER 2

Refinements of Nash equilibrium

Eric van Damme*

1 INTRODUCTION

Non-cooperative game theory studies the question of what constitutes rational behavior in situations of strategic interaction in which players cannot communicate nor sign binding agreements. The traditional answer to this question centers around the notion of Nash equilibrium. Such an equilibrium is a vector of strategies, one for each player in the game, with the property that no single player can increase his payoff by changing to a different strategy as long as the opponents do not change their strategies. The Nash equilibrium concept is motivated by the idea that a theory of rational decision-making should not be a self-destroying prophecy that creates an incentive to deviate for those who believe in it. To quote from Luce and Raiffa (1957, p. 173):

> if our non-cooperative theory is to lead to an *n*-tuple of strategy choices and if it is to have the property that knowledge of the theory does not lead one to make a choice different from that dictated by the theory, then the strategies isolated by the theory must be equilibrium points.

In other words, for a (commonly known) norm of behavior to be self-enforcing it is *necessary* that the norm (agreement) constitutes a Nash equilibrium.

The increased use of non-cooperative game theory in economics in the last decades has led to an increased awareness of the fact that not every Nash equilibrium can be considered as a self-enforcing norm of behavior. Very roughly, the Nash concept is unsatisfactory since it may prescribe irrational behavior in contingencies that arise when somebody has deviated from the norm. In applications, one typically finds many equilibria and intuitive, context depending arguments have been used to exclude the "unreasonable" ones. At the same time game theorists have tried to formalize and unify the intuitions conveyed by applications and examples by means of general refined equilibrium notions. The aim of this chapter is to describe, and comment on the most important concepts that have been put forward as being necessary for self-enforcingness. Although the literature offers a wide variety of different refinements, it will be seen that all of them are based on a small number of basic ideas. (These main ideas are also described in Kohlberg (1989) from which I borrowed the term "norm of behavior.")

Ever since Luce and Raiffa (1957) the intuitive justification of equilibria and the relevance of equilibria to the analysis of a game have been questioned. It has been realized that it is not evident that Nash equilibrium is a necessary consequence of strategic reasoning by rational players, that it is not clear how players would arrive at an equilibrium or how they would select one from the set of equilibria. I do not wish to enter a discussion on these topics here, rather I refer to Aumann (1987, 1988), Bernheim (1986), Binmore (1990), Brandenburger and Dekel (1987), and Tan and Werlang (1988) for extensive discussions on the epistemic foundations of equilibria, i.e., on what the players must know about each other's strategies and each other's rationality for equilibria to make sense. In this author's opinion some of the confusion surrounding the Nash concept can be traced to the fact that the mathematical formalism of non-cooperative game theory allows multiple interpretations and to the fact that the different aspects of non-cooperative analysis are not clearly separated.

Non-cooperative game theoretic analysis has several aspects:

- (i) (The equilibrium definition problem.) Which agreements are self-enforcing?
- (ii) (The equilibrium attainment problem.) How, or under which conditions will the players reach an agreement?
- (iii) (The equilibrium selection problem.) Which agreement is likely to be concluded?

Except for the last section I deal exclusively with the first topic. I do not discuss how self-enforcing norms come to be established nor how the selection among these takes place. The motivation for studying the first question independently is that knowing its answer seems a prerequisite for being able to answer the other questions. (For example, one might hope that in games with a unique self-enforcing equilibrium players will always coordinate on that equilibrium.) I restrict attention to refinements of Nash equilibrium that try to capture further necessary conditions for self-enforcing norms of behavior. Hence, I investigate which conditions Nash equilibria should satisfy such that rational players would have no incentive to deviate from them. Using the terminology of Binmore (1987) I, therefore, remain in the eductive context.

Nash equilibria also admit other interpretations than as self-enforcing norms and in other (non-eductive) contexts different considerations, leading to alternative refinements, may be appropriate. For example, in biology an equilibrium is seen as the outcome of a dynamic process of natural selection rather than as the consequence of reasoning by the players. The basic equilibrium concept in that branch of game theory, viz. the notion of evolutionarily stable strategies or ESS (Maynard Smith and Price, 1973; Maynard Smith, 1982) may formally be viewed as a refinement of Nash equilibrium but it is not further discussed here since it is motivated completely differently (although, mathematically it is related to several concepts discussed below, see van Damme, 1987, chapter 9). Similarly I will not deal with the interpretation of Nash equilibria as stable states of learning processes in a context in which the same game is played repeatedly, but each time with different active players who can use observations from the past to guide their behavior (on learning models, see, for example, Canning, 1989, 1990; Fudenberg and Kreps, 1988; Kalai and Lehrer, 1990; Milgrom and Roberts, 1990, 1991). Of course, this does not imply that I consider such contexts to be unimportant, they simply fall outside the scope of this chapter. Perhaps in economic situations learning and evolution are even more important than reasoning. Finally, I rule out any correlation between players' actions that is not explicitly allowed by the rules. Hence, I do not consider correlated equilibria (Aumann, 1974; Forges, 1986; Myerson, 1986).

Space limitations do not allow an extensive discussion on the applications of the various refinements. Yet, the proof of the pudding is in the eating, it is the applications and the insights derived from them that lend the refinements their validity. As Aumann (1985) writes:

> My main thesis is that a solution concept should be judged more by what it does than by what it is; more by its success in establishing relationships and providing insights into the workings of the social processs to which it is applied than by considerations of *a priori* plausibility based on its definition alone.

The remainder of the chapter is organized as follows. In section 2, I discuss the principle of backward induction, i.e., the idea that an equilibrium strategy should also make sense in contingencies that do not arise during the actual play. Special emphasis is on the concepts of subgame perfect and sequential equilibria, on the definition of consistency of beliefs, and on the assumption of persistent rationality. Section 3 deals with "trembling-hand perfect" equilibria as well as the related notions of properness and persistency. All three concepts require that the equilibrium still makes sense if with a small probability each player makes a mistake. This section also briefly investigates what kind of refinements result if it is required that an equilibrium be robust against slight perturbations in the payoffs or in the structure of the game. Issues related to the Kohlberg/Mertens concept of stable equilibria are discussed in section 4. Stability is a set-valued solution concept and it will be shown that set-valuedness is a natural consequence of several desirable properties. The topic of section 5 is forward induction, i.e., the idea that a player's past behavior may signal either this player's private information or how the player intends to play in the future. For the special class of signaling games several intuitive refinement criteria are reviewed that are all related to Kohlberg/Mertens stability. In section 6 we move from equilibrium refinement to equilibrium selection and briefly discuss a model (originally due to Carlsson and van Damme) in which slight payoff uncertainty forces players to coordinate on a specific "focal" equilibrium in each 2×2 bimatrix game.

This introduction is concluded by specifying the notational conventions that will be used for extensive form games. Attention will be confined to finite games with perfect recall and for the definition of such a game Γ the reader is referred to Selten (1975) or to Kreps and Wilson (1982a). X denotes the set decision points in Γ, Z is the set of endpoints, and $u_i(z)$ is player i's payoff when z is reached. We depict the endpoints by row-vectors, the first component of which is the payoff to player 1, etc. The origin of the game tree is depicted by an open circle. H_i denotes the set of information sets of player i (with typical element h). We depict an information set by a dashed line that connects the points in the set. A behavior strategy s_i of player i assigns a local strategy s_{ih} (i.e., a probability distribution on the set of choices at h) to each $h \in H_i$. If s is a (behavior) strategy vector, $s=(s_1, \ldots, s_n)$, then p^s, the outcome of s, is the probability distribution that s induces on the set of endpoints of Γ. If A is a set of nodes, we also write $p^s(A)$ for the probability that A is reached when s is played. Player i's expected payoff resulting from s is denoted by $u_i(s)$. Hence, $u_i(s)=\Sigma_z p^s(z)u_i(z)$. For a decision point $x \in X$, denote by p^s_x the probability distribution that s would induce on Z if the game were started at x, and write $u_{ix}(s)=\Sigma_z p^s_x(z)u_i(z)$. If μ specifies a probability distribution on the decision points in the information set $h \in H_i$, then we write $u^\mu_{ih}(s)=\Sigma_{x \in h}$ $\mu(x)u_{ix}(s)$. If s is a strategy vector and s_i' is a strategy of player i, then $s \backslash s_i'$ denotes the strategy vector $(s_1, \ldots, s_{i-1}, s_i', s_{i+1}, \ldots, s_n)$, We use S_i to denote the set of all strategies of player i and S is the set of strategy vectors.

2 BACKWARD INDUCTION

A strategy vector s is a Nash equilibrium (Nash, 1950a) of an extensive form game Γ if:

$$u_i(s) \geq u_i(s \backslash s_i') \text{ for all } i \text{ and all } s_i' \in S_i. \tag{2.1}$$

If we interpret a strategy vector s as a (fully specified) norm of behavior then (2.1) is a necessary condition for a commonly known norm to be self-enforcing, i.e., for the norm to be such that no player has an incentive to deviate from it. In this interpretation, s_{ih} (the local strategy of player i at h) may be viewed both as player i's intended action at h as well as the common prediction of all the opponents of what i will do at h (for further comments on the interpretation of strategies, see Rubinstein, 1988). Hence, Nash equilibrium requires common and correct conjectures. It is important to note that, for a Nash equilibrium, it is necessary that different players conjecture the same response even at information sets that are not reached when s is played (cf. the discussion on the game of figure 2.11 in section 5.2). In extensive form games, taking strategy vectors as the primitive concept in particular implies that a player's predictions do not change during the game: Player j's conjecture about the action chosen at h is s_{ih} both at the beginning of the game as well as at any information set $k \in H_j$, even if it is the case that k cannot be reached when s_i is played. Hence, taking strategy vectors as the primitive concept implies an assumption of "no strategy updating," i.e., that at each point in time each player believes that in the "future" all players will behave according to the norm even though he may have seen that players did not observe the norm in the past. We make these remarks to show that some criticisms that have been leveled against subgame perfect equilibria are actually criticisms against using strategy vectors as the primitive concept of a theory.

2.1 Subgame perfect equilibria

Selten (1965) provided an example similar to the game from figure 2.1a to point out that not every Nash equilibrium can be considered a self-enforcing norm of behavior: (D, d) is a Nash equilibrium (player 1 optimizes by choosing D if player 2 chooses d and, if player 1 indeed chooses D then player 2's choice is irrelevant since he doesn't have to move). However, since player 2 cannot commit himself to his choice of d (the game is assumed to be non-cooperative), he will deviate to a if he is actually called to play. Even if there is a prior agreement to play (D, d), player 1 anticipates that player 2 will deviate and he deviates as well, thereby increasing his payoff: the agreement is not self-enforcing.

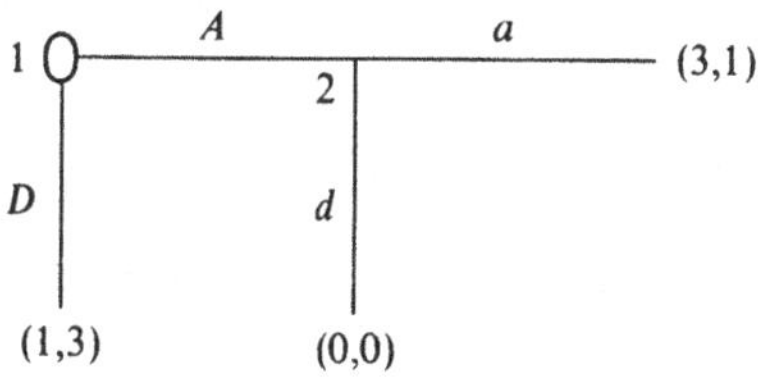

Figure 2.1a Game Γ_1

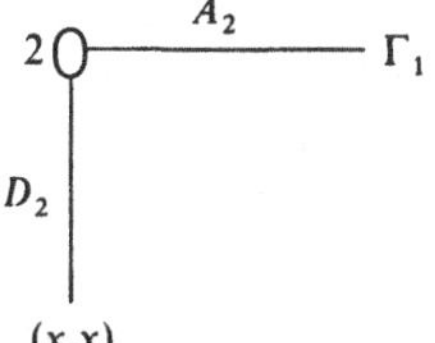

Figure 2.1b Game Γ_2 (x)

Nash equilibrium requires that each player's strategy be optimal from the *ex ante* point of view. *Ex ante* optimality implies that the strategy is also optimal in each contingency that arises with positive probability but, as the example shows, a Nash equilibrium strategy need not be a best reply at an information set that initially is assigned probability zero. A natural suggestion is to impose *ex post* optimality as a necessary requirement for self-enforcingness. For games with perfect information (i.e., games in which all information sets are singletons) this requirement of sequential rationality is mathematically meaningful and may be formalized as:

$$u_{ih}(s) \geq u_{ih}(s \backslash s_i') \text{ for all } i, \text{ all } s_i' \in S_i, \text{ all } h \in H_i. \tag{2.2}$$

Hence, at each information set h, player i's equilibrium strategy maximizes the player's expected payoff conditional on having reached h as long as the opponents play their equilibrium strategies in the future. Clearly, equilibria satisfying (2.2) can be found by rolling back the game tree in a dynamic programming fashion. Selten (1965) noted that the argument leading to (2.2) can be extended to a wider class of games – defining a *subgame* as a part of the tree of an extensive form game that constitutes a game in itself. Selten argued that a self-enforcing norm should induce a self-enforcing norm in each subgame since otherwise some player might find it advantageous to deviate from the norm and thereby reach a subgame with an outcome that benefits him. Selten defined a *subgame perfect equilibrium* as a Nash equilibrium that induces a Nash equilibrium in every subgame.

In condition (2.2) it is assumed that each player at each point in time believes that in the future all players will try to maximize their payoffs. A player is required to have such beliefs even in situations in which he has already seen that some players did not maximize in the past: the information set h may be reached only if a deviation from s has occurred. This assumption of persistent rationality has been extensively criticized in the literature (see, for example, Basu, 1988, 1990; Binmore, 1987; Reny, 1988a, b; Rosenthal, 1981). The critique may be illustrated by means of the game of figure 2.1b. As long as $x > 1$, the unique strategy vector satisfying

(2.2) is (A, D_{2a}). However, if $x=4$, then A_2 is strictly dominated so that player 1 only has to move after player 2 has taken an irrational action. In such a situation it is not compelling to force player 1 to believe that player 2 will certainly behave rationally and play a at his second move. There seems no convincing argument why player 1 could not believe that player 2 will choose d, and in the latter case he would prefer D. Reny (1988a) proposes to weaken (2.2) by demanding optimizing behavior of player i only at information sets h that are not excluded by player i's own strategy, i.e., that do not contradict the rationality of player i. Reny's concept of "weak sequential equilibrium" does not put any restrictions on the conjectures about player i's behavior at information sets $h \in H_i$ that can be reached only when player i deviates from s_i. In the game $\Gamma_2(x)$ with $x>1$ there are multiple weakly sequential equilibria but they all lead to the outcome (x, x). If, however, the game were modified such that the payoff after A_2Aa were (4,4) rather than (3,1), then (D,D_2d) would be a weak sequential equilibrium of $\Gamma_2(1.5)$ and this produces an outcome that differs from the subgame perfect equilibrium outcome. (In the modified game Reny's concept allows player 1 to believe that player 2 will choose d after a defection to A_2.)

In Kohlberg and Mertens (1986) it is also proposed to weaken requirement (2.2). These authors take the position that requiring a theory of rationality to specify a unique choice in every contingency is unduly restrictive and they propose (certain) sets of strategy vectors (rather than single strategy vectors) as the primitive concept of a theory. Hence, according to Kohlberg and Mertens, a self-enforcing norm need not completely pin down the players' behavior and beliefs in those contingencies that will not be reached when the norm is obeyed; we may be satisfied if we can identify the self-enforcing outcomes, i.e., the outcomes that result when everybody obeys the norm. For example, in $\Gamma_2(4)$ the norm that says "player 2 should play D_2" (without specifying what player 1 should do) is self-enforcing in the more liberal sense. In $\Gamma_2(2)$, Kohlberg and Mertens also identify player 2 choosing D_2 as the self-enforcing outcome but now player 1's behavior cannot be completely arbitrary: a self-enforcing norm specifies that player 1 should choose D with a probability of at most $\frac{1}{2}$, since otherwise player 2 will violate the norm. We will return to the Kohlberg/Mertens stability concept in section 5. In that section it will be seen that several desirable properties that we might want self-enforcing norms to possess can only be satisfied by norms that allow some freedom of choice in some circumstances.

The example from figure 2.1b makes clear that the assumptions that players are perfectly rational and that the game is exactly as specified imply that counterfactuals arise naturally in game theory. As Selten and Leopold (1982) write:

In order to see whether a certain course of action is optimal it is often necessary to look at situations which would arise if something non-optimal were done. Since in fact a rational decision maker will not take a non-optimal choice, the examination of the consequence of such choices will necessarily invoke counterfactuals.

In the game $\Gamma_2(4)$, to determine his optimal choice, player 1 has to evaluate the counterfactual "if player 2 would choose A_2, my best response would be A." Philosophers (Lewis, 1973 and Stalnaker, 1969) have suggested evaluating such a counterfactual by investigating whether in a world (or model) that is most similar to the one under consideration and in which player 2 chooses A_2 it is indeed true that the best response is A. Selten and Leopold (1982) suggest a parameter theory of counterfactuals, a slight variation of this idea. To implement this idea, game theorists have suggested to formalize the similarity relation by means of perturbed games: the original game is embedded into a larger perturbed game (in which all information sets are reached), and is approximated by letting the perturbations vanish. Two possible perturbations readily suggest themselves, one may either give up the assumption that the players are perfectly rational (this is the approach taken in Selten's perfectness concept, see subsection 3.1) or one may give up the assumption that the game model fully describes the situation. Some consequences of the latter approach will be investigated in subsection 3.2. Not surprisingly, it will be seen that different approaches may yield different outcomes.

Before turning to perturbations, however, we first discuss the concept of sequential equilibria.

2.2 Sequential equilibria

The *ex post* optimality requirement (2.2) cannot be applied at non-singleton information sets, since there the conditional expected payoff need not be well-defined. As a consequence, the requirement of subgame perfection does not suffice to rule out all non-self-enforcing equilibria. For example, change the game from figure 2.1a, such that player 1 chooses between D, A, and A' with player 2 moving after A and A' but without knowing whether A or A' was chosen and with the payoffs after A' being the same as those after A. Then (D, d) is a subgame perfect equilibrium of the modified game (since the latter admits no subgames), but it clearly is not self-enforcing.

Kreps and Wilson (1982a) suggest extending the applicability of (2.2) by explicitly specifying beliefs (i.e., conditional probabilities) at every information set so that posterior expected payoffs can always be computed and they propose to make these beliefs a formal part of the definition of an equilibrium. Of course these beliefs should not be completely arbitrary, they should respect the information structure of the game and they should be consistent with the equilibrium strategies whenever possible. Formally, a system of beliefs is a mapping μ that assigns a probability distribution to the nodes in h for any information set h and a *sequential equilibrium* is defined as a pair (s, μ) consisting of a strategy vector s and a system of beliefs μ satisfying the following two conditions:

s is *sequentially rational* given μ, i.e., $u^{\mu}_{ih}(S) \geq u^{\mu}_{ih}(s \backslash s_i')$ for all i, all $s_i' \in S_i$, all $h \in H_i$, and: (2.3)

μ is *consistent* with s, i.e., there exists a sequence s^k of completely mixed behavior strategy vectors with $s^k \rightarrow s (k \rightarrow \infty)$, such that $\mu(x) = \lim_{k \rightarrow \infty} p^{sk}(x)/p^{sk}(h)$ for each information set h and each x in h. (2.4)

(s^k is said to be completely mixed if $s^k_{ih}(c) > 0$ for all i, $h \in H_i$ and all choices at h). Condition (2.3) expresses that, given the beliefs μ, the player maximizes his payoff at h by playing according to s as long as the opponents play according to s as well. The consistency requirement means that, at an information set which a player does not expect to be reached, the beliefs can be explained by means of small trembles from the equilibrium strategies. (At other information sets the beliefs coincide with those induced by the equilibrium.) This consistency requirement is inspired by Selten's concept of trembling-hand perfect equilibria (see the next section) but it is not completely intuitive on its own and Kreps and Wilson express some doubts about whether consistency actually "ought" to be defined as in (2.4). In fact Kreps and Wilson's intuitive motivation for where the beliefs come from does not involve any trembles. They argue that at information sets h that are initially assigned probability zero ($p^s(h) = 0$), it is plausible to assume that the player will construct some alternative hypothesis s' as to how the game has been played that is consistent with his observation (i.e., $p^{s'}(h) > 0$) and then use s' and Bayes' rule to compute his beliefs. Formally, define a system of beliefs to be *structurally consistent* if for each information set h there exists some s' with $p^{s'}(h) > 0$ and $\mu(x) = p^{s'}(x)/p^{s'}(h)$ for each x in h. (Kreps and Wilson then go on to strengthen this condition by requiring that alternative hypotheses at diferent information sets be related in certain ways.)

Although this structural consistency requirement seems intuitive at first, further reflection reveals that it actually is not. First, the idea of reassessing the game (i.e., to construct alternative hypotheses) runs contrary to the idea that a rational player can foresee and evaluate all contingencies in advance. (Recall the remarks on strategy vectors from the beginning of this section.)

Secondly, structural consistency conflicts with the sequential rationality requirement (2.3). The latter requires believing that from h on play will be in accordance with s, while the former requires believing that play has been in accordance with s'. Although these requirements are not conflicting in games with a stage structure (in these the past can be separated from the future) they may be incompatible in games in which the information sets cross, since in these deviations in the past are automatically accompanied by deviations in the future. An explicit example is contained in Kreps and Ramey (1987). That paper also contains an example of a game in which there does not exist a sequential equilibrium (s, μ) in which in addition μ is structurally consistent. Hence, structural consistency may conflict with consistency. Since, as seen above, structural consistency does not seem a compeling requirement, one should not be bothered by this discrepancy. Of course there remains the question of whether the consistency requirement (2.4) can be expressed directly in terms of the basic data (i.e., the choices and information sets) of the extensive form of the game. The affirmative answer to this question is given in Kohlberg and Reny (1991).

The literature offers a variety of equilibrium concepts (usually under the common name of "perfect Bayesian equilibrium") that are related to the sequential equilibrium concept but in which milder restrictions are imposed on the way in which beliefs are formed in zero probability events. The weakest of these do not impose any conditions off the equilibrium path and allow, for example, that different players with "identical" information explain an unexpected deviation in different ways. (Note that (2.4), according to the usual "common knowledge" assumption underlying Nash equilibrium, assumes that all players have a common theory to explain deviations). For further details the reader is referred to Fudenberg and Tirole (1989) and Weibull (1990).

Others authors have proposed to impose additional requirements on the way beliefs are revised. In applications, such as the study of dynamic games with incomplete information, frequently the so-called support restriction is imposed. (For example, the concept of perfect sequential equilibrium (PSE) that is often used in applications imposes this restriction, see Grossman and Perry, 1986.) This restriction requires that, if at a certain point in time a player assigns probability zero to a certain type of opponent, then from that time on he continues to assign probability zero to that type. The restriction enables analysis by means of a dynamic programming procedure in which the beliefs are used as a state variable. However, Madrigal, Tan, and Werlang (1987) have shown that imposing this restriction may lead to non-existence: the support restriction may be incompatible with the (very mild) requirement that the beliefs be derived from the equilibrium strategies on the equilibrium path. The following example (taken from Nöldeke and van Damme, 1990) demonstrates why this is the case and makes clear that the support restriction has nothing compelling to it (for a more economic example, see Vincent, 1990).

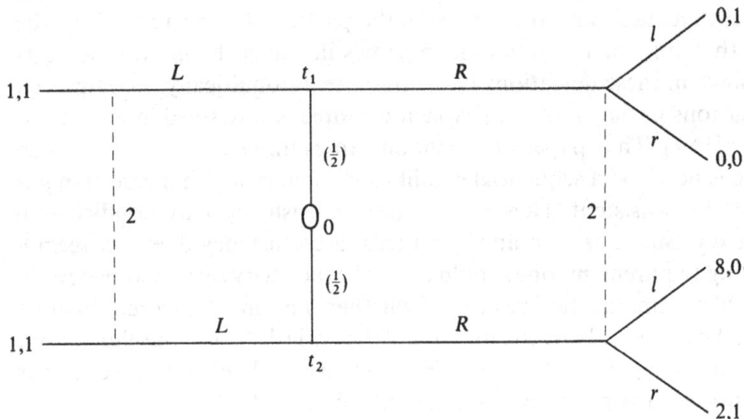

Figure 2.2a A signaling game

L			l	r
1,1	$(t_1,\frac{1}{2})$		0,1	0,0
1,1	$(t_1,\frac{1}{2})$		8,0	2,1
L			R	

Figure 2.2b A matrix representation of the signaling game from figure 2.2a

Consider the signaling game from figure 2.2a: nature first selects a type of player 1, both possibilities being equally likely. If player 1 chooses L the game ends, otherwise player 2 has to choose between l and r. (Figure 2.2b gives a convenient matrix representation of this game following the conventions outlined in Banks and Sobel (1987): the matrices correspond to the choices of player 1, the rows represent the types of this player and the columns are the choices of player 2.) The game has a unique Nash equilibrium, viz. (L, R, r). Now consider the two-fold repetition of this game: Player 1's type is drawn once and for all at the beginning of the game, and before the beginning of round 2 only the actions from the previous round, but not the payoffs, are revealed. We claim that this game has a unique Nash equilibrium outcome, viz. type t_1 chooses L twice and type t_2

chooses R twice. (*Proof*: strict dominance implies that type t_1 chooses L in both rounds and that type t_2 chooses R in the last round. Hence, type t_2 will choose LR or RR, or a mixture of these. LR cannot be type t_2's equilibrium strategy since (when player 2 plays his best response) it yields less than the payoff that type t_2 can guarantee himself by playing LL. Type t_2 cannot mix, since then player 2's unique best response is to choose r whenever R is chosen and this implies that RR is strictly better.) To support the unique equilibrium outcome, player 2 should choose r with a probability of at least $\frac{5}{6}$ in the second round after having observed L in the first round and R in the second. However, such behavior is not optimal if beliefs are required to be consistent with the equilibrium strategies as well as to satisfy the support restriction. Namely, these requirements force player 2 to believe that he is facing type t_1 for sure if he observes LR (since only t_1 chooses L in the first round in equilibrium) and if he has such beliefs he should play l. Hence, the beliefs associated with any Nash equilibrium necessarily violate the support restriction. The example makes clear that such a violation is actually quite natural: after having observed L in the first round, player 2 has no evidence that play is not in agreement with the equilibrium so he adopts equilibrium beliefs. After having observed LR, however, he has such evidence and he corrects his initial beliefs since after all it is only t_2 who might have had an incentive to try to mislead him.

3 PERTURBED GAMES

Selten (1975) proposes to escape from counterfactuals associated with irrational moves of rational players by giving up the assumption that players are perfectly rational and he introduces a model of slight imperfect rationality that is based on the idea that with some very small probability a player will make a mistake. He writes (Selten, 1975, p. 35):

> There cannot be any mistakes if the players are absolutely rational. Nevertheless a satisfactory interpretation of equilibrium points in extensive games seems to require that the possibility of mistakes is not completely excluded. This can be achieved by a point of view which looks at complete rationality as a limiting case of incomplete rationality.

Selten's approach is reviewed in subsection 3.1.

Alternatively, one may escape from the counterfactuals by giving up the assumption that the game fully describes the real situation. One may argue that the model is overabstracted, that there are always some aspects that are not incorporated and that, if a complete model were built, the difficulties associated with unreached information sets would vanish. That there are rewards associated with not taking the description of the game too literally is already known since Harsanyi (1973) in which it was shown that, if the slight uncertainty that each player has about the payoffs of his opponents is actually taken into account, the usual instabilities (and interpretational difficulties) of mixed strategy equilibria vanish. (At least this holds for generic normal form games). In subsection 3.2 we briefly discuss several variants of the idea that a self-enforcing equilibrium should still make sense when the aspects that were abstracted away from (such as payoff uncertainty) are explicitly taken into account. It will turn out that the results depend crucially on which story that one tells, and that even Nash equilibria that are not subgame perfect can make sense in certain contexts. Hence, a main conclusion to be drawn from subsection 3.2 is that, if the game model is not complete, it may not be appropriate to apply equilibrium refinements.

3.1 Perfect equilibria

In Selten (1975) incomplete rationality is modeled by the assumption that at each of his information sets a player will, with a small (independent) probability, suffer from "momentary insanity" and make a mistake. Selten assumes that in the case of a mistake at the information set h the player's behavior at h is governed by some unspecified psychological mechanism which selects each choice at h with a strictly positive probability. Since in such a perturbed game there are no unreached information sets, a Nash equilibrium prescribes the playing of a best response everywhere. Selten proposes to restrict attention to those equilibria of the original game that can be obtained as a limit of a sequence equilibria of perturbed games as the trembles vanish and he calls these perfect equilibria.

It is convenient to define perfect equilibria first for normal form games, i.e., games in which each player has to make just one choice and in which choices are simultaneous. Let $G=(S_i, u_i)_{i=1}^n$ be such a game, let σ be a completely mixed strategy vector (with σ_i representing the choice of player i if he makes a mistake) and let ε be a positive n-vector of mistake probabilities. Denote by $s^{\varepsilon,\sigma}$ the strategy vector that results if each player intends to play s and players make independent mistakes according to (ε, σ). (Hence, $s_i^{\varepsilon,\sigma}$ is the convex combination of s_i and σ_i that assigns weight ε_i to σ_i.) In the perturbed game $G^{\varepsilon,\sigma}$ (i.e., the game in which the players take the mistakes explicitly into account), the strategy vector s is an equilibrium if:

$$u_i(s^{\varepsilon,\sigma}\backslash s_i) \geq u_i(s^{\varepsilon,\sigma}\backslash s_i') \text{ for all } i \text{ and all } s_i' \in S_i. \tag{3.1}$$

The strategy vector s is said to be a *perfect equilibrium* of G if s is a limit of a sequence $s(\varepsilon_n, \sigma_n)$ of equilibria of perturbed games $G^{\varepsilon_n,\sigma_n}$ with $\varepsilon_n \to 0$. Note that for s to be perfect it is sufficient to find *one* mistake sequence that justifies s. Selten (1975) proved that perfect equilibria exist and he showed that the strategy vector s is a perfect equilibrium if and only if s is a best response to a sequence of completely mixed strategy vectors that converges to s. In particular it follows that a perfect equilibrium is undominated (admissible).

Now let us return to an extensive form game Γ. Selten's assumption that trembles at different information sets are independent implies that one may think of different information sets of the same player as being administrated by different agents. The agent ih controling the information set $h \in H_i$ has the same payoff as the original player i but this is the only link between agents, the agent ih cannot directly control the actions of agent ik. Each agent maximizes for himself, counting on the rationality of the other agents, but incorporating the fact that they may make mistakes. It is now natural to look at the normal form game in which the agents are the players. This game $(S_{ih}, u_{ih})_{i=1,\ h \in H_i}^{n}$ (with, of course, $u_{ih} = u_i$ for all i and all $h \in H_i$) is called the *agent normal form* of Γ. A *perfect equilibrium* of the extensive form game Γ is defined as a perfect equilibrium of the agent normal form of Γ. Note that equilibria of a perturbed agent normal form game can be characterized by a condition similar to (3.1). This time we should satisfy the local condition:

$$u_i(s^{\varepsilon,\sigma} \backslash s_{ih}) \geq u_i(s^{\varepsilon,\sigma} \backslash s'_{ih}) \text{ for all } i \text{ and all } h \in H_i, \tag{3.2}$$

where σ is a completely mixed behavior strategy vector. It is easy to see that each perfect equilibrium is a sequential equilibrium; Kreps and Wilson (1982a) proved that the converse holds for generic games.

A perfect equilibrium of the extensive form need not be perfect in the normal form. (Although this property does hold for generic extensive forms.) In figure 2.3 the equilibrium (DL_1, L_2) is perfect in the extensive form: if player 1 fears that he is more likely to tremble than player 2 is, then his choice of D is optimal. The normal form assumes that each player can control his own actions completely. Obviously, in the normal form only (UL_1, L_2) is perfect. Note that in the normal form we represent the "duplicate strategies" DL_1 and DR_1 by their "equivalence class" D. This convention will be followed throughout the remainder of the paper. Hence, our normal form strategies will not specify what a player should do after he himself has deviated. The reader may fill in these actions in any way he wants without affecting the validity of any statements we make below about normal form strategies.

The game from figure 2.4 shows that, on the other hand, equilibria that are perfect in the normal form need not even be subgame perfect in the extensive form: (D_1, D_2) is perfect in the normal form since D_2 is player 2's

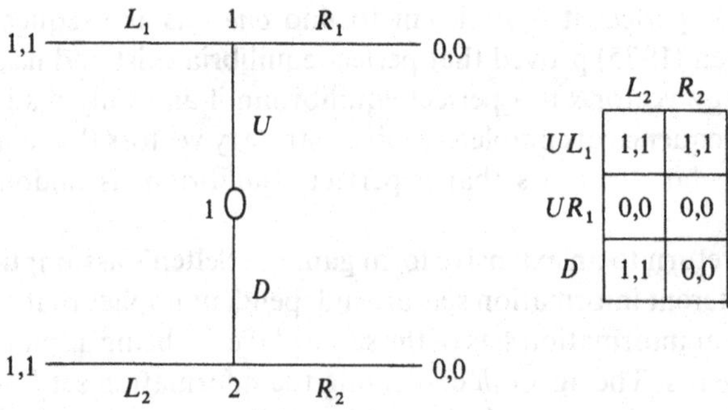

	L_2	R_2
UL_1	1,1	1,1
UR_1	0,0	0,0
D	1,1	0,0

Figure 2.3 An extensive form perfect equilibrium need not be admissible

best strategy if he believes that player 1 is more likely to tremble to A_1d than to A_1a. In the extensive form, perfectness excludes such beliefs: even if player 1 trembled at his first move, player 2 should still consider it very likely that player 1 will play rationally (i.e., choose a) at his second move, i.e., he should play A_2. Only (A_1, A_2) is (subgame) perfect in the extensive form. (Note that the above conclusion would remain valid if the payoffs were slightly perturbed so as to make the game generic. Reny (1988a) has shown that a normal form perfect equilibrium is always "weakly sequential" in the extensive form.)

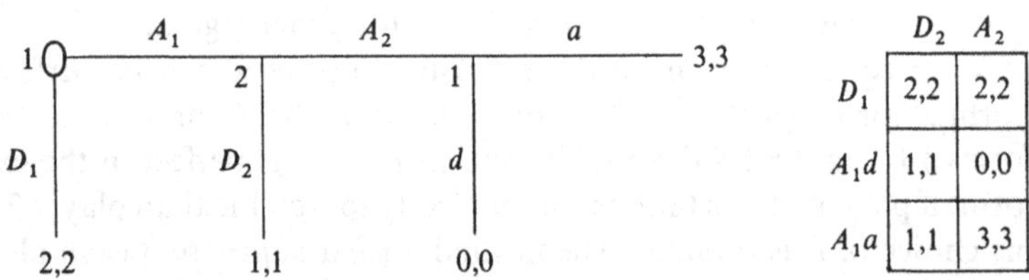

	D_2	A_2
D_1	2,2	2,2
A_1d	1,1	0,0
A_1a	1,1	3,3

Figure 2.4 Normal form perfectness does not imply subgame perfection

Myerson (1978) argued also that in the normal form of figure 2.4 it is nonsensical to believe that A_1d is more likely than A_1a. He argued that A_1d is a more costly mistake than A_1a, that a player will try harder to prevent more costly mistakes and that as a result these will occur much less often. Formally, he defined an ε-proper equilibrium of a normal form game as a completely mixed strategy vector s having the property that, if a pure strategy k of player i is a worse response against s than a pure strategy l, then the probability that s_i assigns to k is at most ε times the probability that s_i assigns to l. A limit of a sequence ε-proper equilibria (as ε tend to zero) is called a *proper equilibrium.* Such an equilibrium exists and is obviously perfect. An important property is that proper equilibria of a normal form game induce sequential equilibrium outcomes in every extensive form game with that normal form. Formally, if Γ is an extensive form game with normal form G and, if s is a proper equilibrium of G, then there exists a sequential equilibrium (s', μ) of Γ such that $p^s = p^{s'}$ (Kohlberg and Mertens, 1986; van Damme, 1984).

Another refinement that is related to the perfectness concept is the persistent equilibrium (Kalai and Samet, 1984). If $G = (S_i, u_i)_{i=1}^n$ is a normal form game and R_i is a compact convex subset of S_i for each i, then $R = X_i R_i$ is said to be an essential retract if there exists a neighborhood R' of R such that for each s' in R' there is some s in R that is a best reply against s'. (Roughly this definition strengthens perfectness by requiring stability against *all* perturbations; simultaneously it weakens perfectness by allowing sets of solutions, this in order to guarantee existence.) A minimal essential retract is called a persistent retract and an equilibrium that lies in such a retract is said to be a *persistent equilibrium.* Persistency does not seem to be a necessary requirement for self-enforcingness. For example, in the Battle of the Sexes Game of figure 2.7a only the pure equilibria are persistent. Hence, a symmetric game need not have symmetric persistent equilibrium. Similarly, in the coordination problem of figure 2.5 the outcome in which player 1 chooses D seems perfectly self-enforcing if players cannot communicate. (Note that player 2 has no incentive whatever to communicate.) However, only the two equilibria with payoff (3,3) are persistent in this game. From these examples it appears that persistency is more relevant in an evolutionary or in a learning context, rather than in a pure eductive context.

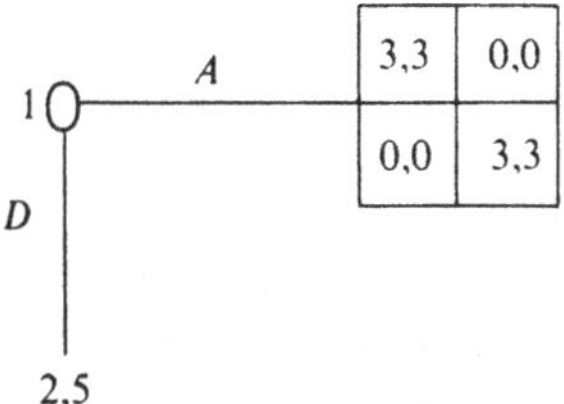

Figure 2.5 A coordination problem

3.2 Correlated trembles

Selten's assumption that mistakes are uncorrelated across different information sets has been criticized and it has been argued (for example, in Binmore, 1987) that in some contexts it may be more natural to allow correlated trembles. Obviously, if perturbations in a more general class are allowed and if only stability against one sequence of perturbed games is required, then typically less outcomes will be eliminated. Correlated trembles arise naturally if there is initial uncertainty about the payoffs and we will now give some examples to illustrate that less equilibria can be eliminated in this context, in fact, that in some cases no Nash equilibrium can be eliminated. The reason is that, when there is initial payoff uncertainty, the players' beliefs may change drastically during the game. Possibilities which are unlikely *ex ante* may have large effects *ex post* when they actually happen. Consequently, it is by no means obvious that the perturbations like the ones discussed below should be considered *slight* perturbations. (That a small amount of payoff uncertainty may have a large effect is also known from the "applications" in Kreps and Wilson (1982b), Kreps *et al.* (1982), and Fudenberg and Maskin (1986). The results below are different since they show that even vanishing uncertainty may have drastic consequences.)

Consider once more the game $\Gamma_2(2)$ from figure 2.1b, but suppose now that player 1 initially has some doubts about the objectives of player 2. He believes that with probability $1-\varepsilon$ player 2 is "rational" and has payoffs as in $\Gamma_2(2)$ and that with probability ε this player is "irrational" and tries to minimize player 1's payoffs (hence, in this case $u_2 \equiv -u_1$). Player 2 knows his own objectives. The subgame perfect equilibrium (A, D_2a) of the original game is no longer viable in this context: if player 2 believes that player 1 chooses A, then he is facing the irrational type of player 2, hence, player 1 should deviate to D. The reader easily verifies that the perturbed game has a unique subgame perfect equilibrium and that in this equilibrium player 1 chooses both A and D with probability $\frac{1}{2}$ while the rational type of player 2 chooses A_2 with probability $2\varepsilon/(1-\varepsilon)$. Hence, with this story, although we obtain the subgame perfect equilibrium outcome of the game $\Gamma_2(2)$ in the limit, we rationalize a strategy for player 1 that is not this player's subgame perfect equilibrium strategy.

By using a construction as above, Fudenberg *et al.* (1988, proposition 4) have shown that, for every extensive form game, each equilibrium that is (strictly) perfect in the normal form can be similarly rationalized by a sequence of slightly perturbed games in which each player has some private, independent, information about his own payoffs. Also outcomes that are not subgame perfect can be "rationalized" by means of slight payoff uncertainty. This result can be illustrated by means of the extensive form game of figure 2.4 which has (A_1a, A_2) as its unique subgame perfect equilibrium outcome. Suppose that player 2 believes that with a small but positive probability player 1 has the payoff 4 if D_2 or d is played. (All other payoffs remain as in figure 2.4 and it is assumed that player 1 knows which payoffs prevail.) This perturbed game has a strict Nash equilibrium (i.e., each agent chooses his unique best response) in which player 2 chooses D_2 while player 1 chooses D_1 if his payoffs are as in figure 2.4. In this equilibrium player 2 correctly infers from the choice of A_1 at player 1's first information set that this player will choose d at his second move; this induces him to choose D_2 which in turn makes D_1 strictly optimal for the "regular type" of player 1. Hence, in the limit, as the uncertainty vanishes we obtain the (normal form perfect) equilibrium (D_1, D_2).

Fudenberg *et al.* (1988) also show that, if the information of different players can be correlated, one can rationalize the larger set of normal form "correlated perfect" equilibria, and that, if it is possible that some player i may have information about the payoffs of player j that is superior to j's information, then one may even rationalize the entire set of pure strategy Nash equilibria. (Formally, if s is a pure strategy Nash equilibrium of game Γ then there exists a sequence of slightly perturbed games in which each player has some private information and an associated sequence of strict equilibria that converges to s [Fudenberg *et al.* (1988, proposition 3)]). This result may be illustrated by means of the game of figure 2.1a. Assume that with a small probability ε the payoffs associated with (A, d) are (2,2) rather than (0,0) and that only player 1 knows what the actual payoffs are. In this perturbed game it makes perfectly good sense for player 1 to choose D if the payoffs are as in figure 2.1a, since he may fear that player 2 may interpret the choice of A as a signal that the payoffs are (2,2) and continue with d after A.

The driving force behind the previous example was that the players could correlate their strategies. Of course, payoff uncertainty is not necessary for correlation to be possible (Aumann, 1974) and, consequently, constructions like the above may be possible if the payoffs are known but there is uncertainty about the game structure. As an example consider the game from figure 2.6 in which the simultaneous move subgame is played between the players 1 and 2 (player 3 is a dummy in that game). Since the subgame has a unique Nash equilibrium with value (3,3,4), the unique subgame perfect equilibrium yields each player the payoff 5. Note, however, that the subgame also admits a correlated equilibrium c in which each of the non-zero entries is played with probability $\frac{1}{6}$. If player 3 believes *ex ante* that there is an ε probability that the players 1 and 2 have a correlation device available that enables them to play c, then he can interpret the choice of A_1

as a signal that this device is available. This interpretation leads him to choose A_3 which in turn induces player 1 to choose D_1 if the correlation device is not available. Hence, this story justifies the outcome (4,4,8). (For an elaboration on this example, and an in-depth study of "sequential correlated equilibria" the reader is urged to consult Myerson, 1986 and Forges, 1986.)

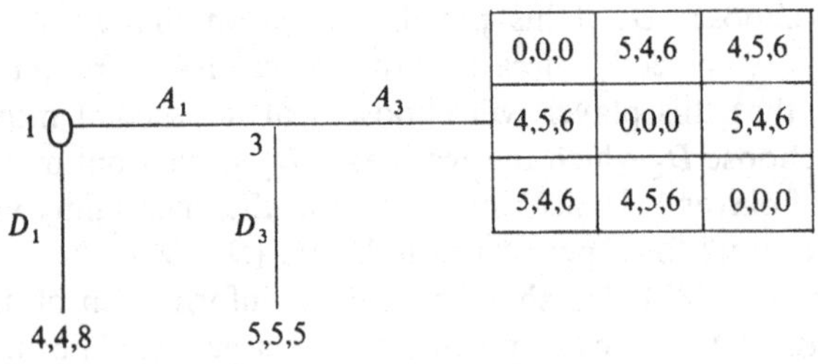

Figure 2.6 Correlation may yield non-subgame perfect equilibrium outcomes

The point of this subsection has been to show that, if the game model is incomplete, then one cannot tell which equilibria are self-enforcing without knowing what the incompleteness of the model consists of, i.e., without knowing the context in which the game is played. Consequently, in the next section we return to the classical point of view that:

> the game under consideration fully describes the real situation, – that any (pre)commitment possibilities, any repetitive aspect, any probabilities of error, or any possibility of jointly observing some random event, have already been modelled in the game tree (Kohlberg and Mertens, 1986, footnote 3).

4 STABLE EQUILIBRIA

The game of figure 2.7b shows that the concepts introduced thus far do not provide sufficient conditions for self-enforcing equilibria. In this game player 1 has to choose between an outside option yielding both players the payoff of 2 or to play the Battle of the Sexes games from figure 2.7a. One equilibrium has player 1 choosing D while the players continue with (w, s) if the BS-subgame is reached. The equilibrium is perfect since perfectness allows player 2 to interpret the move A of player 1 as an unintended mistake which does not affect player 1's behavior at his second move. However, there clearly exists a much more convincing explanation for why the deviation occurred. Player 2 should realize that player 1 (being a rational player) will never play *Aw* since this is strictly dominated by *D*. Hence, he should conclude that the deviation signals that player 1 intends to play *s* in the subgame and he should respond by playing *w*. Clearly, this chain of reasoning upsets the equilibrium.

Figure 2.7a Battle of the sexes (BS) Figure 2.7b BS with an outside option

Note that the above argument involved the normal form of the game, we discussed strategies for the entire game rather than independent actions at different information sets. (Formally, the argument amounts to the observation that, by eliminating dominated strategies, one can reduce the game to the outcome (*As*, *w*). Hence, the example shows that perfect equilibria are not robust to the elimination of dominated strategies.) What is involved is an argument of forward induction: player 2's beliefs and actions should not only be consistent with deductions based on player 1's rational behavior in the future (this is the sequential rationality requirement captured by perfectness) but they should also incorporate (at least as much as possible) rational behavior of player 1 in the past. It seems that the latter type of considerations can only be incorporated by taking a global picture, i.e., by looking at the normal form.

Kohlberg and Mertens (1986) argue forcefully (and convincingly) that the normal form of a game contains sufficient information to find the self-enforcing equilibria of this game. The argument is simply that rational players can and should always fully anticipate what they would do in every contingency; a theory of rationality that would tell a player at the beginning of the game to choose *c* if the information set *h were* to be reached and that would simultaneously advise the player to take a different action *c′* if *h is* actually reached is hardly conceivable. This classical point of view implies that self-enforcing equilibria can only depend on the normal form of the game and entails that (subgame) perfect and sequential equilibria are unsatisfactory. (The two games in figure 2.4 have the same normal form but they have different sets of perfect (resp. sequential) equilibria. Note that in a normal form game every Nash equilibrium is sequential.)

Kohlberg and Mertens argue further that one even needs less information than is contained in the normal form to find the self-enforcing equilibria: since players are always explicitly allowed to randomize over pure strategies, adding such mixtures explicitly as pure strategies in the game should not change the solutions. This requirement implies that the solutions of a game can only depend on the so-called reduced normal form, i.e., on the normal form that results when all pure strategies that are convex combinations of other pure strategies have been deleted. It turns out that this invariance requirement is incompatible with the requirement that the solution of an extensive form game be a subgame perfect equilibrium: there exist two games with the same reduced normal form that have disjoint sets of subgame perfect equilibria. An illustration is provided by the game of figure 2.8a. This is the (reduced) normal form of an extensive form game in which player 1 chooses between an outside option l yielding 2 or to play a 2×2 subgame of the matching pennies type, and the unique subgame perfect equilibrium of this game has player 2 choosing $\frac{1}{2}L+\frac{1}{2}R$. If we add the mixture $s=\frac{1}{2}l+\frac{1}{2}m$ explicitly as a pure strategy of player 1 then we obtain the normal form from figure 2.8b which corresponds to an extensive form game in which player 1 chooses between an outside option or to play a 3×2 subgame (with strategies s, m, and r for player 1 and L and R for player 2). The reduced normal form of this game is as in figure 2.8a; however, the unique subgame perfect equilibrium of the game requires player 2 to choose R.

	L	R
l	6,6	6,6
m	2,0	0,2
r	0,2	2,0

Figure 2.8a

	L	R
l	6,6	6,6
s	4,3	3,4
m	2,0	0,2
r	0,2	2,0

Figure 2.8b

Extensive form games with the same reduced normal form with disjoint sets of SPE

The incompatibility of the two requirements calls again into question whether subgame perfectness is really necessary for self-enforcingness. Like the examples in section 2, this example suggests that one adopts a more liberal point of view and allows multiple beliefs and multiple recommendations for player 2. There is certainly no need to specify a unique action for this player, since his choice doesn't matter anyway when he plays against a rational opponent. His choice may matter if his opponent plays irrationally but then the optimal choice probably depends on the way in which player 1 is irrational and, since no theory of irrationality is provided, the analyst should be content to remain silent. Generalizing from this example one might argue that we may be satisfied if we can identify the outcomes resulting from rational play, i.e., if we can specify which actions a player should take as long as the opponents' behavior does not contradict their rationality. A self-enforcing norm of behavior should not necessarily pin down the players' behavior and beliefs in those instances which cannot be observed when the norm is in effect.

Kohlberg and Mertens also argue that, besides failing to satisfy invariance, a second reason for why perfect (and sequential) equilibria are not satisfactory concepts is that they may allow equilibria in dominated strategies. (Perfectness implies that all moves are undominated; however, the overall strategy may be dominated: cf. the equilibrium (DL_1, L_2) in figure 2.3.) Kohlberg and Mertens consider admissibility of the equilibrium strategies (i.e., those strategies not being weakly dominated) to be a fundamental requirement. Furthermore, as we have seen when discussing the game from figure 2.7b, yet another drawback of perfect (and sequential) equilibria is that they are not robust to the (iterative) elimination of dominated strategies. Kohlberg/Mertens argue that, since (weakly) dominated strategies are never actually chosen by rational players and, since all players know this, such strategies can have no impact on whether or not an equilibrium is self-enforcing. This requirement of "independence of dominated strategies" again points to a set-valued solution concept, since, as is well-known, the outcome of the elimination process may depend on the order in which the strategies are eliminated. For example, in the game of figure 2.8a, the elimination order m, R, r leads to the conclusion that player 2 should play L, while the order r, L, m leads to the conclusion that he should play R. Again one sees that multiplicity is natural: if player 2 eliminates a dominated strategy of player 1 he attributes rationality to this player, but he may have to move only if player 1 actually is irrational. We simply reconfirm that the way in which player 1 is irrational determines player 2's choice and that, if one does not specify what irrational behavior looks like, one should not necessarily specify a unique choice for player 2. A more interesting example, in which different elimination orders actually produce different outcomes is provided by the game from figure 2.9. In this game the notions of forward and backward induction are conflicting. Backward induction (or the elimination order al, AL, d, AR) leads to the conclusion that player 1 should choose D and that the payoffs will be (2,0). Forward induction, or more precisely the fact that player 2 interprets the choice of A as a signal that player 1 will not play R, yields as a possible elimination order AR, ar, D, dl, which gives the conclusion that player 1 should play AL and that player 2 should choose d resulting in the payoffs

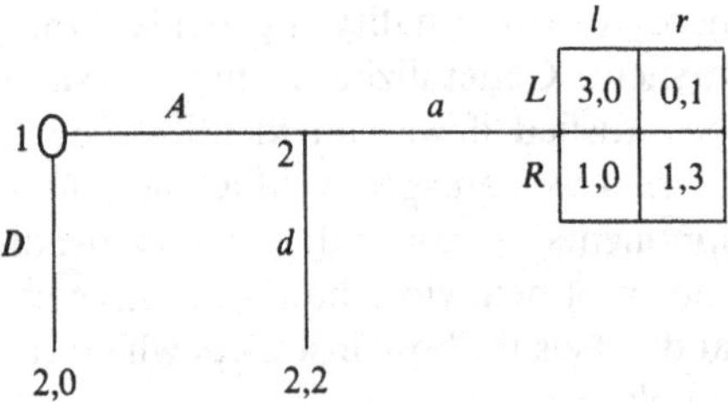

Figure 2.9 Different elimination orders yield different outcomes

(2,2). (This game is non-generic since both D and d yield player 1 the payoff 2, however note that, when one does the backward induction, there are never ties.) This example shows that, if we indeed insist on the requirement that self-enforcing norms should be "independent of dominated strategies," then, in non-generic games, we cannot identify norms with outcomes and this raises the question of how to define norms in this case. Kohlberg and Mertens show that the set of Nash equilibria of a game consists of finitely many connected components and they suggest as candidates for self-enforcing norms (connected subsets of) such components. Since generic extensive form games have only finitely many Nash equilibrium outcomes (Kreps and Wilson, 1982a) it follows that for generic games all equilibria in the same component induce the same outcome, so that for such games the Kohlberg/Mertens suggestion is only a relatively minor departure from the traditional notion of a single-valued solution.

The requirement that the solution be "independent from dominated strategies" is a global requirement: strategies that are "bad" from an overall point of view will not be chosen. Hence, they should play no role. Once a specific norm is under consideration one can be more specific. If the norm is really self-enforcing then a player will certainly not choose a strategy that, as long as the others obey the norm, yields him strictly less than he gets by obeying the norm. Therefore, for a norm to be self-enforcing, it is necessary that it remains self-enforcing after a strategy has been eliminated that is not a best reply against the norm. The power of this requirement of "independence of non-best responses" (INBR) will be illustrated in the next section. The game $\Gamma_2(2)$ from figure 2.1 shows that this INBR requirement is not satisfied by the subgame perfect equilibrium concept: strategy A_2a of player 2 is not a best response against player 1's equilibrium strategy A, but, if A_2a is deleted from the game, player 1 will switch to D. Hence, if one wants to satisfy INBR as well as some form of sequential rationality one is again forced to accept a set-valued solution concept.

Having specified several necesary conditions for self-enforcingness, the obvious question, of course, is whether it is possible to satisfy all these requirements. The answer is yes: there exist norms satisfying the properties discussed above as well as some other desirable properties.

THEOREM (Mertens, 1988, 1989a, 1990) There exists a correspondence that assigns to each game a collection of so-called stable sets of equilibria such that:

(i) (connexity and admissibility) each stable set is a connected set of normal form perfect (hence, undominated) equilibria.

(ii) (invariance) stable sets depend only on the reduced normal form.

(iii) (backward induction) each stable set contains a proper (hence, sequential) equilibrium.

(iv) (iterated dominance) each stable set contains a stable set of a game obtained by deleting a (weakly) dominated strategy.

(v) (INBR) each stable set contains a stable set of a game obtained by deleting a strategy that is not a best response against any element in the set.

(vi) (player splitting property) stable sets do not change when a player is split into two agents provided that there is no path in the game tree in which the agents act after each other.

(vii) (small worlds property) If there exists a subset N' of the player set N such that the payoffs to the players in N' only depend on the actions of the players in N', then the stable sets of the game between the players in N' are exactly the projections of the stable sets of the larger game.

The properties (i) – (v) have already been discussed. Property (vi) implies that it does not matter whether a signaling game (see the next section) is analyzed in normal form (2 players) or in agent normal form, or in any intermediate game form. Note that this property does not hold if two agents of the same player move after each other: the outcome (2,2) is stable in the agent normal form of the game of figure 2.7b. If player 1 consists of two separate agents then the first has no control over the second and he cannot signal this agent's intentions. Property (vii) is a decomposition property that guarantees that the solutions of a game do not depend on things that have nothing to do with the game. Note that we naturally have "contains" rather than "is" in (iv) and (v): stable sets may shrink if "inferior" strategies are deleted. Intuitively, stable sets have to be large since they must incorporate the possibility of irrational play (and there seems no unique best way to play against irrational opponents); however, by eliminating dominated strategies one attributes more rationality to the players, makes them more predictable, and this leads to a smaller set of optimal actions, and hence, to smaller stable sets. The game $\Gamma_2(2)$ of figure 2.1 provides an illustration. The set of normal form perfect equilibria of this game consists of the strategy vectors $s=(s_1, s_2)$ with $s_1=pA+(1-p)D$, $s_2=D_2$ and $p\leq\frac{1}{2}$. Hence (by (i)) each stable set is a subset of this set. Let S^* be a stable set. Since the strategy A_2d is not a best response against S^* and since, in the game in which A_2d is deleted, the unique stable set is (A, D_2) (by admissibility), we have that (A, D_2) belongs to S^*, similarly the strategy $\frac{1}{2}A+\frac{1}{2}D$ of player 1 must belong to S^*. For, if this were the case, then A_2a would be "inferior", so that (by (i) and (v)) (D, A_2d) should belong to S^*. But this is impossible. Hence, it follows by (i) that in $\Gamma_2(2)$ the unique stable set is the set of all normal form perfect equilibria.

Note that the Theorem is stated as an existence theorem. It does not say how to find stable sets. Kohlberg and Mertens (1986) initially defined a stable set of a game G as a "minimal closed set S of equilibria of G with the property that each perturbed game $G^{\varepsilon,\sigma}$ [see section 4] with sufficiently small ε has an equilibrium close to S." This definition is essentially the same as that for perfect equilibria except that one works with the normal form and that one has to look at *all* perturbations rather than just one sequence. However, it turned out that this concept failed to satisfy some essential properties from the Theorem (such as (iii)). Mertens (1988, 1989a) refined the definition to remedy this deficiency and proved the Theorem. For the purpose of this chapter the exact definition is not so relevant, since, in the applications to be discussed next, the properties from the Theorem will suffice to single out the stable outcomes. Finally, Hillas (1990) defines a stable set of a game G as "a minimal closed set S of equilibria of G with the property that for each game G' with the same reduced normal form as G and for each upper-hemicontinuous compact convex valued correspondence that is pointwise close to the best reply correspondence of G' there exists a fixed point that is closed to S". Such stable sets exist and satisfy the properties (i) – (v) from the Theorem.

5 FORWARD INDUCTION

In this section we briefly discuss some applications of forward induction, i.e., of the idea that the inferences players draw about a player's future behavior should be consistent with rational behavior of this player in the past. Informally stated, forward induction amounts to the requirement that for an equilibrium to be self-enforcing there should not exist a non-ambiguous deviation from the equilibrium that, when interpreted in the appropriate way, makes the deviator better off. This attractive idea has proved elusive and, consequently, several formalizations have been proposed in the literature. It has turned out, however, that stability (and in particular "independence of dominated strategies and/or non-best responses") captures at least some of the forward induction logic. In this section we first illustrate some applications of stability in games of complete information, thereafter, we indicate how powerful that concept is to eliminate implausible equilibria in signaling games. Along the way several other formalizations of forward induction that are in some way related to stability will be encountered. Throughout the section attention will be confined to generic games, i.e., to games that have finitely many Nash equilibrium outcomes. We will call an outcome of such a game stable if there exists a stable set of which all elements induce this outcome. (Recall that in generic games all elements in a same stable set yield the same outcome.)

5.1 Signaling intentions

Consider the following modification of the game of figure 2.7b: First chance determines whether player 1 or player 2 will have an outside option available. If a player takes up the outside option each player has the payoff 2. If player i is selected by chance but he does not take up his option then players play the Battle of the Sexes. It is easily seen that in the unique stable outcome the option is not taken up, that the player who has the option available chooses to play BS and gets the payoff 3 (Abdalla *et al.* (1989) provide experimental evidence on the success of forward induction in similar games). In particular, we see that the history of the game determines the way in which the subgame is played: the player's expectations in the subgame are not endogenous, i.e., they are not determined by the subgame alone but depend on the context in which the subgame arises (see Mertens, 1989b for an informal discussion on this topic). The equilibrium selection theory of Harsanyi and Selten (1988) is based on the assumption of endogenous expectations: Harsanyi and Selten impose the requirement of subgame consistency, i.e., a subgame should always be played in the same way no matter how it arose. The example shows that subgame consistency conflicts with stability. Similarly, it may be shown that other concepts that require history independence, such as Markov perfection (Maskin and Tirole, 1989) or stationarity, conflict with stability.

Suppose that the players have to play the Battle of the Sexes game from figure 2.7a, but that before playing this game player 1 has the option of burning one unit of utility and that when BS is played it is common knowledge whether or not player 1 burned utility. It is easily seen that iterative elimination of dominated strategies reduces the normal form to the payoff (3,1). Hence, only the outcome in which player 1 does not burn utility and gets his most preferred outcome is stable. Using this argument,

Ben-Porath and Dekel (1987) have shown that, in games of "mutual interest," the players will succeed in coordinating on the Pareto best equilibrium if one player has the ability to destroy utility. In Van Damme (1989) it is shown that "in the Battle of the Sexes" all stable outcomes are inefficient (i.e., involve some burning) if both players have the opportunity to simultaneously burn utility. Applications of these ideas to more economic contexts are found in Bagwell and Ramey (1990), Dekel (1990), and Glazer and Weiss (1990).

The deletion of dominated strategies in the BS with one-sided burning of utility corresponds to the following intuitive story: if player 2 observes that player 1 burns utility he should conclude that player 1 will continue with s; assuming that player 1 will play w does not make sense, since burning followed by w yields at most the payoff zero, and, hence, is strictly dominated by not burning and randomizing between s and w. This conclusion leads player 2 to play w if burning is observed and burning utility is sure to yield player 1 the payoff 2. At this stage of the reasoning process we are back to a game like that in figure 2.7b and we can continue reasoning as in that example to reach the conclusion that (s, w) should also be played if player 1 does not burn utility. A little reflection reveals that the argument above is not intuitive at all; it is not clear why player 2 should respond to the burning by playing w since, given the conclusion we just reached, burning is a signal that player 1 is not rational, at least it signals that he did not follow the above reasoning. At this point the reader should be reminded of the discussion of counterfactuals in section 2, so it is not necessary to go into details here. Let us just remark that stability does not force player 2 to play w after player 1 has burned utility: the stable set includes both ww and ws for player 2 ($\alpha\beta$ denotes that player 2 responds to not burning by α and to burning by α). Namely, property (iv) of the theorem implies that $(-s, ww)$ belongs to the stable set. ($-s$ denotes the strategy of not burning by α and to burning by β). Namely, property (iv) of the Theorem implies that $(-s, ww)$ belongs to the stable set. ($-s$ denotes the strategy of not burning and playing s.) Furthermore, given that player 2 plays a mixture of ww and ws in any element of the stable set, the strategies bs (i.e., burning and then playing s) and $-w$ are inferior for player 1. If these strategies are eliminated, ws becomes dominated for player 2 and the normal form is reduced to $(-s, ws)$, so that the Theorem implies that this strategy pair also has to belong to the stable set.

When a game with multiple equilibria is repeated the set of subgame perfect equilibrium payoffs expands until in the limit it covers, at least under a mild regularity condition, the entire set of feasible and individually rational payoff vectors. This is the content of the "folk theorem" (Benoit and Krishna, 1985). Hence, in repeated games, the problem of multiplicity of equilibria is ubiquitous. Considerations of forward induction may eliminate some of these equilibria as the twice repeated battle of the sexes may show. As an illustration, let us show that the outcome (path) in which the one-shot equilibrium (s, w) is played twice is not stable. Namely, INBR implies that player 1 should interpret a deviation of player 2 to s in the first round as a signal that player 2 will also play s in the second round. (If he plans to play w then his payoff is at most 1, which is less than the equilibrium payoff. Hence, such a strategy is not a best response.) Consequently, after the deviation player 1 should play w, but then player 2 gains by deviating (his payoff is 3 rather than 2), so that the outcome is not stable. Alternating between (1,3) and (3,1) is a stable outcome, so is playing the mixed equilibrium twice, as well as some other mixtures in which the continuation at time 2 depends on the outcome of stage 1. It seems that stability forces payoffs to move closer to the 45° line but whether this property remains for repetitions with longer duration remains to be investigated.

To this author's knowledge no general results are available for stable equilibrium payoffs of repeated games: mathematically stability is not very easy to work with. Some preliminary results on repeated coordination games are contained in Osborne (1990). In particular, Osborne shows that, in a class of repeated coordination games, paths that consist of pure Nash equilibria of the stage game can be stable only if they yield payoffs that are nearly Pareto optimal. This restriction on paths is unfortunate since for more general games no such path need be stable (van Damme, 1989). Osborne does not use the full power of stability, he works with a weaker criterion of "immunity to a convincing deviation" – which is akin to the Cho and Kreps (1987) intuitive criterion (see the next subsection) and to the formalization of forward induction proposed in Cho (1987). One negative result that is known is that stability conflicts with ideas of renegotiation-proofness: there may not exist a stable equilibrium that is also renegotiation-proof (van Damme, 1988). (Renegotiation-proofness requires that at each stage of the game players continue with an equilibrium that is Pareto efficient within the set of the available equilibria – see Pearce (1990) for an overview of the various concepts formalizing this idea.) In an interesting application Ponssard (1991) shows that forward induction leads to the conclusion that long-term competition in a market with increasing returns to scale forces firms to use average cost pricing. Ponssard, however, develops his own concept of forward induction (also see Ponssard, 1990a, b) and it is not clear that stable equilibria satisfy Ponssard's conditions.

An alternative (preliminary) formulation of forward induction based on an idea originally developed in McLennan (1985) was proposed in van Damme (1989). In that paper it was argued that, in a generic 2-player game in which player 1 has the choice between an outside option o or to play a subgame γ of which a unique viable (say stable) equilibrium e yields player 1 more than his option, only the outcome in which player 1 chooses to play γ and in which e is played in γ is sensible. The justification for this requirement is that by choosing to play γ player 1 can unambiguously signal that he will play according to e in γ. Alternatively one may imagine a context in which there is initial strategic uncertainty about whether the norm o or the norm γe is in effect: even if player 2 originally believes that he is in a world in which o is obeyed, he concludes from the fact that he has to move that the norm must be γe and he responds appropriately. (Telling the story in this way makes it clear that this type of forward induction is related to the risk dominance concept from Harsanyi and Selten (1988). Another paper dealing with this type of situation is Suehiro (1990). Also Binmore (1987) has such a context in mind when he presents an argument in favor of the imperfect equilibrium in Selten's "horse" game.) Van Damme (1989) constructs an example to show that stable outcomes as originally defined by Kohlberg and Mertens do not necessarily conform to this forward induction logic. It is unknown to this author whether Mertens' refined stability concept satisfies this forward induction requirement.

5.2 Signaling private information

A signaling game is a 2-player game in which player 1, who has private information takes an action ("sends a signal") that is observable to player 2 who thereupon takes an action and in which the payoffs depend on both players' actions and the type (i.e., the information) of player 1. (Formally, a signaling game is a tuple $\Gamma = (T, M, (R_m)_m, u_1, u_2, \pi)$ where T is the (finite) set of types of player 1, M is the (finite) set of messages that can be sent, R_m is the (finite) set of responses to m, $u_i = u_i(t, m, r)$ is the payoff function of player i, and π is a probability distribution on T representing the initial beliefs of player 2. An example of a signaling game is the game in figure 2.2a; from now on we will use a matrix representation as in figure 2.2b. to depict signaling games.) Signaling games were introduced by Spence (1974) and they provide stylized models of many interesting economic situations (see Cho and Kreps, 1987 and Kreps and Sobel, 1991). These games typically have large numbers of equilibria and researchers have used intuitive, context dependent arguments to eliminate equilibria. Although a great variety of refinements exist, they all incorporate some form of forward induction. Hence, they can be related to the stability concept from the previous section. Next we briefly discuss these relations. (The reader is referred to Cho and Kreps, 1987; Banks and Sobel, 1987; Kreps and Sobel, 1991; Sobel *et al.* 1990 for more details.) Before starting to discuss the relationships it should however be noted that the "intuitive criteria" are based on a somewhat different point of view, viz. economists have tried to directly define "plausible beliefs" and have proposed to restrict attention to the ("plausible") equilibria that can be supported by "plausible beliefs." Such a requirement is stronger than the ones considered previously which were based on the idea that a candidate equilibrium should be rejected if it can be upset by "plausible" beliefs. The difference is that there may not exist equilibria that can be sustained by "plausible" beliefs since "plausible" beliefs may not exist (cf. the discussion on burning utility in the Battle of the Sexes game).

Let an equilibrium s of a signaling game be given. Typically the intuitive criteria that are used to judge the "plausibility" of this equilibrium start out by assuming that, if player 1 does not deviate from his equilibrium strategy, player 2 will not deviate either. Hence, playing the equilibrium strategy guarantees each type of player 1 his equilibrium payoff. (This assumption certainly makes sense: if the equilibrium is really self-enforcing, then no player will deviate. However, see the discussion in the figures 2.12 and 2.13.) Next, assume that m is a message that is not sent if s is played. If choosing m is sure to yield a certain type t of player 1 less than what the equilibrium guarantees this type, then it is not "plausible" to assume that t will choose m and it should be possible to sustain the original equilibrium by beliefs that assign zero weight to t. Depending on how one defines "to sustain" in the previous sentence, the resulting test is known as "*the intuitive criterion*" or as "*equilibrium dominance*" (Cho and Kreps, 1987). The equilibrium s satisfies the intuitive criterion if for each type t of player 1 there exists a belief in the restricted set (of beliefs that put zero weight on the types for which m is dominated) and an associated best response for player 2 at m that makes type t prefer to choose s rather than m. The test posed by equilibrium dominance is more restrictive and requires that there exists a belief in the restricted set and an associated best response of player 2 such that no type of player 1 wants to deviate to m if that response is taken at m. Hence, the latter test requires that different types conjecture the same response after m, the former allows different types to have different conjectures. In the signaling game of figure 2.10 the outcome in which both types of player 1 choose L does not survive application of the intuitive criterion since the latter requires that, after R, player 2 should put weight 1 on type t_1 and play l. In the game of figure 2.11, the outcome in which all types choose L survives the intuitive criterion (this requires that player 2 puts weight zero on t_3 but it allows that the conjectures of t_1 and t_2 are mismatched., i.e., that t_1 believes that player 2 will play m and that t_2 believes that he will play l), but it does not pass the equilibrium dominance test, since, if t_1 and t_2 conjecture the same (mixed) strategy of player 2, at least one of them will deviate. (Note that the game of figure 2.11 (with t_3 deleted) demonstrates the claim made at the beginning of section 2 that the Nash equilibrium concept depends in an essential way on the assumption that different players (here t_1 and t_2) conjecture the same out-of-equilibrium responses.)

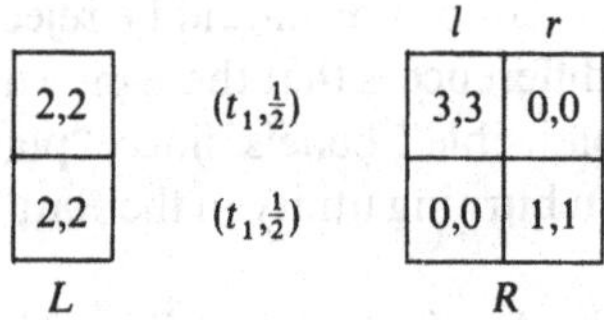

Figure 2.10 Pooling at L is not "intuitive"

L		R: l	m	r
2,2	$(t_1, \frac{1}{3})$	5,5	0,0	0,0
2,2	$(t_2, \frac{1}{3})$	0,0	5,5	0,0
2,2	$(t_3, \frac{1}{3})$	0,0	0,0	1,1

Figure 2.11 Equilibrium dominance is more restrictive than the intuitive criterion

The above tests may be applied repeatedly. Formally, this repeated procedure runs as follows. Given an equilibrium *s* and an unsent message *m*, one first constructs the auxiliary signaling game in which player 1 has the choices *s* and *m*, where *s* guarantees the equilibrium payoffs and where the payoffs after *m* are the same as those in the original game. Next one starts eliminating strictly dominated strategies in the agent normal form of this game (hence, the types of player 1 are considered as independent players). If during the process the action *s* vanishes for some type *t*, then *s* does not satisfy the intuitive criterion. If the game that one obtains at the end of the process does not have *s* as an equilibrium, then *s* fails the equilibrium dominance test. Since only actions are eliminated that are not a best response against any equilibrium in the same component as *s*, the Theorem implies that equilibria failing any of these tests cannot belong to stable sets.

Alternatively, one might construct the normal form of the auxiliary signaling game and eliminate dominated strategies in that game form. This poses a stricter test since more dominance relationships exist in the normal form. Consider the equilibrium *s* of the 3-message signaling game of figure 2.12 in which both types choose L and the auxiliary game corresponding to the message M. (Hence, for the moment we completely neglect the message

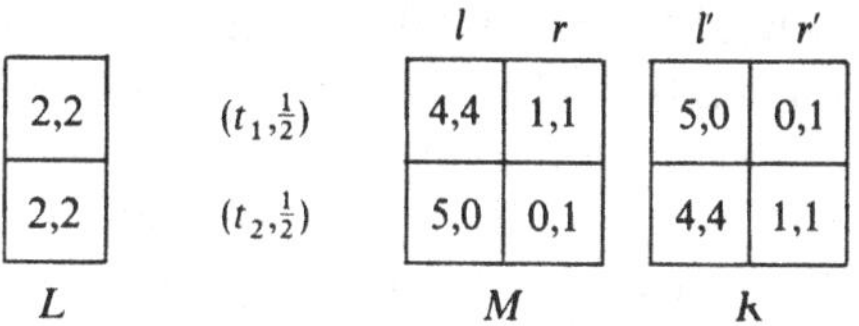

Figure 2.12 Investigating unsent messages separately or simultaneously may make a difference

R.) Then s survives the equilibrium dominance test since choosing M is not dominated for either type. In the normal form, however, the strategy LM (i.e., t_1 chooses L and t_2 chooses M) is dominated (by a combination of ML and MM) and after this strategy has been eliminated one sees that player 2 should play l, thereby upsetting s. The intuitive argument corresponding to the elimination of dominated strategies in the normal form is known in the literature under the name of *codivinity* (Sobel *et al.*, 1990), a criterion that is slightly weaker than that of *divinity* (Banks and Sobel, 1987). These criteria may also be described as follows. Assume that (the types of) player 1 conjecture that player 2 will reply to m with the response r. Letting $u^s(t)$ denote the equilibrium payoff of type t, the propensity $\lambda(t, r)$ for type t to deviate from s is given by:

$$\lambda(t, r) = \begin{cases} 0 & \text{if } u^s(t) > u(t, m, r) \\ \in [0, 1] & \text{if } u^s(t) = u(t, m, r) \\ 1 & \text{if } u^s(t) < u(t, m, r). \end{cases} \tag{5.1}$$

Hence, if player 2 knows that player 1 conjectures that he will play r, then his beliefs will be in the set:

$$\mathcal{B}(\pi, r) = \{\pi' \in \Delta(T);\ \pi' = \pi\lambda(\cdot, r) \quad \text{for some } \lambda \text{ as in (5.1)}\}. \tag{5.2}$$

If there exists a possible conjecture r for which $\mathcal{B}(\pi, r)$ is not empty (i.e., if there exists a type that would not lose from deviating to m), then divinity and codivinity require that the equilibrium s can be sustained by beliefs that belong to $\cup_r \mathcal{B}(\pi, r)$, where r ranges over the possible conjectures. Divinity is a slightly stronger concept since it allows only conjectures r that are (mixed) best responses, while codivinity allows the larger set of all mixtures of (pure) best responses. Banks and Sobel (1987) show that every stable component contains a divine equilibrium.

It will be clear that, because of (5.1), the divinity concepts force the updating to be monotonic: if type t_1 has a "greater incentive to deviate" to

m than type t_2, then player 2 should not revise downward the probability that he is dealing with t_1 after m has been chosen. For example, in the game of figure 2.12 both t_1 and t_2 could possibly gain by deviating from L to M but t_1 has the "greater incentive" to do so (the range of responses where t_1 gains is strictly larger than the range where t_2 gains), so that codivinity requires that the posterior probability of t_1 after M is at least $\frac{1}{2}$. Hence, player 2 should choose l thereby upsetting the equilibrium.

Note that divinity investigates each unsent message separately. (For each such message a separate auxiliary game is constructed, and s is eliminated if it fails the test in at least one auxiliary game.) In figure 2.12, for example, it is thus required that player 2 plays l after M and l' after R. If player 1 foresees this reaction and plays his best response (R if t_1 and M if t_2) beliefs are induced that are incompatible with those of divinity. In fact, player 2's best response against this best response (viz. playing r after M and r' after R) sustains the original equilibrium. (Formally what happens is that, by including the third message, LM becomes undominated in the normal form.) Some readers might conclude from this that divinity is not an intuitive requirement after all. In the author's opinion the above argument simply shows that we do not know what will happen when the pooling equilibrium at L is recommended. However, this should not bother us: we also do not know what will happen if, in an ordinary normal form game, a strategy vector is recommended that is not a Nash equilibrium. Questions concerning "disequilibrium dynamics," i.e., questions dealing with what will happen when a non-self-enforcing equilibrium is proposed, cannot be answered by equilibrium analysis (cf. Von Neumann and Morgenstern, 1948, section 4.8.2.)

The so-called "Stiglitz critique" (Cho and Kreps, 1987, p. 203) on the intuitive criterion (or more precisely on the assumption that not deviating guarantees the equilibrium payoff) also involves such "disequilibrium dynamics." The critique may be illustrated by means of the game of figure 2.13. In one equilibrium of this game, the types of player 1 pool at L and player 2 responds to L with l. The intuitive criterion eliminates this equilibrium: Type t_1 will deviate to R since he foresees that player 2 will switch to l' at R. According to the critique one should not stop the analysis with this disequilibrium outcome. Rather player 2 should realize that only t_2 can have chosen L and he should switch or r after L. But then t_2 also finds it better to deviate to R, whereafter player 2 finds it better to play r' after R, which in turn induces t_1 to choose L again. Continuing the argument two more steps we are back at the original equilibrium choices. Hence, according to the critique, no type of player 1 might have an incentive to deviate from L after all. This author's opinion is that the pooling outcome at L should not be considered self-enforcing: There are players that have an incentive to deviate. What the critique shows is that we do not know what will happen if it is suggested to the players to pool at L, but, as already seen above, equilibrium analysis cannot answer this question.

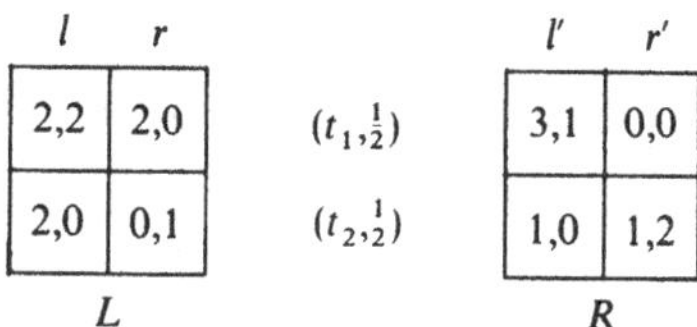

Figure 2.13 Illustration of the "Stiglitz critique"

In this author's opinion, the intuitive criteria that we discussed above may be criticized for the fact that they treat reached and unreached information sets asymmetrically: it is assumed that player 2 follows the recommendation after any message that is chosen in equilibrium, whereas he completely neglects the recommendation, and reoptimizes, after any unexpected message. To check self-enforcing it is more appropriate to follow the symmetric procedure of first assuming that the recommendation is self-enforcing, that player 2 will always, i.e., after every message, follow the recommendation, and then reject the recommendation if this assumption leads to a contradiction. Of course, this latter requirement is simply the INBR condition from the previous section. It is illustrated by means of the game of figure 2.14. Cho and Kreps (1987) provide a similar example and claim that the elimination of the pooling equilibrium at L is not intuitive in this game. Consider the equilibrium outcome in which the types of player 1 pool at L. If we insist that recommendations be admissible (i.e., undominated) strategies, then to sustain pooling at L we should recommend that player 2 randomizes between m and r after R, putting at least half of the weight on r. Given this set of possible recommendations, choosing R is not a best response for type t_2, and, after having eliminated this action, we see that player 2 prefers to choose l. Hence, he wants to deviate from the recommendation. Consequently, if we insist on admissibility and INBR, then pooling at L cannot be self-enforcing. Note that none of the previous arguments discussed in this subsection, nor INBR alone, eliminates this outcome. (If the dominated strategy $\frac{2}{3}l+\frac{1}{3}r$ is allowed as a recommendation for player 2, then sending R is not inferior for type t_2.)

The literature also offers refined equilibrium notions that are not implied by stability. One such concept that is frequently used in applications is that of *perfect sequential equilibrium* or PSE (Grossman and Perry, 1986). It is convenient to describe the slightly stronger notion of PSE* (van Damme,

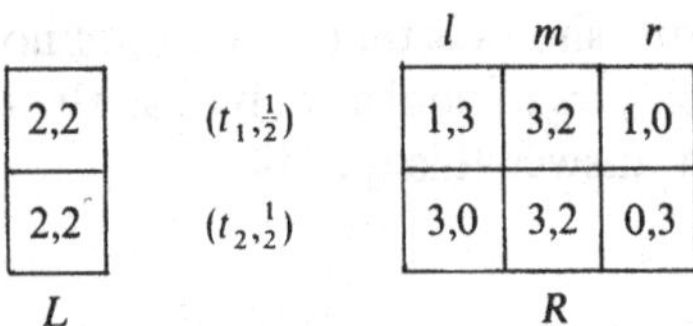

Figure 2.14 The combination of admissibility and INBR eliminates pooling at L

1987). Roughly, an equilibrium s fails to be a PSE* if there exists an unsent message m, a subset T' of types of player 1, and a response r at m, such that (i) if r is chosen at m then T' is exactly the set of types that prefer m to s and (ii) r is a best response against the conditional distribution of π on T'. (The formal definition is slightly different since types may be indifferent between deviating or not; such indifferences are handled as in (5.1), (5.2). The PSE concept is defined similarly but it is weaker since it allows player 1 to conjecture the "wrong" response at m.) Hence, roughly, s fails to be a PSE* if there exists some message m and an equilibrium s' of the auxiliary game determined by s and m, such that at least one type of player 1 prefers s' to s. Clearly, this concept is closely related to the forward induction requirement that was discussed at the end of the previous subsection. The difference is that there we required that there be a unique equilibrium that improves upon s, whereas here we allow there to be multiple improvements.

Grossman and Perry (1986) have given an example to show that PSE need not exist. The game from figure 2.15 shows that a stable set need not contain a PSE. In this game, pooling at L is stable but it is not a PSE. The outcome is stable since (roughly) stability allows player 2 to believe that any type might have deviated. Hence, it allows player 2 to randomize in such a way that actually neither t_1 nor t_2 wants to deviate. The outcome is not a PSE since this concept forces player 2 to put weight 1 on either t_1 or t_2 i.e., to choose either l or r. Clearly in either case at least one type of player 1

L		l	r
2,5	$(t_1, \frac{1}{2})$	3,3	0,0
2,5	$(t_2, \frac{1}{2})$	0,0	3,3
		R	

Figure 2.15 Pooling at L is stable but is not a PSE

will want to deviate from L. This example makes clear that the PSE concept assumes that the players can coordinate their actions, i.e., that communication is possible and that communication indeed takes place. (However, note that player 2 has no incentive whatsoever to communicate.) Hence, PSE is not a purely non-cooperative solution concept. In this author's opinion it is preferable to model communication explicitly by the rules of the game rather than indirectly by means of the solution concept. Such "cheap talk" games typically also have many equilibria and stability is not effective by reducing this set, since every equilibrium outcome can be obtained by "babbling," i.e., by using each message with positive probability. We will not consider cheap talk games any further; we just note that from the seminal papers Farrell (1984, 1990) and Grossman (1981) an extensive literature has sprung up, and that Matthews *et al.* (1990) survey the refinements used in this area. All these refinements assume that players will always accept the literal meaning of each statement unless it is logically contradictory, and the real challenge in this area seems to be to derive this assumption as a conclusion.

6 EQUILIBRIUM SELECTION

Up to now we have dealt exclusively with the self-enforcing aspect of equilibria, we did not discuss how self-enforcing norms come to be established nor how the selection among these takes place. We have seen, however, that considerations concerning self-enforcingness already lead to some conclusion concerning equilibrium selection: the basic idea of forward induction is that the equilibrium that is selected may depend on the context in which the game is played (cf. figure 2.7b). In this section we briefly discuss the approach to equilibrium selection and equilibrium attainment that is proposed in Carlsson and van Damme (1990) (henceforth CD). CD picture players in the context in which the payoffs of the game are only "almost common knowledge" and they show that, when a 2×2 game is played in this context, players reason themselves to the risk dominant equilibrium (Harsanyi and Selten, 1988). (CD obtain results only for the class of 2×2 games. For general attacks on the equilibrium selection problem, see Harsanyi and Selten, 1988 and Güth and Kalkofen, 1989.) In the coordination game of figure 2.16a the equilibrium (L_1, L_2) satisfies the most stringent requirements for self-enforcingness that have been discussed thus far: (L_1, L_2) is a strict equilibrium so that each player strictly loses by deviating if he expects the opponent to obey the recommendation to play this equilibrium. Of course, the question is whether a rational player will indeed expect his opponent to obey this recommendation. There is some evidence that at least human players do not consider such recommen-

	L_2	R_2
L_1	1,1	0,0
R_1	0,0	2,2

Figure 2.16a A coordination game

	L_2	R_2
L_1	9,9	$0,1+\theta$
R_1	$1+\theta,0$	θ,θ

Figure 2.16b Game Γ (θ)

dations credible. Van Huyck *et al.* (1988) report on an experiment conducted with a 3×3 coordination game with (diagonal) payoffs (in dollarcents) of (90,90), (50,50), and (10,10) in which only 1 pair of players (out of 30) follows the recommendation to play (10,10): if (10,10) is recommended, then 47 of the 60 individuals (and 18 of the 30 pairs) deviate to the payoff dominant equilibrium (90,90). It is very likely that similar behavior would be observed in the game of figure 2.16a. One explanation for this behavior is that players are firmly convinced right from the start that only R makes sense in this game, that they consider any suggestion to play something else as being irrelevant, and that such a suggestion can safely be ignored since it will be ignored by the opponent as well. The obvious question of course is how players can know that only R makes sense, and basically the answer that CD give is that players know this from reasoning through similar games. CD argue that the game from figure 2.16a should not be analyzed in isolation: players know what to do in *this* game since they know that it is optimal to play the Pareto best equilibrium in *each* coordination game with Pareto ranked payoffs. CD suggest analysis of classes of games with the same structure simultaneously and they show that self-enforcing norms for how to play classes of games may prescribe a specific equilibrium of each element of the class, roughly because of the fact that norms will require that similar games be played similarly. (Fudenberg and Kreps (1988) present another approach to similarity in games. Of course the idea that a solution of a game should be part of a plan that is consistent across a larger domain occurs already in the seminal work of Nash (1950b) on bargaining and that of Schelling (1960) on focal points.)

The CD approach will now be illustrated by means of the game $\Gamma(\theta)$ from figure 2.16b. (The reader himself can supply the details for how the argument would run if the coordinnation game from figure 2.16a were embedded in a one-dimensional parameter of coordination games.) The game $\Gamma(7)$ has been extensively discussed in Aumann (1989). Aumann argues that if the players are convinced that they should play R then no amount of preplay communication can convince them to switch to L since each player knows that a player who intends to play R will try to induce his opponent to switch to L. In $\Gamma(7)$ both L and R are strict equilibria and each one has something going for it: L Pareto dominates R but R is much safer. Hence, in this game there is a conflict between the intuitive notions of payoff dominance and risk dominance (Harsanyi and Selten, 1988). Formally, in a 2×2 game G, R is said to risk dominate L if the stability region of R (i.e., the set of all strategy vectors s against which R is a best reply) has a larger area than the stability region of L. Hence, in figure 2.16b, R risk dominates L if and only if $\theta > 4$. In their theory, Harsanyi and Selten resolve the conflict between the two intuitive notions in favor of payoff dominance (the reader should consult the postscript to their book for the arguments in favor of this choice).

Now imagine that the players are in the context in which they know that they have to play a game $\Gamma(\theta)$ as in figure 2.16b but they do not yet know which one. Hence, they know that they have to play a game in which the conflict between risk dominance and payoff dominance exists. (The reader may argue that the parametrization from figure 2.16b is not natural; we have chosen this parametrization to simplify the presentation. The assumptions to be discussed next are motivated similarly; the results from Carlsson and van Damme (1990) are more general.) The reader will probably agree that as θ increases playing L becomes less and less attractive and that a natural way to play this game is by specifying a cutoff value $\hat{\theta}$ and play L if and only if θ is less than $\hat{\theta}$. CD show that, if the players can observe the actual parameter value θ only with some slight noise, then the value of $\hat{\theta}$ is uniquely determined in equilibrium. In fact $\hat{\theta} = 4$. Hence, the players always choose the risk dominant equilibrium. (Note that some noise is essential to derive uniqueness: if θ could be perfectly observed, then each game $\Gamma(\theta)$ would occur as a simple subgame and the cutoff value may lie anywhere – in fact, in this case the equilibrium strategies need not be stepfunctions.)

To formally derive the above result let us assume that the set Θ of all possible parameter values is finite, that initially all values of θ are equally likely, and that Θ includes values θ with $\theta < 0$ (which makes L_i strictly dominant) as well as values with $\theta > 8$ (such that R_i is strictly dominant). Furthermore, assume that, if the actual parameter value is θ, then one player receives the signal θ^+ (i.e., the smallest value in Θ that is larger than θ) while the other gets to hear θ^- (i.e., the largest value in Θ that is smaller than θ) with both possibilities being equally likely (with the appropriate modifications at the endpoint of Θ). Since the observations are noisy no player knows exactly which "game" he is playing, however, if the grid of Θ is fine then each player has fairly accurate information about the payoffs in the game. Furthermore, in this case each player also has good knowledge about the information of his opponent and the players know that their perceptions of what the payoffs are do not differ too much. Hence, if the grid of Θ is fine, the game with noisy observations may be viewed as a small perturbation of the game in which observations are perfect and in the latter $\Gamma(\theta)$ occurs as a subgame for each value of θ. However, it should be noted that, from the point of view of common knowledge (Aumann, 1976), the games are completely different. Namely, in the unperturbed, if a player receives the signal θ, then it is common knowledge that the game is $\Gamma(\theta)$, i.e., both players know that both players know ... that both players know that the game is $\Gamma(\theta)$. However, in the game with noise, if a player receives the signal θ, then he knows that the payoffs either are as in $\Gamma(\theta^{-})$ or as in $\Gamma(\theta^{+})$, and that his opponent either received the signal θ^{--} or θ^{++}. Hence, he also knows that the opponent believes that the game is either $\Gamma(\theta^{---})$, or $\Gamma(\theta^{-})$, or $\Gamma(\theta^{+})$, or $\Gamma(\theta^{+++})$, with all probabilities being equally likely, and that the opponent believes that his signal is either θ^{----}, or θ^{++++}, or θ with the latter having probability $\frac{1}{2}$. Continuing inductively it is therefore seen that no matter how fine the grid size of Θ is, basically the only information that is common knowledge is that some game $\Gamma(\theta)$ with θ in Θ has to be played. This lack of common knowledge forces the players to take a global perspective in order to solve the perturbed game: to know what to do if one receives the signal θ one should also investigate what to do at parameter values θ' that are far away from θ. It is this phenomenon that drives the CD results. (A similar "action from a distance" also drives the results in Rubinstein's (1989) electronic mail game.)

The analysis of the perturbed game is simple. Let θ_i be the observation of player i. If $\theta_i^{+} < 0$ (resp. $\theta_i^{-} > 8$) then player i chooses L_i (resp. R_i), since he knows that this action is strictly dominant. Assume that it has already been shown by iterative elimination of strictly dominated strategies that L_1 and L_2 (resp. R_1 and R_2) are strictly dominant at each observation θ with $\theta \leq \alpha$ (resp. $\theta \geq \beta$). Hence, the iterative procedure starts with $\alpha = 0^{--}$ and $\beta = 8^{++}$. Consider $\theta_i = \alpha^{+}$, so that player i knows that either $\theta_j = \alpha^{-}$ or $\theta j = \alpha^{+++}$. Hence, player i knows that player j will choose Lj with a probability p that is at least $\frac{1}{2}$. Choosing L_i yields an expected payoff of $9p$ while R_i yields at most $\alpha^{++} + p$, so that player i will find it strictly dominant to choose L_i if $\alpha^{++} < 4$. Consequently, L_i is iteratively dominant for player i at θ_i if $\theta_i < 4^{-}$ and similarly R_i is iteratively dominant at θ_i if $\theta_i > 4^{+}$. We see that the perturbed game is almost dominance solvable: for all but a small set of parameter values (viz. the interval $[4^{-}, 4^{+}]$) unique iteratively dominant actions exist. By playing these dominant strategies players coordinate on the risk dominant equilibrium of the actual game that was selected by chance. Hence, by just relying on rationalizability (Bernheim, 1984; Pearce, 1984) in the perturbed game we obtain equilibrium selection according to the risk dominance criterion for every game $\Gamma(\theta)$ with $\theta \notin [4^{-}, 4^{+}]$.

Binmore (1990) has argued that in order to make progress in game theory it is necessary to model the way players think: that attention should be focused more on equilibriating processes rather than on equilibria. Although the model outlined above is rudimentary I believe that it captures some relevant aspects of reasoning processes. Certainly I do not want to claim the model's universal applicability: in some contexts the model may be relevant, in other contexts players may reason differently. The point, however, is that classical game theory is rich enough so as to provide models of the ways players might think.

Notes

* Paper presented at the 6th World congress of the Econometric Society, Barcelona, 22–8 August, 1990. The author thanks Helmut Bester, Larry Samuelson, and Jonathan Thomas for comments on an earlier version.

References

Abdalla, A., R. Cooper, D. DeJong, R. Forsythe, and T. Ross (1989), "Forward Induction in Coordination and Battle of the Sexes Games: Some Experimental Results," Working Paper, University of Iowa, nr. 89–22.

Aumann, R. (1974), "Subjectivity and Correlation in Randomized Strategies," *Journal of Mathematical Economics*, **1**: 67–96.

(1976), "Agreeing to Disagree," *Annals of Statistics*, **4**: 1236–9.

(1985), "What is Game Theory Trying to Accomplish?" in K. Arrow and S. Honkapohja (eds), *Frontiers of Economics*, Oxford: Basil Blackwell, pp. 28–100.

(1987), "Correlated Eqiulibrium as an Expression of Bayesian Rationality," *Econometrica*, **55**: 1–18.

(1988), "Irrationality in Game Theory," Paper for conference on Economic Theories of Politics.

(1989). "Nash Equilibria are Not Self-Enforcing," mimeo, Hebrew University of Jerusalem.

Bagwell, K. and G. Ramey (1990), "Capacity, Entry and Forward Induction," University of California at San Diego Discussion Paper 90–22.

Banks, J. S. and J. Sobel (1987), "Equilibrium Selection in Signalling Games," *Econometrica*, **55**: 647–61.

Basu, K. (1988), "Strategic Irrationality in Extensive Games," *Mathematical Social Sciences*, **15**: 247–60.

(1990), "On the Non-Existence of Rationality Definition for Extensive Games," *International Journal of Game Theory*, **19**: 33–44.

Ben-Porath, E. and E. Dekel (1987), "Coordination and the Potential for Self-Sacrifice," Research Paper No. 984, Graduate School of Business, Stanford University.

Benoit, J.-P. and V. Krishna (1985), "Finitely Repeated Games," *Econometrica*, **53**: 905–22.

Bernheim, D. (1984), "Rationalizable Strategic Behavior," *Econometrica*, **52**: 1007–28.
(1986), "Axiomatic Characterizations of Rational Choice in Strategic Environments," *Scandinavian Journal of Economics*, **88**: 473–88.
Binmore, K. (1987), "Modeling Rational Players I," *Economics and Philosophy*, **3**: 179–214.
(1988), "Modeling Rational Players, II," *Economics and Philosophy*, **4**: 9–55.
(1990), "Foundations of Game Theory," Lecture delivered at the 6th World Congress of the Econometric Society in Barcelona.
Brandenburger, A. and E. Dekel (1987), "Rationalizability and Correlated Equilibria," *Econometrica*, **55**: 1391–402.
Canning, D. (1989), "Convergence to Equilibrium in a Sequence of Games with Learning," STICERD Discussion Paper.
(1990), "Social Equilibrium," mimeo, Pembroke College, Cambridge.
Carlsson, H. and E. van Damme (1990), "Global Games and Equilibrium Selection," CentER Discussion Paper nr. 9052, Tilburg University.
Cho, I. K. (1987), "A Refinement of Sequential Equilibrium," *Econometrica*, **55**: 1367–90.
(1990), "Strategic Stability in Repeated Signaling Games," mimeo, University of Chicago.
Cho, I. K. and D. M. Kreps (1987), "Signalling Games and Stable Equilibria," *Quarterly Journal of Economics*, **102**: 179–221.
Cho, I. K. and J. Sobel (1990), "Strategic Stability and Uniqueness in Signaling Games," *Journal of Economic Theory*, **50**: 381–413.
Dekel, E. (1990), "Simultaneous Offers and the Inefficiency of Bargaining: A Two-period Example," *Journal of Economic Theory*, **50**: 300–8.
Farrell, J. (1984), "Credible Neologisms in Games and Communication," mimeo, Massachusetts Institute of Technology.
(1990). "Meaning and Credibility in Cheap-Talk Games," forthcoming in M. Dempster (ed.) *Mathematical Models in Economics*, Oxford University Press.
Forges, F. (1986), "An Approach to Communication Equilibria," *Econometrica*, **54**: 1375–85.
Fudenberg, D. and D. Kreps (1988), "A Theory of Learning Experimentation and Equilibrium in Games," Manuscript.
Fudenberg, D., D. Kreps, and D. Levine (1988), "On the Robustness of Equilibrium Refinements," *Journal of Economic Theory*, **44**: 354–80.
Fudenberg, D. and E. Maskin (1986), "The Folk Theorem in Repeated Games with Discounting and with Incomplete Information," *Econometrica*, **54**: 533–54.
Fudenberg, D. and J. Tirole (1989), "Perfect Bayesian Equilibrium and Sequential Equilibrium," mimeo, Harvard University, forthcoming in *Journal of Economic Theory*.
Glazer, J. and A. Weiss (1990), "Pricing and Coordination: Strategically Stable Equilibrium," *Games and Economic Behavior*, **2**: 118–28.
Grossman, S. (1981), "The Information Role of Warranties and the Private Disclosure about Product Quality," *Journal of Law and Economics*, **24**: 461–83.

Grossman, S. and M. Perry (1986), "Perfect Sequential Equilibrium," *Journal of Economic Theory*, **39**: 97–119.

Güth, W. and B. Kalkofen (1989), "Unique Solutions for Strategic Games," *Lecture Notes in Economics and Mathematical Systems*, **328**, Berlin: Springer Verlag.

Harsanyi, J. (1973), "Games with Randomly Disturbed Payoffs: A New Rationale for Mixed Strategy Equilibrium Points," *International Journal of Game Theory*, **2**: 1–23.

Harsanyi, J. and R. Selten (1988), *A General Theory of Equilibrium Selection in Games*, Cambridge, MA: MIT Press.

Hillas, J. (1990), "On the Definition of the Strategic Stability of Equilibria," *Econometrica*, **58**: 1365–90.

Kalai, E. and E. Lehrer (1990), "Rational Learning Leads to Nash Equilibrium," mimeo, Northwestern University.

Kalai, E. and D. Samet (1984), "Persistent Equilibria," *International Journal of Game Theory*, **13**: 129–41.

Kohlberg, E. (1989), "Refinement of Nash Equilibrium: The Main Ideas," mimeo, Harvard University.

Kohlberg, E. and J.-F. Mertens (1986), "On the Strategic Stability of Equilibria," *Econometrica*, **54**: 1003–37.

Kohlberg, E. and P. Reny (1991), "Consistent Assessments in Sequential Equilibria," unpublished notes.

Kreps, D., P. Milgrom, J. Roberts, and R. Wilson (1982), "Rational Cooperation in the Finitely-Repeated Prisoners' Dilemma," *Journal of Economic Theory*, **27**: 245–52.

Kreps, D. and G. Ramey (1987), "Structural Consistency, Consistency, and Sequential Rationality," *Econometrica*, **55**: 1331–48.

Kreps, D. and J. Sobel (1991). "Signalling," in R. Aumann and S. Hart (eds.), *Handbook of Game Theory*, Amsterdam: North Holland.

Kreps, D. and R. Wilson (1982a), "Sequential Equilibria," *Econometrica*, **50**: 863–94.

(1982b), "Reputation and Imperfect Information," *Journal of Economic Theory*, **27**: 253–79.

Lewis, D. (1973), *Counterfactuals*, Oxford: Blackwell.

Luce, R. and H. Raiffa (1957), *Games and Decisions*, New York: Wiley.

Madrigal, V., T. Tan, and S. Werlang (1987), "Support Restrictions and Sequential Equilibria," *Journal of Economic Theory*, **43**: 329–34.

Maskin, E. and J. Tirole (1989), "Markov Equilibrium," mimeo, Harvard University.

Matthews, S., M. Okuno-Fujiwara, and A. Postlewaite (1990), "Refining Cheap-Talk Equilibria," mimeo, Northwestern University.

Maynard Smith, J. (1982), *Evolution and the Theory of Games*, Cambridge University Press.

Maynard Smith, J. and G. Price (1973), "The Logic of Animal Conflict," *Nature*, London, **246**: 15–18.

McLennan, A. (1985), "Justifiable Beliefs in Sequential Equilibrium," *Econometrica*, **53**: 889–904.

Mertens, J.-F. (1987), "Ordinality in Non Cooperative Games," CORE Discussion Paper No. 8728.

(1988), "Stable Equilibria – A Reformulation," CORE Discussion Paper No. 8838.

(1989a), "Stable Equilibria – A Reformulation, Part I," *Mathematics of Operations Research*, **14**: 575–625.

(1989b), "Equilibrium and Rationality: Context and History-Dependence," mimeo, CORE.

(1990), "The 'Small Worlds' Axiom for Stable Equilibria," CORE Discussion Paper No. 9007.

Milgrom, P. and J. Roberts (1990), "Rationalizability, Learning, and Equilibrium in Games with Strategic Complementarities," *Econometrica*, **58**: 1255–77.

(1991), "Adaptive and Sophisticated Learning in Repeated Normal Form Games," *Games and Economic Behavior*, **3**: 82–100.

Myerson, R. (1978), "Refinements of the Nash Equilibrium Concept," *International Journal of Game Theory*, **7**: 73–80.

(1986), "Multistage Games with Communication," *Econometrica*, **54**: 323–58.

(1989), "Credible Negotiation Statements and Coherent Plans," *Journal of Economic Theory*, **48**: 264–303.

Nash, J. (1950a). "Equilibrium Points in *n*-person Games," *Proceedings from the National Academy of Sciences, USA*, **36**: 48–9.

(1950b), "The Bargaining Problem," *Econometrica*, **18**: 155–62.

Nöldeke, G. and E. van Damme (1990), "Switching Away From Probability One Beliefs," University of Bonn Discussion Paper No. A-304.

Osborne, M. (1990), "Signaling, Forward Induction, and Stability in Finitely Repeated Games," *Journal of Economic Theory*, **50**: 22–36.

Pearce, D. (1984), "Rationalizable Strategic Behavior and the Problem of Perfection," *Econometrica*, **52**: 1029–50.

(1990), "Renegotiation in Repeated Games," Lecture delivered at the 6th World Congress of the Econometric Society in Barcelona.

Ponssard, J.-P. (1990a), "Self Enforceable Paths in Games in Extensive Form: A Behavioral Approach Based on Interactivity," *Theory and Decision*, **28**: 69–83.

(1990b), "A Note on Forward Induction and Escalation Games with Perfect Information," mimeo, Ecole Polytechnique, Paris.

(1991), "Forward Induction and Sunk Costs Give Average Cost Pricing," forthcoming in *Games and Economic Behavior*, **3**: 221–36.

Reny, P. (1988a), "Backward Induction, Normal form Perfection and Explicable Equilibria," mimeo, University of Western Ontario.

(1988b), "Backward Induction and Common Knowledge in Games with Perfect Information," mimeo, University of Western Ontario.

Rosenthal, R. (1981), "Games of Perfect Information, Predatory Pricing, and the Chain-Store Paradox," *Journal of Economic Theory*, **25**: 92–100.

Rubinstein, A. (1988), "Comments on the Interpretation of Game Theory," STICERD Discussion Paper. Forthcoming in *Econometrica*.

(1989), "The Electronic Mail Game: Strategic Behavior Under 'Almost Common Knowledge'," *American Economic Review*, **79**: 385–91.

Schelling, T. C. (1960), *The Strategy of Conflict*, Cambridge, MA: Harvard University Press.

Selten, R. (1965), "Spieltheoretische Behandlung eines Oligopolmodels mit Nachfragetragheit," *Zeitschrift für die Gesamte Staatswissenschaft*, **12**: 301–24 and 667–89.

(1975), "Re-examination of the Perfectness Concept for Equilibrium Points in Extensive Games," *International Journal of Game Theory*, **4**: 25–55.

Selten, R. and U. Leopold (1982), "Subjunctive Conditionals in Decision Theory and Game Theory," in Stegmuller, Balzer, and Spohn (eds.), *Studies in Economics*, Berlin: Springer Verlag. *Philosophy of Economics*, vol. 2.

Sobel, J., L. Stole, and I. Zapater (1990), "Fixed-Equilibrium Rationalizability in Signalling Games," *Journal of Economic Theory*, **52**: 304–31.

Spence, M. (1974), *Market Signalling*, Cambridge MA: Harvard University Press.

Stalnaker, R. (1969), "A Theory of Conditionals," in N. Rescher (ed.), *Studies in Logical Theory*, Oxford: Blackwell.

Suehiro, H. (1990), "On a 'mistaken theories' refinement," mimeo, Kobe University.

Tan, T. and S. Werlang (1988), "The Bayesian Foundations of Solution Concepts of Games," *Journal of Economic Theory*, **45**: 370–91.

Van Damme, E. (1984), "A Relation Between Perfect Equilibria in Extensive Form Games and Proper Equilibria in Normal Form Games," *International Journal of Game Theory*, **13**: 1–13.

(1987), *Stability and Perfection of Nash Equilibria*, Berlin: Springer-Verlag.

(1988), "The Impossibility of Stable Renegotiations," *Economic Letters*, **26**: 321–4.

(1989), "Stable Equilibria and Forward Induction," *Journal of Economic Theory*, **48**: 476–96.

Van Huyck, J. B., A. B. Gillette, and R. C. Battalio (1988), "Credible Assignments in Non-Cooperative Games," Working Paper, Texas A&M University.

Von Neumann, J. and O. Morgenstern (1948), *Theory of Games and Economic Behavior*, Princeton NJ: Princeton University Press.

Vincent, D. (1990), "Bilateral Monopoly, Non-durable Goods and Dynamic Trading Relationships," mimeo, Northwestern University.

Weibull, J. (1990), "On Self-Enforcement in Extensive-Form Games," mimeo, Princeton University.

Discussion of: "Foundations of game theory," by Kenneth J. Binmore and "Refinements of Nash equilibrium" by Eric van Damme

Eddie Dekel*

> [A] unified theory for all non-cooperative games does not seem possible. The only alternative seems to be ... introducing ... information referring to personality traits, psychologies of the players, etc. [E]ven if ... examples ... throw doubt upon the universality of a concept, this does not necessarily undermine its importance. It merely establishes that care must be exerted to check whether the concept is plausible in the specific cases to which it is applied. Ideally, one should attempt to investigate the mathematical restrictions which should be placed on the domain of admissible games so that the concept is plausible.
>
> Luce and Raiffa (1957, pp. 104–5)

1 SWIMMING THROUGH THE FLOOD

Binmore believes "the foundations of game theory to be a mess." He attributes this mess in part to Bayesian foundations being "clinker-built," and in part to their failure to solve the problem of multiple equilibria. Binmore claims that foundations are "clinker-built," because they do "not address the conscious choice question"; and he observes that the problem of multiple equilibria has not been solved because refinements draw "contradictory conclusions from hypotheses said to be 'reasonable' or 'plausible'." Yet, despite this dismal view of the current state of foundations, he emphasizes that providing foundations is important since, "As regards game theory, too many of our wonderful results are wrong."

Binmore concludes that "it is necessary to model the way players think," "we need to be told something about the equilibrating process," and in fact "if the issue of conscious choice is to be faced squarely [it] would involve actively modeling the players as computing machines." Thus, he favors dynamic models of automatons that "classify solution concepts according to the environments in which it makes sense to apply them."

In contrast to Binmore, I do not think that foundations are a mess or clinker-built. Nor would I agree that our results are (in general) wrong. But current foundations are inadequate; so I do agree with Binmore insofar as he concludes that *more* foundations are needed. We need deeper foundations that examine the justifications, implications, and modifications of assumptions underlying game-theoretic tools. My view is that research using the Bayesian framework should continue:[1] assumptions (including common knowledge of rationality) should be examined further, weakened (for example, by considering that information is not correctly or costlessly processed), and added (e.g., people communicate, or strategies may have different costs of implementation).

Binmore proposes foundations that develop machine-based dynamic models of thought processes. While this is important, I will argue that furthering the Bayesian paradigm and developing other non-Bayesian approaches are no less important, despite Binmore's and van Damme's shared skepticism of psychological and behavioral assumptions. Assuming that people make decisions in accordance with an evolutionary model of perturbed automatons is no less problematic than exploring Bayesian learning, psychological assumptions, or other paradigms for decision-making; all require justification. Because I strongly agree with Binmore that we should categorize game-theoretic tools according to the environments in which they are appropriate, I view his focus on how players make decisions, and in particular on modeling players as machines, as too restrictive.

I will first review why foundations can be useful; and I will briefly argue that Binmore's goal of foundations that do not depend on intuition is unattainable: foundations inherently rely on intuition. I will then comment on the issue of conscious choice in Bayesian modeling. The main part of this chapter will raise a few questions regarding Binmore's general and specific proposals that we model how players think using explicit dynamics of game-playing machines. Because of my pessimism that any one approach will come close to solving the problems of foundations and game theory, I will conclude by supporting a more general research agenda.

To place my discussion of foundations in context I should first mention my view of its role in the broader area of economic theory. Models identify important features in economic problems, and verify the implications of those features using assumptions about human interaction. Decision theory synthesizes such assumptions to yield solution concepts. Foundations, in turn, examine these assumptions in depth. Foundations should help us comprehend which assumptions drive our results, evaluate informally (by introspection and intuition) their plausibility in various environments, analyze the robustness of results to modifications in the assumptions, and, at its best, enable us to formally analyze the assumptions using alternative and even more primitive assumptions.

2 FOUNDATIONS: MISPERCEPTIONS, MULTIPLICITY, AND THE PROBLEM OF INTUITION.

Foundations focus our attention on the implicit hypotheses that underlie our assumptions, and on the informal arguments that justify these assumptions. This compels us to examine whether the implicit hypotheses are consistent with other assumptions we make, and whether our informal justifications can be formalized. Several insights have been gained by carefully considering our solution concepts and assumptions. For instance, preceding Bernheim's (1984) and Pearce's (1984) work, there seemed to be little awareness that common knowledge of rationality does not imply Nash-equilibrium behavior. Also, in their talks, both Binmore and van Damme discussed the less-known fact that common knowledge of rationality (appropriately defined for extensive-form games) does not imply backwards induction (see Binmore for references).[2,3]

Another (related) reason to study foundations is to deal with the multiplicity of equilibria. If game theorists don't know which equilibrium is "right," then how do the players? If there are aspects that are not incorporated into the game and that help players know which strategies they should be playing, then explicitly incorporating these aspects may change the game. As Binmore emphasizes, how we choose an equilibrium concept is not independent of how we choose among equilibria.[4]

Most researchers agree that formal modeling is important, and are careful in their modeling assumptions: for example, what aspects of the environment are observable; whether the interaction is one-shot or repeated; whether we should assume that prices are sticky; whether it is valid to restrict attention to a subset of non-optimal mechanisms, or to linear pricing rules. Moreover, many argue that modeling assumptions should be explored (e.g., why are some aspects observable, why are prices sticky); and these researchers often reject unexamined modeling assumptions that simply yield more precise, or even "better," predictions.

By contrast, there seems to be a view that economists need not explore solution concepts because one can adopt those that are "useful." A more balanced view is that economists should be held equally responsible for their modeling assumptions and for their choice of solution concepts; the separation of assumptions about the model from those regarding the solution concept, when both ought to be appropriate for the environment, seems indefensible. I admit (and argue below) that assumptions are necessary; I want to emphasize here Binmore's point that foundations are needed – expediency does not justify leaving any fundamental assumptions unexplored.

There is, however, an important and inherent limitation of any foundations for game theory. Since all work begins with hypotheses, such as Binmore's hypothesis that automatons are – and neural networks are not – a good approximation of human decision-making, in the end we all rely on notions of intuitive appeal, introspection, and reasonableness. Binmore seems to criticize this use of intuition, while I see no way for game theory to avoid it. For example, should we reject *all* understanding gained about incredible threats because backwards induction is not the consequence of Bayesian rationality? The lack of a formal justification of an assumption cannot make it unacceptable, since assumptions at some level are always needed. Unexplored assumptions are, however, a signal to proceed with care. While a thorough comprehension of backwards induction continues to elude us, a paper can warily use backwards induction because of its intuitive appeal. It may, in fact, be an appropriate tool precisely because so many people find it appealing. (Its origin long before other equilibrium concepts supports this view.)

Of course, I agree with Binmore that an interesting and important research question is: "Why is an assumption intuitively appealing?" Without an answer, the assumption should be treated with extreme caution. Comprehension of an assumption's appeal can tell us if a result that relies on the assumption is robust and internally consistent. Most importantly, formal analysis of an assumption can explain why it appears intuitive in some contexts and not in others. In the example of backwards induction, it seems clear that a tension exists: it is appealing in some contexts, but not others; foundations should tell us why this is the case. Until foundations explain the cause of this tension, we can neither categorically reject, nor wholeheartedly accept, backwards induction.

In summary, I agree with Binmore that much can be learned by asking why an assumption is appealing. My disagreement with Binmore is more modest: I do not view dynamic models of thought either as necessary or as promising as does he. Yes, it is important to examine assumptions that underlie a model; however, the search for the most elementary assumptions is (I believe) as elusive as that for elementary particles. Just as physicists rightly do not restrict attention to the search for elementary particles, it could be extremely costly for research on foundations to await the development of a correct description of decision-making, despite the obvious importance of such a model for the discipline of decision theory.

3 WHICH FOUNDATIONS?

Binmore argues that the current state of foundations, as examplified by Aumann's (1987) "common-knowledge-of-Bayesian-rationality approach," is dismal. One major criticism he makes is that the Bayesian framework does not allow for conscious choice, since states are assumed to completely describe the world, including players' actions. This assumption in turn is used to justify the hypothesis that the players' information structure is common knowledge, which is a necessary ingredient in interpreting Bayesian foundations of solution concepts.

This criticism, which leads Binmore to conclude that Bayesian foundations are clinker-built, seems too strong. The Bayesian framework can allow (at least some aspects of) conscious choice, since it does not require that all players face the same state space. Thus each player could be uncertain about the state of the world – which is a complete description of the world *excluding* her own choice. In such a model common knowledge of rationality still leads to rationalizability, while players' choices are not determined by the state space, so that the model allows for free choice.[5] Thus, I take issue with Binmore's argument that a Bayesian Ark *must* be clinker-built.

Nevertheless, I strongly agree with Binmore that Bayesian foundations based on rationality alone have made little progress toward solving the problem of multiple equilibria. In fact, these foundations have exacerbated the problem by questioning backwards induction and showing the implausible nature of assumptions that appear necessary (within the "common-knowledge-of-Bayesian-rationality approach") to justify Nash equilibrium and its refinements. So the question is where to proceed next. Obviously it is time to examine the implications and reasonableness of additional assumptions.

Binmore proposes that we develop dynamic models of the decision-making process in order to understand how players reach an equilibrium. Aware of the various dynamics that can be proposed, he recommends using them to categorize solution concepts according to the environments in which they should be applied. His image is one of an armada of ships – each ship representing a dynamic thought process appropriate for some environments. He contrasts these dynamic models of thought processes with introspection and intuition, which are used to justify the hypotheses made in papers on learning and on refinements of Nash equilibrium. He sees introspection and intuition as providing "just cause" to those who describe game theory as pseudo-scientific.

Although I agree with the importance of dynamic models of thought, I doubt that they will save game theory from the contradictory conclusions that have provoked such criticisms. The same enlightened view of dynamic models, namely as categorizing environments, should be applied to other proposed hypotheses. Moreover, I doubt that the dynamics, let alone the models of our thought processes, will be so clearly related to "reality" that the resulting classification will be much simpler or more natural than alternative classifications based on restrictions on beliefs, physical environments, or behavioral hypotheses.[6] Thus, I fail to see the distinctive advantage of dynamic models of thought over, for example, learning models with assumptions about the way players experiment (see, for example, Fudenberg and Kreps, 1988).

I agree with Binmore that the dynamics by which equilibrium is reached provides a useful, under-explored direction for analysis.[7] Moreover, Binmore is certainly right that it would be good to open the black box of Bayesian beliefs and consider what various assumptions regarding the environment imply about the players' beliefs. However, if the Bayesian paradigm is to be challenged, it should be thoroughly overhauled, so that alternatives do not implicitly adopt a half-Bayesian model. In particular, it is equally important to explore the other sacred cow of the Bayesian paradigm: what determines preferences? In traditional short-run models it may be appropriate to take preferences as given. However, assuming fixed preferences seems questionable in precisely the evolutionary environments that Binmore advocates considering.

In any case, Binmore's more particular thesis is that we should model the dynamics of decision-making using computing machines (Turing machines or automatons for example), in order to have a model which would allow us to characterize what players would do if they were a little different. He cites interesting work in support of this thesis: Binmore and Samuelson (1990) and Fudenberg and Maskin (1990) both derive surprisingly strong results in favor of efficiency by applying an equilibrium concept based on evolutionary arguments (ESS) to an infinitely repeated game without discounting, and that is played by finite automatons.[8] Yet, I fail to see why such "metaphors for an evolutionary process," that explore beliefs using preferences based on computer science, are different at a fundamental level from psychological assumptions, or other restrictions on beliefs, strategy spaces, or learning processes.

I have argued that the Bayesian paradigm, including learning models, are no less appropriate for foundations than are models using machines. I also want to emphasize that the existing literature on automatons lies squarely within the Bayesian paradigm: recall that researchers have already made the intuitive claim that players focus attention on "simple" (e.g., stationary, Markov, or trigger) strategies. Instead of adopting Binmore's view that automatons describe human decision-making, one can take the more conventional view that they are an *assumption* within the Bayesian model: players prefer "simple" strategies. Automatons have some advantages over other *ad hoc* restrictions on strategy spaces. First, they appeared in a different literature, so are less likely to be biased in favor of results that game theorists are seeking. Second, they are easily compared to other models of machines and bounded recall in order to get a sense of their robustness. Finally, since computer scientists rank machines and problems in terms of memory and complexity, it is possible – but questionable – to assume that players' preferences rank them similarly, and hence to use traditional economic arguments regarding tradeoffs.[9]

As an aside, I would like to discuss the distinction Binmore draws between classifying "nearby worlds" according to whether they model differences in the physical world or differences in the players' thought processes. I wonder whether, in the end, such a distinction is meaningful. As far as I know, few game theorists view the literature on reputation and incomplete information as modeling perturbations of the physical environment; rather these perturbations of the payoffs are best thought of as metaphors for perturbing the players. In fact, it seems impossible to distinguish empirically between a player whose payoffs are different and who thereby behaves "irrationally" and a player whose thought process is irrational. When Fudenberg and Levine (1989) prove that a long-run player can achieve high payoffs by "imitating" a player with "Stackelberg payoffs," isn't it reasonable to view the "Stackelberg payoffs" as a summary for a player whose reasoning leads him to play as if his payoffs were as they specify? I conjecture that results that are robust to a wide variety of "physical" perturbations will be robust to a wide variety of "mental" perturbations, and conversely.

Since I feel that we are stuck with relying on intuition at every level – both specifying the model and developing solution concepts – I would like to repeat: insights on solution concepts can be gained by other methods, in addition to formally modeling the decision-making process; and other methods are no more suspect than Binmore's program, since the next level of assumptions that underlie all the models will be justified by intuition, and the models are equally "pseudo-scientific." So I now consider possible sources for intuitive *assumptions* about decision-making other than machines.

Outside of game theory, behavioral hypotheses have proven useful: Machina's (1982) Hypothesis II clarifies the relationships among many empirical "paradoxes" (e.g., preference reversals and the Allais paradox (Safra, Segal, and Spivak, 1989)). In games, for example, one might want to model the psychological feature that the players' expectations over outcomes might affect the games' payoffs (that is, the beliefs enter the payoffs). This interesting idea was proposed and modeled by Geanakoplos, Pearce, and Stacchetti (1989). As another possibility, Kahneman and Tversky (1989) have argued that the value assigned to an object is a function of whether it is owned. A related idea is that the sequence of offers in a bargaining game effects the preferences (or behaviors) in the induced subgame. Based on this, one might argue that offers (even after being rejected and withdrawn) are *perceived* by players as relevant in that they indicate a willingness to concede in the future. This implies that in finite-horizon bargaining games, delay will occur when players are sufficiently patient (Fershtman and Seidmann, 1990).

A category of behavioral assumptions concerns communication, or cheap talk, which has been used informally to justify Nash equilibrium as a solution concept. The argument that models of communication suffer from endless debates over "intuitive" assumptions and from limited success appears to lend support for Binmore's criticisms. I disagree. Although there are cases in which it is not clear which are the right assumptions, there are certainly unambiguous cases where all assumptions yield similar conclusions. (Interestingly, some of these cases correspond to games where other refinements have led to much controversy and ambiguity.) Moreover, cheap-talk models offer interesting negative results: informal claims regarding communication yielding Nash equilibrium and Pareto optimality are not supported by formal analysis, even with fairly strong assumptions about communication.[10] Finally, since communication plays a significant role in economic environments, it seems to me that much remains to be learned by considering behavioral assumptions about how people talk and by developing new models of communication.

There are at least two tempting criticisms of psychological and behavioral assumptions: they introduce the complexity which game theory tried to abstract into the payoffs, and the flexibility allowed by introducing psychological assumptions can destroy some of the discipline that the rational-player model imposes. However, these problems also seem to arise when introducing restrictions on strategies based on computer science. Judicious use of psychological assumptions, even in the absence of a complete model of our psyche, should be no less insightful than using automatons for modeling thought processes. And I agree with Binmore that formal models should not forever avoid the complexities of reality or the care required when a restraining straight-jacket is removed.

Nevertheless, exciting ideas and interesting issues will result not only by imposing assumptions from outside economics (e.g., psychology, cheap talk, and computer science) but also by using more conventional Bayesian methods to explore and relax the assumption that rationality is common knowledge. Binmore's very statement that "what [common knowledge of rationality] means is less than clear" suggests that significant questions remain unanswered. The notion of forwards induction (see Kohlberg and Mertens, 1986) is a recent and important contribution to our understanding of rationality.[11] The traditional approach to relaxing the assumption that rationality is common knowledge is based on games of incomplete information. Using this approach, Carlsson and van Damme provide an interesting justification of risk dominance. They show that in any Nash equilibrium (and in some cases, any rationalizable outcome) of a two-by-two game with incomplete information, as the uncertainty vanishes, players choose the risk-dominant equilibrium of the (almost certain) game. Their global game sets up another flotilla: depending on the environment, modeled by different forms of incomplete information, different selection criteria, such as risk dominance, may be justifiable.[12]

4 CONCLUSION: MANY ARMADAS ARE NEEDED

I disagreed with Binmore's claim that the conscious-choice problem (described in sections 2 and 3) implies that Bayesian foundations are clinker-built. However, I do agree that foundations have so far focused attention on problems, rather than providing positive results. I also agree with Binmore that it will be useful to have formal models of how players think (perhaps as machines). Yet, we will benefit by studying Bayesian learning, by incorporating into the Bayesian model assumptions drawn from many fields, and, of course, by developing new paradigms. Thus, many (contradictory) classifications of solution concepts are appropriate: armadas based on models of machines, learning, incomplete information, psychological features, and other aspects of the environment, will help us intuitively select a solution concept.

It is unlikely that criticisms about the pseudo-scientific nature of game theory will be less forceful even if we pursue dynamics and automatons wholeheartedly. Arguments over what are reasonable restrictions on beliefs will be replaced by arguments over reasonable dynamics. The same contradictory conclusions that Binmore attributes to intuitive restrictions on beliefs will arise from "plausible" dynamics. And I doubt that the dynamics – let alone our models of how we think – will be so well based in reality that we will actually be able to associate the different dynamics with clear-cut economic environments.

Game theory, especially if viewed as a branch of decision theory, would certainly benefit from an understanding of how people reach decisions. But the view that such an understanding, especially based on dynamic models of machines, can – let alone will – actually solve the problems from which decision theory suffers seems overly optimistic. I reject the view that such models are currently *necessary* for further insights, even though they are an admirable objective.

Notes

* I would like to thank Jean-Jacques Laffont for the enjoyable and exciting invitation to discuss these papers. Conversations with Elchanan Ben-Porath, Adam Brandenburger, Faruk Gul, and especially the patience and comments of Matthew Rabin and Suzanne Scotchmer have contributed to this discussion. Financial support from the Sloan Foundation the Econometric Society and NSF grant SES 88-08133 are gratefully acknowledged. My focus will be on Ken Binmore's paper, and I will relate it to two recent papers by Eric van Damme (which I received in lieu of a paper for this session).

1 The Bayesian paradigm examines the decision-theoretic implications of various hypotheses about players' beliefs and utilities, usually including variants of "rationality is common knowledge."

2 Moreover, having accepting backwards induction as a starting point, if a player sees it violated should she continue to believe in it? The traditional logic of backwards induction requires an unambiguous yes, but it is far from clear that this is reasonable. Van Damme and Noldeke show that a similar problem occurs in refinements of equilibrium that impose the "support restriction." This restriction requires that if an equilibrium leads a player to believe an event is impossible then she should never change that view, even off the equilibrium path. This ignores the fact that being off the path violates the equilibrium hypothesis used as a starting point, and hence it is again not clear that such a refinement is reasonable. The problems with the support restriction and with backwards induction both result from the difficulty in analyzing counterfactuals. The fact that very similar problems with apparently intuitive arguments arise repeatedly emphasizes the need to examine the foundations of solution concepts.

3 The literature on cheap talk (begun by Crawford and Sobel, 1982 and Farrell, forthcoming) provides another example of the insights gained from formalizing assumptions. For example, it may be appealing to assume that players choose some Pareto optimal equilibrium; and it may also be appealing to assume that we should allow *any* of the Pareto optimal equilibria. This is the approach of much of the literature on renegotiation in games (e.g. Bernheim and Ray, 1989 and Farrell and Maskin, 1989). However, Rabin (1990) has argued that explicit modeling of symmetric communication (which could be thought of as the reason that these two assumptions are jointly appealing) *cannot* justify them together (except for the trivial case of a unique Pareto dominant equilibrium). For related examples, see footnotes 5 and 11.

4 A simple and natural example concerns the literature on communication: as Myerson (1986) and Forges (1986) have shown, introducing communication changes the game. So, using communication to select among outcomes (in the

modified game) can lead to an outcome that is a correlated, rather than Nash, equilibrium of the original game.

5 A problem is that in such a model there seems to be no appealing analog to the common prior assumption (CPA), let alone a justification for it. But, at the least, as shown by Brandenburger and Dekel (1986), conscious choice seems to be allowed if one is willing to forego the CPA.

A similar point can be made from another, more speculative, perspective. Following his "conscious choice" criticism of Bayesian foundations Binmore discusses the Bayesian model of "knowledge." He claims that foundations must address how knowledge is attained. Binmore therefore proposes modeling knowledge as a consequence of proving theorems, and for this purpose an appropriate logical foundation is the modal logic of provability, (G). Brandenburger, Dekel, and Geanakoplos (forthcoming) show that the set of equilibria attained by allowing for information structures which, in a sense, correspond to (G) (in that they drop the assumption that knowledge implies truth) is equal to the set of equilibria attained using the standard partition model (that corresponds to S5) so long as the CPA is not imposed. Thus, if one is willing to forgo the CPA, Binmore's recommendation that information and knowledge be modeled using (G) need not lead to different sets of equilibria than those which result from the standard partition model corresponding to S5.

6 Dynamic models seem very sensitive to their specification. For example, assuming discrete versus continuous time, or including mutations and other forms of noise can have significant (and non-robust) implications. Can we really say what economic environments correspond to different models of mutation? What forms do mutations in economic environments take? Moreover, the properties of "limit points" may depend on whether one looks at attractors, stable points, asymptotically stable points, accumulation points, cycles, etc. Which characterizes the equilibrium we are at (if, in fact, we are in a convergent environment)?

7 This view is substantiated by the fact that the very originators of evolutionary dynamics, after turning to game theory, have become concerned about what qualifies as reasonable equilibria: "theories of almost limitless craziness can no longer be ruled out on commonsense grounds. If we observe an animal ... standing on its head instead of running away from a lion, it may be doing so to show off to a female. It may even be showing off to the lion." But natural "selection alone is entitled to judge" (Dawkins, 1989, p. 313). Nevertheless, since nature offers biologists many more *real* life experiments than those offered economists, I hope economists do not abandon intuitively informed arguments. A model that, *in the end*, does not convince one of its intuitive appeal should and will be ignored.

8 These papers are interesting and thought provoking. However, it is not clear that the use of infinitely repeated games without discounting is reasonable. Such games may be appropiate as an approximation for how players perceive long finite games. However, since the players receive payoffs and reproduce according to the actual game, not their perceptions, this approximation does not justify using such games in evolutionary models. Moreover, in terms of the

dynamics, it is disconcerting to (implicitly) use an evolutionary model that involves repetition of a game that never ends. An evolutionary model of overlapping generations seems much more "intuitive," and a promising avenue of research that has yet to be investigated. Finally, ESS is no more a "libration" than are other refinements: it is informally motivated using evolutionary arguments, but formal dynamics yield quite different predictions. My point is that this type of research can offer insights, despite hypothesizing a dynamic process that cannot be met in any environment, and despite failing Binmore's "libration" test.

9 Perhaps I should address the criticism that my argument simply lumps everything into the Bayesian paradigm, thereby achieving nothing. My point is that many aspects of how we think can and should be explored by taking beliefs and utilities as a starting point, and imposing assumptions. I conclude that automatons are only one way of formalizing specific types of assumptions. Regarding the more speculative search for new paradigms, I think that focusing on machine-based models of human thinking is no more promising than other, e.g., behavior or psychology-based, lines of research.

10 A commonly known language appears insufficient to guarantee equilibrium outcomes (Farrell, 1988; Rabin, 1990). Rabin, however, has shown that in combination with natural behavioral hypotheses, the set of payoffs a player can expect under rationalizability coincides with the set of expected Nash-equilibrium payoffs to that player. So, in one sense, the distinction between rationalizability and Nash equilibrium disappears due to communication (see also footnote 4).

11 Another recent example is Gul (1990), who focuses on results that do not rely on equilibrium hypotheses.

12 I doubt, however, that *these* forms of incomplete information correspond to real features of a modeling environment, though such a correspondence is necessary for a classification of solution concepts to be useful.

References

Aumann, Robert J. (1987), "Correlated Equilibrium as an Expression of Bayesian Rationality," *Econometrica*, 55(1): 1–18.

Bernheim, Douglas B. (1984), "Rationalizable Strategic Behavior," *Econometrica*, 52(4): 1007–28.

Bernheim, Douglas B. and Debraj Ray (1989), "Collective Dynamic Consistency in Repeated Games," *Games and Economic Behavior*, (4): 295–326.

Binmore, Kenneth G. and Larry Samuelson (1990), "Evolutionary Stability in Repeated Games Played by Finite Automata," University of Michigan Discussion Paper.

Brandenburger, Adam and Eddie Dekel (1986), "Bayesian Rationality in Games," Working Paper, Churchill College, Cambridge University.

Brandenburger, Adam, Eddie Dekel, and John Geanakoplos (forthcoming), "Correlated Equilibrium with Generalized Information Structures," *Games and Economic Behavior*.

Crawford, Vincent and Joel Sobel (1982), "Strategic Information Transmission, *Econometrica*, 50: 1431–51.

Dawkins, Richard (1989), *The Selfish Gene*, 2nd edition, Oxford University Press.

Farrell, Joseph (1988), "Communication, Coordination, and Nash Equilibrium," *Economic Letters*, 27: 209–14.

(forthcoming), "Meaning and Credibility in Cheap Talk Games," in M. Demster (ed.), *Mathematical Models in Economics*, Oxford University Press.

Farrell, Joseph and Eric Maskin (1989): "Renegotiation in Repeated Games," *Games and Economic Behavior*, 1(4): 327–60.

Fershtman, Chaim and Daniel J. Seidmann (1990), "Deadline Effects and Inefficient Delay in Bargaining with Endogenous Commitment," MEDS, KGSM Discussion Paper, Northwestern University.

Forges, Françoise (1986), "An Approach to Communication Equilibria," *Econometrica*, 54(6): 1375–86.

Fudenberg, Drew and David M. Kreps (1988), "Learning, Experimentation and Equilibrium in Games," Working Paper, Massachusetts Institute of Technology.

Fudenberg, Drew and David Levine (1989), "Reputation and Equilibrium Selection in Games with a Patient Player," *Econometrica*, 57(4): 759–78.

Fudenberg, Drew and Eric Maskin (1990), "Evolution and Cooperation in Noisy Repeated Games," *American Economic Review*, 80(2): 274–9.

Geanakoplos, John, David Pearce, and Ennio Stacchetti (1989), "Psychological Games and Sequential Rationality," *Games and Economic Behavior*, 1(1): 60–79.

Gul, Faruk (1990), "Rational Strategic Behavior and the Notion of Equilibrium" Working Paper, GSB, Stanford University.

Kahneman, Daniel and Amos Tversky (1989), "Reference Theory of Choice and Exchange," Working Paper, Department of Psychology, University of California, Berkeley.

Kohlberg, Elon, and Jean-Francois Mertens (1986): "On the Strategic Stability of Equilibria," *Econometrica*, 54(5): 1003–38.

Luce, Duncan R. and Howard Raiffa (1957), *Games and Decisions*, New York: John Wiley.

Machina, Mark J. (1982), "'Expected Utility' Analysis without the Independence Axiom," *Econometrica*, 50: 277–323.

Myerson, Roger (1986), "Multistage Games with Communication," *Econometrica*, 54(2): 323–58.

Pearce, David (1984), "Rationalizable Strategic Behavior and the Problem of Perfection," *Econometrica*, 52(4): 1029–50.

(1987), "Renegotiation-Proof Equilibria: Collective Rationality and Intertemporal Cooperation," Cowles Foundation Discussion Paper No. 855, Yale University.

Rabin, Matthew (1990), "A Model of Pregame Communication," mimeo, Department of Economics, University of California, Berkeley.

Safra, Zvi, Uzi Segal, and Avia Spivak (1989), "Preference Reversal and Nonexpected Utility Behavior," *American Economic Review*, 80(4): 922–30.

CHAPTER 3

Explaining cooperation and commitment in repeated games

Drew Fudenberg[1]

1 Introduction

Repeated games models have been one of the main tools for understanding the effects of long-run interactions, and in particular how long-run interactions make possible forms of trust and commitment that can be advantageous to some or all of the players. The most familiar example of this is the celebrated prisoner's dilemma, displayed in figure 3.1.

	Cooperate	Defect
Cooperate	2,2	−1,3
Defect	3,−1	0,0

Figure 3.1

When this game is played a single time, the unique equilibrium outcome is for both players to defect, but when the game is played repeatedly without a known terminal date and the players are sufficiently patient there are equilibria where both players always cooperate. This cooperative equilibrium has been used to explain observed trust and cooperation in many situations in economics and political science. Examples include oligopolists "implicitly colluding" on a monopoly price, Macaulay's (1963) observations that relations between a firm and its suppliers are often based on "reputation" and the threat of the loss of future business, and non-aggression and trade pacts between competing nation-states, as in the essays in Oye (1986).[2]

Closely related kinds of trust and commitment can arise in models where a single long-run player faces a sequence of short-run or myopic opponents.

Examples include Simon's (1951) explanation of non-contractual relations between a firm and its workers (recast in a game-theoretic model by Kreps (1986)), and the papers by Dybvig and Spatt (1980) and Shapiro (1982) on a firm who produces high-quality output because switching to low quality would cost it future sales. In these models, when the long-run player is sufficiently patient there is an equilibrium where it is always "trustworthy" and honors its contracts or keeps quality high.

In the applications of these models, analysts typically note that there is an equilibrium of the repeated game with the desired properties, and suppose that observed behavior will correspond to that equilibrium. In symmetric games where all players are long run, the equilibrium chosen is usually the most efficient symmetric equilibrium, while in games with a single long-run player the equilibrium chosen is the one that maximizes the long-run player's payoff. While this may be a fruitful way to understand the various applied situations, it raises a problem at the theoretical level, for both classes of games have many other equilibria. In particular, no matter how many times a stage game is repeated, or how patient the players are, repeated play of any of the stage game's equilibria is always an equilibrium of the repeated game. Thus, while repeated games models explain how cooperation, trust, or commitment might emerge, they do not predict that cooperation or commitment will occur.

What then is the basis for the widespread intuition that certain of the repeated-game equilibria are particularly reasonable? This chapter discusses two classes of potential explanations. Sections 2 and 3 discuss the literature on "reputation effects," which models the idea that players in a repeated game may try to develop reputations for certain kind of play. The intuition here, first explored by Kreps and Wilson (1982a), Milgrom and Roberts (1982), and Kreps, Milgrom, Roberts, and Wilson (1982), is that, if a player chooses to always play in the same way, his opponents will come to expect him to play that way in the future, and will adjust their own play accordingly. To model the possibility that players are concerned about their reputation, we suppose that there is incomplete information (Harsanyi, 1967) about each player's type, with different types expected to play in different ways. Each player's reputation is then summarized by his opponents' current beliefs about his type. For example, to model a central bank's reputation for sticking to the announced monetary policy, we assign positive prior probability to a type that will always stick to its announcements. More generally, we suppose that there are different types associated with different kinds of play, which is equivalent to assuming that no player's "type" directly influences any other player's payoff function.[3]

With the reputation-effects approach, the question of why certain equilibria seem particularly plausible is then whether some or all of the players will try to develop the reputations that are associated with particular equilibria. In general, the set of equilibrium reputations will depend on the players' prior beliefs about their opponents' types. It is comparatively easy to obtain restrictions on the set of equilibria by imposing strong restrictions on the players' prior beliefs, and to the extent that we feel comfortable imposing these restrictions, they can help us understand the mechanism supporting the "plausible" equilibria. But, if very strong restrictions on the priors are needed, the restrictions do not seem to constitute an explanation of why the plausible equilibria are plausible.

This raises the question of whether reputation effects have strong implications for a broad class of prior distributions. The case where reputation effects have the strongest general implications is where a single long-run player faces a sequence of short-run opponents, each of whom plays only once, as in the papers by Kreps and Wilson (1982a) and Milgrom and Roberts (1982) on the chain-store paradox.

In these games, there is only one player who has an incentive to maintain a reputation, so it may not be surprising that reputation effects are quite powerful: under a weak full-support distribution on the prior distribution, if the long-run player is patient, he can use reputation effects to obtain the same payoff as if he could publicly commit himself to whatever strategy he most prefers (Fudenberg and Levine, 1989, 1991). The reason is that, if the long-run player chooses to play the same action in every period, eventually his opponents will come to expect him to play that action in the future; and, since the opponents are short-run, they will then play a short-run best response to the action the long-run player has chosen. (This is imprecise – the conclusion requires either that the stage game be simultaneous-move, which the chain-store game is not, or that the extensive form have a special property explained in section 2.3.)

Another case where reputation effects might be thought to allow one player to commit himself is that of a single "large" player facing a great many long-lived but "small" opponents, since the large player's reward for a successful commitment is much greater. One reason for interest in this case of small opponents is that it may be a better description of the situation facing some government entities than the short-run player model. Whether reputation effects allow the big player to commit itself depends rather more on the fine structure of the game, as observed by Fudenberg and Kreps (1987).

When all players are long-run, as in the repeated prisoner's dilemma studied by Kreps, Milgrom, Roberts, and Wilson (1982), there is no distinguished player whose interests might be expected to dominate play, and so it would seem unlikely that reputation effects could lead to strong general conclusions. It is true that strong results can be obtained for specific prior distributions over types. For example, in the repeated prisoner's dilemma, Kreps *et al.* found that if player 2's payoffs are known to be as in the usual complete-information case, while player 1 is either a type who always plays the strategy "tit-for-tat" or is a type with the usual payoffs, then with a sufficiently long finite horizon in every sequential equilibrium both players cooperate in almost every period. However, Fudenberg and Maskin (1986) showed that by varying the prior distribution, any feasible, individually rational payoff of the complete-information game can be obtained. This confirms the intuition that reputation effects on their own have little power when all players are long run. More recently, Aumann and Sorin (1989) have shown that reputation effects do pick out the unique Pareto optimal payoffs in games of pure coordination when the prior distributions on types is restricted in a particular way. Section 3 presents these results.

To summarize sections 2 and 3, reputation effects provide a strong foundation for the intuition that a single long-run player can obtain his commitment payoff, in the sense that this conclusion emerges for a wide range of prior distributions over types. In contrast, reputation effects on their own (i.e., without strong restrictions on the priors) do not help to explain why trust or cooperation might tend to emerge in games with several long-run players.

Several authors have tried to explain the emergence of trust and cooperation using the concept of an evolutionarily stable strategy or ESS. This work is described in section 4. Axelrod and Hamilton (1981), discussed in section 4.1, introduced this concept to the study of repeated games, and showed that evolutionary stability rules out the "always defect" in the repeated prisoner's dilemma with time-average payoffs. However, this is roughly the extent of its power: many other profiles are ESS, including some where players defect most of the time.

As we will see, the reason is that "mutant strategies" attempting to invade a population playing an inefficient strategy profile may be severely "punished" by the prevailing population for deviating from the prescribed path of play. For example, the strategy "alternate between cooperate and defect; if anyone deviates from this pattern, defect forever afterwards" *is* an ESS, even though it uses the non-ESS profile "always defect" to punish deviations. This suggests that, in order for ESS to restrict the set of equilibria in a repeated game, there must be some reason that the punishments for deviation will not be too severe.

Two recent papers develop this idea by introducing different forces that lead to bounds on how strong punishments can be. Fudenberg and Maskin (1990a) introduce "noise" into the model by supposing that players sometimes make "mistakes" and play a different action than they had intended to. Since any prescribed punishment may be triggered by a mistake, certain extreme punishments are ruled out. Returning to the prisoner's dilemma, the strategy that enforced alternation between cooperate and defect with the punishment of "always defect" can be invaded by a strategy that follows the alternation until a mistake is made, but arranges to return to cooperation following a deviation from prescribed play. A more complicated argument shows that the only evolutionarily stable outcome of a pure strategy ESS is for both players to cooperate in almost every period. However, the same assumptions do not imply efficiency in other repeated games. These results are presented in section 4.2.

Section 4.3. presents the model of Binmore and Samuelson (1991), who analyze noiseless repeated games where players incur an implementation cost that depends on the number of "states" (in the sense of automata theory) required to implement their strategy. This cost implies that players will not use a strategy that has states that are not reached in the course of play, and in particular rules out strategies that punish deviations for an infinite number of periods before returning to the equilibrium path. Using this fact, Binmore and Samuelson show that ESS outcomes in any repeated game must be efficient.

2 REPUTATION EFFECTS WITH SINGLE LONG-RUN PLAYER

2.1 The chain-store game

The literature on reputation effects began with the papers by Kreps and Wilson (1982a) and Milgrom and Roberts (1982) on reputation in Selten's (1978) chain-store game. To set the stage for their work, let us first review a slight variant of Selten's original model. Each period, an entrant decides whether to enter or stay out of a particular market. If the entrant stays out, the incumbent enjoys a monopoly in that market; if the entrant enters, the incumbent must choose whether to fight or to accommodate. The incumbent's payoffs are $a>0$ if the entrant stays out, 0 if the entrant enters and the incumbent accommodates, and -1 if the incumbent fights. The incumbent's objective is to maximize the discounted sum of its per-period payoffs; δ denotes the incumbent's discount factor. Each entrant has two possible types, tough and weak. Tough entrants always fight; a weak entrant has payoff 0 if it stays out, -1 if it enters and is fought, and $b>0$ if it enters and the incumbent accommodates. Each entrant's type is private information, and each entrant is tough with probability q^0 independent of the others.[4] Thus the incumbent has a short-run incentive to accommodate, while a weak entrant will enter only if it expects the probability of fighting to be less than $b/(b+1)$. The incumbent faces a different entrant at each period t, and each entrant is informed of the actions chosen at all previous dates.

If this game has a finite horizon, there is a unique sequential equilibrium, as Selten (1978) observed: the incumbent accommodates in the last period, so the last entrant always enters, so the incumbent accommodates in the next-to-last period, and by backwards induction the incumbent always accommodates and every entrant enters. Selten called this a "paradox" because, when there are a large number of entrants and q^0 is small, the equilibrium seems counterintuitive: one suspects that the incumbent would be tempted to fight to try to deter entry, and that the "right" prediction is that the incumbent would fight and the weak entrants would stay out. This intuition is partly supported by the fact that, in the infinite-horizon version of the model, if $a(1-q^0)-q^0>0$, so that the incumbent's average payoff is higher when it fights than when it accommodates, and the incumbent is sufficiently patient, i.e., the discount factor δ is close to 1, there are subgame-perfect equilibria where entry is deterred.[5] One such equilibrium is for the incumbent to fight all entrants so long as he has never accommodated in the past, and accommodate otherwise, and for the weak entrants to stay out if the incumbent has never accommodated, and enter otherwise.[6]

Since the infinite-horizon model also has an equilibrium in which every entrant enters, it does not explain why the entry deterrence equilibrium is the most plausible. To provide an explanation, Kreps and Wilson, and Milgrom and Roberts, modified the finite-horizon model to allow the incumbent to maintain a reputation for "toughness." Specifically, suppose now that the incumbent is either "tough" or "weak." If it is weak, it has the payoff function described above; if it is tough, it has "always fight" as its dominant strategy.[7] The entrants do not know the incumbent's type; each entrant assigns the same probability p to the incumbent being tough. (Note that the incumbent's type is chosen once and for all, and influences its preferences in every market.)

If the game is played only once, the weak incumbent accommodates if entry occurs, so that a weak entrant nets $(1-p^0)b-p^0$ from entry. Thus a weak entrant enters if $p^0<b/(b+1)=p$ and stays out if the inequality is reversed. (Here and henceforth knife-edge cases will be ignored.)

Now suppose that the incumbent will play two different entrants in succession, in two different markets. Entrant 1 is faced first, and entrant 2 observes the outcome in market 1 before making its own entry decision.

The equilibrium of this game depends on the prior probabilities and the parameters of the payoff functions; the equilibrium is unique except for parameters on the boundaries of the regions described below.

(i) If $a\delta(1-q^o)<1$ or $q^0>\bar{q}\equiv(a\delta-1)/a\delta$, the maximum benefit of fighting is less than its cost. In this case, since a weak incumbent would not fight in market 1, a weak entrant 1 enters if $p^0<\bar{p}$, and stays out if $p^0>\bar{p}$. Entrant 2 enters if the incumbent accommodates, and stays out if the incumbent fights.

(ii) If $q^0<\bar{q}$, the weak incumbent is willing to fight in market 1 if doing so deters entry, since accommodating reveals the incumbent is weak and causes entry to occur. The exact nature of the equilibrium again depends on the prior p that the incumbent is tough.

(ii.a) If $p^0>\bar{p}$, then the weak incumbent fights in market 2, weak entrants stay out of both markets, and the incumbent's expected payoff is:

$$[(1-q^0)a-q^0]+\delta(1-q^0)a.$$

(ii.b) If $p^0<\bar{p}$, then in equilibrium the weak incumbent fights in market 2 with positive probability β less than 1.[8] Whether the weak entrant enters in market 2 depends on whether the total probability of fighting in market 2 exceeds $b/(b+1)$, which turns out to be the case if $p^0>(b/(b+1))^2$. Note that for $p\in[(b/(b+1))^2, b/(b+1)]$ the weak incumbent's expected average payoff is positive, while its payoff was zero for the same parameters in the one-entrant game. If $p^0<(b/(b+1))^2$, the weak entrant enters in market 2, and the weak incumbent's payoff is 0.

As the number of markets (and entrants) increases, the size of the prior p^0 required to deter entry (for $q^0<\bar{q}$) shrinks, so that even a small amount of incomplete information can have a very large effect in long games. When $\delta=1$, the unique equilibrium has the following form:

(a) If $q^0>a/(a+1)$, then the weak incumbent accommodates at the first entry, which occurs (at the latest) the first time the entrant is tough. Hence, as the number of markets $N\to\infty$, the incumbent's average payoff per period goes to zero.

(b) If $q^0<a/(a+1)$, then for every p^0 there is a number $n(p^0)$ so that, if there are more than $n(p^0)$ markets remaining, the weak incumbent's strategy is to fight with probability 1. Thus weak entrants stay out when there are more than $n(p^0)$ markets remaining, and the incumbent's average payoff per period approaches $(1-q^0)a-q^0$ as $N\to\infty$.[9]

It is easy to explain the role played by the expression $a(1-q^0)-q^0$ in the above. Imagine that the incumbent is given a choice at time zero of making an observed and enforceable commitment either to always fight or to always acquiesce. If the incumbent always fights, its expected payoff is $a(1-q^0)-q^0$, as it must fight the tough entrants to deter the weak ones. The asymptotic nature of the equilibrium turns exactly on whether a commitment to always fight is better than a commitment to always accommodate, which yields payoff 0. Thus one interpretation of the results is that reputation effects allow the incumbent to credibly choose whichever of the two commitments it prefers.

Note though that neither of these commitments need be the one the incumbent would like most. Suppose that $a(1-q^0)-q^0>0$, so that a patient incumbent is willing to fight the tough entrants to deter the weak ones. Then while it receives a positive payoff from committing to always fight, it could do even better by committing to fight with probability $b/(b+1)$, which is the minimum probability of fighting that deters the weak entrants. This commitment would give it average payoff $a(1-q^0)-bq^0/(b+1)$, which exceeds the payoff of $a(1-q^0)-q^0$ from committing to always fight. Of course, if the only two types of incumbent with positive prior probability are the tough and weak types described above, then the first time the incumbent accommodates its reputation for toughness is gone and all subsequent entrants enter. The next section discusses how reputation effects may permit commitments to mixed strategies.

2.2 Reputation effects with a single long-run player

General simultaneous-move stage games

If we view reputation effects as a way of supporting the intuition that the long-run player should be able to commit himself to any strategy he desires, the chain-store example raises several questions: does the strong conclusion derived above depend on a backwards induction argument from a fixed (and thus perfectly foreseen) finite horizon, or do reputation effects have a similar impact in the infinitely repeated version of the game? Can the long-run player maintain a reputation for playing a mixed strategy when such a reputation would be desirable? How robust are the strong conclusions in the chain-store game to changes in the prior distribution to allow more possible types? How does the commitment result extend to games with different payoffs and/or different extensive forms? What if the incumbent's action is not directly observed, as in a model of moral hazard?

To answer the first question, the role of the finite horizon, consider the infinite horizon version of the chain-store game with $a(1-q^0)-q^0>(1-\delta)/\delta$, so that, as we saw in the last section, even if $p^0=0$ there is an equilibrium in which the weak incumbent fights all entrants. Note now that this is not the only equilibrium of the infinite-horizon model, and that even if $p^0 > 0$ there is an equilibrium in which the weak incumbent accommodates the first entry. Here are the equilibrium strategies: "The tough incumbent always fights. The weak incumbent accommodates to the first entry, and then fights all subsequent entry if it has not accommodated two or more times in the past. Once the incumbent acquiesces twice, it accommodates to all subsequent entry. Tough entrants always enter: weak entrants enter if there has been no previous entry or if the incumbent has already accommodated at least twice; weak entrants stay out otherwise." In this equilibrium, the weak incumbent reveals its type by accommodating in the first period; it is willing to do so because weak entrants stay out even after the incumbent's type is revealed.

These two equilibria shows that reputation effects need not determine a unique equilibrium in an infinite-horizon model. This is potentially troubling, since it raises the possibility that the power of reputation effects in the chain-store game might rely on the power of long chains of backwards induction, and several authors have argued that such chains should be viewed with suspicion.[10] At the same time, note that if the incumbent is patient it does almost as well in the new equilibrium as in the equilibrium where all entry is deterred, so that the new equilibrium does not show that reputation effects have no force in infinite-horizon models. Finally, the multiplicity of equilibria suggests that it might be more convenient to try to characterize the set of equilibria without determining all of them explicitly.

This is the approach used in Fudenberg and Levine (1989, 1991). We extend the intuition developed in the chain-store example to general games where a single long-run player faces a sequence of short-run opponents. To generalize the introduction of a "tough type" in the chain-store game, we suppose that the short-run players assign positive prior probability to the long-run player being one of several different "commitment types," each of which plays a particular fixed stage-game strategy in every period. The set of commitment types thus corresponds to the set of possible "reputations" that the long-run player might maintain.

Instead of explicitly determining the set of equilibrium strategies, we obtain upper and lower bounds on the long-run player's payoff that hold in any Nash equilibrium of the game.[11] The (1989) paper considers reputations for pure strategies and deterministic stage games; the (1991) paper allows for reputations for playing mixed strategies, and also allows the long-run player's actions to be imperfectly observed, as in the Cukierman and Meltzer (1986) model of the reputation of a central bank when the other players observe the realized inflation rate but not the bank's action.[12]

The upper bound on the long-run player's Nash equilibrium payoff converges, as the number of periods grows and the discount factor goes to one, to the long-run player's Stackelberg payoff, which is the most he could obtain by publicly committing himself to any of his stage-game strategies. If the short-run player's action does not influence the information that is revealed about the long-run player's choice of stage-game strategy (as in a simultaneous-move game with observed actions) the lower bound on payoffs converges to the most the long-run player can get by committing himself to any of the strategies for which the corresponding commitment type has positive prior probability. If the stage game is not simultaneous move, the lower bound must be modified, as explained in section 2.3.

Consider a single long-run player 1 facing an infinite sequence of short-run player 2s in a simultaneous-move stage game, where the long-run player's realized choice of stage-game strategy a_1 is revealed at the end of each period. The history $h^t \in H^t$ at time t then consists of past choices $(a_1^\tau, a_2^\tau)_{\tau=1,\ldots,t-1}$. (This would not be the case in a sequential-move game, where the observed outcome need not reveal how a player would have played at some unreached information set, or in a game where actions are only imperfectly observed.) The long-run player's type $\theta \in \Theta$ is private information; θ influences player 1's payoff but has no direct influence on player 2's; θ has prior distribution p which is common knowledge. Player 1's (behavior) strategy is a sequence of maps σ_1^t from the history H^t and Θ to the space of stage-game mixed strategies $\mathscr{A}_1$: a strategy for the period-t player 2 is $\sigma_2^t\colon H^t \to \mathscr{A}_2$. Since the short-run players are unconcerned about future payoffs, in any equilibrium each period's choice of mixed stage-game strategy α_2 will be a best response to the anticipated marginal distribution over player 1's actions. Let $r\colon \mathscr{A}_1 \to \mathscr{A}_2$ be the short-run player's best response correspondence.

Two subsets of the set Θ of player 1's types are of particular interest. Types $\theta_0 \in \Theta_0$ are "sane types" whose preferences correspond to the expected discounted value of per-period payoffs v_1 (a_1, a_2, θ_0). All sane types use the same discount factor δ and maximize their expected present discounted payoffs. (The chain-store papers had a single "sane type" whose probability is close to 1.) The "commitment types" are those who play the same stage-game strategy in every period; $\theta(\alpha_1)$ is the commitment type corresponding to α_1. The set of commitment strategies $C_1(p)$ for prior p are those for which the corresponding commitment strategies have positive prior probability. I will present the case where Θ and thus C_1 are finite; our (1989) paper considers extensions to densities over commitment types.

Define the Stackelberg payoff for $\theta_0 \in \Theta_0$ to be:

$$v_1^s(\theta_0) = \max_{\alpha_1} \left[\max_{\alpha_2 \in r(\alpha_1)} v_1 \; (\alpha_1, \alpha_2, \theta_0) \right],$$

and let the Stackelberg strategy for type θ_0 be one that attains this maximum.[13] This is the highest payoff type θ_0 could obtain if (1) his type were public information and (2) he could commit himself to always play any of his stage-game actions (including mixed actions). Note that, as in the chain-store game, the Stackelberg strategy need not be pure.

Given the set of possible (static) "reputations" $C_1(p)$, we ask which reputation from this set type θ_0 would most prefer, given that the short-run players may choose the best response that the long-run player likes least. This results in payoff:

$$v_1^*(p, \theta_0) = \sup_{\alpha_1 \in C_1(p)} \left[\min_{\alpha_2 \in r(\alpha_1)} v_1(\alpha_1, \alpha_2, \theta_0) \right],$$

which is type θ_0's commitment payoff relative to the set of possible reputations.

The formal model allows the prior p to assign positive probability to types that play mixed strategies. Is this reasonable? Suppose that of the 100 periods to date, where entry has occurred, the incumbent has fought in fifty of them, and that various statistical tests fail to reject the hypothesis that the incumbent's play is the result of independent $1/2-1/2$ randomizations between fight and acquiesce. How should the entrants expect him to play? Arguably it is reasonable to suppose that they predict a 1/2 chance of fighting, which is consistent with a prior that assigns positive probability to a type that mixed in this way.[14]

Let $\underline{N}(\delta, p, \theta)$ and $\bar{N}(\delta, p, \theta)$, respectively, be the lowest and highest payoffs, of type θ in any Nash equilibrium of the game with discount factor δ and prior p.

THEOREM 1 (Fudenberg and Levine, 1991) Suppose that the long-run player's choice of stage game strategy a_1 is revealed at the end of each period. Then for all θ_0 with $p(\theta_0) > 0$, and all $\lambda > 0$, there exists $\underline{\delta} < 1$ such that for all $\delta \in (\underline{\delta}, 1)$:

$$(1-\lambda)v_1^*(p, \theta_0) + \lambda \min_{\alpha_1, \alpha_2} v_1(\alpha_1, \alpha_2, \theta_0) \leq \underline{N}_0(\delta, p, \theta_0), \tag{1a}$$

and

$$\bar{N}_0(\delta, p, \theta_0) \leq (1-\lambda)v_1^s + \lambda \max_{\alpha_1, \alpha_2} v_1(\alpha_1, \alpha_2, \theta_0). \tag{1b}$$

Remarks

(1) The theorem says that if type θ_0 is patient he can obtain about his commitment payoff relative to the prior distribution, and that regardless of the prior a patient type cannot obtain much more than its Stackelberg

payoff. Note that the lower bound depends only on which feasible reputation type θ_0 wants to maintain and is independent of the other types that p assigns positive probability and of the relative likelihood of different types.

(2) Of course the lower bound depends on the set of possible commitment types: if no commitment types have positive prior probability, then reputation effects have no force! For a less trivial illustration, modify the chain-store game presented above by supposing that each period's entrant, in addition to being tough or weak, is one of three "sizes," large, medium, or small, and the entrant's size is public information. It is easy to specify payoffs so that the incumbent's best pure-strategy commitment is to fight the small and medium-sized entrants, and accommodate the large ones. The theorem shows that the incumbent can achieve the payoff associated with this strategy if the associated commitment type has positive prior probability. However, if as in section 2.1 the only commitment type fights all entrants regardless of size, then the incumbent cannot maintain a reputation for fighting only the small and medium entrants, for the first time it accommodates a large entrant it reveals that it is weak.

(3) For a fixed prior distribution p, the upper and lower bounds can have different limits as $\delta \to 1$. In generic[15] simultaneous-move games, $\underline{v}_1^s(p, \theta_0) = v_1^s(\theta_0)$ when the prior assigns a positive density to every commitment strategy.

(4) The Stackelberg payoff supposes that the short-run players correctly forecast the long-run player's stage game action. The long-run player can obtain a higher payoff if its opponents mispredict its action. For this reason, for a fixed discount factor less than 1, some types of the long-run player can have an equilibrium payoff that strictly exceeds their Stackelberg level, as the short-run players may play a best response to the equilibrium actions of other types.

For example, in the chain-store game suppose that $a(1-q^0) < q^0 b/(b+1)$, so that the weak incumbent's Stackelberg payoff is zero. And suppose that the prior probability of the "tough" type is greater than $b/(b+1)$. Then one equilibrium is for the weak incumbent to always acquiesce, and the weak entrants stay out until they have seen a tough entrant enter and the incumbent acquiesce. Then the weak incumbent's equilibrium payoff is positive, since the first entrant might happen to be weak and thus stay out. However, as $\delta \to 1$ the incumbent's average discounted payoff (i.e., the discounted payoff normalized by $(1-\delta)$) tends to 0, as the only way the incumbent can repeatedly deter entry is to fight when a tough entrant enters, and the cost of doing so is outweighed by the benefits. A second example is in Bénabou and Laroque (1989), where an informed insider can use his information to "take advantage" of uninformed outsiders who believe that the insider might be honest. Each time the insider takes advantage, the outsiders attach a lower probability to his honesty, so that outsiders cannot be fooled by very much very often. Intuitively, stage-game payoffs above the Stackelberg level are informational rents that come from the short-run players not knowing the long-run player's type. In the long run, the short-run players cannot be repeatedly "fooled" about the long-run player's play, and the only way the long-run player can maintain a reputation for playing a particular action is to actually play that action most of the time.[16] This is why a patient long-run player cannot do better than its Stackelberg payoff. Reputation effects can serve to make commitments credible, but, in the long run, this is all that they do.

(5) While the theorem is stated for the limit $\delta \to 1$ in an infinite-horizon game, the same result covers the limit as the horizon grows to infinity of finite-horizon games with time-average payoffs.

Sketch of proof I will give an overview of the general argument and a detailed sketch for the case of commitment to a pure strategy. Fix a Nash equilibrium $(\hat{\sigma}_1, \hat{\sigma}_2)$. (Recall that σ denotes a strategy profile in the repeated game, as opposed to the stage game.) This generates a probability distributed π over histories. The short-run players will use π to compute their posterior beliefs about θ at every history that π assigns positive probability. Now consider a type $\bar{\theta}$ with $p(\bar{\theta})>0$, and imagine that player 1 chooses to play type $\bar{\theta}$'s equilibrium strategy $\sigma_1(\cdot|\bar{\theta}, \cdot) \equiv \bar{\sigma}_1(\cdot|h^t)$. This generates a sequence of actions with positive probability under π.

Since the short-run players are myopic, and best response correspondences are upper hemi-continuous, Nash equilibrium requires that the short-run player's action be close to a best response to σ_1 in any period where the observed history has positive probability and the expected distribution over outcomes is close to that generated by σ. Because the short-run players have a finite number of actions in the stage game, this conclusion can be sharpened: if the expected distribution over outcomes is close to that generated by $\bar{\sigma}_1$, the short-run players must play a best response to $\bar{\sigma}_1$.

More precisely, for any h^t with $\pi(h^t)>0$, let $\rho(h^t) = \pi[\hat{\sigma}_1^t(\cdot|\cdot, h^t) = \bar{\sigma}_1(\cdot|h^t)|h^t]$.

> *Lemma* 1: For any $\bar{\theta}$ with $p(\bar{\theta})>0$ there is a $\rho<1$ such that $\hat{\sigma}_2^t \in r(\bar{\sigma}_1^t)$ whenever $\rho(h^t)>\bar{\rho}$.

Conversely, in any period where the short-run players do not play a best response to $\bar{\sigma}_1$, when player 1's action is observed there is a non-negligible probability that the short-run players will be "surprised" and will increase the posterior probability that player 1 is type $\bar{\theta}$ by a non-negligible amount. After sufficiently many of these surprises, the short-run players will attach a very high probability to player 1 playing $\bar{\sigma}_1$ for the remainder of the game. In fact, one can show that for any ε there is a $K(\varepsilon)$ such that with probability $(1-\varepsilon)$ the short-run players play best responses to a in all but $K(\varepsilon)$ periods, and that this $K(\varepsilon)$ holds uniformly over all equilibria, all discount factors, and all priors p with the same prior probability of θ.

Given a $K(\varepsilon)$ that holds uniformly, the lower bound on payoffs is derived by considering θ to be a commitment type which has positive prior probability, and observing that type θ_0 gets at least the corresponding commitment payoff whenever the short-run players play a best response to $\bar{\alpha}_1=\sigma(\theta)$. To obtain the upper bound, let $\bar{\theta}=\theta_0$, so that type θ_0 plays its own equilibrium strategy. Whenever the short-run players are approximately correct in their expectations about the marginal distribution over actions, type θ_0 cannot obtain much more than its Stackelberg payoff.

In general the stage-game strategies prescribed by $\bar{\sigma}_1$ may be mixed. Obtaining the bound $K(\varepsilon)$ on the number of "surprises" is particularly simple when $\bar{\sigma}_1$ prescribes a the same pure strategy $\bar{a}_1$ in every period for every history. Fix an $\bar{a}_1$ such that the corresponding commitment type θ has positive prior probability, and consider the strategy for play 1 of always playing a_1. From claim 1, there is a $\bar{\rho}$ such that in any period where the players 2s do not play a best response to $\bar{a}_1$, $\rho(h^t)<\bar{\rho}$. Then if player 1 plays $\bar{a}_1$ in every period, there can be at most $\ln(p(\theta))/\ln(\bar{\rho})$ periods where this inequality obtains.

To see this, note that $\rho(h^t)\geq p(\bar{\theta}|h^t)$, because $\bar{\theta}$ always plays $\bar{a}_1$. Along any history with positive probability, Bayes rule implies that:

$$p(\bar{\theta}|h^{t+1})=p(\theta|(a^t, h^t))=\pi(a^t|\bar{\theta}, h^t)p(\bar{\theta}|h^t)/\pi(a^t|h^t). \tag{2}$$

Then since player 2's play is independent of θ, and the choices of the two players at time t are independent conditional on h, $\pi(a^t|h^t)=\pi(a_1^t|h^t)\cdot\pi(a_2^t|h^t)$ and $\pi(a^t|\bar{\theta}, h^t)=\pi(a_1^t|\bar{\theta}, h^t)\pi(a_2^t|h^t)$. If we now consider histories where player 1 always plays $\bar{a}_1$, $\pi(a_1^t|h^t)=1$, and (2) simplifies to:

$$p(\bar{\theta}|h^{t+1})=p(\bar{\theta}|h^t)/\pi(a_1^t|h^t). \tag{3}$$

Consequently $p(\bar{\theta}|h^{t+1})$ is non-decreasing, and increases by at least $1/\bar{\rho}$ whenever $\rho(h^t)\leq\bar{\rho}$. Thus there can be at most $\ln(p(\bar{\theta}))/\ln(\bar{\rho})$ periods where $\rho(h^t)\leq\bar{\rho}$, and the lower bound on payoffs follows. (The additional complication posed by types θ that play mixed strategies is that $p(\bar{\theta}|h^t)$ need not evolve deterministically when player 1 uses strategy σ_1.)

Note that the proof does not assert that $p(\bar{\theta}|h^t)$ converges to 1 when player 1 uses type $\bar{\theta}$'s strategy. This stronger assertion is not true. For example, in a pooling equilibrium where all types play the same strategy, $p(\bar{\theta}|h^t)$ is equal to the prior in every period. Rather the proof shows that, if player 1 always plays like type $\bar{\theta}$, eventually the short-run players become convinced that he will play like $\bar{\theta}$ in the future.

2.3 Extensive form games

Theorem 1 assumes that the long-run player's choice of stage-game strategy is revealed at the end of each period, as in a simultaneous-move game. The following example shows that the long-run player may do much less well than predicted by theorem 1 if the stage game is sequential move. This may seem surprising, because the chain-store game considered by Kreps and Wilson (1982a) and Milgrom and Roberts (1982) has sequential moves; indeed the chain-store game and the example below have the same game tree, but different payoffs.

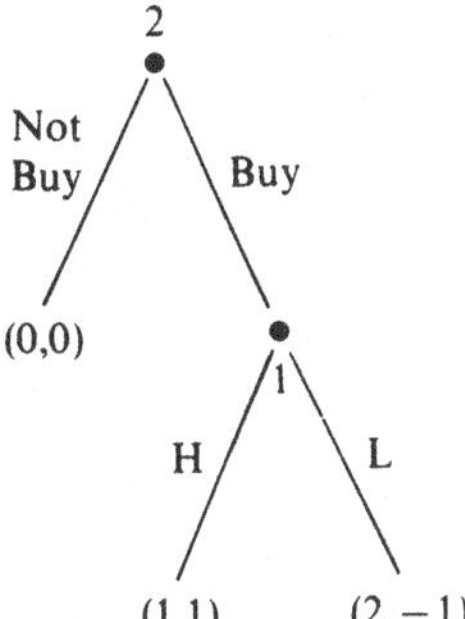

Figure 3.2

Player 2 begins by choosing whether or not to purchase a good from player 1. If he does not buy, both players receive 0. If he buys, 1 must decide whether to produce low or high quality. High quality gives each player a payoff of 1, while low quality gives player 1 a payoff of 2 and gives -1 to player 2. Note that, if player 2 does not buy, player 1's (contingent) choice of quality is not revealed. The Stackelberg outcome here is for player 1 to commit to high quality, so that all player 2s will purchase. Thus if theorem 1 extended to this game it would say that if there is positive probability p^* that player 1 is a type θ^* who always produces high quality, and if δ is close to 1, then a "sane" type θ_0 of player 1 (whose payoffs are as in the figure) receives payoff close to 1 in any Nash equilibrium.

This extension is false. Take $p(\theta_1)=0.99$, $p^*=0.01$, and consider the following strategy profile. The high-quality type always produces high quality: the "sane" type θ_0 produces low quality as long as no more than a single short-run player has ever made a purchase, and produces high quality beginning with the second time a short-run player buys. The short-run players do not buy unless a previous short-run player has already bought, in which case they buy so long as all short-run purchasers but the first have received high quality. This strategy profile is a Nash equilibrium that gives type θ_0 a payoff of 0; the profile can be combined with consistent beliefs to form a sequential equilibrium as well.[17]

The reason that reputation effects fail in this example is that, when the short-run players do not buy, player 1 does not have an opportunity to signal his type. This problem does not arise in the chain-store game, for there the one action the entrant can take that "hides" the incumbent's action was precisely the action the incumbent wished to be played. One response to the problem posed by the example is to assume that some consumers always purchase, so that there are no zero-probability information sets. The second response is to weaken the theorem. Let the stage-game be a finite extensive form of perfect recall without moves by Nature. As in the example, the play of the stage game need not reveal player 1's choice of normal-form strategy a_1. However, when both players use pure strategies the information revealed about player 1's play is deterministic. Let $0(a_1,a_2)$ be the subset of A_1 corresponding to strategies a_1', of player 1 such that $(a_1'$ $a_2)$ leads to the same terminal mode as (a_1,a_2). We will say that these strategies are observationally equivalent. For each a_1 let $W(a_1)$ satisfy:

$$W(a_1)=\{a_2| \text{ for some } \alpha_1' \text{ with support in } 0(a_1,a_2),\ a_2 \in r(\acute{a}_1)\}. \tag{4}$$

In other words, $W(a_1)$ is the set of pure strategy best responses for player 2 to beliefs about player 1's strategy that are consistent with the information revealed when that response is played. Then, if δ is near to one, player 1's equilibrium payoff should not be much less than:

$$v_1^2(\theta_0)=\max_{a_1}\left[\min_{a_2\in W(a_1)} v_1(a_1, a_2, \theta_0)\right]. \tag{5}$$

This is verified in Fudenberg and Levine (1989). Observe that this result, while not as strong as the assertion in theorem 1 that player 1 can pick out his preferred payoff in the graph of B, does suffice to prove that player 1 can develop a reputation for "toughness" in the sequential-move version of the chain-store game. In this game $B(\text{fight})=\{\text{out}\}$ and $B(\text{acquiesce})=\{\text{in}\}$. Also, 0(fight, out)=0(acquiesce, out)={acquiesce, fight}, while 0(fight, in)={fight} and 0(acquiesce, in)={acquiesce}. First we argue that

W(fight) = F(fight). To see this observe that W(fight) is at least as large as B(fight) = {out}. Moreover, "in" is not a best response to "fight," and "acquiesce" is not observationally equivalent to "fight" when player 2 plays "in." Consequently, no strategy placing positive weight on "in" is in W(fight). Finally, since player 1's Stackelberg action with observable strategies is fight, and W(fight) = B(fight), the generalized Stackelberg payoffs and the usual one coincide in this game.

2.4 Reputation effects with a single "big" player against many small but long-lived opponents

The previous sections showed how reputation effects allow a single long-lived player to commit itself when facing a sequence of short-run opponents. An obvious question is whether a similar result obtains for a single "big" player who faces a large number of small but long-lived opponents. For example, one might ask if a large "government" or "employer" could maintain its desired reputation against small agents whose lifetimes are of the same order as the large player's.

Suppose first that an infinite-lived "large" player faces a continuum of infinite-lived "small" players in a repeated game, that all players use the same discount factor δ, and that the small players' payoff functions are public information. The incumbent has various possible reputations, corresponding to "types" with positive probability. One might expect that the small players should behave as if their play had no influence on the play of their opponents, but this need not be the case: if the play of an individual short-run player can be observed, then there can be equilibria where its play influences the play of its opponents, even though its play has no direct effect on the payoff of any other player.[18] We can however restrict attention to games where the actions of the small players are ignored by postulating that each player can only observe the play of the large player and of subsets of small players of positive measure. (Doing so provides only a starting point for the analysis, as one would like to know if there are sequences of equilibria with finitely many short-run players that converge to other limits.) Under this assumption, the small players will behave myopically. That is, each period they will play a best response to that period's expected play. Thus the situation is strategically equivalent to the case of short-run players, and theorem 1 should be expected to apply – the large player should be able to approximate the payoff of her most preferred positive-probability reputation. ("Should be expected to" because at this writing no one has worked out a careful version of the argument, attending to the technical niceties involved in continuum-of-players models.)

Next consider a large player facing a large but finite number of small long-run opponents, each of whose actions can be observed. If the payoffs of the small players are public information, one would expect that there will be equilibria which approximate the commitment result of the previous paragraph, although there could be other equilibria as well. But once the actions of the small players can be observed, they potentially have an incentive to maintain reputations of their own. Thus, instead of requiring the payoffs of the small players to be public information, it seems more reasonable to allow for the possibility that the small players will maintain reputations by supposing that there is some small prior probability that each small player is a "commitment type." The question then becomes whether the large player's concern for his reputation will outweigh the concern of the small players for theirs. Fudenberg and Kreps (1987) study this question in the context of one particular game, a multiplayer version of the two-sided concession game of Kreps and Wilson (1982a).

In the concession game, at each instant $t \in [0,1]$, both players decide whether to "fight" or "concede." The "tough" types always fight, while the "weak" ones find fighting costly but are willing to fight to induce their opponent to concede in the future. More specifically, both weak types have a cost of 1 per unit time of fighting. If the entrant concedes first at t, the weak incumbent receives a flow of a per unit time until the end of the game, so the weak incumbent's payoff is $at-(1-t)$, and the weak entrant's payoff is $-(1-t)$. If the weak incumbent concedes first at t, the weak incumbent's payoff is $-(1-t)$ and the weak entrant's payoff is $bt-(1-t)$, where b is the entrant's flow payoff once the incumbent concedes. Thus each (weak) player would like the other player to concede, and each player will concede if he thinks his opponent is likely to fight until the end. The unique equilibrium involves the weak type of one player conceding with positive probability at date zero (so the corresponding distribution of stopping-times has an "atom" at zero); if there is no concession at date zero both players concede according to smooth density functions thereafter.

In the multiplayer version, a "large" incumbent is simultaneously involved in N such concession games against N different opponents. Each entrant plays only against the incumbent, but observes play in all of the games. The incumbent is tough in all of the games with prior probability p^0, and weak in all of them with complementary probability; each entrant is tough with prior probability q^0 independent of the others. This situation differs from that of the preceding section, in that both the big player and the small ones have the ability to maintain reputations.

The nature of the equilibrium depends on whether an entrant is allowed to resume fighting after it has already dropped out. In the "captured contests" version of the game, if an entrant has ever conceded (i.e., exited from the market), it must concede from then on, while the "reentry" version allows the entrant to revert to fighting after it has acquiesced. Note that, when there is only one entrant, the captured contests and reentry versions have the same sequential equilibrium, as once the entrant chooses to concede it receives no subsequent information about the incumbent's type and thus will choose to acquiesce from then on.[19]

One might guess that if there are enough entrants the incumbent could deter entry in either version of the game. This turns out not to be the case. Specifically, under captured contests, when each entrant has the same prior probability of being tough, then no matter how many entrants the incumbent faces, equilibrium play in each market is exactly as if the incumbent played against only that entrant. To see why, suppose that there are N entrants, and that, at time t, $N-k$ of them have conceded, so that there are k entrants still fighting. Supposing that the equilibrium is symmetric (one can show that it must be) then the incumbent has the same posterior beliefs q_t about the type of each active entrant. Further supposing that the incumbent is randomizing at date t, it must be indifferent between conceding now, in which case it receives continuation payoff of zero in the remaining markets, and fighting on for a small interval dt and then conceding. The key is that whatever happens in the active markets the captured markets remained captured, so the incumbent does not consider them in making its current plans. If we denote the probability each entrant concedes between t and $t-dt$ by σ_t, we have:

$$0=-k+k(1-q_t)\sigma_t at.$$

Note that the number of active entrants k factors out of this equation, so that it is the same equation as that for the one-entrant case. This is why adding more entrants has no effect on equilibrium play.

In contrast, if reentry is allowed, and there are many entrants, then reputation effects can enable the incumbent to obtain approximately its commitment payoff, provided that once the incumbent is revealed to be weak, all entrants who have previously conceded reenter.[20] In this case, when the incumbent has captured a number of markets he has a great deal to lose by conceding. Here the incumbent's myopic incentive is to concede to entrants who have fought a long time and thus are likely to be tough, but the incumbent lacks the flexibility to concede to these active entrants without also conceding to the entrants who have already been revealed to be weak, and this lack of flexibility enables the incumbent to commit itself to tough play. As the number of entrants grows, the equilibria converge to the profile where the incumbent never concedes and weak entrants concede immediately. At this point the remaining entrants are revealed to be tough, and the incumbent would like to concede to them if it could do so without also conceding against the weak entrants. However, since $a(1-q^0)-q^0>0$, the incumbent is willing to fight the tough entrants to retain control of the other markets.

The moral of these observations is that the workings of reputation effects with one big player facing many small long-run opponents can depend on aspects of the game's structure that would be irrelevant if the small opponents were played sequentially. Thus in applications of game theory one should be wary of general assertions that reputation effects will allow a large player to make its commitments credible.

What happens when the incumbent's type need not be the same in each contest is an open question. If the types in each market are statistically independent, then the various contests can be decoupled; the interesting situation is one of imperfect correlation. One issue here is that, when types are imperfectly correlated, the incumbent's payoff aggregates outcomes in markets where it is tough and markets where it is soft, so that the exact specification of the "tough" type's payoffs and strategies becomes more important. For example, is the incumbent willing to sacrifice payoff in a market where it is weak to increase its payoff in a market where it is tough? The answer is presumably is context-specific, it might be interesting to explore some special cases.

3 REPUTATION IN GAMES WITH MANY LONG-RUN PLAYERS

3.1 General stage games and general reputations

So far we have looked at cases where reputation effects can allow a distinguished "large" or "long-run" player to commit himself to his preferred strategy. There are also incentives to maintain reputations when all players are equally large or patient, but here it is more difficult to draw general conclusions about how reputation-effects influence play.

Kreps, Milgrom, Roberts, and Wilson (1982) analyzed reputation effects in the finitely repeated prisoner's dilemma of figure 3.1. If both types are sane with probability one, then the unique Nash equilibrium of the game is for both players to defect in every period, but intuition and experimental evidence suggest that players may tend to cooperate. To explain this intuition, Kreps *et al.* introduced incomplete information about player 1's type, with player 1 either a "sane" type, or a type who plays the strategy "tit-for-tat," which is "I play today whichever action you played yesterday." They showed that, for any fixed prior probability ε that player 1 is tit-for-tat, there is a number K independent of the horizon length T such that, in any sequential equilibrium, both players must cooperate in almost all periods before date K, so that, if T is sufficiently large, the equilibrium payoffs will be close to those if the players always cooperated. The point is that a sane player 1 has an incentive to maintain a reputation for being tit-for-tat, because, if player 2 were convinced that player 1 plays tit-for-tat, player 2 would cooperate until the next-to-last period of the game.

Just as in the chain-store game, adding a small amount of the right sort of incomplete information to the prisoner's dilemma yields the "intuitive" outcome as the essentially unique prediction of the model with a long finite horizon. However, unlike games with a single long-run player, the resulting equilibrium is very sensitive to the exact nature of the incomplete information specified, as was shown by Fudenberg and Maskin (1986).

Fix a two-player stage-game g with finite set of pure actions A_i for each player i and payoff functions u_1 and u_2. Now consider repeated play of an incomplete-information game with the same action spaces as g, but where the players' payoffs need not be the same as in the repeated version of g. Call player i "sane" if his payoff is the expected value of the sum of u_i (We can take the discount factor equal to 1 without loss of generality because we consider a large, but finite horizon.)

THEOREM 2 (Fudenberg and Maskin, 1986) For any feasible, individually rational payoff[21] v and any $\varepsilon > 0$ there exists a $\hat{T}$ such that for all $T > \hat{T}$ there exists a T-period game such that each player i has probability $(1-\varepsilon)$ of being sane, independent of the other, and such that there exists a sequential equilibrium where player i's expected average payoff if sane is within ε of v_i.

Remark Note that this theorem asserts the existence of a game and of an equilibrium; it does not say that all equilibria of the game have payoffs close to v. Note also that no restrictions are placed on the form of the payoffs that players have when they are not sane, i.e., on the support of the distribution of types: no possible types are excluded, and there is no requirement that certain types have positive prior probability. However, the theorem can be strengthened to assert the existence of a game with a strict equilibrium[22] where the sane types' payoffs are close to v, and a strict equilibrium of a game remains strict when additional types are added whose prior probability is sufficiently small.

Partial Proof Much of the intuition for the result can be gained from the case of payoffs v that Pareto-dominate the payoffs of a static equilibrium. Let e be a static equilibrium with payoffs $y = (y_1, y_2)$, and let v be a payoff vector that Pareto-dominates y. To avoid a discussion of public randomizations, assume that payoffs v can be attained with a pure action profile a, i.e., $g(a) = v$. Now consider a T-period game where each player i has two possible types, "sane" and "crazy," and crazy types have payoffs that make the following strategy weakly dominant: "Play a_i as long as no deviations from a have occurred in the past, and otherwise play e_i." Let $u_i = \max u_i$ and $\hat{u}_i = \min u_i$. Set:

$$\hat{T} > \max_i (u_i - (1-\varepsilon)\hat{u}_i)/\varepsilon(v_i - y_i). \tag{6}$$

Consider the extensive game corresponding to $T = \hat{T}$. This game has at least one sequential equilibrium for any prior beliefs; pick one and call it the "endgame equilibrium."

Now consider $T > \hat{T}$. It will be convenient to number periods backwards, so that period T is the first one played and period 1 is the last. Consider strategies that specify that profile a is played for all $t > \hat{T}$, and that if a deviation does occur at some $t > \hat{T}$ (i.e., "before date $\hat{T}$"), then e is played for the rest of the game, while, if a is played in every period until $\hat{T}$, play follows the endgame equilibrium corresponding to prior beliefs. Let the beliefs prescribe that, if any player deviates before $\hat{T}$, that player is believed to be sane with probability one, while if there are no such deviations before $\hat{T}$ than the beliefs are the same as the prior until $\hat{T}$ is reached, at which time strategies are given by the endgame equilibrium thereafter.

Let us check that these strategies and beliefs form a sequential equilibrium. The beliefs are clearly consistent (in the Kreps–Wilson sense). They are sequentially rational by construction in the endgame equilibrium, and are also sequentially rational in all periods following a deviation before $\hat{T}$, where both types of both players play the static equilibrium strategies.

It remains only to check that the strategies are sequentially rational along the path of play before $\hat{T}$. Pick a period $t > \hat{T}$ where there have been no deviations to date. If player i plays anything but a_i, he receives at most $\bar{u}_i$ today and at most y_i thereafter, for a continuation payoff of:

$$\bar{u}_i + (t-1)y_i. \tag{7}$$

If instead he follows the (not necessarily optimal) strategy of playing a_i each period until his opponent deviates and playing e_i thereafter, his expected payoff will be at least:

$$\varepsilon t v_i + (1-\varepsilon)\,[\hat{u}_i + (t-1)y_i], \tag{8}$$

as this strategy yields tv_i if his opponent is crazy and at least $\hat{u}_i + (t-1)y_i$ if his opponent is sane. The definition of $\hat{T}$ has been chosen so that (8) exceeds (7) for $t > \hat{T}$, which shows that player i's best response to player j's strategy must involve playing a_i until $\hat{T}$. (A best response exists by standard arguments.) The key in the construction is that, when players respond to deviations as we have specified, any deviation before $\hat{T}$ gives only a one-period gain (relative to y_i). In contrast, playing a_i until $\hat{T}$ risks only a one-period loss and gives probability ε of a gain $(v_i - y_i)$ that grows linearly in the time remaining. This is why even a very small ε makes a difference when the horizon is sufficiently long.[23]

3.2 Common interest games and bounded-recall reputations

Aumann and Sorin (1989) consider reputation effects in the repeated play of two-player stage games of "common interests," which they define as stage games where there is a payoff vector that strongly Pareto dominates all other feasible payoffs. In these games, the Pareto-dominant payoff vector corresponds to a static Nash equilibrium, but there can be others, as in the game of figure 3.3.

	L	R
U	9,9	0,8
D	8,0	7,7

Figure 3.3

This is the game used by Aumann (1990) to argue that even a unique Pareto-optimal payoff need not be the inevitable result of preplay negotiation: Player 1 should play D if he assesses probability greater than $\frac{1}{8}$ that player 2 will play R. Also, player 1 would like player 2 to play L regardless of how player 1 intends to play. Thus, when the players meet each will try to convince the other that they will play their first strategy, but these statements need not be compeling.

Aumann and Sorin show that when the possible reputations (i.e., crazy types) are all "pure strategies with bounded recall" (to be defined shortly) then reputation effects pick out the Pareto-dominant outcome so long as only pure-strategy equilibria are considered. A pure strategy for player i has recall k if it depends only on the last k choices of his opponents, that is if all histories where i's opponent has played the same actions in the last k periods induce the same action by player i. (Note that, when player i plays a pure strategy and does not contemplate deviations, conditioning on his own past moves is redundant.) When k is large the bounded recall condition may seem innocuous, but it does rule out some simple but "unforgiving" strategies, such as those that prescribe permanent reversion to a static Nash equilibrium if any player ever deviates.

Aumann and Sorin consider perturbed games with independent types, where each player's type is private information, each player's payoff function depends only on his own type, and types are independently distributed. The prior p_i about player i's type is that player i is either the "sane" type θ_0, with the same payoffs as in the original game, or a type that plays a pure strategy with recall less than some bounded μ. Moreover, p_i is required to assign positive probability to the types corresponding to each pure strategy of recall 0. These types play the same action in every period regardless of the history, just like the commitment types considered in section 2.[24] Such priors correspond to "admissible perturbations of recall μ," or "μ-perturbations" for short. Say that a sequence p of μ-perturbations supports a game G if $p^m(\theta^i_0)\to 1$ for all i where $m\to\infty$, and if the conditional distribution $p^m(\theta^i|\theta^i\neq\theta^i_0)$ is constant.

THEOREM 3 (Aumann-Sorin, 1989) Let the stage-game g be a game of common interests, and let z be its unique Pareto-optimal outcome. Fix a recall length μ, and let p^m be a sequence of μ-perturbations that support the associated discounted repeated game $G(\delta)$. Then the set of pure-strategy Nash equilibria of the games $G(\delta,p^m)$ is not empty, and the pure-strategy equilibrium payoff converge to z for any sequence (δ,m) converging to $(1,\infty)$.

Idea of Proof The intuition is clearest in the case where δ goes to 1 much faster than m goes to infinity (the theorem holds uniformly over sequences (δ,m)). Suppose a pure-strategy equilibrium exists, and suppose its payoff is less than z. Consider the strategy for player 1 of always playing the action $a_1(z)$ corresponding to z. Since the equilibrium is pure this strategy is certain to eventually reveal that player 1 is not type θ_0. The commitment type $\theta(z)$ corresponding to $a_1(z)$ has positive probability by assumption, so if $\mu=0$ player 2 will infer that player 1 is $\theta(z)$ and will play $a_1(z)$ from then on (because crazy types play constant strategies when $\mu=0$). However, player 1 could be some other type with memory longer than 0, and to learn player 1's type will require player 2 to "experiment" to see how player 1 responds to different actions. Such experiments could be very costly if they provoked an unrelenting punishment by player 1, but since player 1's crazy types all have recall at most μ, player 2's potential loss (in normalized payoff) from experimentation goes to zero as δ goes to one. Thus if δ is sufficiently large we expect player 2 to eventually learn that player 1 has adopted the strategy "always play $a_1(z)$," and so when δ is close to one player 1 can obtain approximately z by always playing $a_1(z)$.

Remarks Aumann–Sorin give counterexamples to show that the assumptions of bounded recall and full support on recall 0 are necessary, and also show that there can be mixed-strategy equilibria whose payoffs are bounded away from z. They interpret the necessity of the bounded recall assumption with the remark that "in a culture in which irrational people have long memories, rational people are less likely to cooperate." Note that the theorem concerns the case where δ is large compared to the recall length μ, while one might expect that a more patient player would tend to have a longer memory. This is important for the proof: if μ grew with δ, it is not clear that player 2 would try to learn player 1's strategy.

3.3 Reputation effects in repeated bargaining models with two long-run players

Schmidt (1990) extends the logic of the proof of Fudenberg and Levine (1989) to a repeated bargaining model where both players are long-lived but only one of the players has the opportunity to build a reputation. In this model, in each period t a seller whose cost of production is known (and equal to 0 without loss of generality) makes an offer p_t to a buyer whose value v is private information; v takes on finitely many values between $\underline{v}$ and $\bar{v}$. If the buyer accepts offer p_t, the seller's payoff that period is p_t and the buyer's payoff is $v-p_t$; if the buyer rejects each player's payoff that period is zero. The good is not storable, and each period the seller has a new good to offer for sale. Each player's objective is to maximize the expected discounted sum of his per-period payoffs, with discount factor δ_b for the buyer and δ_s for the seller. (Hart and Tirole (1988) solved this game for the case where the buyer and seller have the same discount factor and the buyer has only two possible types.)

Since the seller's payoff function is assumed to be public information, only the buyer potentially has the ability to develop a reputation. If we can show that the buyer always rejects prices above his valuation, then each valuation is a "commitment type" in the sense of section 2.2, and the buyer's most preferred reputation is for $v=\underline{v}$. (This reputation only yields the Stackelberg payoff if $\underline{v}$ equals the seller's cost of zero.) While it seems intuitive that the buyer should behave in this way, the infinite-horizon model has equilibria where this is not the case. However, Schmidt shows that the buyer does reject all prices above his valuation in a Markov-perfect equilibrium of the finite-horizon model, so that $\underline{v}$ does serve as a commitment type when this equilibrium concept is used.[25] The strategy "reject all prices above $\underline{v}$" is the corresponding commitment strategy, and the seller's best response to this strategy is to always charge price $\underline{v}$.

The proof of theorem 1 relies on the fact that short-run players always play a short-run best response to the anticipated play of their opponents, so the short-run players would necessarily be "surprised" in any period where their play was not a best response to the long-run player's play. In the context of the bargaining model, this says that if the seller were a short-run player he would be "surprised" whenever his offer was rejected. Because the seller is a long-run player, it is not necessarily true that he will never make an offer that is certain to be refused, and so there can be periods in which the seller does not play a best response to the buyer's commitment strategy and yet is not surprised when the commitment strategy is played. Nevertheless, as Schmidt shows, even a long-run seller cannot continually make offers that are likely to be refused, as the seller could do better by charging price $\underline{v}$, which is certain to be accepted in any Markov perfect equilibrium. More precisely, for any discount factor $\delta_s<1$, and any $\varepsilon>0$, there is an $M(\varepsilon,\delta_s)$ such that among the first M offers above $\underline{v}$, at least one of them has a probability of acceptance of at least ε. With this result in hand, the proof of theorem 1 can be used to conclude that, in any Markov perfect equilibrium, if the buyer adopts the strategy of always rejecting prices above $\underline{v}$, then eventually the seller must charge $\underline{v}$. This implies that as $\delta_b \to 1$ and the horizon $T\to\infty$ for a fixed δ_s, the buyer's equilibrium payoff converges to its commitment value of $v-\underline{v}$. (The seller's discount factor must be held fixed, as $M(\varepsilon,\delta_s)$ goes to infinity as δ_s goes to 1.)

Moreover, because of the assumption that the game has a finite horizon, this conclusion can be strengthened to obtain for all $\delta_b>1/2$. Schmidt shows that $\delta_b>1/2$ implies that the few "bad" periods where the seller's price exceeds $\underline{v}$ occur towards the end of the game. (More precisely, there is a K independent of the length of the game T such that the seller offers price $\underline{v}$ whenever there are at least $T-K$ periods remaining.) Thus with a sufficiently long horizon even an impatient buyer obtains approximately his commitment payoff.[26]

4 EVOLUTIONARY STABILITY IN REPEATED GAMES

While the idea of applying evolutionary stability to repeated games is roughly as old as the literature on reputation effects, so far it has not been as extensively developed, and it will receive correspondingly less attention in this chapter.

4.1 An introduction to evolutionary stability in repeated games

Consider a symmetric two-player game, meaning that both players have the same sets S and Σ of feasible pure and mixed strategies, respectively, and the same utility function $u(\cdot,\cdot)$, where the first argument is the strategy chosen by the player and the second argument is the strategy of the player's opponent.

A strategy profile σ in a symmetric two-player game is a "strictly evolutionarily stable strategy" or "strict ESS" (Maynard Smith and Price,

1973; Maynard Smith, 1974) if no other strategy profile σ' has as high a payoff as σ against the strategy $(1-q)\sigma+q\sigma'$ for all sufficiently small positive q. When the space of pure strategies is finite, this condition is equivalent to the condition that for all $\sigma' \neq \sigma$, either:

$$u(\sigma',\sigma)<u(\sigma,\sigma), \text{ or} \tag{i}$$
$$u(\sigma',\sigma)=u(\sigma,\sigma) \text{ and } u(\sigma,\sigma')>u(\sigma',\sigma').^{27} \tag{ii}$$

A weak ESS is a profile σ such that for every $\sigma' \neq \sigma$ satisfies either (i) or the weaker condition (ii′).

$$u(\sigma',\sigma)=u(\sigma,\sigma) \text{ and } u(\sigma,\sigma')\geq u(\sigma',\sigma'). \tag{ii′}$$

This definition allows σ to repel invasion by σ' by doing as well as σ' against the mixtures of σ and σ'.[28] Inspection of (i) and (ii′) makes it clear that an evolutionary stable profile is a symmetric Nash equilibrium; the second clause in (ii) gives evolutionary stability additional bite. The intuition for the concept is that, if s is not evolutionarily stable, it can be invaded by a "mutant" strategy s': if a small percentage of a large group of players begins to play s', and players are randomly matched with a different opponent each period, then the expected payoff of s' exceeds that of s, and this may mean that the percentage of players using s' will increase.

In the biological justification of the concept, it is supposed that the strategy each individual plays is determined by its genes, and that individuals reproduce copies of themselves at a rate proportional to their payoff in the game. Moreover, it is supposed that all of the animals belong to the same population, as opposed to there being distinct populations of "player 1s" and "player 2s." (Actually the usual biological model leads not to ESS but rather to something called the "replicator dynamics": the fraction of the population playing strategy s grows at a rate proportional to the difference between the payoff to using s and the average payoff obtained in the whole population. Note that this dynamics is deterministic, and does not allow for "mutations." An evolutionary stable profile is a stable fixed point of the replicator dynamics, but other profiles can be stable as well.[29])

Even in animal populations, it is not clear that the "hard-wired" interpretation of the determinants of behavior should be taken literally, as behavior may be thought to be coded for by several genes that co-evolve in a complex way. Nevertheless, theoretical biologists have found evolutionary stability a useful concept for explaining animal behavior.

When applied to human agents, the hard-wired interpretation is even more controversial. Instead, the assumption that the growth rates of the population fractions using each strategy are proportional to the strategies' payoffs has been defended as the result of various kinds of boundedly rational learning (see, e.g., Sugden, 1986; Crawford, 1989). For example, each period a small proportion of the population might somehow learn the current payoff of each strategy, and choose the strategy with the highest current payoff. A more appealing story might be that players learn the strategies and current payoffs of a few other individuals ("neighbors?") and again myopically choose the strategy with the highest current payoff. However, some other learning processes do not lead to concepts like evolutionary stability, and there is not yet much of a consensus on which economic contexts evolutionary stability is appropriate for. The interest of the results reported below relies on the hope that either a good foundation will be found for the application of evolutionary stability to economics, or that the results will turn out to extend to related equilibrium concepts for which economic foundations can be provided.

The first application of evolutionary stability to repeated games was by Axelrod and Hamilton (1981). They showed that the strategy "always defect" is not evolutionarily stable in the repeated prisoner's dilemma with time average payoffs.[30] In particular, they noted that a population using "always defect" can be invaded by the strategy "tit-for-tat," which cooperates in the first period and then always plays the strategy its opponent played the period before. Tit-for-tat can invade because it does as well against always defect as always defect does against itself (both give a time-average payoff of 0) and tit-for-tat obtains payoff 2 when paired against itself, so that tit-for-tat does strictly better than always defect for any proportion q of mutants playing tit-for-tat.

If players discount their repeated-game payoffs with discount factor δ, this conclusion needs to be modified, as the payoff of tit-for-tat against always defect is then not 0 but $-(1-\delta)$. In this case, tit-for-tat cannot invade if its proportion q is arbitrarily small and strategies are randomly matched with each other, as the probability $(1-q)$ of losing $(1-\delta)$ outweighs the potential gain of $2q$. However, tit-for-tat can still invade if there is a sufficient amount of "clustering," meaning that mutants are matched with each other more often than random matching would predict. (Clustering is discussed by Hamilton (1964); with the payoffs of figure 3.1 it suffices that the probability that tit-for-tat is paired with itself be greater than $(1-\delta)/(3-\delta)$.)

Thus evolutionary stability can be used to rule out the strategy "always defect." Axelrod and Hamilton argued further that evolutionary stability supports the prediction that players will use the strategy tit-for-tat. They noted that tit-for-tat is evolutionarily stable with time-average payoffs, and indeed is evolutionarily stable for discount factors sufficiently close to 1, even if clustering is allowed.[31] They also noted that tit-for-tat was the winning strategy in two computer tournaments organized by Axelrod (1980a, 1980b) (entrants in the second tournament were informed of the results in the first one) and that tit-for-tat eventually dominated play when the strategies submitted in Axelrod (1980b) were allowed to evolve according to the replicator dynamics.

Although the experimental results are interesting, the theoretical argument is weak. The problem is that many strategies besides tit-for-tat are evolutionarily stable with time-average payoffs. In particular, the outcome where players always defect can be approximated arbitrarily closely by an ESS. Consider the strategy "cooperate in period 0, k, $2k$, etc., and defect in all other periods, so long as the past play of both players has conformed to this pattern. If in some past period play did not conform, then defect in all subsequent periods." Call this strategy "$1C,kD$." This strategy yields payoff $2/k$ when matched against itself, which is close to the payoff of always defect if k is large. Yet the strategy is evolutionarily stable, because if an invader deviates from the pattern, it is punished forever afterwards and so obtains a time-average payoff of at most 0.

Note that the ESS strategy $1C,kD$ uses "always D" as a punishment for deviations, even though always D is not itself an ESS. A mutant strategy cannot invade by conforming to $1C,kD$ on the equilibrium path and improving on "always D" in the punishment states following deviations, since so long as both players conform to the equilibrium path the punishment states have probability zero. However, the fact that always D is not an ESS does suggest that $1C,kD$ can be invaded if players sometimes make "mistakes," so that the punishment of always D is triggered with positive probability. This observation is the starting point of the work described in the next subsection.

4.2 Evolutionary stability in noisy repeated games

Fudenberg and Maskin (1990a) use the assumption that players make mistakes (and other assumptions detailed below) to show that players always cooperate in any symmetric ESS of the repeated prisoner's dilemma with time-average payoffs. More generally, we obtained lower bounds on the payoffs in ESS of symmetric two-player stage games. Whether or not these bounds imply efficiency depends on whether there is a unique feasible payoff in the stage game where the sum of the two player's payoffs is maximized.

To begin, it would be helpful to give a precise definition of what is meant by symmetry in this context. Suppose that the stage-game g is symmetric, so that in the stage game both players have the same set A of feasible actions.[32] Then the time-t history h of a player is the sequences of past actions chosen by himself and by his opponent, and a pure strategy s is a sequence of maps from histories to actions. (Note that, with this definition of the history, a given sequence of actions generates two distinct histories, corresponding to the viewpoints of the two players.) A symmetric profile is a profile in which the two players use the same strategy. For example, the profile where both play tit-for-tat is symmetric. Symmetry does not require that the two players choose identical actions in every subgame: if both play tit-for-tat, then in the subgame following the first-period actions (C,D), the second-period actions will be (D,C).

Next, assume that players use strategies of only finite complexity in the sense of Kalai and Stanford (1983).[33] This means the following: say that histories h^t and $\tilde{h}^{t'}$ are *equivalent under s* if for any T and any sequence of action profiles a^T of length T, strategy s prescribes the same action following (h^t,a^T) and following $(\tilde{h}^{t'},a^T)$. The complexity of s is the number of distinct equivalence classes it induces. For example, the strategy tit-for-tat has two equivalence classes, one consisting of all histories where the opponent played D last period, and the other the union of the initial history and any history where the opponent played C last period. For any initial history h^t, the play of a profile of finitely complex strategies will eventually follow a repetitive cycle, so time-average payoffs are well-defined.

Finally, suppose that the game has a very small amount of "noise." "Noise" means that the realized actions are sometimes not the ones that the players intended to choose, and that each player observes only the actions his opponent actually played, and not the intended ones. The noise is small in the sense that the most likely event, with probability almost 1, is that each player never makes a "mistake." The next most likely event, with probability $\varepsilon \simeq 0$, is for exactly one mistake somewhere along the infinite course of play. Each player is equally likely to make this mistake, and it can ocur in any period. Two mistakes has probability about ε^2, and so on. By taking the limit $\varepsilon \to 0$ we have a situation where the preferences of the players are lexicographic: payoffs conditional on no mistakes are infinitely more important than payoffs conditional on one mistake, which are infinitely more important than payoffs conditional on two mistakes, and so on.[34] If we step back from the various limits to consider the case of discount factors $\delta < 1$ and error probabilities $\varepsilon > 0$, the lexicographic preferences describe a situation where the next mistake is unlikely to happen for such a long time that its effect on payoff is negligible, so that the error probability must be tending to 0 "faster" than the discount factor tends to 1.

Say that a payoff vector $(v,v') \in V$ is efficient if it maximizes the sum of the players' payoffs, i.e., $(v,v') \in \arg\max(u+u' \mid (u,u') \in V)$. This definition gives equal weights to both players, which is natural given we have supposed that the "player 1s" and the "player 2s" are drawn from a common population. Let $\hat{u} = \min\{u \mid \text{there exists a } u' \text{ such that } (u,u') \in V \text{ is efficient}\}$. If in some subgame a player's payoff is below $\hat{u}$, not only is there an alternative outcome of that subgame where both players are better off, but any efficient outcome *must* be better for both players. In contrast, when a player's payoff exceeds $\hat{u}$, there are efficient outcomes that he likes less. In the prisoner's dilemma this point is moot, because there is a unique efficient payoff, namely (2,2). However, in the game in figure 3.4, any feasible payoff vector that sums to 5 is efficient, and $\hat{u}=1$. For this reason the following theorem has very different implications in these two games.

THEOREM 4 (Fudenberg and Maskin, 1990a) If (v,v) is feasible and individually rational,[35] and $v>\hat{u}$, and there is *some* finitely complex symmetric profile with payoffs (v,v), then there is a finitely complex pure-strategy ESS with these payoffs. Conversely, each player's payoff in a finitely complex pure strategy ESS is at least $\hat{u}$.[36]

Here is a partial intuition for this result. Consider first how and why some payoff vectors can be supported by ESS. In the prisoner's dilemma of figure 3.1, the unique efficient payoff is (2,2). To see that (2,2) is an ESS of the noisy repeated game, consider the profile in which both players use the strategy "perfect tit-for-tat," which is "cooperate in the first period; in subsequent periods cooperate if and only if in the previous period either both players cooperated or both players defected." Denote this strategy by σ^*. If both players use σ^*, the continuation payoffs in every subgame are (2,2): each mistake triggers one period of mutual punishment, and then cooperation resumes. At the same time, the one period of mutual punishment is enough to deter deviations, so the profile is subgame-perfect.

If perfect tit-for-tat were not an ESS, then for all q there would need to be a σ', such that $u(\sigma',\sigma')-u(\sigma^*,\sigma')>[(1-q)/q](u(\sigma^*,\sigma^*)-u(\sigma',\sigma^*))$. But for $u(\sigma',\sigma^*)$ to be close to $u(\sigma^*,\sigma^*)$, σ' must induce σ^* to cooperate in every period, and so σ' must also cooperate in almost every period. Thus $u(\sigma^*,\sigma')$ will be close to 2, and σ' cannot achieve a higher payoff when matched with itself, so perfect tit-for-tat is an ESS.[37]

It is interesting to note that the "usual" tit-for-tat of the evolutionary biology literature – "cooperate at the start and thereafter play the action the opponent played last period" – is not a Nash equilibrium (and *a fortiori* is not an ESS) in the noisy prisoner's dilemma: the first mistake triggers an inefficient cycle with payoffs $(3,-1)$, $(-1,3)$, etc. For the same reason tit-for-tat is not subgame-perfect in the model without noise.

The next example shows how an ESS can have inefficient payoffs.

In the game of figure 3.4, the payoff (2,2) is inefficient, but gives each player more than $\underline{u}=1$. This payoff vector is the outcome of the ESS profile where players use the strategy: "play d in the first period, and continue to play d so long as last period either both players played d or neither did. If one player unilaterally deviates from d, henceforth he plays b and his

	a	b	c	d
a	0,0	4,1	0,0	0,0
b	1,4	0,0	0,0	0,0
c	0,0	0,0	0,0	0,0
d	0,0	0,0	0,0	2,2

Figure 3.4

opponent plays a." Even though this profile is inefficient, any strategy that tries to promote greater efficiency will be punished with payoff 1 forever; this punishment is consistent with ESS because it is an efficient static equilibrium.

To see the idea behind the converse direction of the theorem, that payoffs below $\hat{u}$ cannot be supported by an ESS, consider a finitely complex pure-strategy profile (s,s) that is "supersymmetric," meaning that both players choose the same actions in *every* subgame, even those where the past play of the players has been different. And suppose there is an action a^* such that (a^*,a^*) is efficient. From the assumption of finite complexity, there is some history (or histories) h^t, where the players' continuation payoffs $v(h)$ are minimized. Now consider a "mutant" strategy s' that plays like s except following history h^t. Given history h^t, s' plays some action $\hat{a} \neq s(h^t)$ at period t. If its opponent plays a as well, it is revealed to be a "fellow mutant," and henceforth s' plays a^*. If its opponent does not play $\hat{a}$ at h^t, at all subsequent dates s' plays just like s. Since h^t is a history where continuation payoffs are minimized, when s' is paired with s it receives the same payoff as s does when paired with itself. And when s' is paired with itself, it does strictly better, since every history has positive probability of being reached.

This argument shows that a "supersymmetric" ESS not only has payoffs above $\hat{u}$ but must be efficient! When general strategies (such as tit-for-tat) are allowed, the continuation payoffs of the players can be different in histories where they have played differently in the past. This is why equilibrium payoffs need only exceed $\hat{u}$.

The restriction to pure strategies makes it easy for a "mutant" to signal its identity; we believe that this restriction is not essential. The restriction to finite complexity *is* essential. Consider the following strategy for the prisoner's dilemma: "Alternate between C and D so long as past play conforms to this pattern. If there is a deviation, switch to playing C every third period, after a subsequent deviation switch to C every fourth period, and so on." Both players using this strategy is an ESS because, regardless of the history, any deviation is punished by a positive amount, but the strategy is not efficient.

Maskin and I believe we will be able to extend theorem 4 to the case of discount factors close to 1 and a 'small but non-infinitesimal' probability of mistake. Since the lexicographic model describes a situation where payoffs conditional on even one mistake are not very important, the model corresponds to a limit where the probability of mistake per period goes to zero much faster than the discount factor goes to 1. And from the discussion of the discounting case in the previous subsection, we know that evolutionary stability will only have bite if "clustering" is allowed. Our hoped-for extension will assert that, for any positive period amount q of clustering for discount factors δ close enough to 1, and error probabilities that are sufficiently small compared to $1-\delta$, ESS exist, and ESS must have payoffs at least $\hat{u}-\varepsilon$, with ε going to zero as q tends to 1.

We are fairly confident that this extension is true, and that it holds without the restrictions to pure strategies and finite complexity. A potentially more difficult extension is to the case of games played by two separate populations, as opposed to the single population assumed above. After all, it does not seem reasonable to assume that players are assigned each period to be either a "consumer" or a "firm." Allowing for distinct populations would also permit the analysis of ESS in repeated games where some of the players are long-lived and the others play only once, as in Fudenberg, Kreps, and Maskin (1990).

4.3 Evolutionary stability in games played by finite automata

Binmore and Samuelson (1991) consider evolutionary stability in repeated games in which less complex strategies are less costly, as in Abreu and Rubinstein (1989). In this model, players choose finite automata (idealized computer programs) to play the repeated game for them, and the cost of the automata is increasing in their complexity, which is the number of internal states the automata requires.[38] Players prefer strategies which maximize their "direct" payoff in the repeated game, but between two strategies with the same direct payoff, players prefer the one whose complexity is lower. Thus complexity here represents a cost of implementing the strategies, as opposed to a cost of computing payoffs or of finding the best response to a strategy of the opponent.

In a Nash equilibrium of the automata game, neither player's machine can have any states that are not used on the path of play, as such unused states could be dropped without reducing the player's direct payoff. For example, both players playing tit-for-tat is not a Nash equilibrium, as the unique best response to tit-for-tat in the presence of implementation costs is the strategy "always cooperate." However, there are Nash equilibria that do result in players cooperating in every period but the first one. It is also a Nash equilibrium for both players to always defect.

The fact that in equilibrium every state of the automata must be reached rules out infinite punishments. Binmore and Samuelson exploit this restriction to show that all pure-strategy ESS profiles must be efficient.

THEOREM 5 (Binmore and Samuelson, 1991)[39] In a symmetric two-player automata game with complexity costs, every pure-strategy ESS has efficient payoffs, and ESS exist.

Sketch of Proof While Binmore and Samuelson discuss symmetrized versions of underlying asymmetric games, in which players are randomly assigned to the roles "player 1" and "player 2" each time they are matched, the proof is easier in the case where the underlying game is symmetric and the players cannot use their labels to correlate their play. Here it is clear that efficient Nash equilibria are evolutionarily stable.

To see why other Nash equilibria are not ESS, note first that in any equilibrium both players will choose the same actions in every period both on and off of the equilibrium path. That is, all pure-strategy Nash equilibria must be "supersymmetric" in the sense discussed in the proof of theorem 4. Suppose also that there is a finite automaton s^* such that (s^*,s^*) has efficient payoffs.[40]

Now consider an ESS s that is not efficient, and consider a mutant strategy $\hat{s}$ that plays as follows. In the initial period, $\hat{s}$ plays an action $\hat{a}$ that differs from the initial action played by s. If the opponent's initial action is $\hat{a}$, $\hat{s}$ plays like the efficient automaton s^* from the second period on. If the opponent's initial action is not $\hat{a}$, $\hat{s}$ computes the state q that automaton s will be in following the initial actions, and plays like s in state q from the next period on. (Because strategy s must be supersymmetric, it specifies the same play for both players even after a unilateral deviation by one of them.) Since state q is certain to be reached when s plays against itself, the strategy $\hat{s}$ obtains the same average payoff when matched with strategy s as s does when matched with itself. Hence $\hat{s}$ can invade s, so s is not an ESS after all.

Note that theorem 5 asserts that every ESS of the game in figure 3.4 must be efficient, and so "always d" is not the outcome of an ESS of the automata game, although it is the outcome of an ESS of the game with noise. The reason is that, without noise, a mutant strategy that attains the efficient average payoff of $2\frac{1}{2}$ when matched against itself can only be repelled by a strategy with an infinite number of periods of punishment, and such infinite punishments are ruled out by implementation costs.

The differing conclusions of the implementation-cost model and the model with mistakes leads to the question of their relative merits. The former model describes a world in which the cost of additional states is high compared to the probability of mistakes, while the latter describes a world in which the probability of mistakes is high compared to the cost of additional states. My own view is that the latter world is a more realistic reduced form, because I think that in most populations of players there is enough randomness in the play of the next opponent that players will not be tempted to switch from tit-for-tat to always cooperate in order to save on internal states.[41] However, the main source of the variation need not be mistakes. Binmore and Samuelson consider "polymorphic" populations in which different types of machines coexist. Such populations, which are analogous to mixed-strategy equilibria, permit more states to be retained, and show that mistakes are not necessary to obtain more intuitive conclusions.

5 CONCLUSIONS

This chapter began by asking how to explain the widespread intuition that certain equilibria of repeated games are particularly likely. In games with a single long-run player, the idea of reputation effects provides a strong foundation for the intuition that the long-run player should be able to obtain his commitment payoff. In games with several equally patient players, reputation effects have strong predictions only if strong restrictions are imposed on the players' prior beliefs. Evolutionary stability may provide an explanation of why long-run players tend to cooperate, but the results require assumptions about the relative magnitude of mutation probabilities and the patience of the players, and the validity of the ESS concept in economic applications is not yet resolved.

There are several other potentially interesting approaches to repeated games, but so far none of them have been able to explain either cooperation when all players are long-run, or commitment by a single long-run player. One approach is to apply equilibrium refinements based on forward induction, such as the "strategic stability" of Kohlberg and Mertens (1986). So far, this concept has only been applied to finitely repeated games, where its results can conflict with efficiency, even where efficiency is a perfect-equilibrium outcome. This makes it seem unlikely that strategic stability would explain cooperation in the infinitely repeated prisoner's dilemma, but verifying this requires an extension of the stability concept to infinite games. However, given such an extension, it seems likely that stability does predict that a single patient player can achieve his commitment payoff against a series of short-run opponents.

A second approach is taken in the literature on "renegotiation" in repeated games surveyed by Pearce in this volume. This literature supposes that equilibrium is the result of negotiation between the players, and assumes that in a static game these negotiations will lead to an equilibrium that is Pareto-efficient in the set of all equilibrium payoffs. If these negotiations can only occur before play has begun, then for sufficiently large discount factors negotiations would lead to efficient outcomes. However, the literature supposes that players can meet and "renegotiate" their original (non-binding) agreement at the beginning of each period, so that equilibria with low continuation payoffs might be overturned. The question is then whether efficiency can be attained in the presence of the renegotiation constraints.

The idea of modeling players as automata is another way to try to obtain sharper predictions in repeated games. The Abreu and Rubinstein (1989) model does yield some predictions, but does not imply that outcomes must be efficient without the addition of the ESS concept. This implementation-cost literature is still in its early stages, and a correspondingly large amount of work remains before its usefulness is established. In particular, while strategies that require an infinite number of states seem implausible, it is less clear that an n-state machine is more costly than a machine with $(n-1)$ states, and that this cost difference is larger than the small probability of mistakes or other random factors. For example, Banks and Sundaram (1989) have shown that, under a measure of complexity that sums the number of states and its number of transition paths, the only Nash equilibrium of the prisoner's dilemma is to always defect. This measure of the cost of a strategy, like counting states, seems to be based on a "hardware" interpretation of complexity costs. To keep with the computer science analogy, it would be interesting to explore complexity measures based on the cost of writing the software to implement the strategy.

Finally, all of the papers I have discussed have used some equilibrium concept as a starting point. An alternative is to explicitly model the process by which equilibrium might be reached. For example, one could consider boundedly rational automata trying to "learn" their opponents' strategies, which would place the complexity cost at the level of the players' calculations instead of at the level of implementation. This approach brings the "automata" literature much closer to that literature on when equilibrium in games can be explained as the result of players having learned one another's strategies, as in Fudenberg and Kreps (1988).

From the viewpoint of learning models, one conjecture is that if the players realize that each is trying to learn the other's strategy, then each player will try to "teach" its opponent in a way that leads the opponent to play "nicely." This is reminiscent of ideas from the reputation-effects models, and poses the following question: in the prisoner's dilemma, why should player 1 be satisfied with teaching his opponent that he plays tit-for-tat, when a higher payoff can be obtained by teaching him that he must allow player 1 to defect occasionally without being punished? A possible answer is that it is harder to teach this "greedy" strategy, but this seems hard to formalize.

Notes

1 It will be clear that David Kreps, David Levine, and Eric Maskin played a major role in the development of the results reported here, but this does not fully reflect their contribution to my own understanding of the field. I would like to thank all three of them, and also Jean Tirole, for many helpful conversations. The discussion of reputation effects here draws heavily on chapter 9 of Fudenberg and Tirole (1991).

2 Recent economic applications of repeated games to explain trust and cooperation include Greif (1989), Milgrom, North, and Weingast (1989), Porter (1983), and Rotemberg and Saloner (1986).

3 This is a narrower meaning of reputation than that suggested by common usage. For example, one might speak of a worker having a "reputation" for high productivity in Spence's (1974) signaling model, and of the high-productivity workers investing in this reputation by choosing high levels of education.

4 This presenation of the chain-store game is based on the summary by Fudenberg and Kreps (1987). Kreps and Wilson consider only the case $q^0=0$, while Milgrom and Roberts consider a richer specification of payoffs.

5 This was observed by Milgrom and Roberts (1982).

6 This is an equilibrium if the incumbent's discount factor δ satisfies $a(1-q^0)-q^0>\frac{(1-\delta)}{\delta}$.

7 By this we mean either that the tough incumbent is unable to accommodate, as in Milgrom and Roberts, or that the incumbent's payoff in the repeated game is such that all strategies but "always fight" are weakly dominated. Fudenberg, Kreps, and Levine (1988) give an algorithm for determining payoff functions with this property.

8 This probability is determined by the requirement that, if the incumbent fights in market 2, the posterior probability that it is tough makes the next entrant indifferent between fighting and staying out. (Recall that the weak incumbent will accommodate in market 1.)

9 Note that we fix p^0 and take the limit as $N\to\infty$. For fixed N and sufficiently small p^0, the weak incumbent must accommodate in each market in any sequential equilibrium. I believe that the characterization extends to any δ by replacing the term $a/(a+1)$ with $[a-(1-\delta)/\delta]/(a+1)$, but I have not checked the details.

10 Following Rosenthal (1981), this point has been made in various ways by Reny (1985), Basu (1985), and Fudenberg, Kreps, and Levine (1988).

11 Recall that the set of Nash equilibria is robust to the introduction of additional types whose prior probability is small, while the set of sequential equilibria is not (Fudenberg, Kreps, and Levine, 1988).

12 Other models of reputation with imperfectly observed actions include Bénabou and Laroque (1989) and Diamond (1989).

13 Because r has a closed graph, the maxima in this definition are attained.

14 For those who are uncomfortable with the idea of types who "like" to play mixed strategies, an equivalent model identifies a countable set of types with each mixed strategy of the incumbent. Thus, one type always plays fight, the next acquiesces the first period and fights in all others, another fights every other opportunity, and so on – one type for every sequence of fight and acquiesce. Thus every type plays a deterministic strategy, and by suitable choosing the relative probabilities of the types the aggregate distribution induced by all of the types will be the same as that of the given mixed strategy.

15 Genericity is needed to ensure that, by a small change in α_1, player 1 can always "break ties" in the right direction in the definition of $v_1^*(p,\theta_0)$.

16 Hal Varian has suggested that this be called the "Abe Lincoln theorem," because it shows that the long-run player can't fool all of its opponents all of the time.

17 These strategies are not a sequential equilibrium if the horizon is finite. They thus do not form a counterexample to the sequential equilibrium version of theorem 1 for finite horizon games. Indeed, Y. S. Kim (1990) has shown that, when this game is played with a long but finite horizon, there is a unique sequential equilibrium, and in it the firm does maintain a reputation for high quality. Kim is working on the question of the best lower bound for sequential equilibria in finite repetitions of general stage games with reputation effects.

18 This point is made in Fudenberg and Levine (1988), who show that such equilibria are not artifacts of the continuum-of-players model, but rather can arise as limits of equilibria of games with a finite number of players. It may be that the common intuition that the play of a small player should be ignored corresponds to a continuum-of-players models with a noise term that masks the actions of individual players yet vanishes in the continuum-of-players limit.

19 If there are several entrants and the incumbent plays them in succession, so that $t \in [0,1]$ is against the first entrant, $t \in [1,2]$ against the second, and so on, then the first entrant might regret having acquiesced if it sees the incumbent acquiesce to a subsequent entrant, but at that point the first entrant's contest is over, and once again the captured contests and reentry versions have the same equilibrium.

20 Backwards induction implies that this is the unique sequential equilibrium in the discrete-time, sequential-move, finite-horizon version of the game. However, the continuous-time formulation has another equilibrium in which the entrants do not reenter.

21 A payoff vector is strictly individually rational if $v_i > \min_{a_{-i}} \max_{a_i} u_i\ (a_i,\alpha_{-i})$ for all players i. Fudenberg and Maskin assumed that each period players jointly observe the outcome of a "public randomization," e.g., a "sunspot." While that

assumption is innocuous in infinitely repeated games with little discounting (Fudenberg and Maskin, 1990b) it may not be innocuous here. In the absence of public randomizations, and if (as assumed throughout this chapter) only the realized actions in the stage game are observed, and not the players' intended randomizations, theorem 2 has only been proved for payoffs such that $v_i > \min_{a_{-i}} \max_{a_i} u_i\ (a_i, a_{-i})$, i.e., the minimization must be restricted to pure strategies for player i's opponents.

22 An equilibrium is strict if each player's strategy is a strict best response to the strategies of his opponents, i.e., no other strategy does as well.

23 Note once again that as $\varepsilon \to 0$ the required $\hat{T} \to \infty$, or conversely that for a fixed T a sufficiently small ε has no effect.

24 In games between long-run players, it can be advantageous to commit to a history-dependent strategy, such as tit-for-tat in the prisoner's dilemma. In contrast, a single long-run player facing a sequence of short-run opponents can obtain the commitment payoff using a strategy of recall 0.

25 See Maskin and Tirole (1989) for a discussion of this equilibrium concept. The Markov-perfect assumption is not needed if the buyer has only two possible types; it is not known whether it is needed with three types or more.

26 The reason that theorem 1 only yields the commitment payoff in the limit as the long-run player's discount factor tends to 1 is that it covers both finite and infinite horizon games, and with an infinite horizon the "bad" periods can occur at the start of play, as in the equilibrium of the chain-store game where the first entrant is not deterred.

27 With an infinite strategy space conditions (i) or (ii) are necessary but not sufficient for the desired inequality to hold over *all* σ' for a given q.

28 Maynard Smith calls this "neutral evolutionary stability."

29 See van Damme (1987) for an excellent survey of the relationship between evolutionary stability and stability in the replicator dynamics. Boylan (1990) proposes a more general dynamics that allows for mutations.

30 In applying evolutionary stability to infinitely repeated games, one supposes that in each "round" players are paired to play the entire repeated game; after the round is over the population fractions of each strategy are updated according to its relative payoff. To allow each round to end in a finite amount of time, we can suppose that the periods of round 1 take place on the interval [0,1], round 2 takes place from $t=1$ until $t=2$, and so on.

An interesting alternative would be for players to reproduce each period, with a stationary probability per period that the current match is broken off and the players are rematched with others in the population.

31 Any strategy that is never the first to defect will always cooperate against tit-for-tat, so that tit-for-tat is weakly stable. It is not strictly stable, and indeed no strictly stable strategy profile exists. (Boyd and Lorberbaum (1987) prove this for pure strategies, Farrell and Ware (1989) for mixed strategies with finite support, and Y. G. Kim (1989) for general mixed strategies.) Sugden (1986) and Boyd (1989) show that strict ESS exist in the discounted repeated prisoner's

dilemma if players make "mistakes." They consider a discounted formulation with "clustering" (defined below), and so their model has a large set of ESS.

The non-existence of strict ESS is a general property of games with non-trivial extensive forms, as it cannot be satisfied by a profile that leaves some information sets unreached. This led Selten (1983, 1988) to define a "limit ESS" as the limit of a sequence of strictly evolutionarily stable strategies in "perturbed games" where players tremble and play all actions with positive probability. Selten's purpose of introducing these "mistakes," like that of Boyd and Sugden, is to *enlarge* the set of evolutionarily stable strategies to avoid non-existence problems, so he defines the limit ESS to include all strict ESS of the unperturbed game. In the work discussed in the next subsection, mistakes are used to restrict the set of (weak) ESS.

32 If the stage game is asymmetric, it can be made symmetric by assuming that at the start of each period nature randomly assigns players to one of the two roles. Then a stage-game action is a contingent map, specifying how to play in each role. The key assumption is that all players are equally likely to play each role, which is not a good description of many economic situations. Also, with this symmetrization process a number of mixed strategies yield the same behavior strategy and are thus equivalent, as noted by Selten (1983), who proposed the notion of a "direct ESS" to get around the resulting non-existence of strictly stable mixed profiles.

33 We believe that the assumption of finite complexity is unnecessary when considering discounting instead of time-averaging.

34 This is a special case of the lexicographic preferences in Blume, Brandenburger and Dekel (1990). Note that if there is an i.i.d. probability ε of mistake in each period, then for any $\varepsilon > 0$ there is probability 1 of an infinite number of mistakes, while in our model in infinite number of mistakes has probability 0.

35 As defined in note 20.

36 The published proof is incomplete: it establishes the existence of a history h that minimizes the player's continuation payoff, but implicitly assumes that this h^* is asymmetric. However, the case of asymmetric h^* is easily handled.

37 So is "perfect n-tit-for-tat," where each mistake or deviation triggers n periods of "both defect." Because we use time average payoffs, no strict ESS exists even though the model has noise. We believe that when we extend our analysis to the limit of discount factors tending to 1 we will be able to construct strict ESS.

38 This complexity measure is similar but not identical to the measure introduced by Kalai and Stanford that was discussed in the last subsection.

39 Like Fudenberg and Maskin, Binmore and Samuelson sidestep the non-existence of strict ESS by using the weak version of the concept. They also extend their result to the limit of discount factors tending to 1 as clustering probabilities tend to 0.

40 This is not the case in the game of figure 3.4, where efficiency requires asymmetric play. To implement this asymmetry requires some way of distinguishing between the players. One way to do this is to assign the players labels. Another is to introduce a probability of mistakes, or to consider mixed strategies, so that symmetric profiles can generate asymmetric histories. Under

any of these alternatives, the equilibria need no longer be supersymmetric.
41 Kalai and Neme (1989) have shown that any individually rational payoffs can be Nash equilibria if there is positive probability of even a single mistake.

References

Abreu, D. and A. Rubinstein (1989), "The Structure of Nash Equilibrium in Repeated Games with Finite Automata," *Econometrica*, 56: 1259–81.

Aumann, R. (1990), "Preplay Communication Does Not Lead to Nash Equilibrium," mimeo, Hebrew University.

Aumann, R. and L. Shapley (1976), "Long-term Competition – A Game Theoretic Analysis," mimeo.

Aumann, R. and S. Sorin (1989), "Cooperation and Bounded Recall," *Games and Economic Behavior*, 1: 5–39.

Axelrod, R. (1980a), "Effective Choice in the Prisoner's Dilemma," *Journal of Conflict Resolution*, 24: 3–25.

(1980b), "More Effective Choice in the Prisoner's Dilemma," *Journal of Conflict Resolution*, 24: 379–403.

(1981), "The Emergence of Cooperation Among Egoists," *American Political Science Review*, 75: 306–18.

Axelrod, R. and W. D. Hamilton (1981), "The Evolution of Cooperation," *Science*, 211: 1390–6.

Banks, J. and R. Sundaram (1989), "Repeated Games, Finite Automata, and Complexity," Working Paper 183, University of Rochester.

Bénabou, R. and G. Laroque (1988), "Using Privileged Information to Manipulate Markets," INSEE Working Paper 137/930.

Blume, L., A. Brandenburger, and E. Dekel (1990), "Lexicographic Beliefs and Equilibrium Refinements," *Econometrica*, 59: 81–98.

Boylan, R. (1990), "Equilibria Resistant to Mutation," mimeo, Caltech.

Chamberlin, E. (1929), "Duopoly: Value Where Sellers are Few," *Quarterly Journal of Economics*, 43: 63–100.

Crawford, V. (1989), "Learning and mixed-strategy Equilibria in Evolutionary Games," *Journal of Theoretical Biology* 140: 537–50.

Cukierman, A. and A. Meltzer (1986), "A Theory of Ambiguity, Credibility and Inflation Under Discretion and Asymmetric Information," *Econometrica*, 54: 1099–121.

Diamond, D. (1989), "Reputation in Acquisition and Debt Markets," *Journal of Political Economy*, August, 828–62.

Dybvig, P. and C. Spatt (1980), "Does it Pay to Maintain a Reputation?" mimeo, Carnegie-Mellon University.

Fudenberg, D. and D. M. Kreps (1987), "Reputation and Simultaneous Opponents," *Review of Economic Studies*, 54: 541–68.

(1988), "A Theory of Learning, Experimentation and Equilibrium in Games," mimeo, Stanford Graduate School of Business.

Fudenberg, D., D. M. Kreps, and D. K. Levine (1988), "On the Robustness of Equilibrium Refinements," *Journal of Economic Theory*, 44: 354–80.

Fudenberg, D., D. M. Kreps, and E. Maskin (1990), "Repeated Games with Long-Run and Short-Run Players," *Review of Economic Studies*, 57: 555–73.

Fudenberg, D. and D. K. Levine (1988), "Open-Loop and Closed-Loop Equilibria in Dynamic Games with Many Players," *Journal of Economic Theory*, 44: 1–18.

(1989), "Reputation and Equilibrium Selection in Games with a Patient Player," *Econometrica*, 57: 759–78.

(forthcoming), "Maintaining a Reputation When Strategies are Imperfectly Observed," *Review of Economic Studies*.

Fudenberg, D. and E. Maskin (1986), "The Folk Theorem in Repeated Games with Discounting or with Incomplete Information," *Econometrica*, 54: 533–54.

(1990a), "Evolution and Cooperation in Noisy Repeated Games," *American Economic Review*, 80: 274–79.

(forthcoming), "On the Dispensability of Public Randomization in Discounted Repeated Games," *Journal of Economic Theory*.

Fudenberg, D. and J. Tirole (1991) *Game Theory*, Cambridge, MA: MIT Press.

Greif, A. (1989), "Reputation and Coalitions in Medieval Trade: Evidence from the Geniza Documents," mimeo, Stanford University.

Hamilton, W. D. (1963), "The Evolution of Altruistic Behavior," *American Naturalist*, 97: 354–6.

Harsanyi, J. (1967), "Games with Incomplete Information Played by Bayesian Players," *Management Science*, 4: 159–82, 320–34.

Hart, O. and J. Tirole (1988), "Contract Renegotiation and Coasian Dynamics," *Review of Economic Studies*, 55: 509–40.

Kalai, E. and A. Neme (1989), "The Strength of a Little Perfection," mimeo, Northwestern University.

Kalai, E. and W. Stanford (1988), "Finite Rationality and Interpersonal Complexity in Repeated Games," *Econometrica*, 56: 397–410.

Kim, Y. G. (1989), "Evolutionary Stable Strategies in the Repeated Prisoner's Dilemma Game," mimeo, UCSD.

Kim, Y. S. (1990), "Characterization and Properties of Reputation Effects in Finitely-Repeated Extensive Form Games," mimeo, UCLA.

Kohlberg, E. and J.-F. Mertens (1986), "On the Strategic Stability of Equilibrium," *Econometrica*, 54: 1003–37.

Kreps, D. M. (1986), "Corporate Culture and Economic Theory," in M. Tsuchiya (ed.), *Technological Innovation and Business Strategy* (Tokyo. Nippon Keizai Shimbunsha Press, in Japanese). Forthcoming in English in Alt and Shepsle (eds.), *Rational Perspectives on Political Science*, Cambridge, MA: Harvard University Press.

Kreps, D., P. Milgrom, J. Roberts, and R. Wilson (1982), "Rational Cooperation in the Finitely Repeated Prisoners' Dilemma," *Journal of Economic Theory*, 27: 245–52, 486–502.

Kreps, D. and R. Wilson (1982a), "Reputation and Imperfect Information," *Journal of Economic Theory*, 27: 253–79.

(1982b), "Sequential Equilibria," *Econometrica*, 50: 863–94.

Macaulay, S. (1963), "Non-Contractual Relations in Business: A Preliminary Study," *American Sociological Review*, 28: 55–67.

Maskin, E. and J. Tirole (1989), "Markov Equilibrium," mimeo, Harvard and MIT.

Maynard Smith, J. (1974), "The Theory of Games and the Evolution of Animal Conflict," *Journal of Theoretical Biology*, 47: 209–21.

(1982), *Evolution and the Theory of Games*, Cambridge University Press.

Maynard Smith, J. and G. R. Price (1973), "The Logic of Animal Conflicts," *Nature*, 246: 15–18.

Milgrom, P., D. North, and B. Weingast (1989), "The Role of Law Merchants in the Revival of Trade: A Theoretical Analysis," mimeo, Stanford University.

Milgrom, P. and J. Roberts (1982), "Predation, Reputation and Entry Deterrence," *Econometrica*, 50: 443–60.

Neyman, A. (1986), "Bounded Complexity Justifies Cooperation in the Finitely Repeated Prisoner's Dilemma," *Economics Letters*, 19: 227–9.

Oye, K. (1986), *Competition Under Anarchy*, Princeton, NJ: Princeton University Press.

Pearce, D. (1991), "Repeated Games: Cooperation and Rationality," this volume.

Rosenthal, R. (1981), "Games of Perfect Information, Predatory Pricing, and the Chain-Store Paradox," *Journal of Economic Theory*, 25: 92–100.

Rotemberg, J. and G. Saloner (1986), "A Supergame-Theoretic Model of Price Wars During Booms," *American Economic Review*, 76: 390–407.

Schelling, T. C. (1960), *The Strategy of Conflict*, Cambridge, MA: Harvard University Press.

Scherer, F. M. (1980), *Industrial Market Structure and Economic Performance*, (2nd edition), Boston: Houghton-Miffling.

Schmidt, K. (1990), "Commitment through Incomplete Information in a Simple Repeated Bargaining Model," mimeo, University of Bonn.

Selten, R. (1978), "The Chain-Store Paradox," *Theory and Decision*, 9: 127–59.

(1983), "Evolutionary Stability in Extensive Two-Person Games," *Mathematical Social Sciences*, 5: 269–363.

Shapiro, C. (1982), "Consumer Information, Product Quality, and Seller Reputation," *Bell Journal of Economics*, 13: 20–35.

Shubik, M. (1970), "Game Theory, Behavior, and the Paradox of Prisoner's Dilemma: Three Solutions," *Journal of Conflict Resolution*, 14: 181–94.

Simon, H. (1951), "A Formal Theory of the Employment Relationship," *Econometrica*, 19: 293–305.

Spence, A. M. (1974), *Market Signaling*, Cambridge, MA: Harvard University Press.

Sugden, R. (1986), The Economics of Rights, Co-operation, and Welfare, New York, NY: Basil Blackwell.

CHAPTER 4

Repeated games: cooperation and rationality

David G. Pearce[1]

1 INTRODUCTION

In economic, political, and personal life, the terms under which individuals or institutions interact are rarely determined fully by explicit, enforceable contracts. Within the bounds of the law, there is enormous scope for variation in the way in which commercial rivalries, international relations, and social affairs are conducted. Often, the same parties interact repeatedly. As a consequence, there is a large role for implicit, self-enforcing contracts to play: agents have an incentive to conform to an implicit agreement today because they believe that this will influence the nature of subsequent interactions. Repeated games provide perhaps the simplest model in which self-enforcing arrangements can be studied formally. It is this aspect of repeated game theory that I attempt to survey here. The chapter focuses on the structural and conceptual issues that have arisen in recent years in the study of repeated discounted games of complete information.

This choice of subject matter embraces a large literature, but excludes some important topics in repeated games. There is a substantial and challenging body of work on repeated games of incomplete information, much of which is surveyed by Mertens (1987). Following Kreps and Wilson (1982) and Milgrom and Roberts (1982), many papers have explored the effects of reputation formation in finitely repeated games with (initially) small amounts of incomplete information. These are covered by Fudenberg (1992) in chapter 3 of this volume. The latter survey also touches on the growing literature that investigates how play evolves as success is rewarded by survival.

The first part of the chapter chronicles the progress that has been made in the past decade in understanding supergame equilibria from a technical point of view.[2] Many problems that had been considered intractable yielded to systematic analysis. Whereas earlier work on discounted repeated games had to content itself with studying artificially restricted behavior, a number of papers revealed that it was possible to drop those restrictions and still obtain strong results. Theorists began to explore more complicated and satisfying models, suggested by features of various economic situations. Players may observe different parts of the history of play, and some of their information may be stochastic, for example. They could meet different partners or rivals over time, or have different time horizons.

Section 2 considers models in which players receive information without any stochastic disturbance, while section 3 is devoted to games with imperfect monitoring. In each case I begin with the analysis of an arbitrary discount factor (or rate of interest) and later address the important case in which players are very patient, relative to the delays between successive plays of the game. Finally, representative applications to applied fields are discussed, as well as some recent attempts to compare the theory with data in various ways.

The second part of the chapter is devoted to some conceptual issues associated with repeated game theory, especially the problem of renegotiation. In a supergame equilibrium involving short-run sacrifices by some player for the good of the group, for example, there is an implicit threat that, if the player fails to cooperate, he will be punished in some way. But *ex post*, will the threat actually be carried out, or will the continuation equilibrium be "renegotiated"? At issue here is the fundamental question of which threats are credible. Game theorists maintained an uncomfortable silence on this point for many years. Recently there has been a small riot of proposals regarding the appropriate formulation of a "renegotiation-proof" solution concept. We are left with an embarrassment of riches, since many of the suggestions are at odds with one another, and lead to entirely different predictions. Section 4 reviews some of the solution concepts. I argue that the diversity of ideas on renegotiation proofness is natural, given the essentially psychological nature of the problem, and suggest that any solution concept in this area be interpreted cautiously. Section 5 concludes briefly.

2 PERFECT MONITORING

This section and the following one are addressed not to the specialist in repeated games, but to scholars who would like a reader's guide to the literature on discounted repeated games of complete information. The emphasis is on the overall picture, and the connections among papers in the field. Those looking for a "nuts and bolts" treatment of the material should consult the expert and up to date coverage in chapter 5 of Fudenberg and Tirole (1991). Also enthusiastically recommended are the concise, specialized piece on folk theorems by Krishna (1987) and the wide-ranging survey of complete information supergames by Sabourian (1989).

In most of the models of this section, all players learn at the end of each period the actions taken in that period by other players. Usually, we are studying situations in which some simultaneous game G is played by the same set $N=\{1,\ldots,n\}$ of players. The *stage game* (or component game) $G=(A_1,\ldots,A_n;\Pi_1,\ldots,\Pi_n)$ is described by the non-empty action sets (or pure strategy sets) A_i, $i\in N$, and the payoff functions Π_i: $A\to\mathbb{R}$, where $A=A_1\times\ldots\times A_n$. If each A_i is finite, G is called a finite game. Extend the functions Π_i in the usual way to the product $M=M_1\times\ldots\times M_n$ of the sets of mixed strategies. Let $F=\text{co}\,\Pi(A)$ be the convex hull of the set of payoff vectors from action profiles in A. Elements in F are called *feasible* values.

Playing G repeatedly produces a stream of payoffs for each player, which in most cases will be discounted by the factor δ, assumed for simplicity to be the same for each player. Payoffs are received at the end of each period, and discounted to the beginning of the first period, period 1. The finitely repeated game consisting of T plays of G, with discount factor $\delta\in(0,1)$, is denoted $G^T(\delta)$. When G is repeated indefinitely, and $\delta\in(0,1)$, we have the infinite horizon game $G^\infty(\delta)$. A pure strategy for player i in a repeated game specifies an action for i in each period t as a function of the actions chosen by all players in all preceding periods.[3] A mixed strategy (more properly, a behavior strategy) in the supergame allows the contingent choices to be stochastic. In this case it must be specified whether other players observe only the outcome of the randomization (this is the standard assumption, and usually the only plausible one) or also the random device used.

Often it is convenient to normalize supergame payoffs so that they are directly comparable to payoffs of a stage game: the average (discounted) value of a stream of payoffs is that number which, if received in every period, would have the same present discounted value as that of the original stream. For any strategy profile $\sigma=(\sigma_1,\ldots,\sigma_n)$ of the supergame let $\Psi(\sigma)$ denote the associated vector of (total) present discounted payoffs, and let $v(\sigma)=\dfrac{1-\delta}{\delta}\Psi(\sigma)$ denote the vector of average values.

Self-enforcing agreements in repeated games are the subjects of inquiry here, but it must be admitted that there is a great deal of controversy about how "self-enforcing" should be *defined* (see section 4). For the moment, let us simply require that the agreements (whether spoken or unspoken) be *subgame perfect equilibria* (Selten, 1965, 1975) of the supergame. This means that, following any $t-1$ period history of play, the agreed-upon strategy profile gives players instructions that constitute a Nash equilibrium (Nash, 1950) of the subgame beginning in period t. In other words, after no history should a player have an incentive to deviate unilaterally from his part of the strategy profile. When a particular player has no incentive to deviate following any history, we say that his strategy is a *perfect best response* to the other players' strategies. The set of average values of subgame perfect equilibria of $G^T(\delta)$ and $G^\infty(\delta)$ are written $V^T(\delta)$ and $V^\infty(\delta)$, respectively. When there is no danger of ambiguity, I simply write V.

Unimprovability

Consider the following requirement that, at first glance, looks much weaker than the perfect best response condition. A strategy for i is *unimprovable* against a vector of strategies of his opponents if there is no $t-1$ period history (for any t) such that i could profit by deviating from his strategy in period t only (conforming thereafter). To verify the unimprovability of a strategy, then, one checks only "one-shot" deviations from the strategy, rather than arbitrarily complex deviations (such as defecting in every period t such that t is prime). The following result simplifies the analysis of subgame perfect equilibria immensely. It is the exact counterpart of a well-known result from dynamic programming due to Howard (1960), and was first emphasized in the context of self-enforcing cooperation by Abreu (1988).

PROPOSITION Let the payoffs of G be bounded. In the repeated game $G^T(\delta)$ or $G^\infty(\delta)$, a strategy σ_i is a perfect best response to a profile γ of strategies if and only if σ_i is unimprovable against that profile.

The proof is simple, and generalizes easily to a wide variety of dynamic and stochastic games with discounting and bounded payoffs. If σ_i is not a perfect best response, there must be a history after which it is profitable to deviate to some other strategy σ_i'. If the deviation involves defection at infinitely many nodes, then for sufficiently large T, the strategy $\hat{\sigma}_i$ that agrees with σ_i' until time T and conforms to σ_i thereafter, is also a profitable deviation (because of discounting and boundedness anything that happens in the distant future has almost no impact on payoffs today). Consider a profitable deviation $\tilde{\sigma}_i$ involving defection at the smallest possible number of nodes, and let x be a node at which $\tilde{\sigma}_i$ disagrees with σ_i for the last time. Not conforming to σ_i at x must be profitable, or else one would have had a profitable deviation with fewer defection nodes than $\tilde{\sigma}_i$, a contradiction. The profitability of deviating from σ_i at x (and never again) means that σ_i is not unimprovable. Thus, if σ_i is unimprovable, σ_i is a perfect best response. The converse is trivial, since the requirements for unimprovability are a subset of those for a perfect best response.

The above equivalence will be exploited frequently in both this and the succeeding section; it does not depend on the structure of players' information.

Cooperation enforced by Nash threats

During the 1950s and 1960s there developed a verbal tradition amongst game theorists to the effect that, if players in an infinitely repeated game considered the future sufficiently important compared to the current period, an extremely wide variety of behavior could be supported in equilibrium. Friedman (1971) formalized this in the context of Cournot oligopoly. How can firms be persuaded to overcome the free-rider problem that drives them away from the joint monopoly output to the less lucrative Cournot–Nash solution? Consider a strategy profile specifying that (i) firms produce some vector of quantities each period that is more profitable for each firm than the Cournot–Nash equilibrium, as long as there has been no deviation from the vector in past periods, and (ii) following any deviation, they revert to playing the static Cournot–Nash solution forever. If players are very patient, a firm's temptation to increase profits today by cheating are outweighed by the permanent loss in profits in succeeding periods. Hence, it is not profitable to deviate once if no one has done so before. If a deviation has occurred earlier, again there is no profitable one-shot deviation, because players are already playing a myopic best response to one another's actions. By the unimprovability criterion described above, we may conclude that the strategy profile is a subgame perfect equilibrium. Thus, although Friedman was concerned only with Nash equilibrium, he actually exhibited "cooperative" strategies that satisfied additional requirements of credibility.

PROPOSITION (Friedman, 1971) Let $G=(A_1,\ldots, A_n; \Pi_1,\ldots, \Pi_n)$ have a Nash equilibrium $e=(e_1,\ldots, e_n) \in A$, and let $q=(q_1,\ldots, q_n) \in A$ satisfy $\Pi_i(Q)>\Pi_i(e)$ for each $i \in N$. Then for δ sufficiently close to 1, there is a subgame perfect equilibrium of $G^\infty(\delta)$ in which q is played in every period on the equilibrium path.

It is convenient (and frequently realistic) to convexify the set of equilibrium values by enriching the structure of the supergame as follows: at the beginning of each period, the realization of some continuous random variable is commonly observed, so players can make their choices conditional on the outcome. Modifying the game in this way is usually called "allowing for public randomization." If we do so, Friedman's argument implies that any element of F that strictly Pareto dominates some Nash equilibrium of G is the average payoff of some subgame perfect equilibrium of $G^{\infty}(\delta)$, for sufficiently high δ. Indeed, arguments of Sorin (1986) and Fudenberg and Maskin (1986) can be used to show that this limit result holds even without public randomization: for values of δ near 1, convexification can be accomplished by varying play appropriately over time.

The folk theorem

A still stronger result was suggested by the verbal tradition alluded to earlier, one eventually proved by Aumann and Shapley (1976) and Rubinstein (1977). Their celebrated "folk theorem" for infinitely repeated games confirms the most optimistic conjecture one could reasonably make regarding which values are average payoffs of (subgame perfect) equilibria when players are ideally patient. Clearly, an average value must be feasible in the physical sense, that is, it must lie in F. The fact that a player always has the option of playing a myopic best response to other players' strategies in each period gives him a *security level* that must also be respected. Formally, let $\underline{v}_i = \min_{\alpha_{-i} \in M_{-i}} \max_{a_i \in A_i} \Pi_i(a_i, \alpha_{-i})$, where $\Pi_i(a_i, \alpha_{-i})$ means $\Pi_i(\alpha_1, \ldots, \alpha_{i-1}, a_i, \alpha_{i+1}, \ldots, \alpha_n)$. Any vector giving each player i at least his security level $\underline{v}_i$ is called *individually rational.* Let F^+ denote the set of feasible and individually rational vectors. Remarkably, if there is "no discounting" in the sense that players care only about their long-run average[4] payoffs, the set of feasible, individually rational payoffs coincides with the set of long-run average payoffs of equilibria of the infinitely repeated game.

PROPOSITION The perfect folk theorem of repeated games (Aumann and Shapley, 1976; Rubinstein, 1977): Let G^{∞} be the supergame in which G is repeated indefinitely and payoffs are evaluated according to the limit of means criterion. Then v is the average payoff of some subgame perfect equilibrium of G^{∞} if and only if it is feasible and individually rational.

The essence of the proof can be conveyed by looking at the simplest case, namely a feasible and individually rational value v for which there exists a pure action profile $c \in A$ with $\Pi(c) = v$. Consider a supergame profile that instructs players to begin by playing c in each period, and to respond to any deviation by forcing the deviant player down to his security level ("minimaxing him") for t^2 periods, where t is the date of his deviation, and then returning to playing c (unless there is some further deviant at time t', who will be minimaxed for $(t')^2$ periods, and so on).[5] If a player deviates an infinite number of times, his long-run average will be at best $\underline{v}_i$, so no such defection would be profitable. If he deviates only a finite number of times, play eventually returns to c forever, and again he has not profited (the limit of means is insensitive to payoff changes in any finite set of periods). To summarize, after no history can anyone gain by a unilateral deviation, so the profile is a subgame perfect equilibrium of G^∞.

Notice that, with no discounting, the criteria "perfect best response" and "unimprovable" are *not* equivalent. The strategy profile according to which each firm in a symmetric Cournot duopoly produces half of the joint monopoly output, regardles of the history of play, is certainly not subgame perfect, and yet the strategies are unimprovable according to the limit of means criterion.

Rubinstein (1979a) also proved a perfect folk theorem akin to the one just discussed, for games with payoffs evaluated according to the overtaking criterion.[6] While also capturing the idea of extreme patience, this criterion seems closer than the limit of means to the case of very little discounting (δ near 1) because it makes players sensitive to what happens in any single period. With this increased realism comes an additional complication: the set of subgame perfect equilibrium values is not closed, and the statement of the theorem must be weakened slightly. When one uses the overtaking criterion, unimprovability is again not useful for checking subgame perfection.

The perfect folk theorems provided an important impetus for further research on *discounted* repeated games, because they suggested vividly that punishments more severe (and hence more effective as deterrents) than permanent reversion to static Nash equilibrium could be credible. Ironically, the proofs of the same theorems probably also threw researchers off track, because the line of attack that eventually proved successful in the discounted case was rather different from methods in the absence of discounting.

Simple strategy profiles

Abreu's work in the early 1980s (ultimately published as Abreu, 1986, 1988) marked a breakthrough in the study of the pure strategy perfect equilibria of discounted supergames. It reduced an ostensible tangle of intertemporal incentive constraints and punishment hierarchies to a comparatively orderly, manageable problem. The first step was to formalize an alternative to viewing a supergame strategy profile as a vector of infinite sequences of functions from histories into action sets. Notice that a strategy profile implicitly specifies what path[7] should be followed, what new path should be followed if someone deviates from the original path, and so on. Indeed, the profile can be thought of as a *collection of paths* and a *rule* governing how to switch amongst them in the event of deviations. On the face of it, this perspective does not look promising: the collection of paths could be infinite, and the rule arbitrarily complex. Abreu (1988) justified the reformulation, however, by showing that, for any pure strategy subgame perfect equilibrium of $G^{\infty}(\delta)$, there is another perfect equilibrium that has the same value, and can be described by $n+1$ paths and an extremely elementary rule. For any $n+1$ paths $Q_0, Q_1, \ldots, Q_n$, define the associated *simple strategy profile* $\sigma(Q_0, Q_1, \ldots, Q_n)$ by the rule:

(i) Q_0 is the initial path;
(ii) after a deviation by a single player i from any ongoing path, play switches to following the path Q_i from the beginning (so if i deviates part way through path Q_i, for example, the path Q_i is restarted).

Working in the space of paths rather than supergame strategies affords a nice proof of the compactness of the equilibrium value set (henceforth, except in the statements of proofs, I often omit the qualifier "subgame perfect"). One implication is that *severest credible punishments for each player exist*. Let $Q_1, \ldots, Q_n$ be the respective paths of some severest equilibria for each player. A central result of Abreu (1988) is that, if Q_0 is the equilibrium path of *any* (perfect) equilibrium γ (simple or not), the simple profile $\sigma(Q_0, Q_1, \ldots, Q_n)$ is also a perfect equilibrium (clearly with the same equilibrium path). Let us check that the profile satisfies the criterion of unimprovability, that is, from no point of any of the $n+1$ paths would a player i wish to deviate, given that path Q_i will subsequently be followed. Each path Q in the collection is the path of some perfect equilibrium, and hence each player i was deterred from cheating at any point on Q by the threat that play would switch to the path of some perfect continuation equilibrium. But at the same point on Q in $\sigma(Q_0, Q_1, \ldots, Q)$, player i is faced with a threat at least as severe (because Q_i is by construction the worst perfect path for i). Thus player i cannot gain by deviating in any contingency.

A proposition summarizes our discussion.

PROPOSITION (Abreu, 1988) Let $G=(A_1, \ldots, A_n, \Pi_1, \ldots, \Pi_n)$ have at least one equilibrium in pure strategies, and, for each i, suppose A_i is compact and Π_i is continuous. Then:

(a) the pure strategy subgame perfect equilibrium value set $V^{\infty}(\delta)$ is non-empty and compact, and

(b) for any equilibrium γ, there is a *simple* strategy profile that is a perfect equilibrium with the same path (and hence the same value).

Why are strategy profiles of the form $\sigma(Q_0, Q_1,\ldots, Q_n)$ called simple? In general the $n+1$ paths might themselves be highly non-stationary and complex. But the way in which deviations are responded to, that is, the implicit punishment hierarchy, is simple in the extreme. A deviation by player i is always treated the same way regardless of the nature of the deviation, the period in which it occurred, the particular path in progress, or the point on the path at which the defection occurred. There is no need to "tailor the punishment to fit the crime."

The preceding analysis does not apply to mixed strategy equilibria, because it is not possible to tell from observing the actions played, whether or not the correct mixed strategies were employed. In other respects, however, the theory is comprehensive in its scope, covering for example all finite games G and all discount factors. A demonstration of its practical value in applied fields was given by Abreu (1986) in a study of optimal collusion among Cournot oligopolists. He considered n identical firms with positive, constant marginal costs c, no fixed costs, and strategy spaces $[0,\infty)$. They face a smooth inverse market demand function P satisfying $\lim_{q\to\infty} P(q)=0$. The conditions of the last proposition above are assumed to hold, except for boundedness of the strategy space; the set of quantities q that a firm could conceivably play in equilibrium is bounded, and this is all that is needed.

In order to derive strong results about the shape of the paths of the worst punishments, it is necessary to restrict attention to *strongly symmetric equilibria*, that is, equilibria which after no history give any player different instructions from any other player. It is easy to check that, without loss of generality, the equilibrium paths of constrained optimal strongly symmetric equilibria may be taken to be *stationary*. But this is emphatically not true for severest punishment paths. The latter have a "stick and carrot" structure that is quite striking: the payoff in the first period is dismal, but the path starting in period 2 is constrained Pareto efficient. In other words, the misery is front-loaded to the maximum extent possible.

PROPOSITION (Abreu, 1986) In a symmetric Cournot oligopoly satisfying the conditions described above, there is a most severe strongly symmetric equilibrium whose continuation value following the first period is constrained Pareto efficient. There is a critical value of δ above which the present value of profits in the severest symmetric equilibrium is zero.

The idea here is that, starting from any equilibrium profile not of the stick and carrot form, one can replace the continuation equilibrium by the

Pareto efficient equilibrium, and restore the entire path to its original value by increasing first-period production sufficiently. A firm's supergame payoff from conformity is the same as before, but the payoff for cheating in period 1 is generally lower (and never higher), because the firm's residual demand curve is lower. So under the new arrangement incentives to conform are at least as strong as in the original equilibrium.

It is sometimes the case that in a stick and carrot regime, the deviant firm is cooperating in its own punishment, that is, in period 1 it is not playing a best response to other firms' production. One might have thought that this was impossible. After all, if you punish someone as severely as possible, how can you expect him to cooperate when there is nothing worse left to threaten him with? The answer is that you can threaten to restart the punishment, a sobering prospect in the case of stick and carrot punishments. One might also have guessed that it is impossible to have an equilibrium with value zero in a Cournot model, since a firm can always choose to play a best response in period 1, pocket the profits and produce nothing thereafter. The strategy can be foiled only by having first-period production so high that the output of $n-1$ firms is enough to reduce price to marginal cost (or below), so no firm can make money in period 1 by any choice of output level. Firms are in effect "mutually minimaxing" one another, a phenomenon that is impossible in some other models, as we shall see later in an example due to Fudenberg and Maskin (1986).

An attractive paper by Lambson (1987) uses simple strategy profiles to characterize optimal collusion in price-setting supergames with capacity constraints and alternative rationing rules. For some, but not all, of the rules considered it turns out that stick and carrot punishments are optimally severe, and using mixed strategies would not expand the set of equilibrium values. In all cases the restriction to strongly symmetric equilibrium is without cost, in contrast to Cournot oligopoly.

There are numerous other applications of repeated games in particular areas, some using simple strategy profiles and others employing trigger strategies. A few examples are Barro and Gordon (1983), which stimulated much interest in strategic monetary theory (see the excellent survey by Rogoff (1989)); Weinberger (1990) on bargaining and delay to agreement, and Rotemberg and Saloner (1989) and Syropoulos (1989) on the relative merits of tariffs and quotas in dynamic trade policy.

Discount factors close to 1

Understanding behavior in repeated games with discount factors significantly different from 1 is important for several reasons, including the fact that the discount factor may represent both impatience in the usual sense, and the chance that the strategic interaction may be interrupted by external factors (new laws, product innovations, and so on). But there are many examples in which the period length is sufficiently short that the players' primary concern is for the future. Thus the perfect discounted folk theorems of Fudenberg and Maskin (1986) occupy a special place in the literature. They demonstrate that, with two qualifications, the classical results of Aumann and Shapley and Rubinstein survive the introduction of a small amount of impatience. An example of Forges, Mertens, and Neyman (1986) showed that values in which some players receive exactly their security levels may not be the payoff of any perfect equilibrium with discounting. For two-person games, this is the only qualification that need be made to the earlier folk theorems.

PROPOSITION Perfect folk theorem in discounted two-person games (Fudenberg and Maskin, 1986): Let g be a finite two-person game, and v be feasible and strictly individually rational (for each i, $v_i > \underline{v}_i$). There exists δ' such that for all $\delta \in (\delta', 1)$, v is the average discounted value of some subgame perfect equilibrium $G^{\infty}(\delta)$.

The proof depends critically on the possibility of players' simultaneously minimaxing one another. This cannot always be done in n-person games. For some such games, the folk theorem fails, as a neat example of Fudenberg and Maskin shows.

	2	
1	1,1,1	0,0,0
	0,0,0	0,0,0

	2	
1	0,0,0	0,0,0
	0,0,0	1,1,1

Figure 4.1

In the simultaneous three-person game of figure 4.1, player 1 chooses the row, 2 the column, and 3 determines which of the two matrices applies. Note that the three players' payoffs are always identical. Each person's security level is 0, but one can verify that, from any strategy profile (pure or mixed), there is some player whose best response payoff is at least $\frac{1}{4}$. Choose any $\delta \in (0,1)$, and any subgame perfect equilibrium, and let i be a player whose myopic best response in the first period gives him at least $\frac{1}{4}$. Since he will get no less than the minimum equilibrium value, call it l_i, from the second period onward, regardless of what he does in the first period, we see that:

$$l_i \geq (1-\delta)\tfrac{1}{4} + \delta l_i, \text{ that is, } l_i \geq \tfrac{1}{4}.$$

In other words, equilibrium payoffs are bounded away from the security level, uniformly in δ.

A sufficient condition for obtaining a full folk theorem in n-person games is that the set of feasible and individually rational payoffs of G be full-dimensional.

PROPOSITION Perfect folk theorem with discounting (Fudenberg and Maskin, 1986) Let $G=(A_1,\ldots,A_n;\Pi_1,\ldots,\Pi_n)$ be a finite game such that the set F^+ of feasible, individually rational payoffs is of dimension n. Then for any feasible, strictly individually rational value v, there exists δ' such that, for all $\delta \in (\delta',1)$, v is the average discounted value of some subgame perfect equilibrium of $G^\infty(\delta)$.

To understand the idea of the proof, take the tidiest case, where the value v is in the interior of F^+ (this set would be empty if the dimensionality condition were violated) and there is some $c \in A$ with $\Pi(c)=v$. Choose $\varepsilon>0$ and n vectors:

$$v(j)=(v_1+\varepsilon,\ldots,v_{j-1}+\varepsilon,\ v_j,\ v_{j+1}+\varepsilon,\ldots,v_n+\varepsilon),$$

such that $v(j) \in F^+, j=1,\ldots,n$. For simplicity assume there are action profiles b^j and $m^j, j=1,\ldots,n$, where $\Pi(b^j)=v(j)$ and m^j minimaxes j (and has j playing a best response). Let $\Delta_j=\max_{a\varepsilon A} \Pi_j(a)-v_j, j=1,\ldots,n$. The simple strategy profile with paths as described below is a subgame perfect equilibrium of $G^\infty(\delta)$ for sufficiently high δ: on the equilibrium path, c is played indefinitely; j's punishment path begins with k periods of m^j, and b^j thereafter, with k chosen large enough so that for each j, $k(v_j-\underline{v}_j)>\Delta_j$. Checking for unimprovability, we note first that no player j wants to deviate from the original path, because he then gets minimaxed for k periods. While being minimaxed, j cannot profitably cheat, because he is already playing a one-shot best response. In the second phase of the punishment path, j has no incentive to cheat because again, the result would be to be minimaxed for k periods instead of receiving v_j. At no time would a player other than j wish to deviate from the jth punishment path, because, for high δ, any short-run gains would be overwhelmed by the loss of an infinite stream of "bonuses" ε. (Note that the second phase of the punishment path is designed to reward players $i\neq j$ for minimaxing j, without also treating j favorably.)

Self-generation

The sweeping characterization of equilibrium values when δ is near 1 has no analogue for arbitrary discount factors. There is, however, a useful sufficient condition for sets of values to be subsets of the supergame value set. The result, called "self-generation" was developed by Abreu, Pearce, and Stacchetti (1986, 1990) for games with imperfect monitoring, but the principle behind it is quite general, and applies in the simple case of perfect monitoring (explicit treatments of self-generation in this setting can be found in Sabourian (1989) and in more detail in Cronshaw and Luenberger (1990)). Self-generation is in the spirit of dynamic programming, in the sense that it depends on the decomposition of a supergame profile into the induced behavior today, and the *value* of behavior in the future, as a function of all possible actions today. The following discussion tries to motivate the result. The analysis can be done for mixed strategies (this is not the case in games with imperfect monitoring) but, for ease of exposition, I consider pure strategies only.

What makes playing the first period of $G^{\infty}(\delta)$ different from playing G in isolation? In the former case, each player is interested in maximizing a weighted sum of his immediate payoff in G, and his continuation payoff in the remainder of the game. In equilibrium, the vector of continuation payoffs after a particular first-period history is drawn from the (subgame perfect) equilibrium value set V *of* $G^{\infty}(\delta)$. Thus, $v \in V$ if and only if for some $a \in A$ (representing first-period actions) and $u: A \rightarrow V$ (contingent continuation payoffs):

$$v = (1-\delta)\Pi_i(a) + \delta u_i(a) \tag{1}$$

and:

$$(1-\delta)\Pi_i(a) + \delta u_i(a) \geq (1-\delta)\Pi_i(a'_i, a_{-i}) + \delta u_i(a'_i, a_{-i}) \quad \text{for all } a'_i \in A_i,\ i = 1, \ldots, n. \tag{2}$$

Notice that when one is allowed to manipulate first-period behavior using continuation values from V, one "generates" exactly the elements of V as values of equilibria created in the augmented static games. More generally, think of augmenting payoffs by values drawn from an arbitrary set $W \subseteq \mathbb{R}^n$, and call the values generated $B(W)$:

$$B(W) = \{(1-\delta)\Pi(a) + \delta u(a) | u: A \rightarrow W, \text{ and } (a,u) \text{ satisfies } (2)\}.$$

We see immediately that V is a fixed point of the map $B: 2^{\mathbb{R}^n} \rightarrow 2^{\mathbb{R}^n}$. Let $B^t(W)$ denote the tth iteration of B on W. For example, $B^2(W) = B(B(W))$.

A non-empty bounded set $W \subseteq \mathbb{R}^n$ is called *self-generating* if $W \subseteq B(W)$. If W is self-generating, there is enough variety in the payoffs in W to create incentives for different equilibria in the corresponding augmented games, indeed enough to generate any value of W. This leads to the conjecture that the values in W are actually equilibrium values, becuase they are able to generate themselves, just the way supergame equilibria generate equilibrium values by using supergame equilibrium values as continuation payoffs.

PROPOSITION Self-Generation (Abreu, Pearce, and Stacchetti, 1990). Let G be a finite game and $\delta \in (0,1)$, and let $B: 2^{\mathbb{R}^n} \rightarrow 2^{\mathbb{R}^n}$ be as defined above. Then if $W \subseteq \mathbb{R}^n$ is self-generating, $B(W) \subseteq V$ (indeed, for $t=1, 2, \ldots,$ $B^t(W) \subseteq V$).

Self-generation has many applications, both theoretical and practical, and will be encountered again in subsequent sections. Here I record one implication that will be helpful later in unifying results from different papers.

PROPOSITION Algorithm: Let G be a finite game, $\delta \in (0,1)$, and B be the associated generation map. For any bounded $W \subseteq \mathbb{R}^n$ with $V \subseteq W$:

$$\bigcap_{t=1}^{\infty} B^t(W) = V.$$

The Proposition gives an algorithm for computing the equilibrium value set: choose any set that is "large enough" (F will do, for example), and apply the map B repeatedly. The limit of this process is V. Recently Cronshaw and Luenberger (1990) have given conditions under which the strongly symmetric equilibrium value set of symmetric repeated games may be computed with a non-iterative procedure. Their technique involves finding the largest solution of a scalar equation, and uses the dynamic programming approach.

Relationships to finitely repeated games

I turn now to finitely repeated games, and their relationship to infinitely repeated games. It was long thought that finite horizon repeated games were of little theoretical interest, because backward induction arguments could be used to show that subgame perfect equilibrium behavior in $G^T(\delta)$ could involve only a string of one-shot equilibria of G. While this is true if G has a unique equilibrium, Benoit and Krishna (1985) and Friedman (1985) showed resoundingly that, more generally, the presumption was false. Benoit and Krishna showed that, if for each player, not all of the equilibria of G have the same value, then folk theorems similar to those of Fudenberg and Maskin (1986) hold for $G^T(1)$ as T becomes large. (Unlike Fudenberg and Maskin (1986), Benoit and Krishna restrict attention to pure strategies.)

PROPOSITION Folk theorem for finitely repeated games (Benoit and Krishna, 1985): Suppose that:

(i) for each player i, there are two equilibria of G with different payoffs for i, and
(ii) $n=2$, or dim $F^+=n$.

Then for any value v that is feasible and individually rational (relative to pure strategies) and any $\varepsilon>0$, there exists T_0 such that for each $T>T_0$, there exists a subgame perfect equilibrium of $G^T(1)$ with average value within ε of v.

This striking theorem is not only a result about finite horizon games, but also a testament to the intimate connection between infinitely and finitely repeated games. Both the statement of the theorem and the line of proof resemble closely those of the perfect folk theorem for discounted infinitely repeated games. In fact, using arguments mimicking those of Benoit and Krishna, one can strengthen their statement as follows: if for each player i there are two equilibria of G with different payoffs for i, then $\lim_{T\to\infty} V^T(1)=\lim_{\delta\to\infty} V^\infty(\delta)$. The equivalence holds regardless of the number of players or the dimension of F^+.

In games G having only one equilibrium, $G^T(\delta)$ has a unique subgame perfect equilibrium. But Radner (1980) pointed out that, even in this case, cooperation is possible if the solution concept is (perfect) ε-equilibrium, that is, if after each history any player's strategy is within $\varepsilon>0$, in *average* value terms, of the best strategy available from then on. In a game $G^T(\delta)$ with T large, anything that happens in the last few periods matters little in average terms, so there are ε-equilibria in which cooperation is induced by the threat that endgame behavior will depend on play earlier in the game. Radner proves that for arbitrarily small $\varepsilon>0$, asymptotically efficient average payoffs can be obtained in ε-equilibria with patient players as T grows large. This is a valuable technical result, but I find the interpretations in Radner (1980), section 8 in terms of search costs and bounded rationality to be forced and unconvincing.

Fudenberg and Levine (1983) elaborated on Radner's idea to produce a powerful equivalence result for finite and infinite horizon games. For present purposes it is specialized to strictly repeated games, and stated in terms of equilibrium values.[8]

PROPOSITION (Fudenberg and Levine, 1983) For any finite game G and $\delta\in(0,1)$, $v\in V^\infty(\delta)$ if and only if there is a sequence $(\varepsilon_T, v_T)_{T=1}^{\infty}$ such that:

(i) $\varepsilon_T > 0$ and v_T is the value of some ε_T-equilibrium of $G^T(\delta)$ for each T, and
(ii) $\varepsilon_T \to 0$ and $v_T \to v$.

Thus, supergame equilibrium values are exactly the limits of ε-equilibria of $G^T(\delta)$ as $\varepsilon \to 0$ and T grows large.

To see why relaxation of the incentive constraints by an arbitrarily small $\varepsilon > 0$ suffices to admit in $G^T(\delta)$ behavior associated with equilibria of $G^\infty(\delta)$, choose any subgame perfect equilibrium σ of $G^\infty(\delta)$, and T large enough so that the average value of any strategy differing from σ only after T is within ε of $v(\sigma)$. Let $\sigma(T)$ be the profile induced on $G^T(\delta)$ by σ. Because σ_i is a perfect best response to σ_{-i} in $G^\infty(\delta)$, our choice of T ensures that σ_i is an ε-perfect best response to $\sigma(T)_{-i}$ in $G^T(\delta)$, that is, $\sigma(T)$ is ε-perfect.

This paragraph is quite difficult, and can be skipped without loss of continuity. A couple of years ago David Kreps suggested to me that the Fudenberg–Levine limit result and the algorithm discussed earlier are related. There are a number of ways of explaining the connection; here is one. Recall that $B(W;\delta)$ is the set of equilibrium values generated by creating new games from G by modifying the payoffs with values from W. Now $B^2(W,\delta)$ is the set of values obtained by augmenting G with the continuation value set $B(W;\delta)$. Equivalently, $B^2(W;\delta)$ is the set of values of perfect equilibria of the *two-period games* obtained by modifying the terminal payoffs of $G^2(\delta)$ by values from W. The same is true for $B^T(W;\delta)$ and the W-augmentation of $G^T(\delta)$. For any positive integer T, and $\varepsilon > 0$, let $W_{T,\varepsilon} = \{w \in \mathbb{R}^n | 0 \le w_i \le \delta^{-T}\varepsilon,\ i = 1, \ldots, n\}$, which is a "cube" of size $\delta^{-T}\varepsilon$. After some reflection, one sees that the ε-equilibria of $G^T(\delta)$ are exactly the equilibria of the $W_{T,\varepsilon}$-augmentation of $G^T(\delta)$. This prompts two observations. First, for a self-generating set $W \subseteq B(W)$, since the $B^T(W)$ converge to the limits of ε_T-equilibria with $\varepsilon_T \to 0$ and $T \to \infty$, the ε-equilibrium limit results says that $B^\infty(W) \subseteq V$, another perspective on the self-generation theorem. Conversely, the Fudenberg–Levine limit theorem can also be appreciated from the point of view of value iteration.

I would like to make some informal remarks aimed at creating an intuition that applies to several of the papers discussed so far. In period t of an infinite horizon game $G^\infty(\delta)$ the one-period incentive constraints of G are loosened to an extent that depends on the size of the continuation value set. This loosening of incentive constraints is mimicked in Fudenberg and Levine (1983) by the use of ε-equilibria, and in Abreu, Pearce, and Stacchetti (1986, 1990) by the extra payoffs drawn from the set W. If the value of ε, or the set W, is too small, the relevant constraints may be violated; the algorithm does not necessarily work "from below" (contrast this with value iteration (Howard, 1960) in dynamic programming, where any initial values are acceptable). How, then, do Benoit and Krishna (1985) guarantee that there is enough "punishment power" to support cooperative behavior in $G^T(1)$ for large T, even if the multiple equilibria of G differ in value only minutely for some or all players? With $T = 10{,}000$ and $n = 5$, for example, play in the last 500 periods could consist of 100 periods of each player's respective favorite equilibrium. In the period preceding this 500-period endgame, each player has a lot to lose (remember that $\delta = 1$). Thus, values of $G^{10{,}000}(1)$ will be a lot like values of $B^{9{,}500}(W,1)$, where W is a large set. Chou and Geanakoplos (1987) show that, in a generic class of games with continuous action spaces, allowing arbitrary behavior *in the last period only* of $G^T(1)$ is enough to generate a folk theorem, even though G may have a unique equilibrium. The subtlety here is that the leeway created by the arbitrary end-period behavior can, by the envelope theorem, be used to disturb behavior slightly in many preceding periods; when summed (without discounting), these changes have large value consequences, and hence can create substantial incentives.

Cooperation amongst mortals

Although the abstraction of a world that continues indefinitely is a useful device, modeling individuals as infinitely lived is less attractive. It seems important to inquire, then, into the possibilities of self-enforcing agreements amongst finitely lived agents in an infinite horizon world. One could avoid the question by arguing that people, no matter how old, have a good chance of living in period $t+1$ *given* that they are alive in t, especially if the period is a day or a week, for example. Another escape route is to note that reputation can be vested in an institution such as a firm, whose mortal owners behave in accordance with implicit understandings (even soon before selling the firm) in order to protect the firm's market value; this is highly plausible, and is one of the ideas explored by Kreps (1987) in his paper on corporate culture. But what of situations where the participants' limited horizons are known precisely, and reputations reside exclusively with the individual? If equilibrium in the component game is unique, as in many free-rider problems, things look discouraging at first glance. Since it is impossible to induce a person to cooperate in the final period of his life, misbehavior having no future repercussions for him, presumably incentives unravel by the backward induction argument familiar from finite horizon games. Crémer (1986) showed that this need not happen, and his work has been generalized by Cooper and Daughety (1988), Salant (1988), Kandori (1989a), and Smith (1990). In an overlapping generations model, suppose that society acknowledges that in the final three periods of his life, say, no individual will act cooperatively. Hence, selfish behavior by the aged is part of the implicit agreement. But, if any young person fails to cooperate, the accord is broken and everyone subsequently optimizes myopically. Young persons will choose not to defect, because they would lose the benefits of social cooperation for the rest of their lives. Folk theorems similar to those discussed earlier hold here, and Kandori (1989a) shows that, if successive individuals are born far enough apart in time, there is no need to invoke any full dimension restriction. Recall that this assumption is usually made to ensure that punishers can be rewarded for minimaxing a defector, without incidentally also rewarding the defector himself. In Kandori's construction, the punishers wait until the defector dies, and then celebrate their earlier self-discipline.

Cooperation in matching models

When large numbers of players are partitioned into pairs who interact strategically perhaps for only one period before the pairings are rearranged, a particular player i may observe, at the end of period t, exactly what his partner j did in that period, while others may be uninformed or only partly informed about j's action. This makes it harder to sustain cooperation, because the group as a whole does not have the information needed to respond immediately and concertedly to a transgression by one individual. Nonetheless, self-enforcing agreements are sometimes possible even under such poor informational conditions. Kandori (1989b) studies trigger strategies in a repeated prisoner's dilemma matching game (always cooperate until someone you meet plays tough, and then play tough against everyone you subsequently meet). He shows that these strategies are a perfect equilibrium when δ is near 1. (The delicate constraint to check here is that, when a person is cheated for the first time, he is willing to accelerate the decay of goodwill in the community by treating his next partner ungenerously.) Okuno-Fujiwara and Postlewaite (1989) focused attention on environments with somewhat better information flows, which they call "local information processing." Each person has a "label" observable by his partner. The label in period $t+1$ depends only on the labels and actions of the individual and his t-partners in period t. (Examples of labels include membership in an organization and possession of a license or credit card.) Folk theorems hold for communities with local information processing and infinite populations (Okuno-Fujiwara and Postlewaite, 1989) or, under additional assumptions, finite populations (Kandori, 1989b). Community enforcement of social norms for bilateral strategic behavior has become the subject of much interest amongst economic historians. Recently a number of papers have traced the development of institutions that promoted community enforcement of fair trade practices, in the absence of adequate legal sanctions (see especially Greif, 1989; Milgrom, North, and Weingast, 1990; and Greif, Milgrom, and Weingast, 1990).

3 IMPERFECT MONITORING

Even during the early development of the theory of cooperation in games with perfect monitoring, researchers became dissatisfied with its scope. In many economic examples of practical interest, the assumption that players observe one another's past actions is inappropriate. Instead, player i observes the outcome of some random variable (team output, number of product failures or consumer complaints, market price, and so on) whose distribution is affected by the private actions of some or all of the players. Positive results for models of this kind again appeared first for games without discounting. The pioneering papers by Rubinstein (1979b), Radner (1981), and Rubinstein and Yaari (1983) proved that in infinitely repeated principal–agent games of various kinds, it is possible to overcome the inefficiency associated with the moral hazard problem in the static model. Rubinstein and Yaari also remarked that their arguments could be extended to yield a perfect folk theorem for agency games with imperfect monitoring.

The Green–Porter model

Green and Porter (1984) and Porter (1983a) were the first papers to study discounted repeated games in which players receive information related only stochastically to others' actions. Whereas the work without discounting had concentrated on one-sided imperfect monitoring (the principal's actions were not private), Green and Porter were interested in seeing whether n players all of whose actions are taken privately, could sustain cooperative (non-myopic) behavior by making their actions conditional on a relevant, commonly observed random variable. They answered the question in the affirmative in a Cournot oligopoly with random shocks to market price. By producing less following some observed prices than others, firms can create an implicit reward function (mapping observed prices into supergame continuation payoffs). For economists, one of the most attractive features of the model is that it escapes the prediction of dynamically uniform behavior on the most collusive equilibrium path, thereby offering a possible interpretation of observed phenomena such as price wars.

Porter investigated symmetric equilibria that are optimally collusive among a restricted set of "trigger strategy" profiles. A trigger strategy is described by a quantity q, a trigger price p, and a positive integer T. Firms begin by each producing q, and do so in every period until the price falls below p. A price realization of less than p triggers a T-period phase of Cournot–Nash behavior, after which cooperation resumes (until the Cournot phase gets triggered again). Should incentives to produce q in the cooperative phase be provided by punishing frequently, or infrequently but with greater severity (larger T)? Porter found that the answer varies with the family of distributions used for stochastic demand, but often it is optimal to set $T=\infty$, that is, revert permanently to the stage game Cournot–Nash equilibrium.

Constrained optimal solutions

Abreu, Pearce, and Stacchetti (1986) dropped the restriction to trigger strategy profiles, and characterized optimal pure strategy symmetric equilibria of a class of games that generalize the Green–Porter model. They found that a constrained efficient solution is described by two "acceptance regions" Ω_1 and Ω_2 in the signal space (price space, in the oligopoly example) and two actions q_1 and q_2. In the efficient equilibrium, players choose q_1 as long as the value of the signal falls in Ω_1. Otherwise, they switch to q_2, and keep playing q_2 as long as the signal falls in Ω_2 (when it falls outside Ω_2 they switch back to q_1, and so on). Thus, behavior on the optimal equilibrium path is a simple first-order Markov process with two states, indexed by the current "target action" q_1 or q_2. Why should the efficient solution take this form?

The value of an equilibrium of the supergame is the weighted sum of the first-period expected payoff and the expectation of the continuation values from period 2 onward. The latter values are drawn from the *symmetric* subgame perfect equilibrium value set $V \subseteq \mathbb{R}$ (elsewhere V was used for equilibrium values in $\mathbb{R}^n$). Thus, in the oligopoly example, with expected payoff function Π and price density function f, we want to choose a first-period quantity q_1 and a continuation reward function $u(p)$ with values in V, to maximize $(1-\delta)\Pi(q,\ldots, q)+\delta\int u(p)f(p, nq)dp$, subject to the incentive constraint that there is no alternative quantity that a firm would prefer to q_1 (given the immediate and future rewards). If it weren't for the need to provide incentives, one would choose $u(p)=\max V$ everywhere. A subset of price space is a good place to assign a lower reward value if its occurrence is much more likely when myopically tempting deviations take place than when q_1 is produced. For example, if there is only one incentive constraint (that is, only one tempting alternative q'), the best places to punish are where the likelihood ratio $\dfrac{f(p,\ (n-1)q_1+q')}{f(p,\ nq_1)}$ is high. In this case, assign the value min V to prices with very high likelihood ratios, and keep adding regions of price space (in decreasing order of likelihood ratio) to the punishment region until the incentive constraint is satisfied. This procedure concentrates the "punishment" into a region Ω_1^c that is as informationally efficient as possible. Using a larger region and a less severe punishment will generally result in a loss of efficiency because of the region's poorer ability to discriminate between good and bad behavior.[9]

Thus, after one period of the best equilibrium, players will be instructed either to begin the worst equilibrium (if price fell in the punishment region) or to restart the best equilibrium (play q_1). Now the worst equilibrium corresponds to the problem of choosing an action q_2 and a reward function $w(p)$ from V, to *minimize* the sum of the current and continuation payoffs, while providing for adequate incentives. Again, we would like to give the minimum reward everywhere, but to create incentives efficiently we give rewards max V in a region Ω_2^c chosen for its discriminatory power. At the end of period 1, players are told to restart the worst equilibrium if price fell in Ω_2, and to start the best equilibrium otherwise. Notice that, in every contingency, players are duplicating the behavior of the first period of one of two equilibria (the best or the worst), so only two quantities are ever produced. Switches between regimes are governed by the regions Ω_1 and Ω_2, as specified earlier.

The requirements this solution places on players' memories is unexpectedly modest. They need only remember which of two quantities they were supposed to produce last period, and what price arose.

Self-generation under imperfect monitoring

Self-generation and related techniques were first developed in the context of unrestricted symmetric equilibria of the Green–Porter model, and then presented in greater generality in Abreu, Pearce, and Stacchetti (1990). Suppose that players take private actions $a_i \in A_i$ (finite), $i \in N$, that determine the density $f(p; a)$ of a commonly observed random variable p with constant support Ω. Player i's realized payoff depends on his action a_i and on the realization p. Let i's *expected* payoff be $\Pi_i(a)$. In pure strategy equilibria of the repeated game, one-shot incentives are supplemented by continuation values drawn from the equilibrium value set $V \subseteq \mathbb{R}^n$. The continuation equilibria in effect create a (measurable) reward function mapping Ω into V. Hence, the natural value generation function to look at in this case is $B: 2^{\mathbb{R}^n} \to 2^{\mathbb{R}^n}$ defined by:

$B(W) = \{w \in \mathbb{R}^n \mid \exists (a,u) \in A \times L^\infty(\Omega, W)$ s.t. $w = (1-\delta)\Pi_i(a) + \delta \int u_i(p) f(p;a)dp$ and $(1-\delta)\Pi_i(a) + \delta \int u_i(p) f(p;a)dp \geq (1-\delta)\Pi_i(b_i, a_{-i}) + \delta \int u_i(p) f(p; b_i, a_{-i})dp \ \forall b_i \in A_i, i \in \mathrm{N}\}$. Again, if W is non-empty and bounded and

$W \subseteq B(W)$, W is called *self-generating*. This value-generation approach led to a number of results summarized below.

PROPOSITIONS (Abreu, Pearce, and Stacchetti, 1990).

Self-Generation. If W self-generating, then $W \subseteq \bigcup_{t=1}^{\infty} B^t(W) \subseteq V$.

Bang-bang rewards. V is compact, and for all $v \in V$ there exists an equilibrium whose implicit reward functions after each history take only values in the set of extreme points of V.

Algorithm. If W is bounded and $V \subseteq W$, then $\bigcap_{t=1}^{\infty} B^t(W) = V$.

Monotonicity. If $0 < \delta_1 < \delta_2 < 1$, then $V(\delta_1) \subseteq V(\delta_2)$.

Under certain conditions the "bang-bang sufficiency" result given above can be strengthened to a necessity result: an equilibrium that maximizes a linear combination of player payoffs (including negative combinations) *must* have implicit reward functions that use only extreme points of V. The rough intuition is the same as the one given earlier for the Green–Porter model: if you are creating incentives by moving rewards in a direction that reduces the objective function of the problem, do so aggressively (move until you can't go any further in V) but in as small and informative a region of signal space as possible. This advice cannot be applied literally in a model with a discrete signal space, so the bang-bang necessity result does not hold. The sufficiency result can be restored trivially in an essentially discrete model if the signal space is taken to include the outcome space of a public randomization device.

The scope of the preceding analysis is limited in three ways in order to preserve the "recursive structure" of the supergame equilibria: players receive no private signals, they use only pure strategies, and the commonly observed signal has constant support. When any of these restrictions is relaxed, some equilibria may, after certain histories, have continuation profiles that are not Nash equilibria of the supergame. This arises because imperfect correlation may develop in the actions of different players who are conditioning their behavior on private signals from earlier periods (including realizations of their own mixed strategy randomizing device). Fudenberg, Levine, and Maskin (1989) impose none of the three restrictions, but avoid the messy consequences in one superbly pragmatic stroke. They consider only the *public equilibria* of the supergame, that is, profiles of strategies that are perfect best responses to one another, and which use information from earlier periods only if it is publicly observed. The continuations of these equilibria are again public equilibria, and a straightforward dynamic programming approach can be used. I return to Fudenberg, Levine, and Maskin's work in some detail later in this section.

Discontinuity at $\delta=1$

Following the appearance of the efficiency results for undiscounted repeated agency problems mentioned at the beginning of this section, Radner (1985a) demonstrated the existence of fully efficient perfect equilibria in a class of partnership games with the limit of means criterion. Especially once Radner (1985b) had shown that asymptotic efficiency could be attained in repeated discounted agency problems as δ approaches 1, it seemed likely that the same could be proved for discounted partnerships. Thus, theorists were particularly intrigued when Radner, Myerson, and Maskin (1986) produced an example of a two-person repeated partnership game whose equilibria are bounded away from the efficient frontier, uniformly in δ. Each player has two strategies: work, or shirk (the latter is a dominant strategy in the component game). The commonly observed signal is the shared output, which may be either high or low; the probability of low output is f_w or f_s if both players work or only one works, respectively, where $0<f_w<f_s<1$. Restrict attention to symmetric equilibria (for expositional ease), and let v be the value of the maximal equilibrium. The best way to get players to work is to give a continuation value of v when high output is observed, and a lower value $v-x$ when low output is observed. Choose x just large enough that the expected loss in continuation value equals the average value of the absolute myopic gain (say g) from shirking:

$$(f_s-f_w)x=g\frac{(1-\delta)}{\delta}.$$

Even when both players work, low output occurs with probability f_w, so if Π is the expected payoff in G when both work, we have (if δ is not too low):

$$\begin{aligned}\bar{v}&=(1-\delta)\Pi+\delta(\bar{v}-f_w x)\\&=(1-\delta)\Pi+\delta\left(\bar{v}-\frac{f_w}{f_s-f_w}g\frac{(1-\delta)}{\delta}\right)\\\therefore\ \bar{v}&=\Pi-\frac{g}{\ell-1},\end{aligned}$$

where ℓ is the likelihood ratio f_s/f_w. Since δ does not appear in the expression for v, we see that the average payoff does not approach the first best as δ approaches 1. The average efficiency loss $g/(\ell-1)$ is proportional to the one-shot gain from cheating, and inversely proportional to the (transformed) likelihood ratio of the punishment region. Abreu, Milgrom, and Pearce (forthcoming) show that this formula applies quite generally to symmetric equilibria of repeated partnership problems; I explain later how they use this to study the effects of changing information and timing in such games.

The limit of means criterion and discounting with δ near 1 are alternative ways of modeling very patient players. Together, the papers by Radner (1985a) and Radner, Myerson, and Maskin (1986) show that they are by no means equivalent; this is sometimes called a "discontinuity at $\delta = 1$." In my opinion the repeated partnership (and most repeated games) are better modeled with discounting than with the limit of means criterion, and the example under discussion illustrates this well. If they are to have incentives to work in period t, players must be punished (sooner or later) if period t output is low. Since low output may occur even under good behavior, this imposes a real cost, one which must be borne every time players are supposed to work. The per-period nature of the problem is nicely reflected in the discounting case, where the loss gets capitalized in the value set. Without discounting, it is *not* necessary to deter shirking period by period: if a player cheats for k periods, it has no effect on his long-run average payoff. Only infinite strings of deviations are a problem, and these Radner detects using a "review strategy" that, according to the law of the iterated log, will yield a first-best equilibrium average payoff. I can think of few economic problems that are well modeled by the assumption that it is safe to ignore incentives in any particular 50,000 periods. For this reason I consider discounted folk theorems (and counterexamples) important advances, even in the presence of the comprehensive theory for $\delta = 1$.

The need to deter single deviations (with discounting) and its absence (with the limit of means) probably explains the difference in methodologies in the respective literatures. Statistical methods are ideally suited to guarding against long-run deviations, whereas dynamic programming methods are largely inapplicable at $\delta = 1$ (recall, for example, the failure of the equivalence of unimprovability and perfect best responses). With discounting, the problem of deterring current deviations leads naturally to the decomposition of a supergame profile into behavior today and continuation values for the future. The dynamic programming perspective has the benefit of unifying the treatment of patient and impatient players, infinite and finite horizon games, and implicit and explicit contracts (of which, more later). This is not to say that the statistical approach cannot be used to advantage when payoffs are discounted; see, for example, the work of Fudenberg and Levine (forthcoming) on folk theorems for approximate equilibria.

Information and timing

In models with perfect monitoring, fixing the players' rate of time preference and shortening the length of the period (of fixed actions) is equivalent to letting the discount factor approach 1: in either case, today's payoff becomes a small part of total payoffs, so the folk theorems have two interpretations. With imperfect monitoring, shrinking the period length still implies less discounting from one period to the next, but also leaves less time for players to observe signals relevant to behavior. For example, if signals arrive according to a Poisson process in continuous time, with the arrival rate determined by players' current behavior, the quality of information (in a sense relevant for incentives, as explained below) available over a period of time of length s deteriorates as s decreases. So there are two effects of reducing the period length: an effective increase in patience, which we know from the monotonicity result stated earlier tends to increase the average value set, and a worsening of information, which Kandori (1988) has elegantly shown to decrease the set of equilibrium values. Either of these two effects can dominate in a particular case.

The upper bound for $\bar{v}$ developed above for a simple partnership problem holds as stated for symmetric equilibria of repeated partnerships with arbitrary signal spaces, as shown by Abreu, Milgrom, and Pearce (1991), and with slight modification for more than two actions. Attaching different punishments (continuation values) to different signal values is equivalent to using the severest punishment with different probabilities, which in turn simply amounts to choosing a region (say Ω_0) of extended signal space (the product of the natural signal space and the range of a public randomizing device) in which to punish uniformly. Once Ω_0 has been chosen optimally, which can be accomplished by solving a linear program, the efficiency loss from providing incentives for cooperation is $g/(\ell - 1)$, as before (if cooperation is possible at all).

Now think of the Poisson example with arrivals interpreted as "good news," such as research breakthroughs or the winning of major contracts. If all members of the team are working, perhaps the arrival rate over a year's time is 10, whereas it drops dramatically to 1 if anyone shirks. If the period of fixed action is a year, under plausible parameter values cooperation could be sustained very profitably. But suppose that instead actions can be changed daily. The only way to encourage cooperation is to punish the event that there is no goods news (zero arrivals), which has probability near 1 whether anyone shirks or not. Thus, the likelihood ratio is little more than 1, so the efficiency loss is enormous (more precisely, as the period length shortens the value falls until *cooperation is no longer possible*, and the formula ceases to apply). Ironically, in this case the players' ability to respond quickly to information destroys all possibility of cooperation. This suggests that *delaying* the release of information might actually be valuable in partnerships; Abreu, Milgrom, and Pearce show that for high δ, information delays can virtually eliminate the inefficiency that Radner, Myerson, and Maskin identified.

Folk theorems with imperfect monitoring

The prospects for a general folk theorem for discounted repeated games with multisided moral hazard seemed dim, in the face of the Radner, Myerson, and Maskin counterexample. But gradually a number of papers challenged the presumption that the troublesome example was representative. First, Williams and Radner (1987) showed that efficiency could be approached in generic static partnerships with enforceable contracts. Matsushima (1989) subsequently used a first-order approach and some fairly palatable assumptions on information and the value set to generate asymptotic efficiency in equilibria of infinitely repeated partnerships. Next, Fudenberg, Levine, and Maskin (1989) independently demonstrated that, under remarkably weak conditions on primitives, a folk theorem holds for a wide class of games including those with moral hazard on all sides. Demougin and Fishman (1988) also showed that, under reasonable conditions, oligopolies with imperfect monitoring could enjoy efficient collusion.

I concentrate here on the paper by Fudenberg, Levine, and Maskin (hereafter FLM) because it is by far the most general, and represents the state of the art in discounted folk theorems for a broad range of information structures. Anyone interested in repeated games should read it closely. In order to avoid the introduction of further notation, I shall simplify their model in a way that makes it easy to describe here. Start with the n-person repeated game with imperfect monitoring studied by Abreu, Pearce, and Stacchetti, discussed earlier, and make two changes:

(i) let the signal take on only k values, k finite, and
(ii) drop the "constant support" assumption.

As FLM explain, this model embraces perfect monitoring games (where the signal is simply the vector of players' actions), oligopolies, partnerships, and principal– agent problems (where the agent's action in the component game is a plan contingent on the compensation function offered by the principal). What I omit here are adverse selection problems, discussed in the final section of FLM.

Logically prior to the possibility of *efficient* cooperation is the question of whether cooperation can be supported at all. If one is allowed to employ arbitrary continuation values in $\mathbb{R}^n$ as threats and promises, can players necessarily be induced to take a particular desired vector of actions? With perfect monitoring, the answer is obviously yes: players will do anything to avoid sufficiently severe punishments. With imperfect monitoring, however, player 1 might have three actions a_1, b_1, and c_1 such that, given some profile of actions for other players, the distribution of the public signal is the same when 1 chooses c_1 as when he randomizes between a_1 and b_1 with probabilities 0.6 and 0.4, for example. If the component game payoff to 1 is higher for both a_1 and b_1 than for c_1, then it is impossible to induce him to play c_1. No matter what rewards are attached to signal realizations, switching from c_1 to the mixture raises player 1's immediate payoff and leaves the distribution of continuation rewards unchanged. Hence, FLM's first informational assumption is one ensuring that a player's different possible actions can be distinguished, and hence encouraged or discouraged. Specifically, they impose the *individual full rank* condition: at each profile $a \in A$ and for each player i, the $k \times m_i$ matrix[10] whose columns are the probability distributions induced by the respective action profiles (b_i, a_{-i}), $b_i \in A_i$, has rank m_i, that is, the probability vectors corresponding to each pure action of i are linearly independent. It is easy to verify that this guarantees that any behavior can be *enforced* if arbitrary continuation payoffs can be used.

Enforceability of this kind is clearly not enough to yield a folk theorem, because the Radner, Myerson, and Maskin counterexample satisfies individual full rank. The problem there was that the only way to enforce good behavior was to punish *both* players in the event that output is low. Efficient (or nearly efficient) cooperation in a model where no player's actions are observed, generally requires that, when one player's continuation payoff is reduced, another's must be increased:[11] surplus should be passed back and forth amongst players, not thrown away. For a transfer of surplus from i to j to be effective in creating incentives, it needs to be associated with information that discriminates statistically between deviations by i and deviations by j. The availability of such information is ensured by the *pairwise full rank* condition: for each pair of players i and j there is some profile $\alpha \in A$ such that the $k \times (m_i + m_j)$-dimensional matrix whose first m_i columns are the respective public distributions induced by the vectors (b_i, α_{-i}), $b_i \in A_i$ and whose final m_j columns are the distributions induced by the vectors (c_j, α_{-j}), $c_j \in A_j$, is of rank $m_i + m_j - 1$. (There is inevitably one linear dependency among the columns, because both i and j can create the distribution associated with α by putting the appropriate weights on pure actions.)

It would have been reasonable to guess that, to prove that a desired profile γ can be enforced (almost) efficiently, it would be necessary to impose pairwise full rank relative to deviations from γ. By contrast, all that is actually assumed is that, for each i and j, there is some "distinguishing" α that allows i's and j's deviations to be distinguished, and not necessarily the same α for each pair of players! FLM demonstrates that a profile as close as desired to γ can be found that puts a little weight on the strategies used in the "distinguishing profiles," and discriminates as required between deviations of different players. They attribute the kernel of this idea to Legros[12] (1989).

With the additional restrictions on the information structure guaranteed by the full rank conditions, FLM prove a folk theorem of virtually the same degree of generality as for perfect monitoring. There is no restriction to pure strategies.

PROPOSITION Perfect folk theorem with imperfect monitoring (Fudenberg, Levine, and Maskin, 1989). For a finite game G satisfying individual full rank and pairwise full rank (see above) and dim $F^+ = n$, for any closed set W in the relative interior of F^+ there exists δ' such that for all $\delta > \delta'$, $W \subseteq V(\delta)$.

Fudenberg and Levine (1989) show how the folk theorem must be weakened if some of the participants in a supergame are "short-run" players; they provide an upper bound for the payoffs attainable by the long-run players, as a function of the information structure.

Agency and repeated contracting

The classic moral hazard problem with one principal and one agent is an important example of a game with imperfect monitoring on one side. Many principal–agent relationships are of an ongoing nature, and much effort has been devoted to understanding the implications of repetition for the shape and performance of optimal contracts. Some of this research was underway at the time of the Fifth World Congress of the Econometric Society, and was included in the authoritative survey by Hart and Holmström (1987). For a taste of what has been done since, see the relevant section of FLM, MacLeod and Malcomson (1988, 1989), Pearce and Stacchetti (1987), Phelan and Townsend (1991), and Rey and Salanie (1990). While not strictly repeated, some games of international debt repayment are closely related; see especially Atkeson (1991).

One of the benefits of the recent overlap of contract theory and repeated games has been a growing understanding of the relationship between what can be accomplished by implicit and explicit (legal) enforcement mechanisms, respectively. Naturally, implicit contracts are advantageous when the concerned parties share information that cannot (for legal reasons, or because verification costs are prohibitive, etc.) be used in an explicit contract. But, when the contracts can be specified in terms of the same information, do self-enforcing agreements achieve what explicit contracts can? The answer depends on whether one can create the same variation in continuation payoffs in self-enforcing agreements as in explicit contracts (and hence provide incentives with the same degree of efficiency). This is not always possible: the equilibrium value set (in the implicit contract environment) might be of less than full dimension, or might be too small to allow efficient exploitation of the game's signal space (recall the earlier discussion of likelihood ratios). Suppose, however, that the conditions of the FLM folk theorem of this section are met. Then as δ approaches 1, self-enforcing agreements achieve almost any feasible, individually rational payoff, so asymptotically implicit contracts perform as well as their explicit counterparts.

Confronting the theoretical predictions with reality

This will be a brief subsection, because reality and I have been out of touch for a long time. A number of investigators have developed econometric tests of the Green–Porter model and applied them to data on the Joint Executive Committee railroad cartel (weekly aggregate time series for the period 1880 to 1886). Porter (1983b), Lee and Porter (1984), and Hajivassiliou (1989), respectively, use switching regression models of increasing sophistication to allow for collusion punctuated by price wars. Berry and Briggs (1988) use the same data to test the hypothesis that the alternation between regimes follows a Markov process, and Hajivassiliou (1989) compares the performance of the Abreu, Pearce, and Stacchetti (1986) and Rotemberg and Saloner (1986) analyses of oligopolistic collusion. Slade (1986, 1987) tests a learning model (Slade, 1989a) with a daily time series on gasoline prices in Vancouver, collected by the author.

I value this body of work principally for its implementation of econometric results appropriate to the study of collusive markets, and for its organization of some facts about intertemporal strategic behavior in a few oligopolies. It seems entirely premature, however, to draw conclusions about the relevance of the particular models tested (and accordingly I do not summarize the results of the various tests here).[13] First, it is highly probable that none of the models comes close to capturing the strategic considerations at work in the oligopolies in question. The environments were far more complicated, in important ways, than any of the models tested, and I think Slade has the right attitude when she describes the process of comparing supergame models to data as follows: "The object of the exercise is not to pick a winner. Instead, the role of industry characteristics in determining pricing dynamics is assessed, and the reasons why simple models may fail to explain complex pricing patterns are examined" (Slade, 1989b). A second reservation is that the collusive theories tested are quite naive from a conceptual point of view, ignoring renegotiation, coalition formation, and other considerations of equilibrium refinement. In my opinion, the pure theory of implicit collusion is at such a primitive stage that it is in no shape to be tested.

Still, I feel that there is a lot to be learned from studying collusion in specific industries, keeping in mind an assortment of questions provoked by modern theory. An exciting example of what can result is Levenstein's (1989) work on the bromine industry in the USA and Germany from 1880 until 1914. By analyzing the internal documents of the Dow Chemical Company and its correspondence with other American and German producers, Levenstein gives us an extraordinary picture of the evolution of competition and collusion among the oligopolists as they gained experience, learned about their rivals, and faced changing market conditions. Other fascinating examples of self-enforcing contracts in the economic history literature include Greif (1989) on reputation among medieval Mediterranean traders, and Milgrom, North, and Weingast (1990) on the role of the Law Merchant and the Champagne fairs in Europe in the middle ages.

4 RENEGOTIATION AND SELF-ENFORCING AGREEMENTS

If an agreement among players in a repeated game is truly self-enforcing, it must be able to withstand the possibility that the players could renegotiate the terms of the agreement after any history. This section principally concerns renegotiation involving all parties to the agreement, although the potential for defections by smaller coalitions is an important and difficult problem as well. An explosion of research in the last six or seven years has produced a baffling variety of criteria for "renegotiation-proofness." Rather than exhaust the space available here by reproducing the details of the many definitions, I will try to provide a conceptual overview of the literature, emphasizing the concerns that prompted the authors to formulate the new solution concepts. There will be no attempt to describe the technical characterizations of the solution sets; under moderate assumptions, existence is not a problem, except where mentioned. Non-specialists will find the discussion herein more meaningful if they first (or concurrently) refer to some of the original papers in the literature.

While all the work on renegotiation is skeptical about the credibility of the kinds of equilibria described in sections 2 and 3, there is an even more radical critique that deserves mention. In the spirit of Harsanyi and Selten (1988) one could say that the behavior of "ideally rational" players in a subgame depends only on the internal *structure* of the subgame, and not on how it was reached. Since all subgames of an infinite horizon, strictly repeated game are identical, it follows that there is no scope for negotiation of any kind: the same (non-cooperative) outcome will occur in each period. Güth, Leininger, and Stephan (1988) provide a formal argument based on a generalization of subgame consistency (Selten, 1973). It is not clear why full rationality necessarily precludes agreements to vary behavior across isomorphic subgames if the result is beneficial to all concerned. But I have some sympathy with the work just described insofar as I think (and argue later) that most other authors err in the opposite direction by overestimating the influence of verbal agreements on the course of play.

The first work on renegotiation in infinitely repeated games[14] was done independently by Bernheim and Ray (1989) and Farrell and Maskin (1989). Their position is that the stationary structure of $G^{\infty}(\delta)$ implies that the set of credible (renegotiation-proof) equilibria is the same in every subgame. Moreover, they assume that, after any history of play, an ongoing agreement would be renegotiated (abandoned) if and only if a Pareto superior credible equilibrium were available. That is, players will stick with the status quo unless everyone can credibly be made better off. In the terminology of Farrell and Maskin, a subgame perfect equilibrium is called *weakly renegotiation-proof* (WRP) if no two of its continuation values[15] (after *any* history) are Pareto ranked. This can be translated into a criterion for sets of supergame (average discounted) values, to facilitate comparison with other solution concepts. A set W of values is WRP if it is self-generating (this imposes the discipline of subgame perfection) and if no two values in W are Pareto ranked. One might say that such a solution set is "Pareto-thin."

Unfortunately, a WRP set W may contain a point w that is Pareto dominated by a point x in some other WRP set X. Why is the value w credible if players can propose the universally preferred continuation value x, which is itself credible according to the WRP criterion? A WRP set none of whose values is Pareto dominated by an element of any other WRP set is called *strongly renegotiation-proof* (SRP). Such a set does not always exist: there may be no "greatest" WRP set, but rather two or more intersecting "maximal" WRP sets, such as W and W' in figure 4.2. This possibility led to several interesting definitions intermediate between WRP and SRP, none of them completely satisfying. These include relative strongly renegotiation-proofness (Farrell and Maskin, 1989) and minimal consistency and simple consistency (Bernheim and Ray, 1989). For technical characterizations of WRP, SRP and their variants see the two papers just mentioned, and also van Damme (1989) and Evans and Maskin (1989).

Bernheim and Ray have reservations about all of the foregoing definitions because in the following sense they require too little. If W is the solution set, it should not be possible to construct an equilibrium σ with value Pareto superior to some value in W, and using only continuation values from W after every non-trivial history. After all, how could one argue against renegotiating to σ (from an equilibrium with the Pareto dominated value), if in all future contingencies it specifies continuation values that are

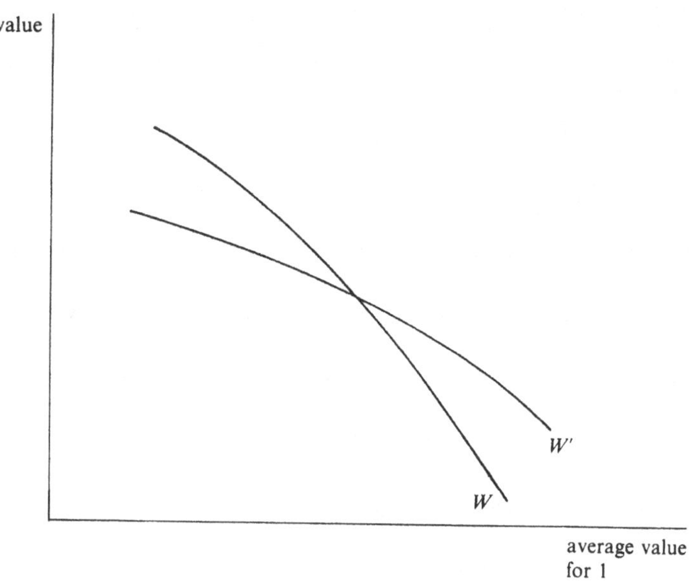

Figure 4.2

credible within the theory? Thus, one needs to require that the solution set W satisfy $W = \text{eff } B(W)$, where eff X means "the (Pareto) efficiency frontier of X." Such a set is called *internally renegotiation-proof* and is studied by Ray (1989). Existence is apparently problematic.

Pearce (1987) suggests a different approach to renegotiation, one that ties the influence of a negotiated agreement to the usefulness of such agreements in the future. For simplicity, think of a very special case, namely, an infinitely repeated game all of whose subgame perfect equilibrium average values are symmetric (if one player gets x in equilibrium, so does everyone else). Players at time t will not follow an equilibrium with continuation value 2, say, if the only reason for doing so is that the threat of triggering the value 2 was needed *earlier* to induce a certain pattern of cooperation. But the continuation equilibrium *will* stand if the value 2 is truly indispensable for the provision of incentives in the *future*, that is, if *every* subgame perfect equilibrium must use continuation values of 2 or less after some histories. In the special case under consideration, Pearce (1987) calls an equilibrium σ *renegotiation-proof* if[16] $\inf C(\sigma) \geq \inf C(\gamma)$ for every subgame perfect equilibrium γ. Implicitly some notion of precedent is being invoked: players should not think that, on the one hand, they can abandon a punishment of 2 now, but that they would never do so again in the future.

I will omit the extension of the solution concept to general repeated games, because (like almost all of the literature) it uses the Pareto criterion in determining when a credible alternative will be adopted by the group of players. There is a need for more plausible criteria, a point discussed briefly below.

Greenberg (1990) presents the results of research over a number of years on the "theory of social situations," which expands on the "stable set" methodology of von Neumann and Morgenstern (1947) and applies it to a variety of strategic settings. This work has had an influence on the debate about renegotiation, particularly through the research of Asheim (1988, 1991), whose analysis of renegotiation relies explicitly on stable sets of equilibria. A solution in his sense is a set of equilibria for each subgame; the set associated with a given subgame is interpreted as those equilibria considered credible in that subgame. Asheim calls a solution "Pareto perfect" (following the terminology of Bernheim and Ray, 1989) if it is both internally and externally stable. Internal stability means that for any subgame g and element σ of the associated solution set, and any subsequent subgame h, no element of the solution set of h Pareto dominates σ. (Thus, no credible equilibrium should be interrupted after some history by a Pareto superior equilibrium considered credible following that history.) External stability requires that, for any equilibrium σ excluded from the solution set for subgame g, there must be some subsequent subgame h such that some element of the solution set of h Pareto dominates the continuation equilibrium induced by σ on h. An attractive feature of the theory, then, is that it explains why no further equilibria were included in the solution sets. Existence has not been established in general, and it seems unlikely that strong results are possible. Asheim (1991) shows that, even in very simple examples, existence is incompatible with stationarity of the solution sets.

Instead of giving up stationarity, perhaps we can exploit it to arrive at an appropriate relaxation of external stability. If an equilibrium σ is not dominated after any history by an "included" equilibrium, σ might still be excluded on the grounds that it is internally inconsistent. Suppose that, for some history h, the continuation equilibrium $\sigma|_h$ is dominated by σ itself. If players found σ credible, then after the history h they would unanimously agree to renegotiate away from $\sigma|_h$ to σ, which contradicts the hypothesis that such a σ could be found credible. One can find arguments for and against weakening external stability by allowing for exclusion on the basis of internal inconsistency. For those who would object that this is a departure from the original spirit of the von Neumann and Morgenstern definition, I should remark that they presumably were thinking principally of strict dominance relations that were irreflexive, so the issue of self-dominating elements did not arise. It is only in the context of objects with a dynamic structure that the question becomes important.

Abreu and Pearce (1991) adopt the stable solution formulation with a number of changes. First, we weaken external stability in the way just described. Secondly, we argue that it is reasonable to look for stationary stable sets of *deviations*, rather than sets of credible plans. The interpretation is that, since a deviation from an ongoing social agreement does not depend upon the old agreement for its legitimacy, it must stand on its own. Thus, if it is credible in one contingency, it is credible in any contingency. (This is not to say that it will be *adopted* independently of the context; the group may not *want* to adopt it if the status quo is sufficiently attractive.) So it seems natural to impose stationarity on the set of deviations that are considered credible. Finally, we suggest that the Pareto criterion be replaced as dominance criterion by some ordering, preferably complete, reflecting considerations of bargaining power in the game.

The use of the Pareto criterion for determining when a credible alternative will be adopted imputes to each player veto power over changes from the old negotiated agreement to a suggested alternative. Why should a verbal agreement embody such commitment power? In my (minority) opinion, it is more plausible to posit that decisions to adopt credible alternatives are governed by some rule that takes into account the bargaining positions of the players, as determined by the structural features of the game. Abreu and Pearce (1991) have nothing constructive to say about precisely what the rule ought to be. The problem is a little easier in symmetric games, where Abreu, Pearce, and Stacchetti (1989) modify the definition of renegotiation-proofness given in Pearce (1987) by replacing the Pareto criterion with a simple (many would say too simple) bargaining rule. DeMarzo (1990) raises another problem concerning veto power and the status quo. Suppose that the initial equilibrium σ is adhered to in the first period, and in the second players are pondering the credibility of an alternative σ'. If they adopt σ', then in the third period can each player insist on the continuation of σ' (against a new proposal σ'', say) or on the continuation of σ? In other words, what should serve as the status quo? Departing from the earlier literature, DeMarzo says that in many circumstances σ is more appropriate, because the original equilibrium has the weight of tradition behind it (it is a "social norm").

Bergin and MacLeod (1989) present an axiomatic system within which they can generate a number of the alternative solution concepts in the renegotiation literature. Although in some cases (such as their axiomatization of my own definition) I find the particular decomposition of the definitions into principles and preferences unnatural or forced, in others it is very helpful, especially in understanding the relationships of formulations of renegotiation-proofness in finite and infinite horizon supergames. Several papers, most notably Benoit and Krishna (1988) have explored the implications of "Pareto perfection" (Bernheim and Ray, 1989) in finitely repeated games.[17] The definition is recursive. In the final period, the credible Nash equilibria are those that are Pareto efficient among all Nash equilibria of G. In the last two periods, the equilibria that are efficient among those whose continuations are credible, are deemed credible, and so on. In technical terms, if W^t is the set of credible average values in the final t-period subgame, then $W^{t+1} = \text{eff}\, B(W^t)$. So, as Bergin and MacLeod point out, the WRP concept is really not analogous to the commonly accepted finite horizon definition. Actually, Bernheim and Ray's internally renegotiation-proof solution is a closer analogue to the latter. Bergin and MacLeod also propose a new solution called recursive efficiency; see their paper for a discussion of its relationship to DeMarzo's point of view.

I cannot end this catalogue without mentioning an intriguing paper by Matsushima (1990). His idea is that just as an equilibrium specifies what will happen if its "instructions" are not obeyed, societies have metacodes indicating what happens when a social convention (equilibrium) is breached. The ensuing analysis is highly ingenious; to my astonishment, Matsushima emerges from a jungle of infinite sequences of social conventions and breaching rules, with an existence result. I will not try to explain the motivation for the solution concept; on that score, despite some enjoyable discussions with the author, I remain mystified.

How are we to choose among the multitude of theories of renegotiation? I don't think this can be done purely on logical grounds: each theory is consistent on its own terms, and respects all the relevant intertemporal incentive constraints. Many strategic situations (as traditionally described) are fundamentally underdetermined, even if one imposes the questionable restriction of equilibrium. What people will believe after observing a particular history of play, and what weight they give to verbal agreements, are partly questions of psychology. Why not leave the problem to the psychologists, then? I find this abdication of responsibility unattractive: the psychological aspects of puzzle are inextricably interwoven with complicated considerations of sequential rationality and bargaining power. Thus, while guidance certainly should be sought from other disciplines, the skills of game theorists and economists are highly relevant in the construction of *educated guesses* about cooperation in supergames.

To guess is unavoidable[18] if we are to make any contribution to many of the most important areas of the social sciences (beyond asserting that nothing can be said with much certainty, sometimes a useful remark in itself). The danger is that the guesses may be taken too seriously. "Equilibrium in dominant strategies" and "weakly renegotiation-proof equilibrium" are worlds apart in the immediacy of their links to basic principles of rationality, and correspondingly in the degree of confidence they ought to command. Yet one term, "solution concept," is used to describe them both (along with scores of other notions). We need to develop a means of communicating the intended interpretations of our various solution concepts, and of distinguishing what is relatively solid in our analyses from what is of a more speculative nature. Such a language is needed not only for studying repeated games, but for game theory in general. Its absence is a stumbling block for the useful fusion of non-cooperative and cooperative theories of strategic behavior.

5 CONCLUSION

Study of the equilibria of repeated games has been intense over the past decade. The results have been rewarding. While progress occurred largely in models chosen for their tractability, a picture has emerged that seems likely to be broadly representative of more general environments. Among other things, we have some sense of what optimal self-enforcing agreements look like, when they are likely to approach the first best, which theoretical simplifications are fairly innocuous, how implicit and explicit contracts compare, and which techniques extend to dynamic and stochastic games. But beneath our understanding of the mechanics of supergame equilibria lie foundational issues of the most immediate relevance.

The multiplicity of equilibria that causes problems in many areas of game theory arises in a dramatic way in repeated games: without multiplicity, self-enforcing cooperative agreements would be impossible. The accompanying conceptual puzzles were long ignored, but recent years have seen an explosion of research on supergame solution concepts, with particular attention devoted to the renegotiation of implicit agreements. After all the activity, there remain more questions than conclusions. Under what conditions are players likely to expect others to behave non-myopically? What do they think when someone departs from an agreed-upon plan? Which negotiation statements are credible? What is an effective precedent? Issues like these float tantalizingly in a multidisciplinary limbo, beyond the reach of purely mathematical analysis. They are too central to ignore, yet too nebulous to have definitive answers. This is at once the most frustrating and the most alluring aspect of the subject.

Notes

1 This chapter was prepared for the Sixth World Congress of the Econometric Society, held in August 1990 in Barcelona, Spain. I am grateful to Dilip Abreu

and Ennio Stacchetti for their expert and patient help. Many thanks to the Alfred P. Sloan Foundation and the National Science Foundation for their financial support.

2 Numerous references can be found in subsequent sections.

3 It is often remarked that it is unnecesary to allow i to condition on his *own* past actions. It is easy to show by example that this is false.

4 Given a stream of payoffs $\{x_t\}$, one can define the sequence of average payoffs $\{y_t\}$ by $y_t = \frac{1}{t}\sum_{k=1}^{t} x_k$. The sequence $\{y_t\}$ may not have a limit, but the limit inferior is always defined, and this is what is meant here by the "long-run average" or "limit of means" associated with the original stream $\{x_t\}$.

5 Simultaneous deviations are ignored, since they are irrelevant for checking subgame perfection.

6 A payoff stream $\{w_t\}$ is strictly preferred to $\{x_t\}$ under the overtaking criterion if $\lim_{T\to\infty} \inf \sum_{t=1}^{T} (w_t - x_t) > 0$.

7 A *path* is a sequence of action profiles, one for each period.

8 Further work on equilibria of convergence sequences of games include Harris (1985) and Fudenberg and Levine (1986).

9 Often the optimal region will consist of prices below some critical value p. When a tail test is *not* optimal, but is imposed arbitrarily, raising the critical value may add some informationally more efficient points to the region. This explains Porter's finding that sometimes $T < \infty$ is optimal; a unique interior solution of this kind can occur only when imposing a tail test is inappropriate.

10 Recall that there are k possible signal values, and m_i pure strategies for each player i.

11 This is true in the context of the present model, in which the range of the public signal is finite (assuming in addition that all realizations occur with positive probability in equilibrium). In games with richer signal spaces, it is sometimes possible as δ approaches 1 to construct a sequence of symmetric punishments that are asymptotically efficient, based on punishment regions whose likelihood ratios are exploding. Recall the famous example of Mirrlees (1974) in which the static agency problem is overcome in the same way.

12 Legros was concerned with a static incentive problem. Recently Legros and Matsushima (1990) have given a nice sufficient condition for the existence of efficient solutions of static partnership problems.

13 Useful summaries and discussion may be found in the surveys by Jacquemin and Slade (1989) and Bresnahan (1989).

14 Around the same time Bernheim, Peleg, and Whinston (1987) were developing their notion of coalition-proof equilibrium, whose extensive form expression can be specialized to a theory of renegotiation-proofness in finitely repeated games. An early note on renegotiation in infinitely repeated games was circulated by Farrell (1984). Cave (1987) deserves mention for studying the minimal punishments necessary to support a given degree of collusion in a dynamic fisheries model.

15 For any profile σ, the set of continuation values of σ is $C(\sigma)=\{v(\sigma|_h)|h$ is some (possibly degenerate) history of play$\}$, where $\sigma|_h$ is the profile induced by σ on the subgame following h. Note that $v(\sigma)$ is included in $C(\sigma)$.
16 Here $C(\sigma)$ is treated as a set of scalars, since everyone's payoff is the same.
17 Abreu and Pearce (1991) suggest that the logic of renegotiation is rather different in finitely, as opposed to infinitely, repeated games. If verbal agreements are influential because of their *prospective* usefulness, what weight can they carry in the final period of $G^T(\delta)$, where there is no future for the players to consider?
18 In his scintillating essay on the foundations of game theory, Binmore (1992) urges that predictions about strategic behavior be informed by careful study of "librations" (equilibrating processes in real time) and of the actual thought process of (boundedly rational) humans. This may well prove productive, but is unlikely to remove the need for guesswork in the foreseeable future. There will remain ample room for debate about what rules of thumb, models of the mind, updating processes, and so on, are reasonable or plausible.

References

Abreu, D. (1986), "Extremal Equilibria of Oligopolistic Supergames," *Journal of Economic Theory*, 39: 191–225.
(1988), "On the Theory of Infinitely Repeated Games with Discounting," *Econometrica*, 56: 383–96.
Abreu, D., P. Milgrom, and D. Pearce (1991), "Information and Timing in Repeated Partnerships," *Econometrica*, 59: 1713–34.
Abreu, D. and D. Pearce (1991), "A Perspective on Renegotiation in Repeated Games," in R. Selten (ed.), *Game Equilibrium Models* vol. 2, Springer-Verlag.
Abreu, D., D. Pearce, and E. Stacchetti (1986), "Optimal Cartel Equilibria with Imperfect Monitoring," *Journal of Economic Theory*, 39: 251–69.
(1989), "Renegotiation and Symmetry in Repeated Games," Cowles Foundation Discussion Paper No. 920, Yale University.
(1990), "Towards a Theory of Discounted Repeated Games with Imperfect Monitoring," *Econometrica*, 58: 1041–64.
Asheim, G., 1988. "Renegotiation-Proofness in Finite and Infinite Stage Games through the Theory of Social Situations," mimeo, The Norwegian School of Economics and Business Administration.
(1991), "Extending Renegotiation-Proofness to Infinite Horizon Games," *Games and Economic Behavior*, 3: 278–94.
Atkeson, A. (1991), "International Lending with Moral Hazard and Risk of Repudiation," *Econometrica*, 59: 1069–90.
Aumann, R. and L. Shapley (1976), "Long-term Competition: A Game-theoretic Analysis," mimeo.
Barro, R. and D. Gordon (1983), "Rules, Discretion, and Reputation in a Model of Monetary Policy," *Journal of Monetary Economics*, 12: 101–21.

Benoit, J. P. and V. Krishna (1985), "Finitely Repeated Games," *Econometrica*, 53: 905–22.

Benoit, J.P. and V. Krishna (1988), "Renegotiation in Finitely Repeated Games", Harvard Business School Working Paper 89–004.

Bergin, J. and W. B. MacLeod, 1989. "Efficiency and Renegotiation in Repeated Games," mimeo, Queen's University at Kingston.

Bernheim, B. D., B. Peleg, and M. Whinston (1987), "Coalition-Proof Nash Equilibrium 1. Concepts," *Journal of Economic Theory*, 42: 1–12.

Bernheim, B. D. and D. Ray (1989), "Collective Dynamic Consistency in Repeated Games," *Games and Economic Behavior*, 1: 295–326.

Berry, S. and H. Briggs (1988), "A Non-Parametric Test of a First Order Markov Process for Regimes in a Non-Cooperatively Collusive Industry," *Economics Letters*, 27: 73–7.

Binmore, K. (1992), "Foundations of Game Theory," in J. J. Laffont (ed.), *Advances in Economic Theory: Sixth World Congress*, Cambridge University Press.

Bresnahan, T. (1989), "Empirical Studies of Industries with Market Power," in R. Schmalensee and R. Willig (eds.), *Handbook of Industrial Organization*, vol. 2, chapter 17. Amsterdam: North Holland.

Cave, J. (1987), "Long-Term Competition in a Dynamic game: The Cold Fish War," *Rand Journal of Economics*, 18: 596–610.

Chou, C. and J. Geanakoplos (1987), "On Finitely Repeated Games and Pseudo-Nash Equilibria," mimeo, Yale University.

Cooper, R. and A. Daughety (1988), "Cooperation in Infinite Horizon Games with Finitely Lived Players," mimeo, University of Iowa.

Crémer, J. (1986), "Cooperation in Ongoing Organizations," *Quarterly Journal of Economics*, 101: 33–49.

Cronshaw, M. and D. Luenberger (1990), "Subgame Perfect Equilibria in Infinitely Repeated Games with Perfect Monitoring and Discounting," mimeo, Stanford University.

Damme, E. van (1989), "Renegotiation-Proof Equilibria in Repeated Prisoners' Dilemma," *Journal of Economic Theory*, 47: 206–17.

DeMarzo, P. (1989), "Coalitions, Leadership and Social Norms: The Power of Suggestion in Games," Working Paper No. 85, Dept. of Finance, Kellogg School, Northwestern University.

Demougin, D. and A. Fishman (1988), "Efficient Budget Balancing Cartel Equilibria with Imperfect Monitoring," mimeo, University of Toronto.

Evans, G. and E. Maskin (1989), "Efficient Renegotiation-Proof Equilibria in Repeated Games," *Games and Economic Behavior*, 1: 361–9.

Farrell, J. (1984), "Credible Repeated Game Equilibria," mimeo.

Farrell, J. and E. Maskin (1989), "Renegotiation in Repeated Games," *Games and Economic Behavior*, 1: 327–60.

Forges, F., J. F. Mertens, and A. Neyman (1986), "A Counterexample to the Folk Theorem with Discounting," *Economics Letters*, 20: 7, 8.

Friedman, J. (1971), "A Noncooperative Equilibrium for Supergames," *Review of Economic Studies*, 38: 1–12.

(1985), "Cooperative Equilibria in Finite Noncooperative Supergames," *Journal of Economic Theory*, 35: 390–8.

Fudenberg, D. (1992), "Explaining Cooperation and Commitment in Repeated Games," in J.J. Laffont (ed.), *Advances in Economic Theory: Sixth World Congress*, Cambridge University Press.

Fudenberg, D. and D. Levine (1983), "Subgame Perfect Equilibria of Finite- and Infinite-Horizon Games," *Journal of Economic Theory*, 31: 251–63.

(1986), "Limit Games and Limit Equilibria," *Journal of Economic Theory*, 38: 261–79.

(1989), "Equilibrium Payoffs with Long-Run and Short-Run Players," mimeo, MIT and UCLA.

(forthcoming), "An Approximate Folk Theorem with Imperfect Private Information," *Journal of Economic Theory*.

Fudenberg, D., D. Levine, and E. Maskin (1989), "The Folk Theorem with Imperfect Public Information," mimeo, MIT and UCLA.

Fudenberg, D. and E. Maskin (1986), "The Folk Theorem in Repeated Games with Discounting or with Incomplete Information," *Econometrica*, 54: 533–56.

Fudenberg, D. and J. Tirole (1991), *Game Theory*, MIT Press.

Green, E. and R. Porter (1984), "Noncooperative Collusion under Imperfect Price Information," *Econometrica*, 52: 87–100.

Greenberg, J. (1990), *The Theory of Social Situations: An Alternative Game-Theoretic Approach*, Cambridge University Press.

Grief, A. (1989), "Reputation and Coalitions in Medieval Trade: Maghribi Traders," *Journal of Economic History*, 59: 857–82.

Grief, A., P. Milgrom, and B. Weingast (1990), "The Merchant Guild as a Nexus of Contracts," mimeo, Stanford University.

Güth, W., W. Leininger, and G. Stephan (1988), "On Supergames and Folk Theorems: A Conceptual Discussion," ZiF Working Paper, University of Bielefeld.

Hajivassiliou, V. (1989), "Testing Game-Theoretic Models of Price-Fixing Behavior," Cowles Foundation Discussion Paper No. 935, Yale University.

Harris, C. (1985), "Perfect Equilibrium in Infinite Horizon Games," *Journal of Economic Theory*, 37: 99–125.

Harsanyi, J. and R. Selten (1988), *A General Theory of Equilibrium Selection in Games*, Cambridge, MA: MIT Press.

Hart, O. and B. Holmström (1987), "The Theory of Contracts," chapter 3 in T. Bewley (ed.), *Advances in Economic Theory: Fifth World Congress*, Cambridge University Press.

Howard, R. (1960), *Dynamic Programming and Markov Processes*. New York: MIT and John Wiley.

Kandori, M. (1988), "Monotonicity of Equilibrium Payoff Sets with Respect to Observability in Repeated Games with Imperfect Monitoring," mimeo, Stanford University.

(1989a), "Repeated Games Played by Overlapping Generations of Players," mimeo, University of Pennsylvania.

(1989b), "Social Norms and Community Enforcement," CARESS Working Paper No. 89–14, University of Pennsylvania.

Jacquemin, A. and M. Slade (1989), "Cartels, Collusion and Horizontal Merger," chapter 7 in R. Schmalensee and R. Willig (eds.), *Handbook of Industrial Organization*, vol. 1. Amsterdam: North Holland.

Kreps, D. (1987), "Corporate Culture and Economic Theory," mimeo.

Kreps, D. and R. Wilson (1982), "Reputation and Imperfect Information," *Journal of Economic Theory*, 27: 253–79.

Krishna, V. (1987), "The Folk Theorems for Repeated Games," mimeo, Harvard Business School.

Lambson, V. (1987), "Optimal Penal Codes in Price-Setting Supergames with Capacity Constraints," *Review of Economic Studies*, 54: 385–98.

Lee, L.-F. and R. Porter (1984), "Switching Regression Models with Imperfect Sample Separation Information – with an Application on Cartel Stability," *Econometrica*, 52: 391–418.

Legros, P. (1989), "Efficiency and Stability in Partnerships," Ph.D. dissertation, California Institute of Technology.

Legros, P. and H. Matsushima (1990), "Efficiency, Limited Liability and Neutrality in Partnerships," mimeo, Cornell University.

Levenstein, M. (1989), "The Feasibility and Stability of Collusion: A Study of the Pre-World War I Bromine Industry," mimeo, Yale University.

MacLeod, B. and J. Malcomson (1988), "Reputation and Hierarchy in Dynamic Models of Employment," *Journal of Political Economy*, 96: 832–54.

(1989), "Implicit Contracts, Incentive Compatibility, and Involuntary Unemployment," *Econometrica*, 57: 447–80.

Matsushima, H. (1989), "Efficiency in Repeated Games with Imperfect Monitoring," *Journal of Economic Theory*, 48: 428–42.

(1990), "Structure of Renegotiation in Infinitely Repeated Games," mimeo, Stanford University.

Mertens, J. F. (1987), "Repeated Games," *Proceedings of the International Congress of Mathematicians*, 86: 1528–77, American Mathematical Society.

Milgrom, P., D. North, and B. Weingast (1990), "The Role of Institutions in the Revival of Trade: The Law Merchant, Private Judges, and the Champagne Fairs," *Economics and Politics*, 2:1–24.

Milgrom, P. and J. Roberts (1982), "Predation, Reputation, and Entry Deterrence," *Journal of Economic Theory*, 27: 280–312.

Mirrlees, J. (1974), "Notes on Welfare Economics, Information, and Uncertainty," in Balch, McFadden, and Wu (eds.), *Essays on Economic Behavior under Uncertainty*, Amsterdam: North Holland.

Nash, J. (1950), "Equilibrium Points in n-person Games," *Proceedings of the National Academy of Sciences, U.S.A.*, 36: 48–9.

Okuno-Fujiwara, M. and A. Postlewaite (1989), "Social Norms and Random Matching Games," mimeo, University of Pennsylvania.

Pearce, D. (1987), "Renegotiation-Proof Equilibria: Collective Rationality and Intertemporal Cooperation," Cowles Foundation Discussion Paper No. 855, Yale University.

Pearce, D. and E. Stacchetti (1988), "The Interaction of Implicit and Explicit

Contracts in Repeated Agency," Cowles Foundation Discussion Paper No. 892, Yale University.

Phelan, C. and R. Townsend (1991), "Computing Multiperiod, Information-Constrained Optima," *Review of Economic Studies*, 58: 853–82.

Porter, R. (1983a), "Optimal Cartel Trigger Price Strategies," *Journal of Economic Theory*, 29: 313–38.

(1983b), "A Study of Cartel Stability: The Joint Executive Committee, 1880–1886," *Bell Journal of Economics*, 14: 301–14.

Radner, R. (1980), "Collusive Behavior in Noncooperative Epsilon-Equilibria in Oligopolies with Long But Finite Lives," *Journal of Economic Theory*, 22: 136–54.

(1981), "Monitoring Cooperative Agreements in a Repeated Principal-Agent Relationship," *Econometrica*, 49: 1127–48.

(1985a), "Repeated Partnership Games with Imperfect Monitoring and No Discounting," *Review of Economic Studies*, 53: 43–58.

(1985b), "Repeated Principal-Agent Games with Discounting," *Econometrica*, 53: 1173–98.

Radner, R., R. Myerson, and E. Maskin (1986), "An Example of a Repeated Partnership Game with Discounting and with Uniformly Inefficient Equilibria," *Review of Economic Studies*, 53: 59–70.

Ray, D. (1989), "Internally Renegotiation-Proof Equilibrium Sets: Limit Behavior with Low Discounting," mimeo, Indian Statistical Institute, New Delhi.

Rey, P. and B. Salanie (1990), "Long-Term, Short-Term and Renegotiation: On the Value of Commitment in Contracting," *Econometrica*, 58: 597–620.

Rogoff, K. (1989), "Reputation, Coordination and Monetary Policy," in R. Barro (ed.), *Modern Business Cycle Theory*, Cambridge, MA: Harvard University Press.

Rotemberg, J. and G. Saloner (1986), "A Supergame-Theoretic Model with Price Wars During Booms," *American Economic Review*, 76: 390–407.

(1989), "Tariffs vs Quotas with Implicit Collusion," *Canadian Journal of Economics*, 22: 237–44.

Rubinstein, A. (1977), "Equilibrium in Supergames," Research Memorandum 25, Center for Research in Mathematical Economics and Game Theory, Hebrew University, Jerusalem.

(1979a), "Equilibrium in Supergames with the Overtaking Criterion," *Journal of Economic Theory*, 21: 1–9.

(1979b), "Offenses That May Have Been Committed by Accident – an Optimal Policy of Retribution," in S. Brams, A. Schotter, and G. Schwödiauer (eds.), *Applied Game Theory*, Würzburg: Physica-Verlag.

Rubinstein, A. and M. Yaari (1983), "Repeated Insurance Contracts and Moral Hazard," *Journal of Economic Theory*, 30: 74–97.

Sabourian, H. (1989), "Repeated Games: A Survey," in F. Hahn (ed.), *The Economics of Missing Markets, Information, and Games*, Oxford: Clarendon Press.

Salant, D. (1988), "A Repeated Game with Finitely Lived Overlapping Generations of Players," mimeo, GTE Labs.

Selten, R. (1965), "Spieltheoretische Behandlung eines Oligopolmodells mit Nachfrageträgheit," *Zeitschrift für die Gesamte Staatswissenschaft*, 121: 301–24.

(1973), "A Simple Model of Imperfect Competition Where 4 Are Few and 6 Are Many," *International Journal of Game Theory*, 3: 141–201.

(1975), "Reexamination of the Perfectness Concept for Equilibrium Points in Extensive Games," *International Journal of Game Theory*, 4: 22–55.

Slade, M. (1986), "Conjectures, Firm Characteristics, and Market Structure: An Empirical Analysis," *International Journal of Industrial Organization*, 4: 347–70.

(1987), "Interfirm Rivalry in a Repeated Game: An Empirical Test of Tacit Collusion," *Journal of Industrial Economics*, 35: 499–516.

(1989a), "Price Wars in Price-Setting Supergames," *Economica* 56: 295–310.

(1989b), "Strategic Pricing Models and Interpretation of Price-War Data," mimeo, University of British Columbia.

Smith, L. (1990), "Folk Theorems in Overlapping Generations Games," mimeo, University of Chicago.

Sorin, S. (1986), "On Repeated Games with Complete Information," *Mathematics of Operations Research*, 11: 147–60.

Syropoulos, C. (1989), "Cooperative Outcomes in Non-Cooperative Supergames of Trade Policy and the (Non) Equivalence of Tariffs and Quotas," Working Paper No. 1-89-2, Department of Economics, Pennsylvania State University.

von Neumann, J. and O. Morgenstern (1947), *Theory of Games and Economic Behavior*, 2nd edition. Princeton: Princeton University Press.

Weinberger, C. (1990), "Reputation and Strikes in an Ongoing Bargaining Relationship," mimeo, U.C. Berkeley.

Williams, S. and R. Radner (1987), "Efficiency in Partnership When the Joint Output Is Uncertain," mimeo, Northwestern University.

Comments on the interpretation of repeated games theory

Ariel Rubinstein

"The Theory of Repeated Games" has already been surveyed at a previous Econometric Society World Congress. Mertens and Aumman spoke on repeated games in 1980 in Aix-en-Provence (see Mertens, 1982). Drew and David's presentations contain far more economics and considerably more discussion on interpretation than we heard in Aix-en-Provence ten years ago. Those who attended the 1980 Congress will certainly share the feeling of being witness to an amazing revolution in the status of this subject, which has moved from the periphery of economic theory to its core. The strengthening of ties between repeated games theory and economic theory makes questions of interpretation more urgent. I would therefore like to take this opportunity to present a brief discussion of some of the most prominent issues.

Comment 1: On the connection between finite and infinite repeated games

I take the view that a model is an approximation of our *perception* of reality and not an approximation of an objective description of reality. I do not, for example, feel that an infinite repeated game can be seen as an approximation of the real life finite repeated game.

My thinking on repeated games has been influenced by the following passage taken from the pioneering work of Aumann (1959):

In the notion of a supergame that will be used in this paper, each superplay consists of an infinite number of plays of the original game G. On the face of it, this would seem to be unrealistic, but actually it is more realistic than the notion in which each superplay consists of a fixed finite (large) number of plays of G . . . Of course when looked at in the large, nobody really expects an infinite number of plays to take place; on the other hand, after each play we do expect that there will be more. A. W. Tucker has pointed out that this condition is mathematically equivalent to an infinite sequence of plays, so that is what our notion of supergames will consist of.

This statement constitutes the fundamental principle of the art of formal modeling. By using infinite horizon games we do not assume that the real world is infinite. Taking the view that models are not supposed to be isomorphic with reality, I see the infinitely repeated game model as a tool for analyzing situations where players examine a long-term situation without assigning a specific status to the end of the world. In contrast, the finitely repeated game model corresponds to a situation in which a finite period enters explicitly into the players' considerations. Using the terminology of formal logic, we can say that finite horizon models are only suitable for modeling situations in which the last period appears as an "individual constant" (a specified element) in the players' reasoning.

There is only a partial correspondence between the real length of a repeated game and the selection of a model with which to analyze it. Even short games may be better analyzed as infinite horizon games. When laboratory subjects receive instructions to play the prisoner's dilemma twenty times with payoffs of between one and four cents, it appears that the infinite horizon game describes their method of reasoning better than a twenty-period repeated game.

Since I view infinite and finite horizon repeated games as two separate models representing two very different scenarios, I have no difficulty with the discontinuities that exist between their outcomes and am unimpressed by the fact that the limit of a sequence of long finite horizon models constitutes an infinite horizon game. The significance or insignificance of the infinite model does not depend on a continuity result. A convergence result, when it exists, is nothing more than a convenient tool for approximating the perfect equilibrium outcomes of finite horizon models in cases where the horizon is very long.

Comment 2: What are folk theorems for?

Repeated game literature starts from the so-called folk theorems. This (inappropriate) name is given to theorems which state that, under certain conditions, nearly all reasonable payoff vectors can be sustained as equilibrium payoff vectors. This is interpreted to mean that under such conditions the model lacks predictive power. If so, it cannot be applied to economic models and is therefore useless.

I firmly disagree with this approach. I view folk theorems as a means of revealing the logic behind patterns of behavior associated with long-term interactions. Let me clarify my position through a very simple example of the repeated game version of the overlapping generations model (which was analyzed first by Peter Hammond (1975) and later by Cramer (1986), Salant (1988), Kandori (1990), and Lones Smith (1990)). Each player lives for only two periods. In his first period he produces two indivisible units of food and in the second none. The young person can contribute food to the old person. Each player is fully informed of all past events.

This model has one perfect equilibrium in which all young people behave selfishly and give nothing to their parents. There is, however, another perfect equilibrium whereby each young person gives one unit to his father. Should he fail to do so, his own son will in turn withhold food from him in his old age, while the grandson will behave as if it were the beginning of the game. This code of behavior requires one member of society to behave toward another in a manner which is conditional on the second member's behavior. This code of behavior requires a person to look not only at his father's action, but also at his motives. The mistreatment of one member of society by another does not always merit punishment.

Here we have a mini folk theorem. It does not, however, possess any predictive power. Its importance lies in its ability to verify the logic behind this type of intergenerational relationship, precisely in the same way that the classic overlapping generations model has clarified the role of money.

Comment 3: Strategies versus payoffs

In my opinion, the main contribution of repeated games lies in explaining those institutions which prevail in long-term interactions. Characterizing the exact set of equilibrium payoff vectors is therefore less important than discussing the equilibrium *strategies*. Unfortunately, most literature on repeated games deals with the details of the set of equilibrium *payoff* vectors while the plausibility of the strategies is ignored. Thus, for example, we do not mind proving the folk theorem concerning the limit of the means by suggesting an equilibrium in which a deviation at the n-th period is met with punishment for n^2 periods. We do it for the convenience of proving the folk theorem in its maximal range. In general, many of the surveyed papers include unintuitive strategies which lack reasonable verbal interpretations.

In order to clarify the nature of long-term interactions, we must deal with equilibrium strategies schemata. In referring to a scheme of strategy I allude to its structure, stripped of the details which arise from a particular payoff matrix. In this respect, the value of the early folk theorems lies exclusively in their ability to clarify the rationale of codes of behavior in which a deviator is punished for a finite number of periods before the world returns to routine behavior, and not in proving that each individual rational feasible payoff vector is sustained by some perfect equilibrium.

Few of the works on repeated games emphasize the structure of strategies. Abreu (1988) is an exception in this respect. Abreu shows that all equilibrium payoffs can be sustained by simple structured equilibria. The beauty of Dilip's work lies in its achievement of a major goal of economic theory – that of deriving simplicity from complexity.

Exploring the structure of the equilibrium strategies is also one of the main themes in the finite automata and repeated games literature which has not been surveyed here. Presenting a strategy as an automaton enables us to discuss more explicitly the structure of the strategies and to incorporate considerations of complexity into the model (see Rubinstein (1986) and Abreu and Rubinstein (1988)).

Comment 4: On the meaning of equilibrium

I would like to point out a change in the interpretation of equilibrium which has appeared in the recent repeated games literature. There are two possible interpretations of the actions planned by a repeated game player after a deviation. One interpretation, which is emphasized in the early repeated games literature, is a plan of punitive actions carried out by the non-deviators against the deviator. Another interpretation avoids the term punishment. A strategy describes a tree of changes in the social order caused by players' deviations. Thus, when a duopoly switches from a cooperative mode to the one-shot Cournot equilibrium, it is more of a change in the regime or norm rather than an act of punishment. This interpretation appears explicitly in Kandori (1989) and Okuno and Postlewaite (1989) on repeated games with pair-wised matches (see also Rubinstein and Wolinsky (1990) for a discussion of the closely related sequential models of bargaining and matching). The symmetric equilibrium which David describes is a more persuasive interpretation. The switch from a high payoff equilibrium to a low payoff continuation is more a change of the norm than punishment of the single deviator. In the model of one long-run player playing against many short-run players, a deviation of the long-run player is met with a change in the behavior of the short-run players. It is hard to interpret the change as a punishment since it is the behavior of a player who lives only once responding to something which has happened to another independent player and which may deter other players in future games after his death. I would argue, therefore, that an equilibrium in most of the surveyed literature should be interpreted as a method of switching between different social regimes which are constructed for protecting some form of social order.

Comment 5: The reputation models

In discussing reputation models, Drew argues that some outcomes are more plausible than others when they are close to the equilibria of repeated games in which a player, with some small probability, is of a type which is committed to a prespecified strategy. The literature covered by Drew is impressive; however, like Drew, I have doubts as to its effectiveness in isolating equilibria in repeated games. First, recall the important result of Fudenberg and Maskin (1986), which shows that we may support any payoff vector by choosing the proper type of "craziness." Second, the structure of the equilibrium strategies is problematic; the change in beliefs along the equilibrium is tailored to support sequential rationality but is highly unintuitive. Drew's argument only delivers the goods in situations where only one player can build a reputation. In contrast, as Drew points out, Aumann and Sorin (1989) had to limit the "crazy" players to those who remembered the actions of some prior K periods in order to derive strong results for even the most obvious coordination game. This is a very strong restriction since, by depending on the last state of mind rather than the last few outcomes, a player's behavior can result from events of the distant past. Allowing the "crazy" players to remember their previous states of mind (rather than the previous outcome) destroys the result completely. To summarize, I doubt that the reputation models are the vehicle for pointing out the more reasonable equilibria in a repeated game between two long-lived players.

Comment 6: Renegotiation proofness

David discusses the new subfield of repeated games and renegotiation proofness. I have two mild criticisms:

(1) If we require renegotiation proofness against the grand coalition renegotiation, why do we not require proofness against a deviation of a partial coalition? What is so special about coalitions of one player and those including all players?
(2) If renegotiation is possible, why do we not include the renegotiation moves in the model?

The first point calls for a comeback of cooperative game theory while the second calls for the reemergence of non-cooperative game theory.

Nevertheless, I feel this literature is of great value. Consider, for example, David's notion of an "acceptable deviation." It formalizes the following type of argument, often used in real life: We may object to pardoning a deviator, for fear of future deviators claiming the right to pardon based on this precedent. In real life, the main concern of this debate is over what constitutes a precedent. Different notions of precedent lead to different social orders. Thus, I view positively the existence of a multiplicity of solution concepts. They clarify the effect of having various notions of precedent. For me this is the essence of the theory. I would also add that the renegotiation literature (as well as the new approach suggested by Greenberg (1990)) is returning to the internal and external consistency ideas suggested by von Neumann and Morgenstern.

Comment 7: What next?

Whether we want to deepen our understanding of the institutions or whether we want to single out more plausible equilibria, I think that there is no escape from formulating the reasoning processes used by decision-makers, embedding complexity issues, and studying methods of learning. We have already seen the beginning of such a trend in research. I venture to suggest that this will be a central theme in the session on repeated games at the Econometric Society World Congress in the year 2000.

References

Abreu, D. (1988), "On the Theory of Repeated Games with Discounting," *Econometrica*, 56, 383–96.

Abreu, D. and A. Rubinstein (1988), "The Structure of Nash Equilibrium in Repeated Games with Finite Automata," *Econometrica*, 56, 1259–82.

Aumann, R.J. (1959), "Acceptable Points in General Cooperative N-Person Games," in R. D. Luce and A. W. Tucker (eds.), *Contributions to the Theory of Games IV*, Annals of Mathematics Studies, No. 40, Princeton University Press, pp. 287–324.

Aumann, R.J. and S. Sorin (1989), Cooperation and Bonded Recall", *Games and Economic Behavior* 1, 3–39.

Cramer, J. (1986), "Cooperation in Ongoing Organizations," *Quarterly Journal of Economics*, 101, 33–49.

Fudenberg, D. and E. Maskin (1986), "The Folk Theorem in Repeated Games with Discounting or with Incomplete Information," *Econometrica*, 54, 533–54.

Greenberg, J. (1990), *The Theory of Social Situations and Alternative Game Theoretic Approach*, Cambridge University Press.

Hammond, P. (1975), "Charity: Altruism or Cooperative Egoism", in E. Phelps (ed.), *Altruism, Morality and Economic Theory*, New York: Russel Sage Foundation.

Kandori, M. (1989), "Social Norms and Community Enforcement," Stanford University.

(1990), "Repeated Games Played by Overlapping Generations of Players," Princeton University and Pennsylvania University.

Mertens, J. F. (1982), "Repeated Games: An Overview of the Zero-Sum Case," in W. Hildenbrand (ed.), *Advances in Economic Theory*, Cambridge University Press.

Okuno-Fujiwara, M. and A. Postlewaite (1989), "Social Norms and Random Matching Games," mimeo, University of Tokyo and University of Pennsylvania.

Rubinstein, A. (1986), "Finite Automata Play the Repeated Prisoner's Dilemma," *Journal of Economic Theory* 39, 83–96.

(1991), "Comments on the Interpretation of Game Theory," *Econometrica*, 59, 909–24.

Rubinstein, A. and A. Wolinsky (1990), "Decentralized Trading, Strategic Behavior and the Walrasian Outcome," *Review of Economic Studies*, 57, 63–78.

Salant, D. (1988), "A Repeated Game with Finitely Lived Overlapping Generations of Players," GTE Laboratories and VPI.

Smith, L. (1990), "Folk Theorem in Overlapping Generations Games," University of Chicago.

CHAPTER 5

Implementation, contracts, and renegotiation in environments with complete information*

John Moore

READER'S GUIDE

Part one of the chapter is written in an easy style, to try to demystify the subject (it is based on the lecture given at the World Congress). The Biblical story of the Judgement of Solomon is used as a running example for presenting different notions of implementation. Inevitably, perhaps, this part of the chapter contains a number of statements that are rather loose. This is compensated for by the more formal part two, which amplifies certain results and topics – though here, too, some degree of detail has been sacrificed for the sake of readability.

The chapter deals with situations in which agents are presumed to have complete information about each other's preferences. Thomas Palfrey's chapter in this volume, "Implementation in Bayesian Equilibrium: The Multiple Equilibrium Problem in Mechanism Design," is a companion to this, and looks at environments with incomplete information.

Even though the complete-information environment is a restrictive case, the literature on it is vast and still growing. I have therefore had to be quite selective. The chapter should be seen as an overview of recent research, not as a comprehensive survey; I regret that I have not been able to do justice to the work of a number of authors.

PART ONE

The text is taken from the Old Testament: the First Book of Kings, chapter 3, verses 16–28. It is the story of the Judgement of Solomon. Two women came before the King, disputing who was the mother of a child. Quoting from the Jerusalem Bible:

"If it please you, my lord," one of the women said, "this woman and I live in the same house, and while she was in the house I gave birth to a child. Now it happened on the third day after my delivery that this woman also gave birth to a child. We were alone together; there was no one else in the house with us.... Now one night this woman's son died.... And in the middle of the night she got up and took my son from beside me while I was asleep; she put him to her breast and put her own dead son to mine. While I got up to suckle my child, there he was, dead. But in the morning I looked at him carefully, and he was not the child I had borne at all." Then the other woman spoke. "That is not true! My son is the live one, yours is the dead one"; and the first retorted, "That is not true! Your son is the dead one, mine is the live one." And so they wrangled before the king.... "Bring me a sword" said the king; and a sword was brought into the king's presence. "Cut the living child in two," the king said "and give half to one, half to the other." At this the woman who was the mother of the living child addressed the king, for she burned with pity for her son. "If it please you, my lord," she said "let them give her the child; only do not let them think of killing it!" But the other said, "He shall belong to neither of us. Cut him up." Then the king gave his decision. "Give the child to the first woman," he said "and do not kill him. She is his mother." All Israel came to hear of the judgement the king had pronounced, and held the king in awe, recognising that he possessed divine wisdom for dispensing justice.

That is an early example of implementation theory at work.[1]

The formal theory has its roots at least as far back as the 1930s and 1940s, with the Hayek–Mises–Lange–Lerner debates concerning the feasibility of market socialism.[2] In the 1950s and 1960s, Hurwicz took up these ideas and extended them to other mechanisms. It was he who pointed out that one should think of the mechanism as being the unknown – that is, the economic organization/institution by which economic activity is to be coordinated; and of the economic environment (technology, preferences, and endowments) as being the parameters, or coefficients. It is fair to say that Hurwicz is the father of modern implementation theory.[3] There were, however, other crucial earlier contributions. Hayek's classic 1945 paper focused attention on the informational requirements of mechanisms. Samuelson (1954, 1955) pointed out that individuals would want to misrepresent their preferences in the provision of public goods. J. Marschak (1954, 1955) began the theory of teams, systematically elaborated in Marschak and Radner (1972). The pioneering work by Farquharson (1957, published in 1969) on voting, and the work by Vickrey (1961) on auctions, were both forerunners of the later literature on implementation.

During these years, the questions that were asked mostly concerned the "big" issues, like: Are there alternative mechanisms to the price system which would lead not only to efficient but also to equitable outcomes? Can we interpret institutions that we see around us as examples of such mechanisms? Are these mechanisms able to perform well in a variety of economic environments, in particular, in those environments where the price mechanism breaks down – where there are externalities, increasing returns or non-convexities generally? What are the costs of running these mechanisms – can they be decentralized so as to reduce the informational requirements? And, perhaps the central question, how can we design mechanisms that are not vulnerable to strategic manipulation?[4]

In the past few years, the focus has shifted. Now the same theoretical apparatus is being applied to a set of economic problems which have a rather different orientation. Typically, these problems are small scale, in the sense that they involve only a few agents – often just two – and the problems are arguably more down to earth. Implementation theory is pertinent to many areas of economic analysis: public good provision, taxation, auction design, and monopoly pricing; voting theory, constitution design, and political science in general; and finally the whole area of bargaining, agency theory, contracts, and the theory of organizations.

In this chapter, I shall only have space to touch on some of these directly. But the wider implication should be clear: this is a branch of economic theory which has the potential for important practical application. What is more, the theory itself is intriguing.

I

So what exactly is implemention? Let us begin with King Solomon and his judicial dilemma. With some trepidation, I would like to suggest that his divine wisdom was a little flawed. One snag with his mechanism comes to mind straightaway: what would he have done had *both* women pleaded with him not to cut the child up? As it was, the day was saved because the woman who was not the mother of the living child did not behave as cleverly as she might, given the way Solomon was going to use the information. A better strategem for her would have been to mimic whatever the true mother did. Solomon's mechanism could not have coped with that – he would still be in the dark as to which of them was telling the truth.

Let us consider the problem more formally.

The two women are *agents*. Biblical exegetes cannot come up with their names, but I have taken the liberty of calling them Anna and Bess.

There are two possible *states of nature*, which we will call α and β. In state α, Anna is the mother of the living child; and in state β, Bess is the mother.

Solomon, the *planner*, only employed three possible *outcomes*:

a = Anna is given the child,
b = Bess is given the child,
c = The child is cut in half.

For future reference, I would like to include a fourth possible outcome in the set:

d = Anna, Bess, and the child are killed.

It is all very macabre, but c stands for cutting up the child and d stands for death all round.

We can safely presume that the women's preferences over the four outcomes are as follows:

Anna		Bess	
state α	state β	state α	state β
a	a	b	b
b	c	c	a
c	b	a	c
d	d	d	d

The convention is that if, for example, outcome b appears above outcome c in Anna's state α column, then this means that when she is the mother of the living child, she prefers that the child be given to Bess rather than cut in half. Notice that when Bess is the mother (state β), Anna's preferences over b and c are reversed. It is these reversals in the women's preferences that distinguish one state of nature from another.

Solomon would like that in state α, outcome a happens, and in state β, outcome b happens. To put this formally, Solomon has a *choice function f*, mapping from the set of states of nature, $\{\alpha,\beta\}$, to the set of outcomes $\{a,b,c,d\}$:

$$f(\alpha) = a$$
$$f(\beta) = b.$$

The crucial informational assumption is that both women know the state – that is, they know who is the mother of the living child. But Solomon does not know the state. His *implementation problem* is to devise a *mechanism*, or game form, g, which has the property that:

> when g is played in state α the unique equilibrium outcome is a,
> when g is played in state β the unique equilibrium outcome is b.

For the moment, I shall be deliberately vague about what I mean by "equilibrium." We will see that the choice of equilibrium concept turns out to be crucial.

The nub of the matter is that Solomon has to design the mechanism g independently of the state – because he does not know what the true state is.

Notice that we are requiring that the equilibrium outcomes be *unique*. It does not matter if, in any given state of nature, there is more than one pair of equilibrium strategies, provided all equilibria yield the same desired outcome; but equilibria leading to undesirable outcomes are not allowed.

The question of uniqueness is moot. We will see that the requirement of uniqueness can severely limit the set of choice functions that can be implemented. It could be argued that uniqueness of the equilibrium outcome does not matter, as long as the desired outcome is *an* equilibrium. (Presumably, this outcome might be a focal equilibrium, particularly if it involves the agents reporting the truth about their preferences.) For the most part, however, the implementation literature has not admitted this degree of leniency, even though it would make mechanism design a lot easier. One reason is that there may be unwanted equilibrium outcomes which, from the agents' perspective, Pareto dominate the equilibrium outcome which the planner wishes to implement.[5] We shall follow the literature and adopt the more stringent requirement of uniqueness of equilibrium outcome.

Another point of view would be that not only do we want there to be a unique equilibrium outcome, but also we want there to be a unique equilibrium – i.e., a unique pair of equilibrium strategies for each state of nature. This even more stringent requirement has generally not been imposed in the literature (although a number of recent mechanisms have satisfied it), and we shall not do so here.

II

The general implementation framework, then, is as follows. Consider an environment with agents $1, \ldots, i, \ldots, I$, and a set of feasible outcomes, or decisions, A. There are a number of possible states of nature, Θ. In a given state, the profile of agents' preferences over A is indexed by $\theta \in \Theta$.[6] A choice function f associates an outcome $f(\theta)$ to each θ in Θ. (More generally, f may take on many values, but for the moment we ignore choice correspondences.[7] We shall deal with these in part two.) A mechanism, or game form, g endows each agent with a strategy set, and maps each vector of strategies chosen by the agents into an outcome in A. The question is: given a choice function f, does there exist a mechanism g such that when the agents with preference profile indexed by θ play the corresponding game, the unique equilibrium outcome is $f(\theta)$? Notice that what gives the implementation problem its bite is that the mechanism g cannot be tailored to the profile θ; the same g has to cope with all profiles in Θ.

This framework encompasses an extraordinarily diverse number of situations. The most immediate example is that of a planner deciding on the level of provision of a public good, together with who should contribute what. In this case, θ indexes how much each household is willing to pay, and

$f(\theta)$ denotes both the scale of provision of the public good and the vector of contributions. Auction models, monopoly pricing, and many optimal taxation problems can all be couched in similar terms. Typically, in these examples the agents' (or households') individual preferences will be privately known, and so it would be appropriate to design the mechanism g so that $f(\theta)$ is a Bayesian equilibrium outcome under profile θ; see Thomas Palfrey's chapter in this volume.[8]

There are, however, circumstances in which the agents may know each other's preferences, even though the planner does not. Solomon's problem is a case in point. Also, consider a manager devising an incentive scheme for a team of I employees. θ indexes the employees' collective working environment. One might reasonably suppose that all the employees know θ even though the manager does not. In this chapter, I shall focus on such *complete information* environments.

More compelling examples of environments with complete information arise when there is no planner (auctioneer, monopolist, government, Solomon, or manager). Consider a club with I members designing its constitution – a mechanism g for making future decisions. Here $f(\theta)$ denotes the collective decision which they would like to take in the event that the members' future preferences are indexed by θ.[9] Typically g will be a voting procedure. It is designed *ex ante* by the I members for use *ex post* – i.e., once θ has been realized. Notice that we do not delve into the question of how the choice function f is chosen *ex ante*; we might presume that either the entire function f is a social standard on which all the club members agree *a priori*, or that it is the outcome of *ex ante* negotiation and compromise. The question arises: why not simply write a contract specifying that $f(\theta)$ should be enforced conditional on the realization θ? We assume that such a contract is infeasible because θ is never observed by outsiders – in particular, the courts.[10] Thus the club members have to resort to an indirect way to implement f, by using a mechanism g. The point is that g can be contractually enforced (e.g., by penalizing a member for not voting), whereas f cannot.

Of course, the agents could avoid specifying any mechanism, and instead negotiate an outcome once θ is known. However, although this may be *ex post* efficient, in general there will be inefficiencies *ex ante*. Consider two firms that are not vertically integrated. Let θ_1 index the upstream firm's *ex post* situation (which may include such things as input prices, productivity, and technology), and let θ_2 index the downstream firm's circumstances (e.g., its productivity, technology, and the state of demand for the final product). As in the club example, we suppose that, although both firms observe $\theta = (\theta_1, \theta_2)$, this is not observable to outsiders; so a contract cannot be conditioned on θ. $f(\theta)$ denotes the desired price and quantity of the goods traded, together with their quality, time of delivery, and so forth. An optimal $f(\theta)$ will involve not just efficient *ex post* trading, but also take into account certain key *ex ante* efficiency considerations such as risk sharing and/or inducing the firms to make appropriate (non-contractible) specific investments after they have signed the contract. The firms can settle the overall division of surplus by means of a side payment at the time of contracting.[11] Once this is settled, there is typically no ambiguity about the optimum f. But the point is that the firms must contractually specify a mechanism g which implements f; leaving decisions to *ex post* bargaining would in general not lead to the desired outcomes.

I postpone a fuller examination of this contractual example until section VII of part one. Before this, I want to demonstrate a number of different notions of implementation at work, in the context of Solomon's problem, each distinguished by the equilibrium concept employed.

Ideally, one would like to be able to implement the choice function f using the weakest of all concepts, dominant strategy equilibrium. The great merit of dominant strategy implementation is that it is robust – it assumes very little about agents. It does not ascribe to an agent any particular knowledge of what the other agents know, or any particular theory of how the other agents strategically behave. Unfortunately, the use of dominant strategies does not allow for very much flexibility in the design of mechanisms. We shall see in section 1 of part two that choice functions typically cannot be *both* efficient *and* strategy-proof (i.e., implementable in dominant strategy equilibrium) unless they are dictatorial. That is, desirable normative properties of choice functions usually have to be sacrificed in order to meet the stringent incentive requirements of dominant strategy implementation.

To make progress in implementing desirable choice functions, one may therefore need to make use of the fact that agents play strategically (in particular when, as here, they are presumed to have complete information about each other's preferences over the feasible set A). Just how this can be done will depend on what one assumes (or knows) about the way in which the agents strategically interact. At this point, implementation theory is on a different footing from game theory. Whereas game theory is concerned with how a *given* game will be played, implementation theory deals with the *design* of games. If a certain mechanism has awkward conceptual problems, and one cannot be sure how the agents will play it, then one is free to abandon it and try another mechanism. The choice of mechanism will be driven by the choice of equilibrium concept. Understandably, the literature has been preoccupied with conventional notions of equilibrium – implementation in Nash equilibrium, subgame perfect equilibrium, undominated Nash equilibrium, iteratively undominated equilibrium, and the like. However, one's preference may be for cooperative equilibrium concepts, or for evolutionary stability, or for myopic behavior in an adjustment process. No matter, one could still examine what could be implemented using, say, an adjustment mechanism g in which agents behaved myopically.[12] The literature has burgeoned recently, largely because researchers have been picking off an ever wider set of equilibrium concepts. This is not an unhealthy development, particularly given the lack of any strong consensus about how games are played. Implementation theory should, I believe, be largely driven by applications; and in principle each application should bring with it some assumption about how the agents in that specific situation will plausibly behave.

III

We start by looking at Nash implementation.

The pathbreaking work on Nash implementation was done by Maskin in 1977. If Solomon had had the benefit of Maskin's advice, he could have been told that his choice function f is not Nash implementable. Let us see why (see figure 5.1).

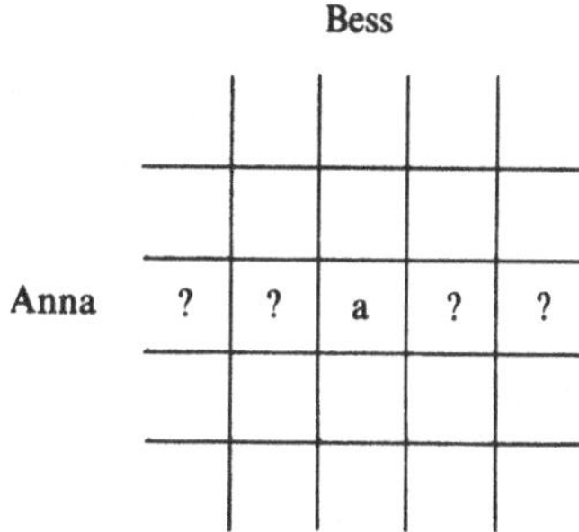

Figure 5.1

This matrix represents a potential mechanism. Anna plays the rows, Bess the columns. The entries in the matrix are the *outcomes* of the mechanism (not payoffs). a is to be the equilibrium outcome in state α. So a must appear somewhere in the matrix. What about the rest of the row containing this a? Remember that in state α Bess strictly prefers b or c to a, so we cannot put either b or c in this row. That leaves us with just a's or d's. But then think how the mechanism would be played in the other state, β. a is Anna's top preference, and Bess prefers a to d. This means that a is an equilibrium outcome in state β too. But then the mechanism is not working: a should not be an equilibrium outcome in state β. Solomon cannot implement his choice function f in Nash equilibrium.

The reason why f is not Nash implementable is that it does not satisfy a condition called monotonicity. Roughly speaking, monotonicity requires that if, as here, the desired outcome $f(\alpha) = a$ moves up both women's rankings in switching from state α to state β, then a must continue to be the desired outcome in state β. But in Solomon's problem, $f(\beta) = b \neq a$. The logic is simple: if nothing beats outcome a (in the sense of being ranked higher for some agent) in state β which did not already beat it (for the same agent) in state α, then the equilibrium strategies which yield outcome a in state α will also constitute a Nash equilibrium in state β.

Maskin's remarkable contribution was to prove that if there are three or more agents then monotonicity is not only necessary but is also, for most practical purposes, sufficient for the choice rule to be Nash implementable. More details of Nash implementation are given in section 2 of part two.

IV

Notice that if Solomon uses a single-stage mechanism like this, he faces the problem of too many equilibria. (Generally speaking, this is *the* main problem in designing a good mechanism: getting rid of unwanted equilibria.) However, in the Bible, Solomon did not use a single-stage mechanism, he used a *multi*-stage mechanism:

> the first woman said something,
> *then* the second retorted,
> *then* Solomon asked for a sword,
> *then* the first woman pleaded with him not to cut the child in half,
> *then* the second woman spoke, and
> *finally* Solomon made his judgment.

The advantage of a multi-stage mechanism like this is that we can insist the agents' strategies have to be credible; i.e., we can restrict attention to the *subset* of Nash equilibria that are subgame perfect. Since the problem with single-mechanisms is that they have too many Nash equilibria, it may therefore be helpful to add stages.

Sad to say for Solomon, we now know from recent research (Moore and Repullo, 1988; Abreu and Sen, 1990) that even adding stages does not solve his problem. If Solomon insists on using just the four outcomes a, b, c, and d, then he cannot solve his judicial dilemma by designing a stage mechanism and applying subgame perfection. In section 3.1 of part two it is explained why not.

V

Solomon might ask for a second opinion from Palfrey and Srivastava, who have recently taken a closer look at Nash implementation (Palfrey and Srivastava, 1991). They have thrown in the extra requirement that agents would never use weakly dominated strategies in equilibrium – which, it might be argued, is a sensible-enough restriction. The following diabolically clever mechanism implements Solomon's choice function in undominated Nash equilibrium:

Each woman has to announce:

> *either* "it is state α" (i.e., Anna is the mother)
> *or* "it is state β" (i.e., Bess is the mother)
>
> together with an integer from $\{1,2,3,\ldots,\}$.

If they disagree on their announced state then outcome d is implemented.

If they announce the same state, the outcome is determined according to figure 5.2.

Both announce α

Anna's integer \ Bess's integer	1	2	3	4	.
1	a	a	a	a	.
2	c	a	a	a	.
3	c	c	a	a	.
4	c	c	c	a	.
.	.	.	.	.	.

Both announce β

Anna's integer \ Bess's integer	1	2	3	4	.
1	b	c	c	c	.
2	b	b	c	c	.
3	b	b	b	c	.
4	b	b	b	b	.
.	.	.	.	.	.

Figure 5.2

The mechanism works as follows. Imagine placing each woman in a separate cell – out of earshot of one another. Each woman has to shout out who is the true mother. If they both shout Anna – i.e., "it is state α" – then the outcome is given by the left-hand matrix. Likewise, if they both shout Bess, the outcome is given by the right-hand matrix. In the matrices, we represent how loudly a woman shouts – or, equivalently, for how long she shouts – by a number 1,2,3,... If they both shout Anna, then she gets the child – unless she shouts louder or longer than Bess, in which case the child is cut in half. Similarly, if they both shout that Bess is the true mother, then she gets the child – unless she shouts louder or longer than Anna, in which case again the child is cut in half. A way to remember all this is: if Solomon hears a woman shouting on and on, he figures: "methinks she doth protest too much," and he proceeds to cut the child in half. If they disagree on who is the true mother, it is death all round, so that cannot be an equilibrium (since either woman would do better to agree with the other, whatever integers are announced).

The analysis is quite simple. In state α, Anna has no undominated strategy if they both say Bess: she would always want to shout a little louder or a little longer. If Anna is the true mother, the only undominated Nash equilibrium is the top left-hand corner of the left-hand matrix, where she gets the child: in this equilibrium they both whisper "Anna." So the truth is out. Similarly, in state β they both whisper "Bess." Palfrey and Srivastava have solved Solomon's dilemma for him.

What would Solomon say? One might guess that he would have been impressed by the ingenuity of all this, but he would probably have cut off Palfrey and Srivastava's heads too, for being too clever by half. Solomon was a practical King, who wanted practical solutions. (However, mechanisms which discriminate between people on the basis of how much fuss they create are not unknown – as an intriguing news item from the *Los Angeles Times* illustrates.[13])

VI

At this point, had Solomon hired an economist as a consultant, he or she would no doubt be tempted to introduce money, and side payments, as a lubricant – on the grounds that everyone has their price. In the context of babies, this seems sordid, but it works.

Luckily we can avoid all the unsavoury aspects of Solomon's mechanism. In fact, we can put the sword away completely and concentrate just on outcomes a and b.

For simplicity, let us assume a certain degree of symmetry. Consider the true mother of the living child. No matter whether this is Anna or Bess, we will assume that she attaches a money value, v^{m}, say, to her getting the child rather than the other woman. And the woman who is not the mother attaches a money value, v^{n}, say, to her getting the child. We will also assume there are no wealth effects in the domain of interest.

The women know each other's valuations (which may be anything), but Solomon knows nothing beyond the fact that $v^{m} > v^{n}$.[14] Nevertheless, he can exploit this fact.

Remember that Solomon's aim is to give the child to its true mother. It is not part of his choice function that the mother should make any payment – that is what stops him from simply using an auction or getting the women to bargain. The following mechanism works (see figure 5.3):[15]

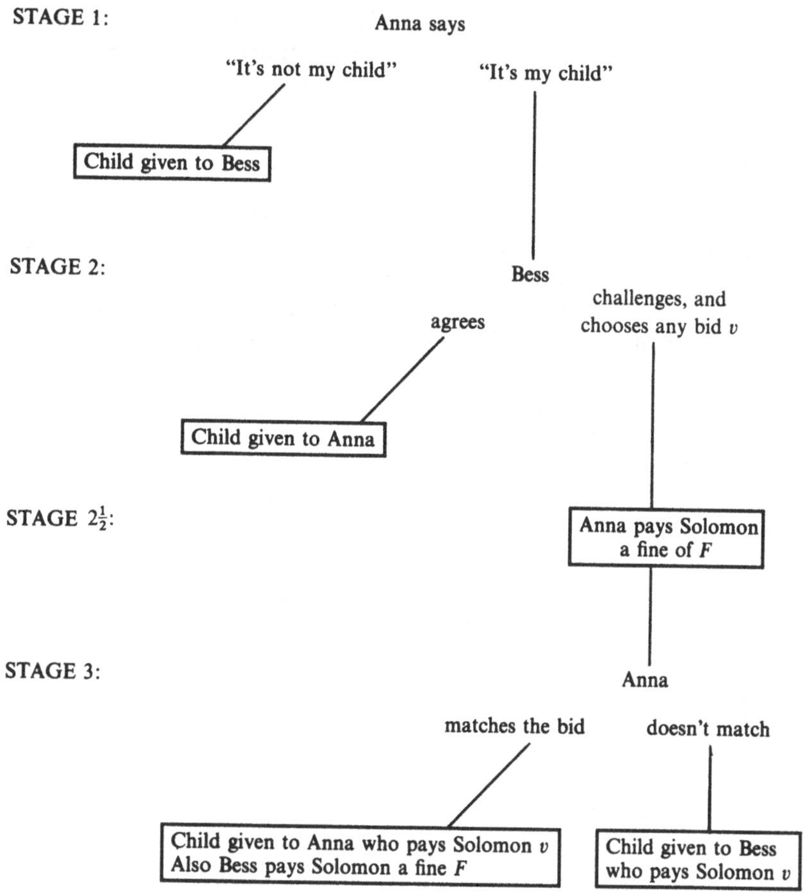
STAGE 1:
Anna says
"It's not my child"
"It's my child"
Child given to Bess
STAGE 2:
Bess
agrees
challenges, and
chooses any bid v
Child given to Anna
STAGE $2\frac{1}{2}$:
Anna pays Solomon
a fine of F
STAGE 3:
Anna
matches the bid
doesn't match
Child given to Anna who pays Solomon v
Also Bess pays Solomon a fine F
Child given to Bess
who pays Solomon v

Figure 5.3

The mechanism starts with Anna, who announces whether or not it is her child. If she says not, the child is given to Bess and the mechanism ends. If she says it is her child, Bess has to agree or challenge. If Bess agrees, the child is given to Anna, and the mechanism ends. If Bess challenges, then she has to put in a bid for the child – say she bids an amount v. Anna is fined a fixed amount $F>0$ whenever she is challenged, after which she must choose between either matching the bid and getting the child by paying Solomon v, or dropping out, in which case the child is given to Bess who pays Solomon v. If Anna does match Bess's bid, then Bess is fined F too.

It is important to stress that before the women play the mechanism,

Solomon explains to them the details of all its stages. That way, the women know what is at stake, and are not led into any traps. In this respect, the Bible story seems a little different – Solomon seems to have pulled a fast one when he decided not to cut the child in half.

Notice that, if she can get away with it, Anna would always want to claim that it is her child at stage 1, no matter who is actually the mother.

Suppose that she is the mother – i.e., suppose that it is state α. Then Bess will not challenge at stage 2. After all, what could Bess bid? If Bess loses the auction – in the sense that her bid is matched by Anna at stage 3 – then she ends up being fined F and not even getting the child; she would be better off simply acquiescing at stage 2. Bess's only prospect of getting the child would be to bid more than Anna's valuation, so that Anna drops out at stage 3. But why should Bess bid that much, when it is not her child and she does not value it as highly as Anna does?

In short, if Anna is the mother, she can tell the truth with equanimity at stage 1, and get the child without paying anything in equilibrium. This is just what Solomon wants.

Things work differently if Bess is the mother – i.e., if it is state β. Suppose that Anna has lied at stage 1, and claimed that the child is hers. Now there *is* a bid that Bess can safely make at stage 2. As long as she puts in a bid that is a little above Anna's valuation, Bess will get the child for less than it is worth to her. Anna will end up being fined F at stage $2\frac{1}{2}$ and not even getting the child. Realizing this, Anna will not lie at stage 1; she will simply give the child to Bess, who pays nothing. Again, this is just what Solomon wants.

To summarize: here we have a mechanism which solves Solomon's dilemma for him. The mechanism is fully explained to the women in advance: there is no need to trick them.[16] And they will play it differently depending on who is the true mother. If Anna is the mother, then in equilibrium Anna first will say that it is her child, and then Bess will agree. But if Bess is the mother, then in equilibrium Anna will simply say at the outset that it is Bess's child.

A number of comments about the mechanism:

First, notice that the later stages of the mechanism merely provide suitable threats to sustain the required equilibrium outcomes. They are never actually reached in equilibrium.

Second, one reason why the mechanism works so well is that it is played in stages. Notice that in state β there is a *second* Nash equilibrium in which Anna always threatens to match any bid for the child at stage 3, no matter how high that bid is. This threat deters Bess from challenging at stage 2, because of the fine of F that would be imposed on her if Anna matches her bid. But the threat is not credible in state β – if it came to the crunch Anna would not match a high enough bid – and we should rule it out. We are restricting our attention to those Nash equilibria that are subgame perfect.

Third, there is no need for the fine F to be large. Indeed, it would be enough if F were arbitrarily small (but positive). This means that we could essentially drop the assumption that there are no wealth effects.

Fourth, the mechanism works even in the more general case where the women do not know each other's valuations precisely. (Of course, in this case, it would be inappropriate to expect the women to play a Nash equilibrium. We should instead perhaps look at the perfect Bayesian equilibrium.) All that matters is that the true mother's valuation is strictly greater than the other woman's valuation with probability one.[17] In fact, it is possible to adjust the mechanism so that it can handle certain non-symmetries (e.g., the values of v^{m} and v^{n} may vary between the two women).

Fifth, the reason why subgame perfect implementation could not solve Solomon's original problem (as was claimed in section IV above) is that Solomon did not, or perhaps could not, use money; it is the fact that money can be exchanged, and fines levied, which makes the problem much easier. To be more precise: money places considerable structure on agents' preferences over feasible outcomes. This additional structure facilitates the implementation of a much wider class of choice functions.

Before I move on, let me point out that mechanisms with side payments like the one we have just analyzed have been used in practice, though it was a long time ago. In Athens in the fifth and fourth centuries BC, at the time of their festivals, the wealthiest man in the city (it was never a woman) had to sponsor a theatrical production known as the *choregia*. The problem was, although everyone had a shrewd idea as to who was the wealthiest man, the man concerned might be slow to step forward. However they had a mechanism to deal with this. Someone nominated the man who was reputed to be the richest. Let us call him Spyros. Spyros would then have to pay up graciously, or claim "I am not the richest, old Timon over there is richer than me. Let him pay for the choregia!" (This was known as the *antidosis* procedure.) If Spyros threw down the gauntlet like this, then Timon was faced with a choice. Either he could pay for the theatre. Or, and this is the interesting bit, he could insist that Spyros put his money where his mouth was. That is, Timon could insist that Spyros exchange all his wealth with him – after which Spyros would have to pay for the theatre.

It is a simple argument to show that the threat of exchange was enough to ensure that the richest man did indeed foot the bill.[18]

This method of taxation was known as a *liturgy* – meaning a service that one performs. And it was used to finance other things too: equipping warships (*treirarchy*), the maintenance of a horse for military purposes (*hippotrophia*), providing facilities for athletes (*gymnasiarchy*), and paying for a tribal banquet at festivals (*hestiasis*).[19]

The liturgical system became widespread, as a means of taxing the rich. The Romans appear not to have continued with the antidosis procedure as such. Instead, they used a simpler mechanism to ensure payment. A nominating official appointed someone to a liturgy. If that person refused – and was unsuccessful in proving either that he had immunity[20] or that he had been maliciously nominated instead of another better qualified person – then he had to surrender all his property to the nominating official, *who then paid the liturgic tax in full*. That is, the nominator was made responsible for his choice.[21] On occasion, though, the surrender of property (*cessio bonorum*) was less than complete: the person nominated was allowed to keep back up to a third of his wealth.[22]

VII

It is important to realize that in the previous section we managed to get away with using a very simple mechanism, with small fines, only because the two women's preferences took such a particular form. In general, even if there is money and preferences are quasi-linear, we typically cannot implement what we want unless we use a more complex mechanism, with significantly large fines. Nonetheless, we can achieve a great deal this way – as we shall see.

Now is the time to leave the ancient world, and to look at a more conventional class of economic models. We return to the contractual example given in section II above. Recall that one of the principal distinctions between a contract model and, say, Solomon's problem is that the latter has a planner (Solomon), whereas the former does not. The contract model is of central importance to a number of branches of economics, over and above the pure theory of contracts – for example, to bargaining; to the theory of organizations; and to voting and constitution design. The next three sections will be devoted to a discussion of the issues surrounding implementation via contracts.

Consider two firms that are not vertically integrated. The upstream firm 1, the seller, supplies goods to the downstream firm 2, the buyer. Denote the quantity supplied by q, and the price paid by p. The seller's *ex post* profits are:

$$p - c(q, \theta_1),$$

where c is a cost function, indexed by a variable, θ_1, say. And the buyer's *ex post* profits are:

$$v(q,\theta_2) - p,$$

where v is a (monetary) benefit function, indexed by another variable, θ_2. Thus, what we call the "state of nature" $\theta \in \Theta$ is the pair (θ_1,θ_2). Of course, the underlying state of nature, $\omega \in \Omega$, say, will be much richer than θ; ω will include all information such as the state of demand, the prices of raw materials, what other firms in the industry are doing, changes to technologies, etc. Ω will typically be complex, and of high dimension. Θ is a coarse partition of Ω which merely indexes the firms' costs and benefits (and their knowledge about each other's costs and benefits).

At the time of contracting, *ex ante*, there may be any degree of statistical dependence between θ_1 and θ_2, ranging from independence to perfect correlation.

Although we shall be thinking of q as a quantity, there is no need to interpret it that narrowly. I shall put almost no structure at all on the cost and value functions c and v – so q could in principle include such things as quality, technical specification, the time of delivery, and so forth.

The firms will in general want the quantity and price to be functions of the state θ. For example, they may well want to implement the bilaterally efficient decision $q(\theta)$, say, which maximizes their joint surplus $v(q,\theta) - c(q,\theta)$, together with the transfer $p(\theta)$, say, which provides the best incentives for the firms to take *ex ante* investments.[23] In that case the choice function that the firms want to implement is $f = (q,p)$.

How can the firms implement this choice function? The simplest way would be to write a contract specifying the terms of trade – that is, a contract contingent on θ specifying that the quantity $q(\theta)$ should be traded at the price $p(\theta)$. However, in reality, a fully contingent contract can be ruled out in many cases. Although the firms may observe their cost and benefit functions – i.e., observe θ – *ex post*, outsiders may not; in the event of a dispute, the courts would then be unable to verify that some particular θ had occurred.[24]

It is conceivable that the courts may be able to observe, and therefore verify, all the components of the underlying ω *ex post*. If so, the firms might in principle specify a quantity and a price contingent on the realization of $\omega \in \Omega$. But, given a highly complex Ω, this could entail huge transaction costs in simply writing the contract down in the first place. In short, it would be impractical to specify q,p as a function of ω – or, for that matter, θ as a function of ω.

Thus, although the firms would ideally like to write a fully contingent contract, it may be at best too expensive, or at worst useless, to try. They will inevitably end up writing a contract which is incomplete.

Can their situation be rescued? That is, can the firms write an incomplete contract which is effective? At this juncture, they can turn to implementation theory.

What the firms need is a mechanism – a mechanism that implements their choice function $f=(q,p)$. The whole point of a mechanism is that it is defined independently of the state of the world: if they can find a mechanism g that works, all the firms then have to do is to specify it in their contract. That is, *ex ante*, they write a contract of the form:

> CONTRACT
>
> We, the undersigned, agree to play the mechanism g tomorrow (*ex post*). If one party refuses to play, that party will incur a crippling fine, which is given to the other party.
>
> *Signed*: Firm 1 (Seller)
> Firm 2 (Buyer)

Notice that this is not a contingent contract, since the firms have committed themselves to play the same mechanism in all states. Moreover, the contract will be enforceable, because the courts can ascertain whether or not the mechanism was played, and if not, who was at fault.

To summarize: if the firms can find a mechanism that implements their choice function $f=(q,p)$, then they can sidestep the problem of having to write any statements contingent on $\omega \in \Omega$ in their contract.

Happily, there *is* such a mechanism.[25] And it does not matter much what the functions q and p actually are. (There is no need, for example, that $q(\theta)$ should equal the bilaterally efficient level.) The mechanism has some similarity to the one we used earlier to solve Solomon's problem.

Broadly, there are three stages (the first two of which have substages): The first stage elicits firm 1's type θ_1. The second stage elicits firm 2's type θ_2. Once $\theta=(\theta_1,\theta_2)$ is known, at the third stage the choice function $f(\theta)=(q(\theta),p(\theta))$ is implemented. The first two stages are symmetric, so I shall concentrate on stage 1. Refer to figure 5.4.

The claim is that, for finite Θ, this mechanism will implement the desired quantity $q(\theta)$ and price $p(\theta)$ in each state $\theta \in \Theta$ provided the fine F is large enough, and $\varepsilon>0$ is small enough.[26]

The argument is as follows. Consider firm 1 at stage 1.1, deciding whether or not to announce the truth about its own preferences. Firm 1 is worried about being challenged at stage 1.2, because, whatever the test pair (q,p), $(\hat{q},\hat{p})$ picked by firm 2, the mechanism will end at stage 1.3 by firm 1 having to pay a fine of F. For large enough F, this is an outcome which firm 1 would want to avoid if at all possible. The question is: will firm 2 challenge?

If firm 1 announces the truth, and firm 2 challenges, then whatever the

STAGE 1 (eliciting firm 1's costs):

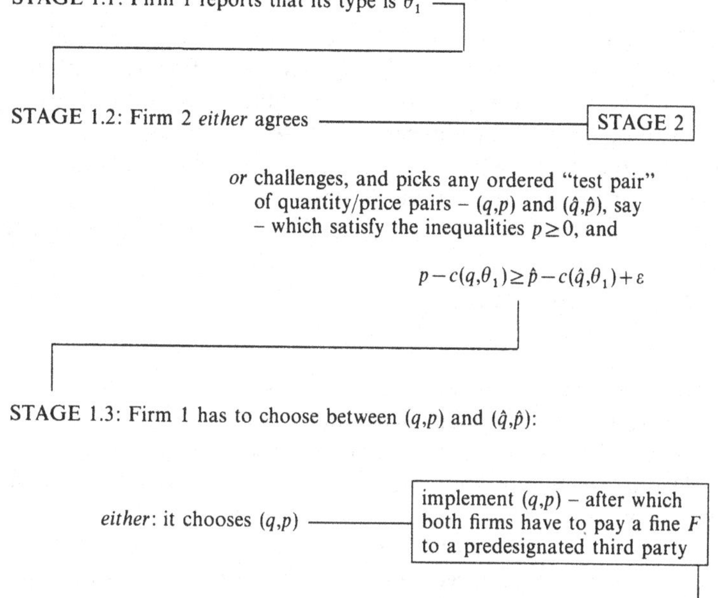
STAGE 1.1: Firm 1 reports that its type is θ_1
STAGE 1.2: Firm 2 *either* agrees
STAGE 2
or challenges, and picks any ordered "test pair" of quantity/price pairs – (q,p) and $(\hat{q},\hat{p})$, say – which satisfy the inequalities $p \geq 0$, and
$p - c(q,\theta_1) \geq \hat{p} - c(\hat{q},\theta_1) + \varepsilon$
STAGE 1.3: Firm 1 has to choose between (q,p) and $(\hat{q},\hat{p})$:
either: it chooses (q,p)
implement (q,p) – after which both firms have to pay a fine F to a predesignated third party

or: it chooses $(\hat{q},\hat{p})$

implement $(\hat{q},\hat{p})$ – after which firm 1 has to pay a fine F to firm 2

STOP

STAGE 2: (eliciting firm 2's benefits): Same as STAGE 1, except reverse the roles of firms 1 and 2. Any test pair (q,p), $(\hat{q},\hat{p})$ must now satisfy the inequalities $p \leq 0$ and $v(q,\theta_2) - p \geq v(\hat{q},\theta_2) - \hat{p} + \varepsilon$ if firm 2 announces θ_2 at stage 1.2.

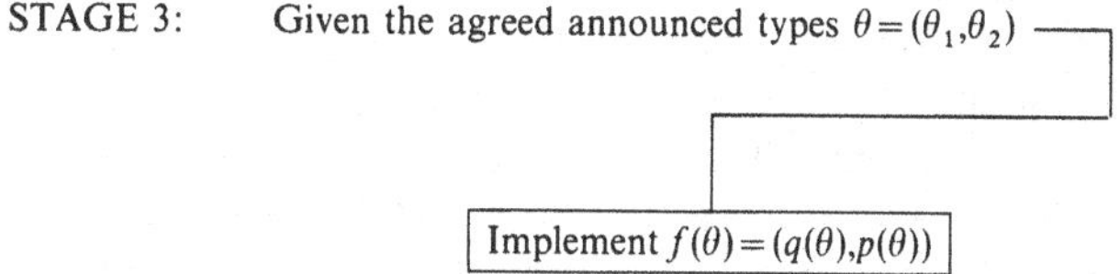
STAGE 3: Given the agreed announced types $\theta = (\theta_1,\theta_2)$
Implement $f(\theta) = (q(\theta),p(\theta))$

Figure 5.4

test pair (q,p), $(\hat{q},\hat{p})$ which firm 2 picks, firm 1 will choose (q,p) at stage 1.3, since any permissible test pair must satisfy:

$$p-c(q,\theta_1)-F>\hat{p}-c(\hat{q},\theta_1)-F.$$

Thus firm 2 – along with firm 1 – will be fined F. For large enough F, firm 2 would be better off not challenging. (Some lower bound on p is important, so that firm 2, the buyer, does not make unlimited money from (q,p) to offset a fine of F. That is why any permissible test pair must satisfy $p \geq 0$.)

If firm 1 lies, then firm 2 will be able to make a challenge which leads to a reward of F. For suppose the truth is ϕ_1; then, given a small enough $\varepsilon>0$, firm 2 can pick a test pair (q,p) and $(\hat{q},\hat{p})$ satisfying the following "preference reversal":

$$p-c(q,\theta_1)\geq\hat{p}-c(\hat{q},\theta_1)+\varepsilon$$
$$p-c(q,\phi_1)<\hat{p}-c(\hat{q},\phi_1).$$

(There must exist a preference reversal if θ_1 differs from the truth ϕ_1.[27]) The second of these inequalities means that firm 1 will choose $(\hat{q},\hat{p})$ at stage 1.3: the fact that firm 1 pays out F subsequently will not affect its choice. Firm 2 receives F from firm 1; and so for large enough F, this is an outcome which firm 2 will want.

In sum, firm 2 challenges if and only if firm 1 lies. Knowing this, firm 1 announces the truth, firm 2 agrees, and the mechanism proceeds to stage 2. By the same argument, firm 2 announces the truth at stage 2.1, firm 1 agrees at stage 2.2, and the mechanism proceeds to stage 3 where the desired quantity and price are implemented. The mechanism works, as claimed.

The power of the mechanism again lies in the fact that it is played in stages. Look at stage 1.3: firm 1 would like to be able to commit itself always to choose the pair (q,p) – because then firm 2 would be fined F, which will always deter firm 2 from challenging at the previous stage, 1.2. Armed with this threat, firm 1 can announce whatever it pleases at stage 1. But the threat is not credible. Once again, we have singled out just one of the many Nash equilibria by imposing subgame perfection.

The fine F has to be big enough both to deter lying and to encourage challenges in the event of lying. In this respect, the mechanism differs from the one we used to solve Solomon's problem; there, recall, the fine could have been arbitrarily small.

The fact that F has to be large calls into question our assumption that there are no wealth effects – that is, our assumption that ordinal (risk-free) preferences are quasi-linear in income. But an inspection of the mechanism reveals that we are not using this linearity in any essential way. Roughly speaking, all that we need is that one agent can be adequately rewarded by sufficiently penalizing another agent. In effect, if the choice function is thought to be in a "payoff box," then more extreme allocations, outside this box, must be feasible. This is a plausible enough requirement.

The mechanism is in fact rather general. Almost no restrictions have been placed on the dimensionality of q, preferences over q, or the choice function f. A mechanism like this could in principle be used in many situations, not just in a contract model. One application would be to the provision of a public good, q. We can easily generalize the mechanism to have many stages – in the extreme, we could have a stage to elicit, in turn, each citizen's willingness to pay. $(p_1, \ldots, p_I)$ would then be a vector of contributions, which will balance the cost of supplying q (rather than to zero, as in the above contract example; the efficacy of the mechanism does not depend on having the transfers sum to zero). In fact, there is a small advantage to having more than two agents playing the mechanism: if, for example, agent 1 were ever to pick (q,p) at stage 1.3, the total fine $2F$ can be shared out among the agents $3, \ldots, I$, rather than given to a predesignated outside third party. That is, the mechanism can be balanced both on and off the equilibrium path.[28]

For most public goods applications, it would be preposterous to assume that every citizen knows everyone else's preferences. However, we do not need to assume anything like that much information. Look back to stage 1 of the mechanism. We were able to discover firm 1's preferences by turning to firm 2 for corroboration. This is a general feature: all the mechanism requires is that for each person, there is at least one other person who knows his or her preferences (and the identity of this other person is known *ex ante*).

Let me summarize what I think this mechanism broadly delivers. For a public goods or contract model without wealth effects, almost anything can be implemented as long as for each agent there is another agent who knows his preferences. Moreover, quasi-linearity of preferences is not all that critical – usually wealth effects will not matter.

Some caveats are in order. First, what this conclusion forgets is that parties who know each other's preferences are usually in enduring relationships, and their long-run interests militate against taking short-run gains – one party challenging the other in order to get the reward F. (Although, taking the assumption of quasi-linearity literally, the fine F could be made large enough to make short-term gains/losses outweigh longer-term interests.)

Second, there is a danger that agents have somewhat less than complete information about each other's preferences, which could lead to gross inefficiencies. Nonetheless, all may not be lost: it is likely that, in any given application, there would be considerably more structure on preferences, which can be exploited. (The strength of the above example comes from the fact that it places so few restrictions on preferences; but this is its weakness too.) Also, if there is some degree of incomplete information, we can broaden the scope of the analysis to consider Bayesian implementation. Other similar, but less jagged and more robust, mechanisms may be available.

VIII

A third caveat about what we have done is more basic, and concerns the use of subgame perfection in this context: in practice, would the agents actually play according to their subgame perfect equilibrium strategies? Arguably, this is placing more weight on the game theory than it can bear. We ought not to posit "rational" forms of strategic behavior which we fear are either too clever or too open to question. Here is an "irrational" strategy for the above mechanism which has a ring of truth:

> Firm 1 – having, say, lied at stage 1.1 – is sufficiently annoyed by a challenge from firm 2 at stage 1.2 that it simply wants to drag firm 2 down with it. Accordingly, it chooses (q,p) at stage 1.3 out of pique in order that both of them are fined, rather than allowing firm 2 to collect the reward.
>
> If agent 2 thinks that this is how firm 1 will behave, then firm 2 will not challenge. But then firm 1 can lie with impunity. Indeed, the very fact that firm 1 does lie at stage 1.1 suggests to firm 2 that firm 1 may be about to behave in this "irrational" manner at stage 1.3.

(Notice how firm 1's "irrationality" is working to its advantage![29])

One of the difficulties here is that within stage 1 of the mechanism, firm 1 may end up playing twice – at stages 1.1 and 1.3. (This is even leaving aside stage 2.) If firm 1 plays "irrationally" at stage 1.1, what is firm 2 to deduce about firm 1's likely subsequent behavior at stage 1.3?[30]

It would be good to sidestep this kind of problem, and use mechanisms in which agents take turns to play, but only play once each. Unfortunately, not as much can be implemented in this way. But it may be helpful to give an example of what can be achieved.

Take a special case of the above buyer–seller contracting example, in which the quantity traded is either 0 or 1 unit. Fix the value v of this unit to the buyer (firm 2) at 100. Suppose the cost c to the seller (firm 1) of producing it may be anything in an interval $[\underline{c},\bar{c}]$, where $0<\underline{c}<\bar{c}<100$.[31] So it is always efficient to trade *ex post*: the optimal $q(c)=1$ for all c. Both firms are risk averse, however, and they want to share risk. Suppose that the buyer is less risk averse than the seller, and that optimal risk sharing entails trading at a price:

$$p(c) = K + 2c/3 \text{ for some constant } K.$$[32]

(Any non-decreasing price function $p(c)$ would do here; I only choose this particular form for the purpose of illustration.) The buyer's *ex post* surplus is $100 - K - 2c/3$, and the seller's is $K - c/3$. The constant K is determined according to the *ex ante* division of surplus. Let $\bar{c}/3 < K < 100 - 2\bar{c}/3$; so *ex post* trade at the desired price $p(c)$ is individually rational.

As before, we assume that the state (in this case, c) is only observable to the firms, and so a contingent contract can be ruled out. What kind of mechanism could the firms write into their contract which would implement their desired choice function $f(c) = (q(c), p(c))$?

The mechanism detailed in figure 5.5 does the job nicely.

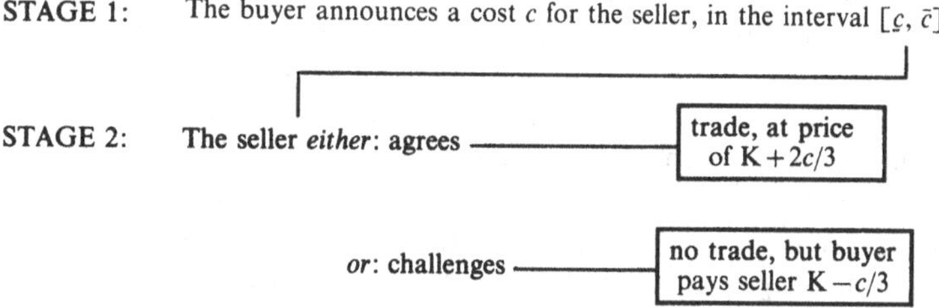

Figure 5.5

To see why, notice that, for any given announcement $c \in [\underline{c}, \bar{c}]$, the buyer's payoff is $100 - K - 2c/3 > 0$ if the seller agrees, and $-K + c/3 < 0$ if the seller challenges. Thus the buyer will only announce a cost c which is commensurate with the seller agreeing; i.e., if the true cost is c^t, the buyer will only announce a c satisfying:

$$K + 2c/3 - c^t \geq K - c/3. \tag{†}$$

Moreover, since the buyer's payoff, $100 - K - 2c/3$, is decreasing in c, the buyer will announce the lowest c satisfying (†), viz. $c = c^t$. That is, the buyer announces the truth, c^t, and there is trade at price $K + 2c^t/3$, as desired. Efficient risk sharing has been implemented.

The mechanism is quite simple: if the seller challenges the announced cost c, it can refuse to trade, and instead insist on being paid an amount equal to the surplus $K - c/3$ it would have earned had c been its true cost. If the seller does challenge, the buyer in effect incurs the loss of the social surplus (since trade does not take place).

The great merit of this mechanism is that the agents take turns to play, and they both play only *once*. Here it is much less controversial to argue that the parties would play the subgame perfect equilibrium.[33]

One can see that this kind of mechanism is likely to work in a wide variety of contractual situations where only one of the parties faces uncertainty, or where the two parties' preferences are perfectly correlated. See theorem 3.3 in part two.

IX

The obvious difficulty with this argument – and indeed with most of the mechanism design literature, particularly when there is no "planner" – is that the mechanism is vulnerable to renegotiation. Consider what would happen if the seller challenges. The buyer pays the seller $K-c/3$, and then – ostensibly – there is no trade. At least, that is what the mechanism in the old contract lays down. But at this point it will be in both parties' interests to renegotiate a fresh contract, rescinding the no-trade outcome specified in the old contract, and agreeing to trade at some new price.[34] (Note that the seller will only choose to enter into negotiations *after* the buyer has paid over the amount $K-c/3$ prescribed in the old contract.) Presumably, the seller will enjoy some of the surplus from this trade. So our earlier critical inequality (†) no longer correctly determines whether or not the seller will challenge under the terms of the old contract: in particular, the seller will be willing to challenge more often if it anticipates the possibility of subsequent renegotiation. It is easy to check that the mechanism fails to implement the trade price $p(.)$ which shares risk efficiently.

It is tempting to think that renegotiation spoils everything, and that the parties might as well abandon their attempts at *ex ante* contracting, and instead simply rely on negotiating a spot price *ex post*. In the present example, given anything other than a two-to-one division of *ex post* bargaining power in favor of the buyer (which is extremely unlikely),[35] this would mean losing efficient risk sharing.

However, an *ex ante* contract *does* help. The contractually specified mechanism steers the parties towards an *ex post* "status quo" point, from which they then bargain. The equilibrium outcome of the mechanism – the status quo point – will typically be sensitive to the parties' preferences (i.e., sensitive to the state of nature). A well-designed mechanism may thus implement some choice function *indirectly* (although of course the outcome of this choice function now has to be on the parties' *ex post* Pareto frontier). Naturally, the mechanism will depend on the nature of the renegotiation – that is, on who has what degree of bargaining power in which *ex post* state.[36]

This is the approach adopted in Maskin and Moore (1987): we characterize what is implementable in a general framework where there is some arbitrary, but *exogenously given*, renegotiation process. The renegotiation takes place outside the mechanism, i.e., after the mechanism has been played. At the time of designing (and subsequently playing) the mechanism, the agents are presumed to have rational expectations about what outcome the bargaining will lead to *ex post*.[37] For further details, see section 7 of part two.

It may be possible to *derive* the renegotiation process from a close examination of the circumstances of the agents (in particular, how and when they communicate and trade) – and then to see what can be implemented. In Hart and Moore (1988), we investigate a simple buyer/seller model with a given technology: specifically, gainful trade of a single item can only occur before a certain deadline, and trade must be voluntary (i.e., $q=1$ cannot be enforced by the courts). Negotiation between the parties is assumed to take place using a time-consuming communications channel. Although we find that only a restricted class of price functions can be implemented, nevertheless this class is broad enough to admit first-best risk sharing; see part two, section 7.1.

There is a related line of enquiry, which is more ambitious: can the mechanism be used to control – i.e., *endogenize* – the renegotiation process itself? Rubinstein and Wolinsky (forthcoming) argue that any bargaining process only works because there is some friction in the model – i.e., some potential efficiency loss (off the equilibrium path) which cannot be negotiated away – and such a friction can be exploited. In particular, lost time can never be recovered. Like Hart–Moore (1988), they take a simple buyer/seller model in which a single item is traded.[38] The parties are impatient. Any informal renegotiation is assumed to take an irreducible short amount of time – with a concomitant small loss of surplus, because of the parties' impatience. The idea is to design a sequential mechanism, to be played out in real time, according to which bargaining power is momentarily allocated to either the buyer or the seller by granting the contractual right to make a price offer to the other party. If the timing of these offers is arranged to be sufficiently frequent, then, loosely speaking, the formal renegotiation process specified in the mechanism will dominate any informal one, and the renegotiation can be controlled. Rubinstein and Wolinsky show that a wide class of price functions can be thus implemented.[39]

I fear that this may be too ambitious. Mechanisms only work if they can be policed – either by a planner (if there is one), or by outside parties (the courts). Arguably, the idea of, say, getting the courts to breathe over contractual parties' shoulders whilst they play the mechanism in "real time" is too unrealistic.[40] Moreover, pre-appointed agents can be bribed. I see merit in simple mechanisms, with very few stages, which arrive at some status quo point, from which the parties renegotiate outside the mechanism.

There may be cruder ways of tilting the renegotiation process in favor of one or other of the parties. Aghion, Dewatripont, and Rey (forthcoming) (see also Chung, 1991) take a trading model like the upstream/downstream model given in section VII, and introduce the idea of a financial hostage, or a large deposit, which is held by, say, the seller pending agreement. This deposit is only given back to the buyer without interest, so this makes the buyer very impatient, and in effect the seller can dictate terms. (A variant on this would be for the contract to impose *per diem* penalties on, say, the seller pending agreement. This would then make the seller impatient, and the buyer could dictate terms.)

An example will help illustrate their idea. (Please note that, in this example, although the functional forms and numbers may look odd, they have been chosen simply to ensure that the levels of investment and the traded quantities are all integer-valued. Beyond this, the example is not at all rigged; it is easily generalized.)

A risk-neutral buyer and seller contract at date T_1 to trade on or after some later date T_3. At T_1 there is uncertainty about their respective values and costs at T_3. There are two states of nature, which are equiprobable. Both parties learn the state of nature at date T_3, but this is not verifiable by outsiders and so state-contingent contracts are ruled out. At some date T_2, after the contract has been signed but before they learn the state, the buyer and seller each make a non-contractible investment, say $\beta \geq 0$ and $\sigma \geq 0$ respectively, at a private cost of $B(\beta)$ and $S(\sigma)$. These investments affect their gains from trade at T_3.

The time line is:

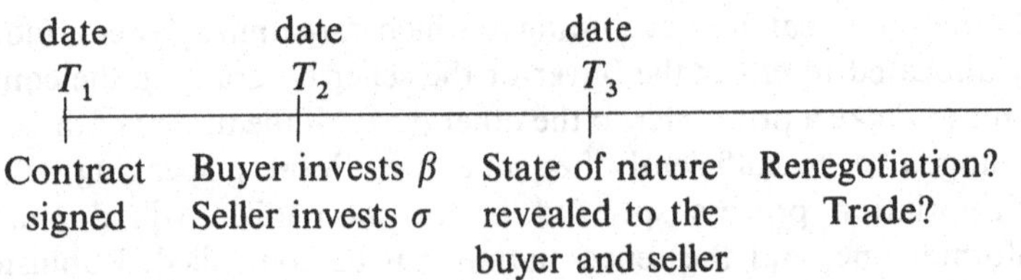

(The nature of the contract will be discussed shortly.)

Suppose that, for a level of trade $q \geq 0$, the buyer's (gross) value and the seller's (gross) cost in each of the two states of nature are:

	Good state	Bad state
Buyer's value	$35(1+\beta)q$	$28(1+\beta)q$
Seller's cost	$14(1+\frac{1}{\sigma})q^2$	$32(1+\frac{1}{\sigma})q^2$

Notice that, as one might expect, the higher the investment β, the greater is the buyer's value in each state; and the higher the investment σ, the smaller is the seller's cost. Also, for a given pair of investments, β and σ, the efficient level of trade in each of the two states is as follows:

	Good state	Bad state
Efficient level of trade, q	$\frac{5\sigma(1+\beta)}{4(1+\sigma)}$	$\frac{7\sigma(1+\beta)}{16(1+\sigma)}$

We can safely assume that, with efficient *ex post* renegotiation, the parties will end up trading at these efficient levels in both states. The difficulty they face, however, is that investments cannot be contracted upon, and are chosen non-cooperatively. In the absence of a contract, and assuming (say) a 50 : 50 division of surplus, they will underinvest. To see why, consider the buyer. From every marginal dollar he adds to his value by investing at a higher level, 50 cents are lost to the seller in the *ex post* bargain. This dilution of his incentives leads him to underinvest. A similar "hold-up" problem arises for the seller. They therefore need a contract to induce efficient investment. Can such a contract be written, given that only the two parties observe the state of nature?

Yes. Let us take a particular example, in which the date T_2 costs of investment $B(\beta)$ and $S(\sigma)$ are $14\beta^2$ and $7\sigma^2/144$ respectively – measured in date T_3 dollars. It is straightforward to show that the first-best investment levels are $\beta=\sigma=144$.[41] Notice that, given these investments at T_2, the efficient levels of trade at T_3 are:

	Good state	Bad state
Efficient level of trade, q	180	63

The buyer and seller can sign the following contract at date T_1; we will see that the contract indirectly implements both the first-best investment levels ($\beta=\sigma=144$) *and* the first-best levels of trade (180 in the good state, and 63 in the bad state).

CONTRACT

1 Each of us has the (unilateral) right to oblige the other party to trade 128 units at any date on or after T_3, for a fixed total price of P. (P is independent of when trade actually occurs.)

2 Meantime, the seller will hold a (large) cash deposit, to be put down by the buyer today (i.e., at date T_1).

3 Once 128 units have been traded, the deposit will be immediately returned to the buyer with interest (at the market rate). However interest will only be paid on the deposit covering the period $T_3 - T_1$; that is, if trade occurs at some date T later than T_3, no interest will be paid for the period $T - T_3$.

Signed: Buyer
Seller

Dated: T_1

The effect of having no interest on the deposit after T_3 is to make the buyer eager to consummate trade. At any time $T \geq T_3$, he can unilaterally insist that the contract is enforced – i.e., he can have 128 units traded for a total price P, and have his deposit returned to him (with interest covering the period $T_3 - T_1$). However, the contractually agreed quantity of 128 will not be efficient in either state – and so the parties will choose to renegotiate. The buyer's impatience means that the seller obtains all the additional surplus from this renegotiation. That is, the buyer is held down to his "reservation" payoff – viz., $[35(1+\beta)128 - P]$ in the good state and $[28(1+\beta)128 - P]$ in the bad state. Taking expectations, the buyer's expected payoff (net of investment cost) at date T_2 is then:

$$\tfrac{1}{2} \times [35(1+\beta)128 - P] + \tfrac{1}{2} \times [28(1+\beta)128 - P] - 14\beta^2.$$

But notice that this is maximized at $\beta = 144$. That is, the contractually agreed quantity of 128 has been judiciously chosen so as to induce first-best investment from the buyer, even though he has no *ex post* bargaining power.

What of the seller's incentives to invest? Since he is in effect the residual claimant *ex post*, his private incentives are aligned with the social objective. He therefore will invest at the first-best level too: $\sigma = 144$.

Given these levels of investment at T_2, the parties renegotiate the old 128-unit contract at T_3, so that actually 180 units will be traded in the good state, and 63 units will be traded in the bad state. It does not matter that the seller obtains all the additional surplus *ex post*, since the parties are risk neutral: any required *ex ante* division can be effected by means of a suitable choice of P. (Alternatively, there could be a transfer payment made at T_1, when the original contract is signed.)[42]

In sum, we have an attractively simple contract which works well, thanks to the possibility of renegotiation. My choice of example was not peculiar: Aghion, Dewatripont, and Rey (forthcoming), and also Chung (1991), show that, for two risk-neutral agents, first-best investments can be implemented with renegotiation under reasonably general circumstances.[43]

There is a caveat. Implicit in the analysis of the above example are two important, but debatable, assumptions: (i) the court can impose a trade level of 128; and (ii), once imposed, there is no scope for the buyer and seller to agree to change this quantity afterwards (either to increase or to decrease it). Assumption (ii) seems particularly strong – it appears to run counter to the whole idea of implementation and renegotiation, that agents can always negotiate away from an inefficient outcome. Aghion, Dewatripont, and Rey defend this assumption on the grounds that, once the court has imposed a trade level of (say) 128, $q = 128$ becomes *ex post* efficient. For example, the seller or buyer may be able unilaterally to take an action which irreversibly makes $q = 128$ the *only* efficient level of trade.[44]

X

Let me end part one with a few general remarks.

The latest developments in implementation theory have been striking. We suddenly seem capable of implementing anything, provided that we appeal to the right notion of equilibrium.[45] This is quite a contrast with the earlier literature. (For more details, see part two.)

Although I have not stressed the fact in part one, these general results are obtained at a cost in terms of realism. Consider, for example, implementation in subgame perfect equilibrium. The general theorem entails the construction of an enormously elaborate mechanism, with several stages of simultaneous moves. Worse, the mechanism appeals to clever but unpalatable devices which exploit the fine detail of what constitutes – or, rather, does not constitute – an equilibrium. Let me list a number of such devices which are frequently used in the design of mechanisms to prevent unwanted equilibria (these things are explained in part two):

(a) integer games,
(b) roulette wheels, and the *a priori* ruling out of mixed equilibria,
(c) infinite mechanisms in finite environments,
(d) absence of best-response strategies (open choice sets),
(e) infinite chains of weak domination,
(f) excessively large out-of-equilibrium penalties.

(There are variants on these.) Unfortunately, from a positive perspective, these devices seem esoteric. To my mind, we should be very wary of using them in our modeling – otherwise we may well be fooled by our own "success." A standard reply to this criticism is that they are used to prove *general* theorems, and it is to be expected that in an abstract environment the mechanism will also have to be abstract. But this begs the question: can the devices be dispensed with in specific applications? We have for too long relied on tricks that verge on the fanciful, and this has given implementation theory a bad name.

Leaving aside more arcane constructions, even familiar revelation mechanisms do not square well with reality. Consider, for example, an incomplete contract. The last few years have seen significant developments in the theory of incomplete contracts, despite the fact that the formal models of contractual incompleteness really amount to not much more than complete contracts in which very little can be verified by the courts: "observable but not verifiable" is a usual assumption.[46] Implementation theory would suggest that, in a world where things are "observable but not verifiable," a revelation mechanism would be highly effective in getting contractual parties to reveal the truth. Yet we do not see firms making simultaneous announcements to a third party – each firm announcing both its own and the other firm's preferences. Why not?

This is the deep question. Why are mechanisms akin to revelation mechanisms, or devices such as (a)-(f), typically *not* used in practice – especially since they appear to deliver so much at a theoretical level?

Arguably, the answer has something to do with their lack of robustness.[47] That is, intricate mechanisms may perform poorly in the "imperfect" world of reality – either because (i) there are flaws in the agents' reasoning; or because (ii) mistakes are made in the specification of the agents' preferences, knowledge, or situation.[48] (Incidentally, the dichotomy between (i) and (ii) is not at all clear cut.) I believe the most important open issue in the area is to find a framework for thinking about *robust* mechanisms. To make a start, we will need to model the "imperfections."

To incorporate (i) – flaws in the agents' reasoning – into our design of mechanisms, we probably first require a model of bounded rationality. In which case, we may be in for a long wait. A better research strategy might be to model (ii). We need to find a tractable way (*not* involving an infinite regress of Bayesian reasoning) of studying the nature of mechanisms that are robust to mistakes in the specification of agents' preferences/knowledge/situation. I am optimistic that this can be done.

My expectation is that mechanisms that are robust in this sense will turn out to be *simple* mechanisms.[49] There may be a parallel here with the recent work by Holmström and Milgrom (1990, 1991) on multi-task agency. Their argument can be roughly construed: the more high-powered are the incentives in areas of performance that can be monitored, the more agents will act to meet their performance targets, at the expense of taking other actions which cannot be monitored but which are nonetheless very important. If the principal misspecifies the agents' actions, he may end up writing a contract which is too high-powered. The parallel message for implementation theory is this: mechanisms which fail to allow for misspecifications in agents' preferences/knowledge/situation, and which build in complex devices to deal with the foreseen states of nature, may perform poorly in the unforeseen states.

A related consideration is *side contracting*. It would be interesting to know whether the possibility of covert side contracting between subcoalitions forces mechanisms to be simple. A leading example of this is in the area of non-linear pricing. If customers can side contract, then arbitrage forces the price schedule to be linear.

It must be stressed that not all implementation papers are vulnerable to the criticism that the mechanisms use implausible devices such as (a)-(f) above. On the contrary: a number of exciting new lines of enquiry have opened up recently, precisely in response to the general misgivings about these devices. Jackson (forthcoming), for example, persuasively argues that mechanisms should be "bounded" – that is, whenever a strategy is weakly dominated, it must be dominated by some other strategy which is itself not weakly dominated – so that, *inter alia*, (a), (c), and (e) would be ruled out. The mechanisms introduced in Sjöström (1991b) for economic environments, and in Jackson, Palfrey, and Srivastava (1991) for so-called "separable environments," are both simple and bounded. Moreover, they lead to unique outcomes irrespective of whether one appeals to the concept of (undominated) Nash equilibrium, or whether one appeals solely to the successive elimination of weakly dominated strategies. Their mechanisms do, however, involve large penalties or fines (see (f)). Abreu and Matsushima (1990) present an ingenious mechanism which is also bounded, but which involves only small fines; they too appeal to the iterative elimination of weakly dominated strategies. (But their mechanism is not simple; the number of iterations needed grows large as the fines become small.) These new mechanisms are all significant discoveries; they will be further discussed, along with other related work, in sections 4, 5, and 6 of part two.

Research on implementation should, I believe, become more orientated towards *applications*. Looking at specific problems puts more restriction on environments, and enables us to think about particular institutions. In general environments the mechanisms seem unworldly, and we have less idea about how agents would actually play such mechanisms. In the context of a specific problem, we can ask important questions about the knowledge and situation of the agents: What do they know about each other? Can they communicate outside the mechanism? For how long will they be together after the mechanism has been used? Can they collude? Can they affect the realization of θ? (For an illustration of how pre-play communication can affect the outcome of a mechanism, see Matthews and Postlewaite (1989) on auctions. On collusion, see Tirole (1992).) It is also worth asking: how do they think? For example, if they do not consciously put time into their strategic calculations, there may be little point in appealing to backward-induction arguments driven by subtle end-point considerations. This is one of many thought-provoking comments that Rubinstein (1991) makes on the interpretation of game theory, and which apply equally well to the design of mechanisms.

The nature of the application in question should aid us in prescribing the class of allowable mechanisms. For instance, if there is a small degree of uncertainty in the agents' knowledge of each other's preferences, then knife-edge mechanisms with large penalties should perhaps be ruled out – especially if we cannot model this uncertainty explicitly (i.e., well enough to permit a fully fledged Bayesian analysis).[50]

One very promising development has been the resurgence of interest in dominant strategy implementation and strategy-proof mechanisms.[51] There is now evidence that, in many specific applications, useful strategy-proof mechanisms do exist. See, for example, the work of Moulin and Shenker (1991) on serial cost-sharing mechanisms, Moulin (1991) on excludable public goods, and the work of Barberà, Sonnenshein, and Zhou (1991) on voting by committees. The strategic advantages of dominant strategy implementation are clear; moreover, the mechanisms are typically simple and interpretable. For these reasons, it would be desirable to have a full characterization of the choice functions that are dominant-strategy implementable in economic environments – with a view to identifying second-best choice functions.[52]

There have also been a number of papers which use multi-stage mechanisms in specific applications. The most familiar such mechanism is the classic divide-and-choose procedure (analyzed by Crawford, 1977); several variants on this have been developed. Papers by Bagnoli and Lipman (1989), Jackson and Moulin (forthcoming), and Varian (1990a and b) introduce simple multi-stage mechanisms for specific public goods problems. Howard (forthcoming) implements a specific bargaining rule using a sequential mechanism. See section 3 of part two for more details. My guess is that these applications will proliferate. The goal should be to find computationally simple mechanisms which people can use.

In this regard, I see merit in sequential mechanisms; i.e., mechanisms in which agents take turns to move ("tree mechanisms"). We lack good characterization theorems here, beyond the case of transferable utility.[53] It would be especially useful to know more about what class of choice rules can be implemented using simple sequential mechanisms in which agents move *once* only. This is what the ancients used (Spyros and Timon never moved together, and each moved once only); and by and large it is what we see in practice.

In conclusion, the application of implementation theory to specific situations, in which there are small numbers of agents, has been a healthy development. The limiting case of two agents is of particular interest: indeed, we might regard it as a leading case given its use for contract theory. Implementation theory has gained a new edge, and in a sense has been brought down to earth. There is much research to do – at both the abstract level and, particularly, at the applied level. The emphasis must be on robustness and simplicity. Solomon and the Greeks knew a thing or two.

PART TWO

Part two is meant as a supplement to part one of the paper, to introduce or amplify certain results and topics:

- Section 1: Dominant strategy implementation
  - Section 1.1: Dominant strategy implementation with quasi-linear preferences
  - Section 1.2: Dominant strategy implementation with other domain restrictions
- Section 2: Nash implementation
  - Section 2.1: Nash implementation with two agents
  - Section 2.2: Nash implementation of single-valued choice rules
- Section 3: Subgame perfect implementation
  - Section 3.1: General extensive form mechanisms
  - Section 3.2: Sequential mechanisms
  - Section 3.3: Simple sequential mechanisms
- Section 4: Undominated Nash implementation
  - Section 4.1: Undominated Nash implementation with bounded mechanisms
  - Section 4.2: Undominated Nash implementation with domain restrictions
- Section 5: Undominated strategy implementation
  - Section 5.1: A single round of elimination of dominated strategies
  - Section 5.2: Iterative elimination of dominated strategies
- Section 6: Virtual implementation and perfect implementation
- Section 7: Implementation and renegotiation
  - Section 7.1: An application

Two remarks are in order:

First, the reader will notice a significant gear-change between parts one and two. This partly reflects the fact that much of the recent research (presented in section 3 onwards) has been aimed at finding ever more permissive theorems showing what can be implemented using alternative equilibrium concepts; and relatively little attention has been paid to questions of realism, robustness, or simplicity. Inevitably, the focus in part two is on what has been done, even though I believe this gives a somewhat distorted picture of the appropriate research agenda.

Second, it should be noted that sections 1 and 2 in part distill "old" material: several of the results presented here predate the last World Congress in 1985. Moreover, the perspective is quite partial.[54] The aim is to draw out certain ideas which pertain to the later sections.

The abstract framework is as follows. Consider an environment with a finite set $\{1, \ldots, i, \ldots, I\}$ of *agents*, and a set A of feasible *outcomes*, with typical element a.

The profile of the agents' preferences over outcomes is indexed by the *state* $\theta \in \Theta$: in state θ, agent i has preference ordering $R_i(\theta)$ on the set A. Let $P_i(\theta)$ and $I_i(\theta)$ respectively denote the strict preference relation and the indifference relation corresponding to $R_i(\theta)$.

Each of the agents is assumed to observe the state θ, so there is *complete information* among the agents about their preferences over A.

The above formulation allows for any degree of correlation across the agents' preferences. Θ may, for example, comprise all possible vectors of preference orderings over A: the *universal* domain. Or there may be perfect correlation, in which case knowing one agent's preference ordering over A would be enough to deduce all the other agents'. We shall say that preferences in Θ have *independent domains* if agent i's set of possible preference orderings over A is fixed – independent of how the other agents $j \neq i$ happen to rank A.[55]

A *choice rule* is a correspondence f: $\Theta \twoheadrightarrow A$ that specifies a non-empty choice set $f(\theta) \subseteq A$ for each state θ. Notice that implicit in this formulation is an assumption that a choice rule depends only on the agents' ordinal preferences over A.[56] However, it will be clear from the definition of implementability that any implementable choice rule would have to be ordinal anyway.

The implementation problem is as follows: does there exist a *mechanism*, or game form, g such that in any state θ, the set of equilibrium outcomes of g coincides with $f(\theta)$? If so, then g (fully) *implements* f. This is a general notion of implementation, in that we have left open the choice of equilibrium concept.

A natural place to start is with a *revelation mechanism*, g^*, in which each agent i's strategy set comprises his set of possible preference orderings, $\{R_i(\theta) | \theta \in \Theta\}$: that is, each agent simply announces what are his preferences over A. (Arguably, revelation mechanisms make most sense if preferences in Θ have independent domains, because then any vector of preferences reported by the agents could in principle be the truth.) If, in each state θ, truth-telling is an equilibrium, whose outcome is in $f(\theta)$, then g^* *truthfully implements* f. Notice that this is weaker than (full) implementation, because there may be other, untruthful equilibria in state θ whose outcomes are not in $f(\theta)$.[57]

1 DOMINANT STRATEGY IMPLEMENTATION

The most appealing notion of implementation is the one that makes the weakest assumptions about the agents' behavior: implementation in *dominant strategy* equilibrium.[58] The great merit of a dominant strategy equilibrium is that agents do not need to have any theory about how the other agents behave; indeed, they do not even need to know the other agents' preferences. To assume that agents play dominant strategies places no restriction on how they resolve their strategic uncertainty: the maximiner, the maximaxer, and the Bayesian (or Nash player, in the case of complete information) will all play their dominant strategies if they have them.

Another great virtue of dominant strategy mechanisms is that they are simple. We know from the Revelation Principle (below) that, at most, agents need report only their own preferences; i.e., if any mechanism works, a revelation mechanism will work as well. (This simplicity is lost once we try to exploit the strategic interaction among agents; for example, in section 2, we will see that the kinds of mechanisms that have been used for Nash implementation are much more complex, and, to an extent, unconvincing.)

Given all these advantages of dominant strategy mechanisms, it is disappointing to report that in general relatively little can be implemented this way, especially if the choice rule is required to be efficient. However, if restrictions are placed on the domain of preferences then it is now emerging that there do exist useful dominant strategy mechanisms, albeit inefficient ones. This is currently an important area of research; see section 1.1 and, particularly, section 1.2 below.

To discover what can be implemented in dominant strategy equilibrium (and other equilibrium concepts), a useful ground-clearing result comes from the *Revelation Principle*. This provides a set of necessary conditions – in effect, incentive constraints – which a choice rule must satisfy if it is to be (fully) implementable. In particular, consider the case where preferences in

Θ have independent domains, and where the choice rule f is *single-valued* (i.e., where $f(\theta)$ is a single outcome for all θ). Then if f is (fully) implementable in dominant strategy equilibrium, it must also be truthfully implementable in dominant strategy equilibrium. To see why, replace the non-revelation mechanism g which (fully) implements f in dominant strategies by a revelation mechanism g^* which mimicks it. That is, if, in state θ, the I agents choose the vector of (dominant) strategies $(s_1(\theta), \ldots, s_I(\theta))$, say, in g, then announcing the truth in g^* leads to the same outcome: $g^*[R_1(\theta), \ldots, R_I(\theta)] \equiv g[s_1(\theta), \ldots, s_I(\theta)]$. Clearly, for each agent i, announcing the truth $R_i(\theta)$ in g^* must be a dominant strategy, because $s_i(\theta)$ is a dominant strategy in g – hence g^* truthfully implements f in dominant strategy equilibrium, as required. However, in moving from g to g^*, we may admit new, unwanted, untruthful dominant strategy equilibria: g^* need not (fully) implement f.

Nevertheless, one senses that for a rich enough choice rule and associated mechanism g^*, there is unlikely to be a multiplicity of dominant strategy equilibria. In particular, there will only be a gap between (full) implementation and truthful implementation in dominant strategy equilibrium if there are indifferences in the agents' preference orderings. If Θ only contains *strict* preference orderings,[59] then dominant strategies are essentially unique: it can easily be shown that a choice rule f is (fully) implementable in dominant strategy equilibrium if and only if it is single-valued and truthfully implementable in dominant strategies.[60] Laffont and Maskin (1982a, pp. 42–3) present other conditions guaranteeing that if truth-telling is a dominant strategy equilibrium of the revelation mechanism g^*, then it is the only one. Given these results, we can sensibly focus on the truthful implementation of single-valued rules in dominant strategies.

We should also keep in mind another, rather compelling, reason for being especially interested in single-valued choice rules: quite simply, this is what most *applications* demand. That is, for most contractual or public economics applications, first-best or constrained second-best choice rules are almost everywhere single-valued.

Unfortunately, for dominant strategy implementation, the necessary conditions (the incentive constraints) provided by the Revelation Principle are very demanding. For a single-valued choice rule f to be truthfully implementable in dominant strategy equilibrium, it must be *strategy-proof*:

> For any agent i, if $\theta, \phi \in \Theta$ are such that $R_j(\theta) = R_j(\phi)$ for all $j \neq i$, then $f(\theta)\ R_i(\theta)\ f(\phi)$ and, symmetrically, $f(\phi)\ R_i(\phi)\ f(\theta)$.

This follows straight from the definition: if f is truthfully implementable, then in state θ agent i cannot gain from misreporting his preferences as

$R_i(\phi)$, thereby changing the outcome from $f(\theta)$ to $f(\phi)$. Moreover, it is clear that, if preferences in Θ have independent domain, then strategy-proofness is also sufficient for f to be truthfully implementable in dominant strategy equilibrium: simply use the revelation mechanism $g^*[R_1(\theta), \ldots, R_I(\theta)] \equiv f(\theta)$.

An early, and fundamental, result, suggested that most choice rules are unlikely to be strategy-proof if the domain is rich enough:

THEOREM 1.1 (Gibbard, 1973; Sattherthwaite, 1975) Suppose Θ includes all possible strict preference orderings over A. Then no single-valued choice rule f, whose range contains at least three distinct outcomes, can be truthfully implemented in dominant strategy equilibrium unless it is dictatorial.[61]

This result was first conjectured by Dummett and Farquharson (1961) (see also Pattanaik, 1973). Subsequent to Gibbard (1973) and Satterthwaite (1975), there have been a number of other proofs.[62] Below, I will present a short proof which is an immediate consequence of theorem 1.2.

The assumption made in theorem 1.1 that Θ includes *all* possible strict preference orderings over A is very strong. It turns out that the theorem is nevertheless robust. For example, Zhou (1991) proves that, if A is a convex set in a finite-dimensional Euclidean space, and if Θ contains all continuous, convex preferences, then any single-valued, strategy-proof choice rule whose range has more than one dimension must be dictatorial. Zhou extends this result to the case where preferences are also monotonic, thus encompassing many pure public goods environments.[63]

When there are private goods as well, a number of papers have demonstrated the impossibility of finding non-dictatorial *Pareto efficient* choice rules that can be implemented in dominant strategy equilibrium.[64] The seminal paper here is Hurwicz (1972), who showed, in the context of a two-person, two-good, pure exchange economy, that no single-valued, individually rational, Pareto efficient choice rule f can be dominant strategy implemented – including, *a fortiori*, the Walrasian choice rule – if both agents' preferences are continuous, strictly convex, and increasing.[65] Subsequent research has revealed that the requirement of individual rationality can be weakened to non-dictatorial.[66] And the requirement of Pareto efficiency can be weakened too. Satterthwaite and Sonnenschein (1981) proved that, in classical economic environments, with both private and public goods, if the domain Θ contains an open set of utility functions then any strategy-proof choice rule has to exhibit some weakened form of dictatorship. Specifically, the choice rule either is a "serial dictatorship," or is "bossy." (The reader is referred to Satterthwaite and Sonnenschein (1981) for the definition of these two.) The former typically rules out Pareto efficient choice rules; and, in a private goods economy, the latter rules out Walrasian choice rules.[67]

1.1 Dominant strategy implementation with quasi-linear preferences

Little can be implemented in dominant strategy equilibrium unless we place some further structure on the domain of preferences. One such domain restriction is to *quasi-linear preferences*: each agent has a utility function $u_i(a,\theta)+t_i$, say – where a is the *decision* (think of a public good decision), and t_i is a *transfer* of some private good (e.g., money) which may be either positive or negative. To be true to our earlier terminology, an outcome in the feasible set A now comprises the decision a together with the vector of transfers $(t_1,\ldots,t_I)$. Denote the set of feasible decisions by $D=\{a,b,c,\ldots\}$. In what follows, we take D to be finite. Any single-valued choice rule f will comprise a decision $d(\theta)$, say, together with a vector of transfers $t_1(\theta),\ldots,$ $t_I(\theta)$, say, for each $\theta\in\Theta$. K. Roberts (1979) proves the following powerful result for generically single-valued choice rules.[68]

THEOREM 1.2 (Roberts, 1979) Consider the domain of *all* quasi-linear preferences. Let the set D of decisions be finite, but contain at least three outcomes. Take some generically single-valued choice rule $f=(d,t_1,\ldots,t_I)$ for which the range of d is the whole of D. If f is truthfully implementable in dominant strategies, then there exists some non-negative vector $(k_1,\ldots,$ $k_I)\neq 0$ and some real-valued function u_0 defined on D such that, generically:

$$d(\theta)=\underset{a\in A}{\operatorname{argmax}}\ u_o(a)+\sum_{i=1}^{I}k_iu_i(a,\theta)$$

and, if $k_i>0$, $t_i(\theta)=\dfrac{1}{k_i}\left(u_o(d(\theta))+\sum_{j\neq i}k_ju_j(d(\theta),\theta)\right)+H_i(\theta)$,

where $H_i(\theta)$ is some real-valued function independent of $u_i(.,\theta)$.

It is clear from the form of the transfer functions $t_i(\theta)$ that the converse of the theorem is also true: any such choice rule $f(\theta)$ is strategy-proof, and hence truthfully implementable in dominant strategy equilibrium.

A sketch proof of theorem 1.2 is instructive (although it should perhaps be skipped on first reading), and will be of value when we come to theorem 2.7 on Nash implementation in section 2.2. Roberts first exploits the fact that $f=(d,t_1,\ldots,t_I)$ must be (generically) strategy proof: i.e., for any agent i, if θ, $\phi\in\Theta$ are such that $u_j(.,\theta)=u_j(.,\phi)$ for all $j\neq i$, then:

$$u_i(d(\theta),\theta)+t_i(\theta)\geq u_i(d(\phi),\theta)+t_i(\phi)$$

and:

$$u_i(d(\phi),\phi)+t_i(\phi)\geq u_i(d(\theta),\phi)+t_i(\theta).$$

Adding and rearranging, we have that $u_i(d(\theta),\phi)-u_i(d(\theta),\theta)\leq u_i(d(\phi),\phi)-u_i(d(\phi),\theta)$. Hence, if $u_i(d(\theta),\phi)-u_i(d(\theta),\theta)>u_i(a,\phi)-u_i(a,\theta)$ for all decisions $a\in D$ other than $d(\theta)$, it must be the case that $d(\phi)=d(\theta)$. Now take some other agent $j\neq i$. Keeping $R_i(\theta)$, $R_i(\phi)$ fixed, and keeping $R_k(\theta)=R_k(\phi)$ for all $k\neq i, j$, we can repeat the above argument. Proceeding through all the I agents in this fashion, we deduce that d must (generically) satisfy the following condition. Take any pair of states $\theta,\phi\in\Theta$; if:

$$u_i(d(\theta),\phi)-u_i(d(\theta),\theta)>u_i(a,\phi)-u_i(a,\theta)$$

for all i and for all $a\in D$ other than $d(\theta)$, then $d(\phi)=d(\theta)$. This is a *monotonicity* condition on d: if, in moving from state θ to state ϕ, decision $d(\theta)$ moves up everyone's rankings more than any other decision $a\neq d(\theta)$, then $d(\theta)$ must continue to be selected by the choice rule.

Roberts next uses a social-choice argument to show that monotonicity of d, together with the range condition specified in the theorem, implies that there must exist a function $F:\mathbb{R}^I\rightarrow\mathbb{R}$, mapping from the vector of utility *levels*, such that, for each θ, $d(\theta)$ maximizes $F[u_1(d,\theta),\ldots, u_I(d,\theta)]$. Moreover, monotonicity implies that $d(\theta)$ is unchanged by adding a constant to any agent's utility function. Consider the indifference surfaces of F. Subject to a translation of each $a\in D$ by amounts which are independent of the state (hence the inclusion of the function u_o), these indifference surfaces must be planes (hence the constants $k_1,\ldots, k_I$).

The rest of theorem 1.2, concerning the admissible form of transfers $t_i(\theta)$, follows using a proof similar to that first used by Green and Laffont (1977).

In the special case where the k_i's are equal and $u_o\equiv 0$, the *decision* $d(\theta)$ will be the Pareto efficient one, $d^*(\theta)$ say, in each state θ (but the entire choice rule f need not be – see below). Here, the transfers $t_i(\theta)$ reduce to the classic form of mechanism proposed by Groves (1973). Clarke (1971) exhibited the particularly interesting member of this class in which:

$$H_i(\theta)=-\underset{a\in D}{\text{maximum}}\sum_{j\neq i} u_j(a,\theta),$$

the so-called "pivotal" mechanism because only agents who actually influence which decision in D is taken get transfers – which are, in fact, negative.[69] If the k_i's are equal and $u_o\equiv 0$, the last part of theorem 1.2 is thus a special case of earlier results by Green and Laffont (1977) and Walker (1978) to the effect that, when the domain of quasi-linear preferences is sufficiently rich, only the Groves mechanisms can (truthfully) implement the Pareto efficient decision rule d^* in dominant strategy equilibrium.[70]

Another important result demonstrated by Hurwicz (1975), Green and

Laffont (1979), and Walker (1980) for the Groves mechanisms applies to the choice rules specified by Roberts: if $k_i > 0$ for all i, then the sum of the transfers cannot always be zero. That is, mechanisms cannot be balanced.[71] It is important to stress that balancedness is a prerequisite for Pareto efficiency of the choice rule f (i.e., in the case where the k_i's are equal and $u_o \equiv 0$). This means that – as we saw without quasi-linearity – Pareto efficient strategy-proof choice rules do not exist for the "universal" quasi-linear domain of theorem 1.2. Indeed, we now know from a recent paper by Hurwicz and Walker (1990) that this non-existence result is "generic" on a large set of classical economies with quasi-linear preferences. Roughly speaking, they show that, if the agents cannot be separated into groups across which there are no potentially conflicting interests – which is a weak enough requirement – then every continuous, strategy-proof choice rule will select *in*efficient allocations in an open dense set of states.

All this suggests that one should perhaps cut one's losses, and examine choice rules that are second-best. That is, "second-best" according to some welfare criterion – e.g., maximize the sum of the agents' expected utilities prior to the realization of the state – within the class of strategy-proof choice rules.

To make progress in this direction, it helps to place more structure on preferences. (This will mean that typically a wider class of choice rules $f = (d, t_1, \ldots, t_I)$ can be truthfully implemented in dominant strategy equilibrium, compared with theorem 1.2.) Laffont and Maskin (1982a, section 3) provide a nice treatment of the particular case where D comprises only two decisions, $d = 0$ or 1 – i.e., whether or not to proceed with some indivisible project (although randomization is allowed for in their analysis). They show that, within the Groves class (i.e., those implementing the Pareto efficient decision d^*), nothing uniformly gives the agents more aggregate surplus (or rather, less of a loss) than Clarke's "pivotal" mechanism;[72] moreover, there is no way of avoiding losses in at least some state(s) if, as seems reasonable, the mechanism is to be individually rational for the I agents. However, if one abandons trying to implement d^*, more is possible. Laffont and Maskin give an example in which the best balanced mechanism dominates (in the expected utility sense) the Clarke mechanism. (Recall that the latter implements d^*, whereas the former cannot do so.)[73]

How robust are these positive results about dominant strategy implementation with quasi-linear preferences? Green and Laffont (1977, theorem 5) have shown that, if preferences are non-separable then Groves mechanisms are no longer strategy-proof. Adapting their proof to Roberts's framework (theorem 1.2), it can be shown that in the non-separable case, k_i can only be strictly positive for one agent i; that is, in each state θ, agent i's preferences solely determine the outcome. This is reminiscent of our earlier discussion of dictatorial results, following theorem 1.1. It suggests that, unfortunately, the positive results for quasi-linear preferences are rather knife-edge to that domain. Nonetheless it can be argued that quasi-linearity approximately captures many situations, and is therefore a leading case that deserves special attention.

As promised, a spinoff of theorem 1.2 is that it gives an immediate proof of the Gibbard–Satterthwaite theorem, theorem 1.1. The argument is as follows. Suppose that the use of transfers were ruled out ($t_i \equiv 0$). Then the set of outcomes A is just the set D, and in effect one loses the structure of quasi-linearity: one is back to a perfectly general domain of preferences. Now take some agent i for whom $k_i > 0$. In any state θ, assuming that f is truthfully implementable in dominant strategy equilibrium, agent i must not gain by (mis)reporting his preferences to be $Su_i(.,\theta)$, say, where $S > 0$ is some scaling factor. But for sufficiently large S, the ordering of:

$$u_0(a) + Sk_i u_i(a,\theta) + \sum_{j \neq i} k_j u_j(a,\theta)$$

over $a \in A$ is dominated by the ordering of $u_i(.,\theta)$ – and so by theorem 1.2 the outcome resulting from agent i reporting $Su_i(.\theta)$ must be top-ranked for him in A. Thus $f(\theta)$ must also be top-ranked; agent i is a dictator, and $k_j = 0$ for all $j \neq i$. Theorem 1.1 is proved.

1.2 Dominant strategy implementation with other domain restrictions

Arguably, the Gibbard–Satterthwaite theorem led to a fascination for negative results, seeing how far impossibility type results could be pushed. There was a particular emphasis on demonstrating that *efficient* choice rules could not be implemented in dominant strategies. As a consequence, the search for more positive results may have been somewhat held back. Recently, however, the mood has changed, and there is some very promising work being done to discover what the class of strategy-proof choice rules looks like under a variety of domain restrictions. The aim is to characterize this class, with a view to identifying *second-best* rules. A fuller understanding of the nature of dominant strategy mechanisms is now starting to emerge – although there remain many open questions.

If preferences are single-peaked, then Moulin (1980a) and, subsequently, Barberà and Jackson (1991a) provide characterization results for choice rules in specific public goods environments. In a sense, this work can be viewed as the one-dimensional (positive) counterpart to the multi-dimensional (negative) results in Zhou (1991). Border and Jordan (1983) consider a multi-dimensional problem, and obtain positive results by making separability assumptions over preferences. The strategy-proof mechanisms that emerge in these public goods models are shown to be variants on median voter models. Specifically, it is as if, in addition to the genuine agents who vote, the planner includes "phantom" agents, endowed with fixed (single-peaked) preferences, who also "vote." Thus, a whole class of mechanisms is generated, by varying the number and type of phantom voters.

Barberà, Sonnenshein, and Zhou (1991) consider a particular framework in which a (not necessarily fixed) number of objects has to be selected from a total set K – for example, K may comprise bills considered for adoption by a legislature, or candidates considered for membership of a club. Assuming that voters' preferences satisfy a natural form of separability, it is shown that strategy-proof mechanisms do exist, and take the form of "voting by committees." (A special case of this is "voting by quota" – a mechanism used by some clubs. A candidate is elected if he receives more than a predetermined number of votes, and voters are allowed to vote for as many candidates as they choose.) Barberà, Gul, and Stachetti (1991) conduct a general analysis of strategy-proof mechanisms when the choice set A is a lattice; by generalizing the notion of single-peaked preferences and median voter schemes, they are able to unify Barberà, Sonnenshein, and Zhou (1991) with the earlier work of Moulin (1980a) and Border and Jordan (1983).

Turning now to private goods environments, Sprumont (1991) considers a classic division problem.[74] For example, imagine a group of agents participating in a joint project which requires a fixed total labor input. It has been agreed that they should each be paid in proportion to the amount that they individually work; the problem is to divide up the work according to the vector of their preferences. (Notice that, given the exogenous payment rule, the problem is really one-dimensional; moreover, it is natural that the agents' preferences are single-peaked.) Sprumont addresses the question of what division rules can be implemented in dominant strategy equilibrium. Barberà and Jackson (1991b) pursue this line of enquiry more generally: they are currently investigating classical exchange economies. It appears that, in these private goods models, the kinds of strategy-proof mechanisms that emerge are variants on fixed-price rationing schemes (see, e.g., Benassy, 1982).

Finally, Moulin and Shanker (1991) address the question of what kinds of cost-sharing, or surplus-sharing, mechanisms can be devised which are strategy-proof and budget-balanced (or at least, make no aggregate loss). In a cost-sharing mechanism, users demand a quantity of output after which they share the production cost; for example, a computer network, a telephone system, a chain store. In a surplus-sharing mechanism, users offer a quantity of input after which they share the output; for example, fishing or pumping oil from a common pool. (Notice that, unlike in Sprumont (1991), these are *two*-dimensional private-goods problems.) It turns out that, if the technology has decreasing returns, an attractive strategy-proof mechanism emerges, which has a *serial* cost-sharing (surplus-sharing) structure. This is most easily understood in a two-agent cost-sharing example, where $C(\cdot)$ is the (convex) total cost function. Let agent 1 demand q_1, and agent 2 demand q_2; and suppose, without loss of generality, that agent 1 demands the smaller quantity. Then agent 1 pays an amount equal to what the per capita cost would have been had – hypothetically – *both* agents demanded q_1: that is, agent 1 pays $\frac{1}{2}C(2q_1)$. And agent 2 also pays this amount, together with the incremental cost $C(q_1+q_2)-C(2q_1)$; that is, he pays $C(q_1+q_2)-\frac{1}{2}C(2q_1)$ net.[75] (Notice that there is no presumption here that preferences are quasi-linear: however, convexity and monotonicity are assumed.) These mechanisms typically do not yield first-best efficient outcomes; however, Moulin and Shenker argue that their mechanisms are second-best efficient, within the class of strategy-proof mechanisms. Moulin (1991) extends these ideas to a more classic public good framework (with and without excludability).

To summarize section 1

(i) Dominant strategy mechanisms have great advantages. Agents do not need to know about the other agents' preferences or strategic behavior. And the mechanism can be simple.[76]

(ii) Unfortunately, choice rules are unlikely to be implementable in dominant strategy equilibrium if the domain is very rich and/or the choice rule is efficient. However, it is known that useful strategy-proof mechanisms do exist for particular domains (e.g., quasi-linear or single-peaked preferences), for particular voting or public good problems, and for particular cost-sharing (or surplus-sharing) problems. We do not yet have a full picture of what can be dominant-strategy implemented in general economic environments, but there are grounds for being more optimistic than the early impossibility results might have suggested. It is clear, though, that in the tradeoff between the efficiency properties and the incentive properties of mechanisms, the former will have to be sacrificed to the latter given the stringency of requiring that mechanisms always have dominant strategy equilibria.

(iii) In order to strike a happier medium between the normative and the incentive goals, we may need to turn to mechanisms that exploit the mutual knowledge and strategic interaction of the agents. Given our assumption of complete information, the natural place to start is with *Nash* implementation.

2 NASH IMPLEMENTATION

Although revelation mechanisms are attractively simple, they turn out to be of limited value for Nash implementation: a choice rule can be truthfully implemented in Nash equilibrium only if it can be truthfully implemented in dominant strategy equilibrium.[77] To see why, suppose preferences in Θ have independent domains; and suppose some revelation mechanism g^* truthfully implements a choice rule f in Nash equilibrium. Then for all $\theta \in \Theta$, truth-telling – viz., the vector of announcements $(R_1(\theta), \ldots, R_I(\theta))$ – constitutes a Nash equilibrium of g^*, with an outcome $g^*[R_1(\theta), \ldots, R_I(\theta)] \in f(\theta)$. Given that preferences in Θ have independent domain, it follows that for each i:

$$g^*[R_1, \ldots, R_{i-1}, R_i(\theta), R_{i+1}, \ldots, R_I] R_i(\theta) \quad g^*[R_1, \ldots, R_{i-1}, R_i(\phi), R_{i+1}, \ldots, R_I]$$

for all $\phi \in \Theta$ and for all possible preference orderings R_j in Θ, $j \neq i$. Hence truth-telling is a dominant strategy equilibrium too.

Thus, for Nash implementation, we need to use more general mechanisms than revelation mechanisms in which each agent reports his own preference ordering. It is useful to note that there is a version of the Revelation Principle which applies here, provided we enlarge the strategy set of each player so that he reports the vector of *all* the agents' preference orderings – in effect, he reports the state θ.[78] (This is natural, since, in an environment with complete information, an agent i's "type" includes his knowledge of θ, not just his personal preference ordering $R_i(\theta)$.) However, the Revelation Principle now has very little cutting power: once the agents' strategy sets have been enlarged in this way, it is only too easy to "truthfully implement" any choice rule in Nash equilibrium. The incentive constraints are very weak. For example, take any single-valued choice rule f, and consider the following "revelation mechanism."[79] Everyone reports a state in Θ. If they agree on some common θ, outcome $f(\theta)$ is implemented. If they disagree, then a "bad" outcome (from the agents' perspectives) is implemented. Clearly, in state θ it is a Nash equilibrium for everyone to announce the truth. The snag is that every other common report $\phi \neq \theta$ is also a Nash equilibrium. We have been successful in "truthfully implementing" f in Nash equilibrium, but we are very far from (fully) Nash implementing f.[80]

The classic paper by Maskin (1977) appealed to two conditions on f, monotonicity and no veto power:

f is *monotonic* if, whenever $a \in f(\theta)$ for some outcome a in some state θ, but

$a \notin f(\phi)$ for some other state ϕ, then there must exist some agent i and outcome y such that:

$$aR_i(\theta)\ y \text{ and } yP_i(\phi)\ a.$$

That is, when switching from θ to ϕ, there is preference reversal (from weak to strict) across the pair (a,y) for agent i. Let us call agent i the *test agent*, and (a,y) the *test pair*. Incidentally, another common way of expressing monotonicity is in terms of nested lower contour sets. Define $L_i(a,\theta) \equiv \{\hat{a} \in A \mid a\ R_i(\theta)\ \hat{a}\}$ to be the lower contour set of agent i at outcome a in state θ. Suppose f is monotonic. Take any pair of states $\theta, \phi \in \Theta$, and any outcome $a \in f(\theta)$; if:

$$L_i(a,\theta) \subseteq L_i(a,\phi) \text{ for all agents } i,$$

then $a \in f(\phi)$ too.

f satisfies *no veto power* if, whenever some outcome a is top-ranked in A for at least $(I-1)$ of the agents in some state θ, then $a \in f(\theta)$.

Maskin proved the following fundamental result:

THEOREM 2.1 (Maskin, 1977) Any Nash implementable choice rule must be monotonic. Moreover, given three or more agents, any monotonic choice rule satisfying no veto power is Nash implementable.[81]

Notice that no veto power is typically a weak requirement when there are three or more agents. For example, if there is a private good from which the agents derive positive benefit then no veto power is vacuously satisfied, since no outcome can simultaneously be at the top of more than one agent's ranking of A. (For two agents – a case which is not covered by Maskin's sufficiency result – no veto power would be a hopelessly strong condition; it would be tantamount to both agents being "dictators" in the sense that the choice rule would have to select any outcome that either of them prefers most. We postpone until section 2.1 a discussion of two-agent implemention; generally speaking, it is a lot harder.)

Thus, for three or more agents, monotonicity will in practice be both a necessary and a sufficient condition for some choice rule to be Nash implementable. How satisfactory is this conclusion? Monotonicity means that if an outcome chosen by f moves up everyone's rankings, then it should continue to be chosen. At first glance, this appears to be an innocuous requirement: if it is decided to build a bridge (say) given some configuration of households' preferences, then surely the bridge ought still to be built if their preferences change in a way that makes the bridge a yet more attractive proposition to everyone? However, this simple public good example may be misleading. It overlooks richer questions involving distribution as well as efficiency. For example, consider a (single-valued) choice rule that specifies not only the decision whether to build the bridge, but also how much each household should contribute. Then, if households' payments are positively related to their willingness to pay for the bridge, the choice rule will be non-monotonic. To see why, suppose that in state θ the vector of households' willingness to pay is $(1,1,\ldots,1)$, whereas in state ϕ the vector is $(100,1,\ldots,1)$. If the cost of the bridge is less than I, it is efficient to build the bridge in both states. But then monotonicity does not allow that the first household pays more in the second state – since it requires that $f(\phi)=f(\theta)$.

The necessity of monotonicity is clear. Let a mechanism g Nash implement f. For any θ and $a \in f(\theta)$, there is a Nash equilibrium of g in state θ whose outcome is a. Take some ϕ for which $a \notin f(\phi)$. Suppose there were no test agent i or test pair (a,y), as per the above definition of monotonicity. Then the strategies which lead to outcome $a \in f(\theta)$ being a Nash equilibrium of g in state θ also constitutes a Nash equilibrium in state ϕ. (In short, if the Nash equilibrium outcome a moves up everyone's rankings when switching from state θ to state ϕ, then it must continue to be a Nash equilibrium outcome.) But this would mean that g has an unwanted equilibrium in state ϕ, and so does not Nash implement f – a contradiction.

The sufficiency part of the theorem 2.1 requires the construction of a mechanism g. Here is a simple mechanism based on that in Repullo (1987):

Each agent i announces a state of nature, an outcome, and a non-negative integer:

> If all agents announce the same state θ, together with the same outcome $a \in f(\theta)$, then the outcome a is implemented.
>
> If all but one of the agents agree on θ and $a \in f(\theta)$, but the remaining agent i announces another state of nature ϕ, then outcome a is still implemented – unless $a \notin f(\phi)$ *and* i happens to be the test agent (as defined above) *and* i announces the outcome y from the test pair (a,y), in which case outcome y is implemented.
>
> Otherwise, implement the outcome announced by the agent who announces the highest integer. That is, they play an *integer game*. (It does not matter how ties are broken.)

If the true state is θ, then it is a Nash equilibrium for all the agents to announce θ together with some $a \in f(\theta)$: no test agent i can benefit from announcing (ϕ,y) since $a\ R_i(\theta)\ y$. However, if the true state is ϕ, this cannot be a Nash equilibrium, since the test agent i could announce (ϕ,y) and y would be implemented, which would be better for him since $y\ P_i(\phi)\ a$. The only other possible Nash equilibrium is where all but one of the agents are content not to exercise their option to win the "integer game," i.e., the outcome of g is top-ranked in A for them – in which case no veto power implies that this outcome is in the choice set of f anyway.

Notice that the integers are no more than "nuisance strategies": they are tacked on to what is in essence a "revelation mechanism." Their role is to help rule out certain unwanted equilibria.[82] Integer games are another controversial device, like tail-chases, which are much used in mechanism design. (One difference between integer games and tail-chases is that integer games are played among agents, whereas tail-chasing is a solo pursuit.) What would imposing some form of boundedness do? One finite substitute for an integer game is a *roulette*, or *modulo game*. Each agent announces an integer in the range $\{1, \ldots, I\}$; if the sum of these integers turns out to be Σ, say, then the "winning" agent – whose announced outcome is implemented – is given by $1 + \text{mod}_I(\Sigma)$. Clearly, whatever the other agents announce, any agent i can win by announcing the appropriate integer, and so there are no pure strategy Nash equilibria. Although finite, the roulette thus mimicks the role of the integer game. However, there is a problem: the roulette has a compeling – and unwanted – mixed-strategy equilibrium in which everyone uniformly randomizes across $\{1, \ldots, I\}$. This could of course be arbitrarily ruled out by simply ignoring mixed-strategy equilibria in mechanism design. For the most part, this has been the position adopted in the literature. But I believe this is mistaken; by moving from an integer game to a roulette, we merely substitute one problem by another. In general, we should be looking for mechanisms which avoid using devices such as tail-chases, integer games, roulettes, and the like.[83]

There has been a great deal of work on Nash implementation in "classical" economic environments, with both private and public goods. This literature has been concerned with matters such as the Nash implementation of Walrasian or Lindahl choice rules (which, as we have seen in section 1, are typically not strategy proof and so cannot be dominant strategy implemented). This line of enquiry, and indeed much of the work on incentives and Nash equilibrium, was inspired by the key paper by Groves and Ledyard (1977). I will not survey the material here.[84] Much of it can be seen implicitly or explicitly to revolve around Maskin's characterization theorem (theorem 2.1). There are difficult questions in this area – particularly relating to the case of unknown endowments, where the vexed issue of infeasible off-the-equilibrium-path allocations crops up.[85] Other lines of enquiry include:

The design of mechanisms which have desirable properties – for example:

mechanisms with minimal strategy spaces;[86]

mechanisms that are continuous.[87]

The analysis of descriptive competitive mechanisms.[88]

The Nash implementation of choice rules that are equitable.[89]

Before moving on to a discussion of the particular difficulties of two-person Nash implementation (section 2.1), and the Nash implementation of single-valued choice rules (section 2.2), we should ask: for the many-agent case, can the gap between Maskin's necessary condition (monotonicity) and his sufficiency condition (monotononicity + no veto power) be closed?[90] This is done in Moore and Repullo (1990), where a new condition – which lies strictly between the two – is found to be both necessary and sufficient. Sjöström (1991c) provides an equivalent condition, which has the merit that there is an algorithm for checking whether or not it holds.

Another, elegantly simple, necessary, and sufficient condition has been found by Danilov (1992) for the case where the domain Θ is universal (see also Yamato, 1991a). The following is a variant on Danilov's result.

For a given choice rule f, define outcome x to be *essential* for an agent i in a set X if there exists some profile ξ for which $x \in f(\xi)$, x is maximal for i in X, and x is maximal in A for all the other agents $j \neq i$.

f is *strongly monotonic* if, whenever $a \in f(\theta)$ for some outcome a in some state θ, but $a \notin f(\phi)$ for some other state ϕ, then there must exist some agent i and outcome y such that y is essential for i in the lower contour set $L_i(a,\theta)$, and $y \; P_i(\phi) \; a$.

THEOREM 2.2 (cf. Danilov, 1992) Given a universal domain Θ, and three or more agents, a choice rule is Nash implementable if and only if it is strongly monotonic.[91]

2.1 Nash implementation with two agents

Theorem 2.1 leaves open the question of whether there are any sufficient conditions for a choice rule to be Nash implementable when there are just two agents (beyond the necessary condition of monotonicity). As already indicated, life is typically much more difficult with two agents, since, in the event of disagreement, the "planner" (if there is one) cannot tell who is misreporting. (Cf. the mechanism sketched out earlier to prove the sufficiency part of theorem 2.1 for the many-agent case – where it was clear who, if any, was the odd agent out.) Nonetheless, the two-agent case is now seen to be an important one, on account of the contractual applications.

One early, and unfortunately negative, result for the two-agent case – due to Maskin (1977) and Hurwicz and Schmeidler (1978) – showed that if Θ comprises all strict orderings over A, then the only Pareto efficient choice rules that can be Nash implemented are dictatorial. (Notice that this result is reminiscent of dominant strategy implementation.) For more general two-agent cases, Moore and Repullo (1990) and Dutta and Sen (1991b) provide a complex condition which is both necessary and sufficient for Nash implementability. Again, Sjöström (1991c) provides an equivalent condition, together with an algorithm for checking whether or not it holds.

Rather than discuss these general results here, I shall instead present a couple of more transparent – and therefore perhaps more useful – sufficiency results: corollary 3 from Moore and Repullo (1990), and proposition 5.1 from Dutta and Sen (1991b). The first result employs a *bad outcome*: an outcome which is always worse for both agents than anything in the range of f. (For example, the bad outcome may involve both agents giving a large fine to a predesignated third party.) Bad outcomes are useful in two-agent mechanisms because they force a certain degree of agreement upon the agents: "if you disagree too much, I'll shoot both of you." This kind of construction is amusing, but arguably rather unsatisfactory: it begs the question as to whether the agents would be "shot" out of equilibrium. We will return to this issue when we discuss renegotiation in section 7.[92] For the moment, we appeal to the existence of a bad outcome, as is common to many two-agent mechanisms.

A choice rule f satisfies *restricted veto power* if, whenever some outcome a is maximal for least $(I-1)$ of the agents in some state θ, and a is not strictly worse than everything in the range of f for the remaining agent, then $a \in f(\theta)$. Notice that restricted veto power becomes a weaker condition as the range of f becomes narrower.[93] In many practical economic applications, where there is a reasonable conflict of interest between the agents, an allocation which is a bliss point for agent 1 (say) will be very poor for agent 2 – worse than anything in the range of f. In these circumstances, agent 2 can veto such an allocation. Thus, in practice, restricted veto power will be much weaker than no veto power.

THEOREM 2.3 (Moore and Repullo, 1990) Suppose there are two agents, and a bad outcome. Then any choice rule satisfying monotonicity and restricted veto power is Nash implementable.

The second sufficiency result is useful for more standard economic environments. We make the following *assumption B*:

> A is a compact subset of a finite-dimensional Euclidean space, and all preference orderings in Θ are continuous. Moreover, for any closed ball $B \subseteq A$,[94] it cannot be the case that, in any state θ, some outcome $b \in B$ is maximal for *both* agents in B. Finally, we assume that, if monotonicity is satisfied (see our earlier definition), the outcome y can be found such that $a\ P_i(\theta)\ y$ (as well as $y\ P_i(\phi)\ a$).

Notice that all three parts of assumption B will typically be satisfied if there is a suitable conflict of interest between the two agents – e.g., they each hold some divisible private good like money.

THEOREM 2.4 (Dutta and Sen, 1991b) Consider two agents in an economy satisfying assumption B. A choice rule f will be Nash implementable if it satisfies monotonicity and *non-empty lower intersection* – viz., for any pair of states θ,ϕ, and any pair of outcomes $a \in f(\theta)$ and $b \in f(\phi)$, there exists some outcome c such that $a\ P_1(\theta)\ c$ and $b\ P_2(\phi)\ c$.[95]

Non-empty lower intersection would hold, for example, in an exchange economy for which indifference curves never touch the axes and for which the choice rule always allocates positive vectors of commodities. (It would also hold if there were a bad outcome, since this bad outcome could play the role of c in theorem 2.4.)

Theorem 2.4 is related to corollary 4 in Moore and Repullo (1990); and has features in common with results in Maskin (1979b) and Roberts (1984, appendix). However, the mechanism Dutta and Sen use to prove theorem 2.4 has the merit that, *for finite* Θ, it does *not* involve the use of an "open set" device – a device used to prove the three other cited sufficiency results.[96] This unattractive device deserves comment, since it has been used elsewhere in the literature. Certain strategy configurations are ruled out from being (unwanted) Nash equilibria on account of the fact that some agent i, say, is failing to achieve a maximum in an open set. That is, for some strategy combinations of the other agents, agent i does not have a best response. This seems at odds with the use of Nash equilibrium as a solution concept, in which agents are meant always to choose best responses. It is important to avoid these kinds of features if at all possible, since the mechanisms seem neither robust nor realistic. We should always insist on the existence of best responses. More on this in section 4.1 below.

2.2 Nash implementation of single-valued choice rules

Recall that in most applications we are likely to be interested in implementing choice rules that are (almost everywhere) single-valued. Unfortunately, it turns out that relatively few single-valued choice rules can be Nash implemented if the domain Θ is sufficiently rich. In particular, Dasgupta, Hammond, and Maskin (1979) prove the following important result (theorem 7.2.3) showing that Nash implementation delivers no more than truthful implementation in dominant strategy equilibrium.

A domain Θ is *monotonically closed* if the following is true. Preferences in Θ have independent domains (defined at the start of part two). Take any agent i, and any pair of states $\theta,\phi \in \Theta$. Pick any pair of outcomes a,b for which it is *not* the case that *either* $a\ R_i\ (\theta)\ b$ and $b\ P_i(\phi)\ a$ *or* $a\ P_i(\theta)\ b$ and $b\ R_i(\phi)\ a$. Then there exists some state ξ such that:

$$L_i(a,\theta) \subseteq L_i(a,\xi) \text{ and } L_i(b,\phi) \subseteq L_i(b,\xi).$$

For example, the universal domain is obviously monotonically closed. So too is any domain which contains all possible strict preference orderings over A. As a third example, consider an I-agent exchange economy in which A comprises all non-negative allocation vectors. If, for each agent, the domain comprises all preferences represented by strictly quasi-concave, strictly monotonic (continuous) utility functions, then it is monotonically closed.[97]

THEOREM 2.5 (Dasgupta, Hammond, and Maskin, 1979) Suppose a single-valued choice rule f is (fully) Nash implementable on a monotonically closed domain Θ. Then f is also truthfully implementable in dominant strategies.

Theorems 1.1 and 2.5 combine to give the important result:

THEOREM 2.6 (Muller and Satterthwaite, 1977; Roberts, 1979)[98] Suppose Θ includes all possible strict preference orderings over A. Then no single-valued choice rule f, whose range contains at least three distinct outcomes, can be Nash implemented unless it is dictatorial.[99]

Although it can be shown that the domain of quasi-linear preferences is not monotonically closed,[100] and so theorem 2.5 does not apply, nevertheless K. Roberts (1979) proves that the set of decisions $\{d(\theta) | \theta \in \Theta\}$ which can be Nash implemented is no greater than the set which can be truthfully implemented in dominant strategy equilibrium (cf. theorem 1.2 above):[101]

THEOREM 2.7 (Roberts, 1979) Consider the domain of *all* quasi-linear preferences. Let the set D of decisions be finite, but contain at least three outcomes. Take some generically single-valued choice rule $f = (d, t_1, \ldots, t_I)$ for which the range of d is the whole of D. If f is Nash implementable, then there exists some non-negative vector $(k_1, \ldots, k_I) \neq 0$ and some real-valued function u_0 defined on D such that, generically:

$$d(\theta) = \underset{a \in A}{\text{argmax}}\ u_0(a) + \sum_{i=1}^{I} k_i u_i(a,\theta).$$

Roberts uses the same argument to prove both theorem 1.2 (first part) and theorem 2.7. Recall the "monotonicity condition" which we derived at the start of the earlier sketch proof of theorem 1.2:

Take any pair of states $\theta, \phi \in \Theta$; if:

$$u_i(d(\theta),\phi) - u_i(d(\theta),\theta) > u_i(a,\phi) - u_i(a,\theta)$$

for all i and for all $a \in D$ other than $d(\theta)$, then $d(\phi)=d(\theta)$.

This is no more than Maskin's notion of monotonicity applied to a *single-valued* decision rule d. The proof of the first part of theorem 1.2 also serves to prove theorem 2.7.

A simple proof of theorem 2.6 follows directly from theorem 2.7. The argument is similar to our earlier proof of the Gibbard–Satterthwaite theorem, theorem 1.1. Rule out transfers. Take some agent i for whom $k_i>0$. Unles i is a dictator, we can find a state θ and an outcome a for which $u_i(f(\theta),\theta)<u_i(a,\theta)$. Assuming that f is Nash implementable by some mechanism g, the Nash equilibrium of g in state θ, whose outcome is $f(\theta)$, must continue to be a Nash equilibrium if agent i's preferences u_i are scaled by some factor $S>0$. (Rescaling u_i does not affect ordinal preferences.) Therefore $f(\theta)$ must continue to be the outcome chosen by f after the rescaling. But for sufficiently large S:

$$u_o(a)+Sk_iu_i(a,\theta)+\sum_{j\neq i} k_ju_j(a,\theta)$$
$$>u_o(f(\theta))+Sk_iu_i(f(\theta),\theta)+\sum_{j\neq i} k_ju_j(f(\theta),\theta)$$

contrary to the theorem 2.7. Hence i must be a dictator, and $k_j=0$ for all $j\neq i$. Theorem 2.6 is proved.

To summarize section 2

(i) In general, more can be implemented in Nash equilibrium than in dominant strategy equilibrium – although the necessary condition of monotonicity is quite a serious restriction in that we may be unable to Nash implement choice rules that are concerned with distribution as well as efficiency.

(ii) Single-valued choice rules may be particularly troublesome in that if the domain of preferences is sufficiently rich, the move from dominant strategy to Nash may not help at all: only the restricted class of strategy-proof choice rules may be Nash implementable. The case of two agents also poses particular difficulties. Unfortunately, choice rules will typically be single-valued in most applications; and the two-agent case is the leading case for contractual applications. So our results are disappointing.

(iii) Moreover, the mechanisms used in the literature on Nash implementation are for the most part highly complex – often employing some unconvincing device such as an integer game, a roulette, or an open set.

3 SUBGAME PERFECT IMPLEMENTATION

As we have seen, the usual difficulty with Nash implementation is that a normal form game may have too many Nash equilibria: it is in order to knock out unwanted equilibria that nuisance strategies have to be built into a mechanism.

Another way to knock out unwanted equilibria is to add stages to the mechanism, and impose the requirement that off-the-equilibrium-path strategies (threats) must be credible – i.e., restrict attention to the subgame perfect equilibria of extensive form mechanisms.

An important distinction can be drawn between general extensive form mechanisms in which agents may make simultaneous moves at some point (section 3.1 below), and those in which agents always take turns (sections 3.2 and 3.3).

The latter kind of mechanism is special, because, in each state of nature, the agents play a game of *perfect information*. I shall refer to these special mechanisms as *sequential mechanisms*, or *trees*.

There has been considerable work done on the use of sequential mechanisms in specific environments, especially in the context of voting – either to analyse specific voting procedures, or to implement specific choice rules. An important precursor was Farquharson's 1957 thesis on the theory of voting (published as a book in 1969). He introduced the concept of "sophisticated voting," which Moulin (1979) later termed dominance solvability – the successive elimination of weakly dominated strategies to yield a unique outcome. For sequential games, Moulin showed that there is almost an equivalence between dominance solvability and subgame perfection.[102] In a number of papers (Moulin 1979, 1980b, 1981a), and in his 1983 book, Moulin extensively studied implementation using dominance solvability – explicitly showing that, in contrast to the results for Nash implementation, non-monotonic choice rules could be implemented. In particular, he examined sequential voting procedures – successive voting over binary choices,[103] and successive voting by veto.[104] (Notice that these mechanisms can easily be redefined as trees, in which no one moves simultaneously.) Howard (1990) provides a more recent application of a tree-mechanism, to implement the result of a system of voting known as "alternative voting" (the single-transferable vote). Section 4 of Hererro and Srivastava (forthcoming) provides a general analysis of what can be implemented using multi-stage voting procedures.

Another, related, line of enquiry was begun by Crawford (1977), who analysed the classic divide-and-choose procedure – which is perhaps the most familiar of stage mechanisms. In Crawford (1979), he extended this idea by, among other things, introducing the possibility of auctioning off the role of the divider. His mechanism was applied and further developed by Demange (1984) and, for the case of public goods, by Moulin (1981b, 1984a).

Sequential mechanisms have recently been used in a number of other specific contexts. Glazer and Ma (1989) study the efficient allocation of a prize (King Solomon's dilemma). The papers by Bagnoli and Lipman (1989), Jackson and Moulin (forthcoming), and Varian (1990a and b) examine the provision of public goods. In Moulin (1984b) and Howard (forthcoming), specific bargaining outcomes are implemented.

The use of sequential mechanisms in general environments will be discussed further in section 3.2 below.

3.1 General extensive form mechanisms

When simultaneous as well as sequential moves are allowed, Moore and Repullo (1988) provided a partial characterization of the choice rules that can be implemented in subgame perfect equilibria. Their results were refined by Abreu and Sen (1990) in the following result:

THEOREM 3.1 (Moore and Repullo, 1988; Abreu and Sen, 1990) Any choice rule f that is implementable in subgame perfect equilibrium must satisfy the following condition. There is a subset of outcomes $B \subseteq A$, containing the range of f, such that, whenever $a \in f(\theta)$ for some outcome a and some state θ, but $a \notin f(\phi)$ for some other state ϕ, there must exist a sequence of outcomes, $a=a_0, a_1, \ldots, a_T=x, a_{T+1}=y$, in B such that for each $t=0, \ldots, T$,

in state θ: $a_t \; R_{j(t)}(\theta) \; a_{t+1}$ for some agent $j(t)$;
in state ϕ: a_t is not maximal in B for $j(t)$,
and $a_{T+1} \; P_{j(T)}(\phi) \; a_T$.[105]

Conversely, if f satisfies this condition and no veto power, and if there are three or more agents, then f is implementable in subgame perfect equilibrium.[106]

Although the statement of the theorem is very long, there is much in common with Maskin's theorem on Nash implementation (theorem 2.1): a condition is found to be necessary for subgame perfect implementability, which, together with no veto power and at least three agents, is also sufficient.

This new condition is much weaker than Maskin's monotonicity condition, however. Consider some outcome $a \in f(\theta)$ for which $a \notin f(\phi)$. Monotonicity would require there to be another outcome y such that (a,y) are a test pair for some test agent i – i.e., $a \; R_i(\theta) \; y$ and $y \; P_i(\phi) \; b$. In the above theorem, there still has to be a test pair (x,y) and test agent $j(T)$ – i.e., $x\ R_{j(T)}(\theta)\ y$ and $y\ P_{j(T)}(\phi)\ x$ – but it is no longer necessary that $a=x$. This considerably enlarges the set of implementable choice rules, particularly in economic environments, where there is some conflict of interest among the agents – for example, if there is at least one divisible private good (e.g., money) from which agents derive positive benefit.

To see why, consider the following example, of a two-agent exchange economy, depicted in the Edgeworth box (figure 5.6):

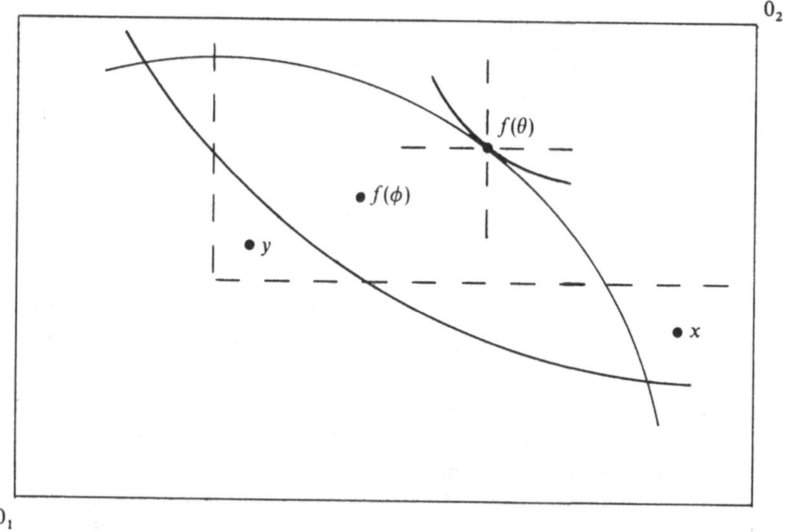

Figure 5.6

There are two possible states $\Theta=\{\theta,\phi\}$: in state θ both agents have Cobb–Douglas preferences (the solid indifference curves); and in state ϕ both agents have Leontief preferences (the dashed indifference curves). $f(\theta)$ and $f(\phi)$ are the respective allocations of a choice rule f. Note that at $f(\theta)$, the θ-lower contour sets are contained in the ϕ-lower contour sets, and so f is not monotonic (there is no y such that $f(\theta)\ R_i(\theta)\ y$ and $y\ P_i(\phi) f(\theta)$ for either agent i). f therefore cannot be Nash implemented.

f does, however, satisfy the necessary condition for subgame perfect implementation given in theorem 3.1. Let **B** be the entire Edgeworth box. For example, consider the ordered pair (θ,ϕ) for which $a=f(\theta)$ is not contained in $f(\phi)$. Set T equal to 1, and the sequence (a_0,a_1,a_2) equal to $(f(\theta),x,y)$. Set agent $j(0)$ to be agent 2, and agent $j(1)$ to be agent 1. Note that

$f(\theta)\ R_2(\theta)\ x$, $x\ R_1(\theta)\ y$, and $y\ P_1(\phi)\ x$, as required. (In fact the first two of these are strict preferences, and agent $j(0)$ could have been agent 1. No matter.) Further, note that in state ϕ outcome $f(\theta)$ (resp. x) is not maximal in B for agent 2 (resp. agent 1), also as required. Thus for this ordered pair (θ,ϕ), the necessary condition is satisfied. [The same B must work for the (only) other ordered pair, (ϕ,θ). It does: for this case, set T again equal to 1, set $(a_0,a_1,a_2)=(f(\phi),y,x)$, and set $j(0)=j(1)=1$.] Had there been three agents in this example, we would know from theorem 3.1 that this f can be subgame perfect implemented. In fact it turns out that, even though there are only two agents, it can be implemented using a very simple mechanism which I will present shortly.

This example is typical of a choice rule in an economic environment. Section 3 of Moore and Repullo (1988) shows that usually the sequences $(a_0, \ldots, a_T, a_{T+1})$ need not be more than of length three, i.e., $T+1 \leq 2$. Only in very unlikely cases will $T+1$ need to be as great as 3. This is useful to know, since $\max\{T+1\}$ equals the number of stages in the mechanism used to prove the sufficiency part of theorem 3.1. That is, in economic environments, mechanisms usually need not have more than two stages, or, in very unlikely cases, three.

In passing, we should confirm that Solomon's problem (before the introduction of side-payments) cannot be solved using stage mechanisms. His choice rule $f(\alpha)=a$, $f(\beta)=b$ does not satisfy the necessary condition given in theorem 3.1. To see this, take the ordered pair $(\theta,\phi)=(\alpha,\beta)$, for which $f(\alpha)=a \notin f(\beta)$. Agent $j(0)$ could not be Anna since $a_0=a$ has to be contained in any chosen set B, and a is Anna's top-ranked outcome in state β (remember a_0 must not be maximal in B for $j(0)$ in state β). Therefore $j(0)$ would have to be Bess. But then, since $a_0\ R_{j(0)}(\alpha)\ a_1$, the only candidate for $a_1\ (\neq a_0)$ would be outcome d. As Bess prefers a to d in state β, this rules out truncating the sequence at $a_{T+1}=a_1$ (there must be preference reversal across a_T and a_{T+1}). Unfortunately, d is always bottom-ranked for both agents. So one cannot find a third outcome $a_2\ (\neq a_1)$ in the sequence for which $a_1\ R_{j(1)}(\alpha)\ a_2$. In sum, the necessary condition in theorem 3.1 is violated, and Solomon's choice rule f is not subgame perfect implementable.[107]

The mechanism constructed to prove the sufficiency part of theorem 3.1 is complex: the three or more agents move simultaneously at each stage, and their strategy sets are unconvincingly rich. In particular, the mechanism has an integer game at each stage. It is therefore vulnerable to the same criticisms that were levelled at some of the mechanisms given earlier. The general two-agent case is even more troubling: the mechanism used in Moore and Repullo (1988) relies on the existence of a bad outcome – cf. theorem 2.3.

Nevertheless, the great attraction of extensive form mechanisms is that often they can be designed to be refreshingly simple, yet highly effective. Consider again the Edgeworth box example. The following mechanism implements the choice rule f in subgame perfect equilibrium, without recourse to integer games or to bad outcomes. It even avoids the agents making simultaneous moves (see figure 5.7).

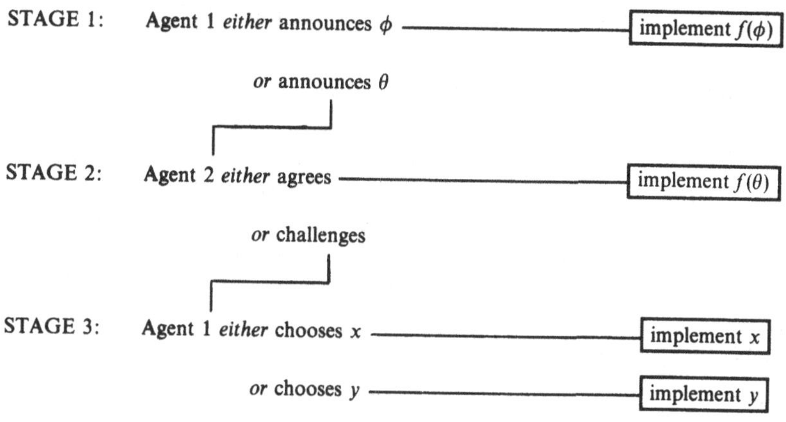

Figure 5.7

As usual, to find the subgame perfect equilibria, one works back from the end, from stage 3 (assuming the mechanism reaches that far). Agent 1 will choose outcome x in state θ, and choose outcome y in state ϕ. At the previous stage 2, agent 2 will therefore agree in state θ (leading to outcome $f(\theta)$), and challenge in state ϕ (leading to outcome y). Hence at stage 1 agent 1 will announce θ in state θ (leading to outcome $f(\theta)$), and announce ϕ in state ϕ (leading to outcome $f(\phi)$. In sum, the mechanism implements f in subgame perfect equilibrium.

The important point is that if the game were in normal form, there would be a second equilibrium in state ϕ. Namely, agent 1 announces θ and threatens to choose x in preference to y; and agent 2 does not challenge. This second equilibrium involves agent 1 making an incredible threat: if preferences were Leontief and stage 3 were ever reached, he would in fact choose y. The unwanted equilibrium has been knocked out by appealing to the fact that threats have to be credible: the subgame perfectness requirement.

3.2 Sequential mechanisms

This last mechanism, together with the examples in sections VI – VIII of part one, suggest that a lot can be achieved using mechanisms in which agents take turns to move: they therefore have perfect information when they play. We shall refer to these kinds of mechanisms as sequential mechanisms, or trees.

In particular, for the domain of quasi-linear preferences, anything can be implemented. The kind of mechanism used in section VII of part one can be used to prove:

THEOREM 3.2 (Moore and Repullo, 1988, section 5) Suppose the domain Θ of preferences is quasi-linear and finite. Consider any single-valued choice rule $f = (d, t_1, \ldots, t_I)$, where d is the decision rule and the t_i's are transfers to the agents. Then, if there are three or more agents, f can be subgame perfect implemented using a sequential mechanism in which the sum of the transfers can be chosen to balance to any amount required at each point of the mechanism (i.e., on and off the equilibrium path). If there are two agents the same is true, except that, off the equilibrium path, there may be an additional surplus generated.

As was pointed out in section VII of part one, this result is robust to small perturbations in the agents' preferences: quasi-linearity is not being delicately exploited, unlike in the literature on dominant strategy and Nash implementation (see theorems 1.2 and 2.7 above).

It would be very desirable to know more about what can be achieved using sequential mechanisms for general preferences. Moulin's work on dominance solvability takes us some way (Moulin, 1979, 1980b, 1981a, 1983): his mechanisms can all be made into trees.[108] Further progress has recently been made by Herrero and Srivastava (forthcoming) and, particularly, by Srivastava and Trick (1991). The task remains, however, of finding a full and workable characterization of the choice rules that can be implemented in trees; in my view, this is one of the most fascinating open problems in implementation theory.

3.3 Simple sequential mechanisms

In section VIII of part one, I made a case for mechanisms in which agents not only took turns to move, but also each moved once only. This avoids subtle questions like: what ought I to think about an agent who has already made an "irrational" move; will he play "rationally" next time? If there is no next time, then it does not matter. Let us call these *simple sequential* mechanisms.

For ease of exposition, we begin by assuming that there are two agents $i=1,2$, and that their preferences are quasi-linear. (Both of these assumptions can be significantly relaxed; see below.) That is, in state θ, they have utility functions $u_i(d,\theta)+t_i$, say, where $d \in D$.[109] We also confine attention to single-valued choice rules $f(\theta)=(d(\phi),t_1(\theta),t_2(\theta))$, $\theta \in \Theta$.

For any given $f=(d,t_1,t_2)$, consider the simple sequential mechanism detailed in figure 5.8.

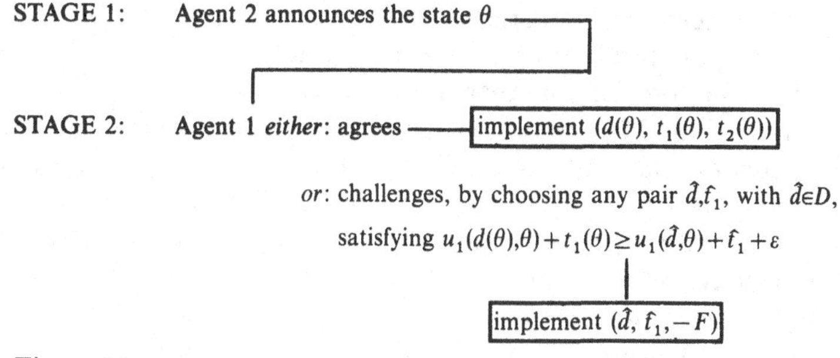
STAGE 1:
Agent 2 announces the state θ
STAGE 2:
Agent 1 *either*: agrees
implement $(d(\theta), t_1(\theta), t_2(\theta))$
or: challenges, by choosing any pair $\hat{d},\hat{t}_1$, with $\hat{d} \in D$,
satisfying $u_1(d(\theta),\theta)+t_1(\theta) \geq u_1(\hat{d},\theta)+\hat{t}_1+\varepsilon$
implement $(\hat{d}, \hat{t}_1, -F)$

Figure 5.8

Here, $F>0$ is a (large) fine imposed on agent 2 if agent 1 challenges at stage 2; and $\varepsilon>0$ is chosen to be small. (Any surplus generated from the fine F would go to a predesignated third party.)

It is straightforward to show that, given a sufficiently large fine F and a sufficiently small $\varepsilon>0$, the above mechanism implements f if Θ is finite and the following condition holds:

Condition M: For each state θ, there is some partition $\Theta^+ \cup \Theta^-$ of $\Theta\backslash\{\theta\}$ such that:

for each $\theta^- \in \Theta^-$: $u_2(d(\theta),\theta)+t_2(\theta)>u_2(d(\theta^-),\theta)+t_2(\theta^-)$; and

for each $\theta^+ \in \Theta^+$: if $f(\theta) \neq f(\theta^+)$ there exists some pair $(\hat{d},\hat{t}_1)$, with $\hat{d} \in D$, such that

$$u_1(d(\theta^+),\theta^+)+t_1(\theta^+)>u_1(\hat{d},\theta^+)+\hat{t}_1$$
$$\text{and } u_1(\hat{d},\theta)+\hat{t}_1>u_1(d(\theta^+),\theta)+t_1(\theta^+).$$

The logic behind condition M is straightforward. If the true state is θ, agent 2 has no incentive to lie at stage 1 by announcing some state $\theta^- \in \Theta^-$, because (for large enough F) the best that can happen at stage 2 is that agent 1 agrees and $f(\theta^-)$ is implemented; but since $f(\theta)\ P_2(\theta)\ f(\theta^-)$, agent 2 would have been better off announcing the truth. (The $\varepsilon>0$ deters agent 1 from challenging if agent 2 is truthful.) Equally, agent 2 dare not announce some

$\theta^+ \in \Theta^+$, because (for small enough ε) agent 1 would have an incentive to challenge, and agent 2 would be fined F.

A special case of condition M is worth noting. If, for each θ, the set Θ^+ can chosen to equal $\Theta \backslash \{\theta\}$ (so that Θ^- is the empty set), then f will be monotonic. In fact, this will be a particular form of monotonicity in which agent 1 is the test agent over *every* (ordered) pair of states (θ^+,θ) for which $f(\theta) \neq f(\theta^+)$. The most natural examples of when this is likely to hold are if either agent 1's are the preferences that are state-dependent, or if both agents' preferences are perfectly correlated.

The most natural example of when the general condition M is likely to hold is if θ is a scalar, and there is an ordering $\theta^1 < \theta^2 < \ldots < \theta^T$, say, of Θ. Then condition M would hold if, given a true state θ^t: agent 2 strictly prefers the outcome $f(\theta^t)$ to any other $f(\theta^{t-s})$, $s>0$; and agent 1 exhibits the preference reversals required by monotonicity for each of the ordered pairs (θ^{t+s},θ^t), $s>0$.[110] (In particular, if $d(\theta)$ were scalar and, say, increasing in θ, then it may well be enough that agent 1's preferences satisfy a standard single-crossing property condition.)[111]

Theorem 3.3 summarizes our findings. Notice that it is not necessary to have only two agents: indeed, with several agents the (out of equilibrium) fine F need not go to a predesignated third party, but could be shared out among agents $\{3,\ldots, I\}$.

THEOREM 3.3 Suppose the domain Θ comprises quasi-linear preferences, and that Θ is finite. Consider any single-valued choice rule $f=(d,t_1,\ldots,t_I)$, where d is the decision rule and the t_i's are transfers to the agents. If, for some pair of agents, agents 1 and 2 say, condition M is satisfied, then f can be subgame perfect implemented using a simple sequential mechanism.

The assumption of quasi-linearity is hardly needed for theorem 3.3. All that we have used it for is to ensure that a large enough fine F can be levied on agent 2 to deter him from misreporting the state at the first stage of the mechanism. This is a plausible enough requirement, and does not need quasi-linearity *per se*. The other agents' domain of preferences can be anything.[112]

4 UNDOMINATED NASH IMPLEMENTATION

The power of multi-stage mechanisms derives from the fact that sequential rationality (subgame perfection) eliminates unwanted Nash equilibria. This suggests that certain other refinements of Nash equilibrium ought to yield strong implementation results too. (Although it should be noted that changing the equilibrium concept will typically have ambiguous effects. On the one hand, it may make it easier to rule out unwanted equilibria; but, on the other hand, it may be more difficult to sustain the desired outcome(s).)

In particular, we could stick to single-stage mechanisms and confine our attention to those equilibria that are trembling-hand perfect (see Sjöström, (forthcoming)) – or even to those equilibria meeting the less stringent requirement that no agent's Nash equilibrium strategy is weakly dominated.

Palfrey and Srivastava (1991) prove the strong result that, with three or more agents, essentially any choice rule satisfying no veto power is implementable in *undominated Nash* equilibrium:

THEOREM 4.1 (Palfrey and Srivastava, 1991) Suppose there are three or more agents, and that in the domain Θ it is never the case that an agent is indifferent across all outcomes in A.[113] Then any choice rule satisfying no veto power is implementable in undominated Nash equilibrium.

In section V of part one of the chapter we saw an example of the ingenious kind of mechanism Palfrey and Srivastava devise to prove theorem 4.1. There, Solomon's problem was solved by placing Anna and Bess in separate cells and asking each of them to shout out who is the true mother. One reason for skepticism about this kind of mechanism is that it appeals to the device of *tail-chasing* to rule out unwanted equilibria. That is, in certain states, agents have no best response in the sense that whichever strategy is chosen there is always another which weakly dominates. The definition of undominated Nash equilibrium rules out such choices.

4.1 Undominated Nash implementation with bounded mechanisms

Jackson (forthcoming) argues that we ought not to admit mechanisms like this. The fact that in Solomon's problem, even though the environment is finite, the mechanism has to be infinite in order to work, gives the clue that something is wrong. To avoid these unconvincing tail chases, Jackson proposes that mechanisms should be *bounded*:

> whenever a strategy is weakly dominated, it must be by some other strategy which is itself not weakly dominated.

Notice that the definition of a bounded mechanism is made with reference to the environment in which it is to be used. Clearly any finite mechanism must be bounded, but not vice versa.

Jackson, Palfrey, and Srivastava (1991) have investigated what can be implemented in undominated Nash equilibrium using bounded mechanisms. In fact they go further, and also require that a best response must always exist (in and out of equilibrium) for any agent. This additional requirement – the *best response property* – precludes "open sets" to rule out certain strategy combinations as (undominated) Nash equilibria; see the discussion following theorem 2.4.[114]

Although it is of course restrictive to confine attention to mechanisms that are both bounded and satisfy the best response property, nevertheless the class of implementable choice rules is quite wide. The following condition, which is weaker than monotonicity, turns out to be sufficient for a choice rule f to be implementable if it satisfies no veto power and there are at least three agents:

A choice rule is *chained* if, whenever $a \in f(\theta)$ for some outcome a in some state θ, but $a \notin f(\phi)$ for some other state ϕ, then:

either (i) there must exist some agent i and outcome y such that:

$$a\ R_i(\theta)\ y \text{ and } y\ P_i(\phi)\ a;$$

or (ii) there must exist some pair of agents $\{i,j\}$ and set of outcomes $\{x,y,b\}$ such that:

$$x\ P_i(\theta)\ y \text{ and } y\ R_i(\phi)\ x$$
$$\text{and } b\ R_i(\phi)\ a \text{ and } b\ P_j(\phi)\ a.$$

Notice that (i) is just monotonicity. If monotonicity fails, then for the alternative condition (ii) to hold, one merely needs preference reversal for some agent i over some test pair $\{x,y\}$ (with strict preference in state θ); and there must be some other outcome b which in state ϕ dominates outcome a for both the test agent i and some other agent j. Happily, (ii) is a very weak requirement in economic environments where there are many agents, since there will almost always be some suitable preference reversal (with, in fact, strict preference in both states θ and ϕ); and a suitable outcome b can easily be found by simply allocating sufficient private resources to agents i and j from all the other agents.

THEOREM 4.2 (Jackson, Palfrey, and Srivastava, 1991) Suppose there are three or more agents, and a choice rule f is chained and satisfies no veto power. Then f can be implemented in undominated Nash equilibrium using a mechanism that is both bounded and satisfies the best response property.[115]

One nice spinoff of the proof of theorem 4.2 is that, if f is monotonic as well as satisfies no veto power, the *same* (bounded) mechanism can be used to implement f in both Nash and undominated Nash equilibria. This extends the results of Yamato (1991b).

Jackson, Palfrey, and Srivastava also show that the chained condition is close to being necessary for f to be implementable in undominated Nash equilibrium using a bounded mechanism.

(It should be noted that the related paper by Sjöström (forthcoming) on implementation in perfect equilibrium uses a bounded mechanism. He is thus able to implement more than Jackson, Palfrey, and Srivastava can with a bounded mechanism: there is no equivalent to the chained condition in Sjöström (forthcoming). For further discussion of Sjöström's paper, see section 6.)

4.2 Undominated Nash implementation with domain restrictions

An appealing feature of using undominated Nash implementation is that, under certain natural restrictions on the domain of preferences, the mechanisms can be simple and intuitive. Important illustrations of this are provided by two related (but independently discovered) mechanisms, from section 4 of Jackson, Palfrey, and Srivastava (1991) and Sjöström (1991b).

Jackson, Palfrey, and Srivastava (1991) define *separable environments*. Roughly speaking, this means that an agent or group of agents can be penalized (for misreporting) without disturbing the remainder of the agents. Economic environments will typically be separable – e.g., quasi-linear preferences with fines; or exchange economies with free disposal. Jackson, Palfrey, and Srivastava show that, in separable environments, any choice rule can be implemented in undominated Nash equilibrium using a bounded mechanism, even if there are just two agents. (Moreover, the mechanism can be constructed so that there are no mixed strategy Nash equilibria which only use undominated strategies.)

As an example, consider again Solomon's problem, with monetary side payments. The simple mechanism detailed in figure 5.9 implements his choice function f in undominated strategy equilibrium:

		Bess	
		t_α	t_β
Anna	s_α	a	b Bess pays Solomon v Anna pays Solomon ε
	s_β	b	b

Figure 5.9

where $\varepsilon > 0$; and the amount v is chosen to lie strictly between the valuation of the woman who is the mother of the living child and the valuation of the other woman (i.e., $v^m > v > v^n$).[116]

The logic is simple. In state α (when Anna is the mother), strategy t_α weakly dominates strategy t_β for Bess; and in state β (when Bess is the mother), strategy t_β weakly dominates strategy t_α. Thus the only undominated Nash equilibrium in state α is (s_α, t_α); and the only undominated Nash equilibrium in state β is (s_β, t_β). Notice that in state α, there is an unwanted Nash equilibrium, viz. (s_β, t_β); but this is knocked out once we impose the requirement that Bess does not play a dominated strategy.

Sjöström (1991b) introduces an attractive mechanism for use in economic environments when there are three or more agents. These environments could have production, private goods, and/or (excludable) public goods. Sjöström's mechanism is related to that used by Jackson, Palfrey, and Srivastava for separable environments: imagine placing the agents around a circle, and ask each agent i to report his own preferences, R_i^i, and those of his immediate neighbors, R_{i-1}^i and R_{i+1}^i. (The superscript i denotes a component of agent i's strategy.) Agent i's allocation is given by the maximal outcome in some set B_i according to the preference ordering R_i^i that he reports – provided that his reports R_{i-1}^i, R_{i+1}^i of his neighbors' preferences agree with what they report about themselves (viz., R_{i-1}^{i-1} and R_{i+1}^{i+1} respectively). If there is any disagreement on this score, agent i gets nothing.[117] The set B_i is a function of the *other* agents' reports *only*. Notice that the only way agent i's report R_i^i affects his payoff is via the selection of a maximal outcome in B_i. So if there is enough richness in the set of *possible* (out of equilibrium) sets B_i, then lying about R_i^i will be weakly dominated. Given that everyone reports the truth about their own preferences, noone will want to lie about his neighbors' preferences either – for fear of receiving nothing. Hence, provided that the selection of the sets B_i is made judiciously, any single-valued choice rule can be implemented in undominated Nash equilibrium. (Moreover, the mechanism can be constructed so that there are no mixed strategy Nash equilibria which only use undominated strategies.)

Aside from its simplicity, there are other strong features of Sjöström's mechanism. First, if Θ is finite, then the strategy sets will also be finite: there are no integer games or roulettes. Second, the mechanism has a natural interpretation as a "taxation mechanism."[118] Third, the informational requirements can be relaxed significantly: an agent need only know his two neighbors' preferences.[119]

The mechanisms of Sjöström and Jackson, Palfrey, and Srivastava have a further desirable property: they are dominance solvable (see the start of section 3 above). That is, the successive elimination of weakly dominated strategies yields a unique outcome. (In the case of Sjöström's mechanism, for example, uniqueness is guaranteed after at most two rounds of elimination.) In the next section we turn to the question of implementation using domination arguments alone. Before doing so, one unsatisfactory feature of the mechanisms of Sjöström and Jackson, Palfrey, and Srivastava should be highlighted: they both employ severe off-the equilibrium-path punishments ($\cong$ large fines). As we will see in section 5.2 below, Abreu and Matsushima (1990) have discovered an alternative mechanism which requires only small fines.

5 UNDOMINATED STRATEGY IMPLEMENTATION

One may be skeptical of Nash equilibrium (and refinements thereof) as a solution concept, and instead wish to presume a less demanding notion of rationality. In particular, suppose one merely assumed that agents never play weakly dominated strategies. Some recent papers have investigated what can be implemented with this assumption – either using a single round of elimination of weakly dominated strategies (implementation in *undominated strategy* equilibrium), or appealing to successive rounds of elimination (implementation in *iteratively undominated strategy* equilibrium).

5.1 A single round of elimination of dominated strategies

Jackson (forthcoming) has studied what can be implemented using mechanisms in which a *single* elimination of weakly dominated strategies leads to the desired set of outcomes specified by the choice rule. He confines attention to preference domains Θ that are *strictly value distinguished*: (i) no agent is ever indifferent across all outcomes in A; and (ii) if an agent i's preferences change when switching from one state θ to another state ϕ, then there must be a *strict* preference reversal – i.e., $a\ P_i(\theta)\ b$ and $b\ P_i(\phi)\ a$ for some $a,b \in A$. With this mild restriction on agents' preferences, Jackson proves a clever, and apparently strong, result:

THEOREM 5.1 (Jackson, forthcoming) If agents' preferences are strictly value distinguished, then *any* choice rule can be implemented in undominated strategy equilibrium.

However, there are some disturbing features of the mechanism used to prove this theorem. Indeed, the main purpose of Jackson in presenting the result was to offer a colorful critique of the kinds of construction employed in implementation theory generally. Consider the following example of his:

Suppose there are two agents, 1 and 2, two outcomes a and b, and two states, θ and ϕ. Agent 2 strictly prefers a to b in both states. Only agent 1's preferences reverse: $a\ P_1(\theta)\ b$ and $b\ P_1(\phi)\ a$. The choice rule f is nasty: $f(\theta)=b$ and $f(\phi)=a$. That is, f goes directly against the incentives of agent 1, even though it is only his preferences that change between states. Consider the following mechanism:

		Agent 2									
		s_2									
	$s_1(\theta)$	b	a	a	a	$\dots$	a	a	a	a	$\dots$
		b	a	a	a	$\dots$	b	b	b	b	$\dots$
		b	b	a	a	$\dots$	b	b	b	b	$\dots$
		b	b	b	a	$\dots$	b	b	b	b	$\dots$
		$\vdots$	$\vdots$	$\vdots$	$\vdots$		$\vdots$	$\vdots$	$\vdots$	$\vdots$	
Agent 1											
	$s_1(\phi)$	a	b	b	b	$\dots$	b	b	b	b	$\dots$
		a	a	a	a	$\dots$	a	b	b	b	$\dots$
		a	a	a	a	$\dots$	a	a	b	b	$\dots$
		a	a	a	a	$\dots$	a	a	a	b	$\dots$
		$\vdots$	$\vdots$	$\vdots$	$\vdots$		$\vdots$	$\vdots$	$\vdots$	$\vdots$	

Notice that each agent's strategy set is divided into two countable subsets, and the outcome matrix therefore comprises four regions. It is easily checked that agent 2 only has one undominated strategy: viz., the left-hand column of his first subset, marked s_2. For agent 1, the only undominated strategy in state θ is the top row of his first subset, marked $s_1(\theta)$; and in state ϕ the only undominated strategy is $s_1(\phi)$, the top row of his second subset. Thus the (unique) undominated strategy equilibrium outcomes are a and b in states θ and ϕ respectively – as required by the choice rule f.

One worrying aspect to the mechanism is that in state θ, given that agent 1 is playing $s_1(\theta)$, agent 2 could do better by switching from s_2 to another strategy. Equally, given that agent 2 is playing s_2, agent 1 could do better in state θ by switching from $s_1(\theta)$ to $s_1(\phi)$; and vice versa in state ϕ. In short, the undominated strategy equilibria are not Nash equilibria.

Another unsatisfactory feature of the mechanism is that it again uses the device of tail chasing to rule out unwanted equilibria. Consider agent 2. In state θ, he would, for example, be better off choosing *any* strategy in his first subset other than s_2; his difficulty is that he is spoiled for choice, since whichever one he chooses it is weakly dominated by a strategy further up the same subset. The definition of an undominated strategy equilibrium rules out such choices. Notice that the mechanism is infinite, even though the environment is finite.

Jackson's thesis is that we should place restraints on the kinds of mechanisms which we admit, to rule out this kind of tail chasing. In particular, they should be bounded (the definition of a bounded mechanism was given in section 4.1 above). Unfortunately, if mechanisms have to be bounded, little can be implemented in undominated strategy equilibrium:

THEOREM 5.2 (Jackson, forthcoming) Any choice rule that can be implemented in undominated strategy equilibrium using a bounded mechanism must be *strategy resistant*:

> For any agent i, if $\theta,\phi \in \Theta$ are such that $R_j(\theta)=R_j(\phi)$ for all $j \neq i$, then for each $b \in f(\phi)$ there exists $a \in f(\theta)$ such that $a\ R_i(\theta)\ b$.

To see why, consider some bounded mechanism g which implements f in undominated strategy equilibrium. In state ϕ there is a vector of undominated strategies $(s_1,\ldots, s_I)$, say, of g such that $g[s_1,\ldots, s_I]=b$. Consider agent i in state θ. If s_i is undominated, then $(s_1,\ldots, s_I)$ is an undominated equilibrium in state θ too, and $b \in f(\theta)$. If s_i is dominated, it must be by some other strategy $\hat{s}_i$ which is undominated, implying that $(s_1,\ldots, s_{i-1},\hat{s}_i,s_{i+1},\ldots, s_I)$ is an undominated strategy equilibrium in state θ with an outcome a, say, for which $a \in f(\theta)$ and $a\ R_i(\theta)\ b$. Either way, f is strategy resistant, as claimed.

The necessity of strategy resistance (theorem 5.2) reveals just how important unboundedness was to the earlier permissive result (theorem 5.1). In fact, if f is a *single-valued* choice rule, then strategy resistance boils down to strategy proofness, and f must therefore be truthfully implementable in dominant strategy equilibrium. (As we have seen in section 1, relatively little can be implemented in dominant strategy equilibrium: choice rules that are strategy proof are typically inefficient.) So we conclude that a single elimination of weakly dominated strategies is not very powerful with bounded mechanisms.[120]

5.2 Iterative elimination of dominated strategies

This conclusion is overturned, however, if we *iteratively* eliminate weakly dominated strategies. Abreu and Matsushima (1990) examine what can be implemented if the choice set A includes all lotteries over outcomes, and small fines are admitted. They prove a striking result:

THEOREM 5.3 (Abreu and Matsushima, 1990) Let there be three or more agents. Suppose that A includes all lotteries over outcomes, and that it is feasible to levy small fines. If the domain Θ of preferences is finite, strictly value distinguished, and the expected utility hypothesis is satisfied in each state, then any single-valued choice function can be implemented in *iteratively undominated strategy* equilibrium. Moreover, the fines (which are only levied out of equilibrium) can be made arbitrarily small.

The Abreu–Matsushima mechanism has several strong features in common with the mechanism in Sjöström (1991b) for economic environments, and with the mechanism in Jackson, Palfrey, and Srivastava (1991) for separable environments (see section 4.2 above). None of the mechanisms falls foul of the standard criticisms which we have discussed. Given a finite domain Θ,[121] the mechanisms are finite and so are bounded (in Jackson's sense); there is no tail chasing and there are no integer games. They satisfy the best response property: optimal strategies always exist, even out of equilibrium. Roulette games are not employed: in fact, the mechanisms have no unwanted mixed-strategy equilibria. And, reassuringly, the order of elimination does not matter (which can be a problem with the iterative elimination of weakly dominated strategies).

As stated in theorem 5.3, the particular merit of the Abreu and Matsushima mechanism is that fines can be made arbitrarily small. (The subtlety of the construction is that the *same* (small) fine is used repeatedly as a deterrent without ever getting "used up.") However, to offset this advantage, it can be argued that a drawback of the Abreu and Matsushima mechanism – relative to the mechanisms in Sjöström (1991b) and Jackson, Palfrey, and Srivastava (1991) – is that a large number of rounds of elimination are required.

Let us now look at the details of the construction.[122] Imagine the agents placed around a circle. Each agent i makes a report of:

> his own preference ordering, R_i^i, over A
> his right-hand neighbor's preference ordering, R_{i+1}^i, over A
> a K-vector $(\theta_1^i, \ldots, \theta_k^i, \ldots, \theta_K^i)$ of profiles in $\Theta \times \ldots \times \Theta$

where K is an arbitrary (large) fixed number. (Notice that the superscript i denotes a component of agent i's strategy.)

The heart of the mechanism lies in the construction of a grand lottery,[123] with K equiprobable outcomes which depend on the agents' reported K-vectors of profiles. Specifically, the kth outcome of the lottery is determined as follows:

> If at least $(I-1)$ of the agents report some common profile θ – i.e., if $\theta_k^i \equiv \theta$ for at least $(I-1)$ agents i – then $f(\theta)$ is implemented (with probability $1/K$). In all other cases, some fixed outcome is implemented (with probability $1/K$).

Notice that, if all the agents report the same K-vector $(\theta, \ldots, \theta)$, say, then $f(\theta)$ will be implemented with probability 1. (Indeed, this is what we want to happen in the (iteratively undominated) equilibrium: we want everyone to report K replications of the *true* state.)

The mechanism has some other features. The first is designed to ensure that each agent i reports the truth about himself; i.e. that R_i^i is the truth. Let $\rho \in \Theta$ correspond to the profile $(R_1^I, R_2^1, R_3^2, \ldots, R_I^{I-1})$ made up by the agents' reports of their *neighbor*'s preference orderings.[124] Then if, for *any* i and k, the report θ_k^i does not coincide with ρ, an additional side lottery comes into operation:

> for a small $\varepsilon > 0$, each agent $i = 1, \ldots, I$ has a probability ε/I of dictating the outcome – i.e., his best outcome in A, according to his reported ordering R_i^i, is implemented. (The "grand" lottery, as defined above, is scaled down by the probability $1-\varepsilon$.)

This has the effect of ensuring that it would be a weakly dominated strategy for an agent to lie about his own preference ordering. (The point is that, from some agent i's perspective, the only way his report R_i^i can affect his own payoff is via this side lottery; and so, by construction, he has no interest in lying.)

The second feature is designed to ensure that each agent i reports the truth about his neighbor; i.e., that R_{i+1}^i is the truth. To this end, small fines are levied in the event of disagreement. If some agent i's report R_{i+1}^i of his neighbor's preference ordering does not match with what his neighbor claims about himself (viz., R_{i+1}^{i+1}), then agent i is fined; moreover, the size of this fine, F' say, is just large enough to deter agent i from disagreeing with his neighbor. That is, since we know that everyone reports the truth about their own preference ordering (a consequence of the first round of eliminating weakly dominated strategies), we can deduce (from the second round of elimination) that everyone will report the truth about their neighbor's preference ordering too. In other words, ρ is the true state.

Having elicited the truth in this fashion, the rest of the construction is designed so that no one wants to be the *first* to deviate from the truth along their reported K-vectors $(\theta_1^i, \ldots, \theta_k^i, \ldots, \theta_K^i)$. A kind of free-rider mechanism is brought into effect. Specifically, any agent who is the first to report a profile different from ρ is fined – i.e., if $\theta_h^i \equiv \rho$ for all i and all $h \leq k$, but $\theta_{k+1}^j \neq \rho$, then agent j is fined an amount F'', say. This is enough to ensure that the only weakly undominated strategy (after a suitable number of rounds of elimination) for an agent i is to report $\theta_k^i = \rho$ for each k.[125]

The point of this entire construction is that the fines can be kept small if K is chosen large enough, because no single reported profile θ_k^i makes much difference to the outcome of the grand lottery given a large K. At the margin, it is better to avoid fines rather than to try to change the outcome of any particular component of the lottery (whose probability of occurring is only $1/K$).

In conclusion, after a sufficient number of rounds of eliminating dominated strategies, we have a unique equilibrium: everyone reports the truth about themselves and their neighbor; and moreover everyone reports K replications of the true state. In each state $\theta \in \Theta, f(\theta)$ is implemented with probability 1, as required.

This ingenious mechanism is not without its critics. See Glazer and Rosenthal (1990) – who, in addition to their critique, give a nice exposition of the kind of construction used by Abreu and Matsushima.[126]

6 VIRTUAL IMPLEMENTATION AND PERFECT IMPLEMENTATION

So far we have required that a mechanism "exactly" implements a choice rule f; that is, for a given state θ, the outcome of the mechanism is precisely $f(\theta)$. It turns out that by using lotteries (cf. theorem 5.3), strong results can be obtained for approximate, or *virtual*, implementation – that is, where the outcome of the mechanism is arbitrarily close (in probabilistic terms) to $f(\theta)$.

Matsushima (1988) and Abreu and Sen (1991) investigate what can be virtually implemented in *Nash* equilibrium. Here we briefly review the results in Abreu and Sen (1991); for further discussion, the reader is urged to consult the introduction to their paper.

For simplicity, consider a case where: (i) for each $\theta \in \Theta$, the choice rule f selects a single, deterministic outcome $f(\theta)$;[127] and (ii) the set of deterministic outcomes is finite. Let A denote the set of all lotteries over these deterministic outcomes. Any $a \in A$ can be viewed as a vector of probabilities over the deterministic outcomes – that is, a point in a simplex of appropriate dimension. f is virtually implementable if, for any given $\varepsilon > 0$, the equilibrium outcome of the mechanism in each state θ is within ε of $f(\theta)$ in this simplex.

A necessary condition for a choice rule f to be Nash implementable is that it is monotonic: i.e., if for some pair of states θ and ϕ, the θ-lower contour sets at $f(\theta)$ are nested inside the ϕ-lower contour sets for all agents, then $f(\phi)$ must equal $f(\theta)$ (see theorem 2.1 above). Consider the case where f is *not* monotonic. The crucial insight made in Matsushima (1988) and Abreu and Sen (1991) is that there will always be some other (single-valued) choice rule $\tilde{f}$, which, in each state, picks *lotteries* arbitrarily close to f, and which has the following property: for any pair of states θ and ϕ, some agent's lower contour sets at $\tilde{f}(\theta)$ under θ and ϕ are not nested.[128] Hence $\tilde{f}$ vacuously satisfies monotonicity. Abreu and Sen show that, under very mild conditions, $\tilde{f}$ can be Nash implemented if there are three or more agents. This result should be contrasted with its counterpart for (exact) Nash implementation, theorem 2.1, which required that the choice rule satisfy both monotonicity *and* no veto power.

The mechanism Abreu and Sen use has an attractive additional property: the Nash equilibria can be made *strict* – i.e., in equilibrium, each agent strictly prefers his Nash strategy. In effect, then, their result embraces implementation using refinements of Nash equilibrium.[129]

There is a comparably clean result for the otherwise vexed case of Nash implementation with two agents (see section 2.1), given that f is single valued. Namely, almost any single-valued choice rule f can be virtually implemented in Nash equilibrium if it satisfies *weak non-empty lower intersection* – viz., for any pair of states θ and ϕ, and any pair of outcomes $a \in f(\theta)$ and $b \in f(\phi)$, there exists some outcome c such that $a\ R_1(\theta)\ c$ and $b\ R_2(\phi)\ c$. This result should be contrasted with one of our earlier results for exact Nash implementation, theorem 2.4, where (in addition to a number of other requirements) the choice rule had to satisfy monotonicity as well as the non-empty lower intersection property.

There are two aspects of these virtual implementation results which give concern. First, the constructive proofs make use of an integer game, which, as we have discussed, is an unappealing device. Second, the virtual implementation of some choice rule f does not necessarily mean that the outcome of the mechanism will always be close to the desired outcome. In Abreu and Matsushima's mechanism, for each state $\theta \in \Theta, \tilde{f}(\theta)$ picks *every* deterministic outcome in A – including, therefore, very "undesirable" outcomes, far from $f(\theta)$ – with positive (albeit small) probability.

The paper of Sjöström (forthcoming) on implementation in perfect equilibrium closely relates to the work on virtual Nash implementation. In both cases, trembles are used to knock out unwanted Nash equilibria. However, whereas Matsushima (1988) and Abreu and Sen (1991) introduce trembles explicitly into the mechanism via lotteries, Sjöström has the agents themselves trembling. If the agents' trembles are hypothetical rather than real, then Sjöström's mechanism has the merit that the choice rule is implemented exactly, not approximately. (Also see Bagnoli and Lipman (1989), who use implementation in perfect equilibrium for a public good problem.)

The idea of approximate, or virtual, implementation is powerful for equilibrium concepts other than Nash (and its refinements). Abreu and Matsushima (1989) have investigated the use of lotteries in iteratively undominated strategy equilibrium. They prove a result comparable to theorem 5.3, but with two differences. First, there is no longer any need for fines, even small ones. Second, and more significantly, the (iterative) elimination is now of *strictly* dominated strategies.[130] Obviously, the drawback of the result, relative to theorem 5.3, is that implementation is not exact.

7 IMPLEMENTATION AND RENEGOTIATION

The small literature on this topic was briefly reviewed in section IX of part one. Here, I will present the two main theorems from Maskin and Moore (1987), and then give an application.

The issue of renegotiation is most apparent in a contractual context, where there is no planner, and the contractual parties – typically just two of them – are free to rescind their mechanism to exploit any *ex post* gains.

In almost all of the mechanism-design literature, it has been implicitly assumed that if some terminal node (either on or off the equilibrium path) of the mechanism were reached, then the corresponding outcome would be implemented, and that would be that. But there is every chance that the outcome will not be Pareto efficient from the agents' perspective – in which case, they may decide to renegotiate. More importantly, the agents will rationally anticipate any renegotiation and this will in general change the equilibrium strategies of the mechanism itself.

A good example of this is the two-agent simple sequential mechanism given in section 3.3 above (see figure 5.8): if, at stage 2, agent 1 challenged, then agent 2 would be fined F – which, from the agents' *combined* perspective, is inefficient. Rather than pay the fine, agent 2 would be willing to renegotiate the outcome of the mechanism with agent 1. This may well distort their incentives to play the mechanism truthfully.

The question arises: how is the implementation problem changed if we assume that whenever the parties have an incentive to renegotiate, they will do so?

Consider a single-valued choice rule f, which for each state $\theta \in \Theta$ selects an outcome $f(\theta)$ that is strongly Pareto efficient under θ, or *θ-efficient* for short. That is, we assume that there is no other $a \in A$ such that a $R_i(\theta) f(\theta)$ for all agents i and $a\, P_j(\theta) f(\theta)$ for at least one agent j.[131] We also make the mild assumption that no two distinct outcomes yield the same vector of utilities on the Pareto frontier:

Assumption R0:

> For any θ, and any θ-efficient outcome $a \in A$, if $\hat{a} \in A$ is such that $\hat{a}$ $I_i(\theta)$ a for all i, then $\hat{a} = a$.

A variety of convexity assumptions on preferences would be enough to ensure that assumption R0 is satisfied.

The mechanisms we design will depend on how they are renegotiated. To an extent, the process of renegotiation is a black box, and we should not be too dogmatic about its eventual outcome. However, we assume three things: that renegotiation is unique, efficient, and individually rational.

Specifically, suppose that in state θ an outcome a is renegotiated to $h(a|\theta) \in A$, say. Then we assume:

*Assumption R*1 (renegotiation is unique):
$h(\cdot|\theta)$ is a function for all $\theta \in \Theta$, not a correspondence.

*Assumption R*2 (renegotiation is efficient):
$h(a|\theta)$ is θ-efficient for all $\theta \in \Theta$, and all $a \in A$.

*Assumption R*3 (renegotiation is individually rational):
$h(a|\theta)\ R_i(\theta)\ a$ for all i, all $\theta \in \Theta$, and all $a \in A$.[132]

Of these three assumptions, assumption R3 is arguably the least controversial: no agent need be forced into a renegotiation process that is going to make him worse off, since he could always insist on the contractually specified outcome. Assumption R2 also seems quite reasonable in the present context: there are no asymmetries of information (a usual source of inefficiency in bargaining), and if the agents commonly anticipated that the renegotiation process were going to end up at an inefficient outcome, then one of them could surely propose a Pareto improvement which the others would accept. Assumption R1 is fairly strong. It amounts to a kind of rational expectation that the agents jointly have concerning the outcome of future bargaining. Behind the assumption lies the idea that these agents know one another well – they know each other's preferences, and, it may be supposed, they know each other's bargaining strengths.[133]

Actually, our formulation admits a broader interpretation: the state θ may signify not merely the agents' underlying preferences over A, but also the nature of the renegotiation. In other words, two (distinct) states θ,ϕ could share common preferences (i.e., $a\ R_i(\theta)\ b$ if and only if $a\ R_i(\phi)\ b$ for all i and for all $a,b \in A$) – and differ only according to how some outcome is renegotiated (i.e., $h(a|\theta) \neq h(a|\phi)$ for some a).

The implementation problem can now be posed: does there exist a mechanism g such that in any state θ, the equilibrium outcome of the *composite* game $h.g$ is $f(\theta)$? [In the composite game $h.g$, the terminal node outcomes $\{a\}$ of g, which were state independent, have been replaced by $\{h(a|\theta)\}$, which may be state dependent. That is to say, in each state θ, when the agents play g, in their strategic calculations they replace any "final" outcome a of g by the outcome to which a will be renegotiated, viz., $h(a|\theta)$.] If so, then g *implements* f *with renegotiation* h. (This is leaving open the choice of equilibrium concept.)

It must be stressed that h is part of the data of the problem. Although f may be implementable with renegotiation h, this does not necessarily mean that it would be with some other $h' \neq h$. Certainly, the choice of mechanism g will in general depend on the given h.

In Maskin and Moore (1987), we examine implementation with renegotiation in both Nash equilibrium and subgame perfect equilibrium. For Nash equilibrium, a modified form of monotonicity is introduced:

(f,h) satisfy *renegotiation monotonicity* if, for each state θ, there exists an outcome a with $h(a|\theta)=f(\theta)$; and if $h(a|\phi)\neq f(\phi)$ for some other state ϕ then there must exist some agent i and some outcome y such that:

$$h(a|\theta)\ R_i(\theta)\ h(y|\theta) \text{ and } h(y|\phi)\ P_i(\phi)\ h(a|\phi).$$

In line with theorem 2.1, we have:

THEOREM 7.1 (Maskin and Moore, 1987) Suppose there are three or more agents. Then any single-valued, strongly Pareto efficient choice rule f can be Nash implemented with renegotiation h if and only if (f,h) satisfy renegotiation monotonicity.

Notice that this is a clean characterization: there is no need for an additional assumption (like no veto power) for the sufficiency result.

Interestingly, the two-agent case is equally clean:

THEOREM 7.2 (Maskin and Moore, 1987) Suppose there are two agents, 1 and 2. Then any single-valued, strongly Pareto efficient choice rule f can be Nash implemented with renegotiation h if and only if for any ordered pair of states θ,ϕ there exists an outcome $y=y(\theta,\phi)$ such that:

$$f(\theta)\ R_2(\theta)\ h(y|\theta) \text{ and } f(\phi) R_1(\phi)\ h(y|\phi).$$

The proof of necessity in theorem 7.2 is straightforward. Consider the outcome matrix to any g which Nash implements f with renegotiation h (figure 5.10).

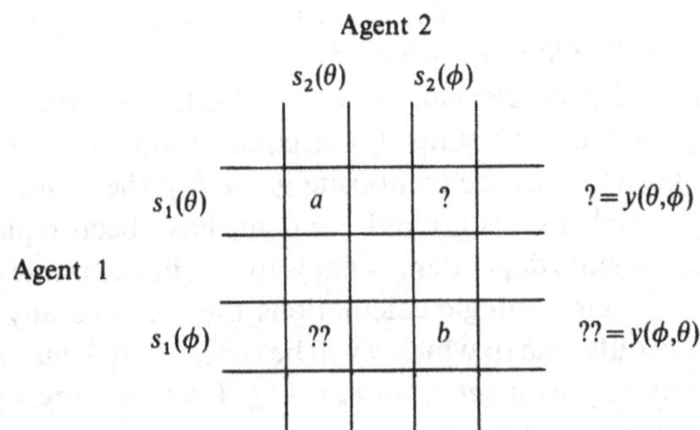

Figure 5.10

In state θ [resp. ϕ], let the equilibrium strategies of $h.g$ be $s_i(\theta)$ [resp. $s_i(\phi)$], $i=1,2$, with final outcome $h(a|\theta)=f(\theta)$ [resp. $h(b|\phi)=f(\phi)$]. Put

$g[s_1(\theta),s_2(\phi)]=y(\theta,\phi)$ (the entry ? in the matrix). The conditions on $y(\theta,\phi)$ given in theorem 7.2 follow directly from the facts that in state θ, strategy $s_2(\theta)$ has to be no worse for agent 2 than $s_2(\phi)$, and that in state ϕ, strategy $s_1(\phi)$ has to be no worse for agent 1 than $s_1(\theta)$.

The proof of sufficiency relies on the fact that all outcomes, both on and off the equilibrium path, end up being renegotiated to the Pareto frontier. We construct a revelation game based on the above payoff matrix; we confirm that in each state θ truth-telling constitutes a Nash equilibrium leading to outcome $f(\theta)$; and finally we use a variant of the classic minmax theorem to prove that any other Nash equilibrium must lead to the same point on the Pareto frontier.[134]

This last argument shows that, for two agents, there is no gain from turning to multi-stage mechanisms g. Subgame perfection may indeed rule out certain Nash equilibria of the mechanism in some state θ, but, given that the renegotiation process $h(\cdot|\theta)$ is θ-efficient, all the Nash equilibrium outcomes of $h.g$ equal $f(\theta)$ anyway. This does mean, though, that a simple sequential mechanism (cf. section 3.3 above) can be used instead of a simultaneous-move mechanism.

7.1 An application

Given the importance that I attach to this kind of mechanism, I now end by looking at an example. The example is related to that in Hart and Moore (1988), and concerns the implementation of first-best risk-sharing (cf. section VIII of part one).

Consider a buyer and seller, who contract to trade a single item at some future date. At the time of contracting, both the buyer's value v and the seller's cost c are uncertain. Since they are both risk averse, they wish to share risk efficiently. Unfortunately, neither v nor c is publicly verifiable, and so a contingent contract cannot be written. However, both parties observe v and c; so there is scope for writing some mechanism into the contract which will implement the first-best risk-sharing prices, which are

a trade price of $p_1^*(v,c)$ if $v \geq c$;
and a no-trade price of p_0^* if $v < c$.

Efficient risk-sharing means that p_0^* is constant for all $v<c$; and $p_1^*(v,c)$ satisfies the Borch (1962) condition:

$$\frac{U_b'[v-p_1^*(v,c)]}{U_b'[-p_0^*]}=\frac{U_s'[p_1^*(v,c)-c]}{U_s'[p_0^*]} \text{ for all } v \geq c,$$

where $U_b(\cdot)$ and $U_s(\cdot)$ are, respectively, the buyer's and seller's (concave) von Neumann–Morgenstern utility-of-income functions. An immediate consequence of the Borch condition is that for all $v \geq c$ and $\hat{v} \geq \hat{c}$:

$$p_1^*(\hat{v},\hat{c}) - p_1^*(v,c) \leq \max\{\hat{v}-v,\ \hat{c}-c\}; \tag{i}$$

and:

$$p_1^*(\hat{v},\hat{c}) - p_1^*(v,c) \geq \min\{\hat{v}-v,\ \hat{c}-c\}. \tag{ii}$$

We assume that, if trade does not take place, the courts cannot determine after the event who refused to trade. Accordingly, if the contract specifies a trade price of p_1 and a no-trade price of p_0, then trade can take place if and only if both parties wish to trade. That is, trade is voluntary:

trade occurs if and only if $v \geq p_1 - p_0 \geq c$.

Notice that if $v > c$ (so that it is efficient to trade) and either $p_1 - p_0 > v$ or $p_1 - p_0 < c$, no trade will occur *unless the parties renegotiate the prices*. Given that both agents observe v and c, it is sensible to assume that they will renegotiate. The question is: how?

In Hart and Moore (1988), we give an argument to suggest that the outcome of the renegotiation might be as follows:

if $p_1 - p_0 > v \geq c \Rightarrow p_1$ is renegotiated down to $v + p_0$;
if $v \geq c > p_1 - p_0 \Rightarrow p_1$ is renegotiated up to $c + p_0$.

Notice that, as a result of the renegotiation, the price difference *will* lie in $[c,v]$, and so trade occurs. (Assume that if $v < c$, or if $c \leq p_1 - p_0 \leq v$, then there will be no renegotiation: the outcome will be efficient anyway so there is nothing to bargain over.)

For our present purposes, the reasons why renegotiation might lead to this particular form of price revision are not important. We are only concerned here with the implementation question – namely, *given* that this is the outcome of renegotiation, can first-best risk-sharing be implemented?

If it useful to translate the problem into our earlier notation. The pair v,c corresponds to a state θ. Let the no-trade price p_0 and the *price difference* $p \equiv p_1 - p_0$ together correspond to an "outcome." For $v \geq c$, the renegotiation function h is given by:[135]

$$h(p|v,c) \equiv \begin{cases} v \text{ if } p > v \geq c \\ p \text{ if } v \geq p \geq c \\ c \text{ if } v \geq c > p \end{cases}$$

For notational convenience, let the RHS of this identity be written simply as $c[p]v$.

Take two states, v,c ($=\theta$, say), and $\hat{v},\hat{c}$ ($=\phi$, say). Suppose for sake of argument that $v \geq c$ and $\hat{v} \geq \hat{c}$, so that trade is efficient in both states. (A similar argument can be used for the other possibilities.) Then, give some no-trade price f_0, what kind of price differences $f(v,c)$ and $f(\hat{v},\hat{c})$ can be Nash implemented with renegotiation h?

Theorem 7.2 gives us the answer. There must exist a no-trade price y_0 and a price difference y – together corresponding to $y(\theta,\phi)$ in the theorem – such that:

$$\text{for the seller: } f_0 + f(v,c) - c \geq y_0 + c[y]v - c; \tag{1}$$

$$\text{and for the buyer: } \hat{v} - f_0 - f(\hat{v},\hat{c}) \geq \hat{v} - y_0 - \hat{c}[y]\hat{v}. \tag{2}$$

(Notice that on the LHS (1), we are appealing to the fact that if the price difference $f(v,c)$ is to be implementable with renegotiation, then the voluntary trade condition must be satisfied: $v \geq f(v,c) \geq c$. And in (2), it must be the case that $\hat{v} \geq f(\hat{v},\hat{c}) \geq \hat{c}$.)

Likewise, reversing the roles of θ and ϕ, there must exist a no-trade price z_0 and a price difference z – together corresponding to $y(\phi,\theta)$ – such that:

$$\text{for the seller: } f_0 + f(\hat{v},\hat{c}) - \hat{c} \geq z_0 + \hat{c}[z]\hat{v} - \hat{c}; \tag{3}$$

$$\text{and for the buyer: } v - f_0 - f(v,c) \geq v - z_0 - c[z]v. \tag{4}$$

Adding (1) and (2) gives:

$$f(\hat{v},\hat{c}) - f(v,c) \leq \hat{c}[y]\hat{v} - c[y]v \text{ for some } y. \tag{5}$$

Adding (3) and (4) gives:

$$f(\hat{v},\hat{c}) - f(v,c) \geq \hat{c}[z]\hat{v} - c[z]v \text{ for some } z. \tag{6}$$

By the necessity part of theorem 7.2, then, (5) and (6) are *necessary* conditions for $f(v,c)$ and $f(\hat{v},\hat{c})$ to be Nash implementable with renegotiation h.

In fact, this argument runs backwards. Given (5) and (6), there exist no-trade prices y_0 and z_0 satisfying (1)–(4) for any f_0. Hence, by the sufficiency part of theorem 7.2, (5) and (6) are also *sufficient* conditions for $f(v,c)$ and $f(\hat{v},\hat{c})$ to be Nash implementable with renegotiation h.

Now it is straightforward to show that, for $f_0 = p_0^*$ and $f_0 \equiv p_1^* - p_0^*$, conditions (5) and (6) are implied by (i) and (ii). Since the pairs v,c and $\hat{v},\hat{c}$ were chosen arbitrarily, this means that first-best risk-sharing is Nash implementable with renegotiation h, as claimed.[136] In fact, rather than using a simultaneous mechanism, one could instead use a simple sequential mechanism g in which, say, the buyer moved first and the seller followed. Renegotiation happens after the play of g is over. Moreover, g could be designed so that there is no renegotiation along the equilibrium path (cf. Green and Laffont, 1991a).

Notes

* This chapter could not have been written without the great advantage of having as coauthors Oliver Hart, Eric Maskin and Rafael Repullo. I am in their debt. I have used up many hours of the time of Matthew Jackson, Steven Matthews, Hervé Moulin, Andrew Postlewaite, Kevin Roberts, Klaus Schmidt and Tomas Sjöström discussing implementation, and I warmly thank them for their patience, generosity and expert help. Finally, I am grateful to Dilip Abreu, Mathias Dewatripont, Aditya Goenka, Ian Jewitt, Albert Ma, Georg Nöldeke, Thomas Palfrey, Ariel Rubinstein, Mark Satterthwaite, Sanjay Srivastava, William Thomson and Lin Zhou for very useful conversations and for kindly giving comments on earlier drafts. Financial assistance is acknowledged from the Suntory-Toyota International Centre for Economics and Related Disciplines at the London School of Economics.

1 Ariel Rubinstein suggested that the story of the Judgement of Solomon could be viewed as an exercise in implementation theory.

2 See von Mises (1920), Hayek (1935), Lange (1936, 1937), Lange and Taylor (1938), Lerner (1936, 1944). For two recent surveys, see Brus (1987) and Kowalik (1987).

3 "Hurwicz's presence is as pervasive as that of Hamlet's father" (from the preface to *Information, Incentives and Economic Mechanisms: Essays in Honor of Leonid Hurwicz* (1987), edited by T. Groves, R. Radner, and S. Reiter). The early, seminal papers are Hurwicz (1960 and 1972). For an informative historical perspective, see, for example, the first sections of Hurwicz (1973).

4 Useful introductions to the earlier literature – in addition to Hurwicz (1973) – include: Groves and Ledyard (1987), Hurwicz (1985), T. Marschak (1987), Radner (1987), and Reiter (1977, 1987). There has been a great deal of work done on the informational (as distinct from the incentive) properties of mechanisms. A classic paper here is Mount and Reiter (1974). Unfortunately, this branch of the literature is outside the scope of the present survey.

5 For example, see pages 16, 17, and 31 of Postlewaite and Schmeidler (1986); and see Ma, Moore, and Turnbull (1988) (based on the model in Demski and Sappington (1984)). Also, problem 16.3 and, particularly, section 18.2 in Kreps (1990) are very useful.

6 The traditional social choice literature would take θ to index the agents' utility

functions; i.e., states of nature would be distinguished solely by changes in agents' underlying preferences. I would like to broaden this interpretation. States of nature may also be distinguished by changes in endowments or technology. For example, suppose there are two firms (the agents) and an "outcome" is the quantity they trade together with the price. A firm's preferences over A will vary with its productivity/technology, which is indexed by θ. But notice that the firm's underlying preference – for profit maximization – is fixed.

In this connection, it is important to observe that A does not vary with θ: any outcome in A is assumed to be feasible – though it may have a very low payoff. That is, the two firms must in principle be able to trade any of the quantities (at their respective prices) in A, without violating either a technological or a bankruptcy constraint. Of course, it would be desirable to generalize the analysis to the case where A depends on θ, but the difficult problem is how to deal with infeasible outcomes off the equilibrium path.

7 If f were a correspondence, then the literature has typically imposed the requirement that, in each state of nature, the set of equilibrium outcomes coincides with the set of desired outcomes given by f.

8 That is, information is incomplete insofar as each agent will typically only know that part of θ pertaining to his own preferences. If attention is restricted to implementation in dominant strategy equilibria (see section 1 of part two), then the distinction between incomplete and complete information becomes less important.

9 This is assuming that such an f exists; we abstract from the difficulty of aggregating preferences (see Arrow, 1951). Our concern is not with the reasons why any particular f should be preferred, but with the question of whether it can be implemented.

10 To use the jargon, the θ's are observable (by the members) but not verifiable (by outsiders). There are other reasons why fully contingent contracts can be ruled out – e.g., the costs of writing such a contract in a sufficiently clear and unambiguous way that it can be enforced. More on this in section VII below.

11 If there are other firms with whom to contract, then this division may be determined in an *ex ante* contract market.

12 See, for example, J. Roberts (1987).

13 A Reuters report appeared in May 1990, under the headline "Philippine Soldiers Told To Sort Out Wives":

> *Manila* – A Philippine general has told his men to put on record who their real wives are, saying that it confuses the military when more than one woman shows up to claim the body of a dead soldier.
>
> "The problem here is that we used to reckon that the one who wails the loudest ought to be the legitimate wife," said Gen. Pantaleon Dumlao. "Lately, however, mistresses have been outcrying the real wives."
>
> Dumlao, chief investigator of the paramilitary constabulary, told soldiers in Iloilo province to straighten out their personnel forms specifying their beneficiaries.

"Before you die, choose among your 'wives' you love most, to forestall problems," Manila's Philippine Star newspaper quoted Dumlao as saying.

14 He may not even know the values of v^m and v^n.

15 This mechanism is similar to that in Glazer and Ma (1989), which they used for the general problem of allocating a prize.

16 In a sense, though, Solomon's trickery served him well – perhaps that was part of his divine wisdom. The notion of the planner changing the rules of the mechanism midstream is an interesting avenue for further research. (Presumably, such behavior would be less effective if the mechanism were to be used repeatedly.) Andrew Postlewaite gives the example of the market for used stamps, in which a second-price auction was ostensibly conducted by post for each stamp or group of stamps. Not surprisingly, sellers exploited the possibility of corrupting the auction midstream, by covertly placing fictitious bids in order to push the prices up to just below the winners' bids. Now the market has become in effect a first-price auction: buyers are no longer being duped.

17 See also the recent paper by Yang (1991), which solves Solomon's dilemma in an incomplete information setting, using the successive elimination of weakly dominated strategies. His mechanism is not dissimilar to the one given in the text.

18 There is a small glitch. In the relatively unlikely event that Timon's wealth is only *just* bigger than that of Spyros (the gap being less than the cost of the choregia), then Spyros will claim that Timon is richer and Timon will protest. They will then exchange wealth – after which Spyros has to foot the bill. But notice that at the end of the day the two men's wealths will be ranked as they were at the start; and, to be precise, *at the moment of payment* the financing of the choregia *is* undertaken by the richest man (viz. Spyros). Rough justice is seen to be done.

19 See Littman (1988, pp. 800–2); and also see Finley (1951, p. 1 and note 1). I thank Robert Wilson for first bringing the Greek antidosis procedure to my attention, and William Thomson for the reference to Finley (1951).

Scholars still dispute whether the antidosis ever led to an actual exchange of property or was merely a formal challenge serving to initiate judicial determination of which party should perform the liturgy. (In the text, I abstracted from the third possibility, viz. judicial procedure. This simplification was made to keep the story tidy – but, interestingly, the analysis would not unravel if the possibility of judicial procedure were to be included.) For a detailed examination of the source materials and conflicting theories, see Goligher (1907, in particular section 4) – who strongly argues that the prospect of exchange was real enough.

The fact that exchange may only rarely have happened (if at all) does not mean that it was irrelevant. Out-of-equilibrium moves can be just as important to the play of a mechanism as equilibrium moves. Indeed, our "analysis" of the subgame perfect equilibrium confirms that, if Spyros and Timon shared complete information about each other's wealth, then the exchange would typically *not* occur in equilibrium.

20 If someone had five children, or was a prize athlete or a member of a learned profession, then he was exempt.

21 In addition, the nominator could be fined. There was an instance in Egypt (AD 143) when the nominating official not only had to pay the liturgic tax in full, but also had to pay a fine of four times the value of the property surrendered by the person who was nominated. See Lewis (1983, p. 181).

22 For references to the Roman system, see: Abbott and Johnson (1926, pp. 89–90, 99–103, and documents 181, 185, 198); Jones (1974, pp. 15 and 173); and Lewis (1983, pp. 177–84). I thank Anne Sheppard and Susan Hardman Moore for their research.

23 $p(\theta)$ might also share risk *ex ante*, if the firms are risk averse – i.e., if the seller (resp. buyer) has some concave von Neumann–Morgenstern utility of profit function $U_s[p-c(q,\theta_1)]$ (resp. $U_b[v(q,\theta_2)-p]$).

24 Expert witnesses, if there are any, can be bribed.

25 The following is adapted from section 5 of Moore and Repullo (1988).

26 In fact, Θ need not be finite; this assumption is made only to keep the exposition uncluttered. (Notice that the mechanism given in the text essentially comprises only the function f, an ordering of moves, and the two numbers F and ε.) For the general case, section 5 of Moore and Repullo (1988) presents a mechanism in which the set of permissible test pairs is prescribed in the *ex ante* contract. (Inter alia, this avoids the use of ε's at stages 1.2 and 2.2.)

However, it *is* necessary that the costs c and values v are bounded – which would be true if, for example, Θ were compact and c,v were continuous in θ. In addition, there must be preference reversal (see below).

27 This is making the assumption that $c(.,\theta_1)$ and $c(.,\phi_1)$ cannot merely differ by a constant.

28 It is important to realise that, even with only two agents, the mechanism is self-financing. Off the equilibrium path, the "planner" (actually, the predesignated outside third party) can *receive* $2F$.

29 One way to tackle this issue would be to try to incorporate agents' preferences over how other agents play the mechanism.

30 Although the difficulties associated with using backward induction have been largely ignored in the literature on implementation (so the material in section VIII here is new, along with theorem 3.3 in part two), these difficulties are by no means new to game theorists. Rosenthal's "centipede game" (Rosenthal, 1981) provided one of the classic paradoxes.

31 We have simplified our earlier notation so that c now plays the role of θ_1 directly: $c(0,\theta_1)\equiv 0$ and $c(1,\theta_1)\equiv c$. Also, θ_2 is degenerate: $v(0,\theta_2)\equiv 0$, and $v(1,\theta_2)$ is fixed at $v=100$.

32 The seller has a (constant) coefficient of absolute risk aversion equal to twice that of the buyer.

33 It should be pointed out that having each agent move only once need not completely avoid the difficulties of using backward induction. Consider the

following two-player game: player 1 can either choose the payoffs (100,100) and the game ends; or he can ask player 2 to choose between (0,0) and (101,ε). Subgame perfection requires that the equilibrium outcome is (101,ε). But might player 2 not be sufficiently annoyed at having been denied 100 that (given a small ε) she chooses (0,0) in order to punish player 1?

34 Similarly, in Solomon's problem outcome *d*, for example, is always inefficient; one might imagine that the two women would be able to bargain with Solomon not to kill them and the child – presuming that Solomon derives no pleasure from death all round.

35 Even in this knife-edge case, a constant amount $K-100/3$ would have to be paid over in advance – which itself suggests some form of *ex ante* contract.

36 For two short papers which introduce and survey this material, see Aghion, Dewatripont, and Rey (1990) and Bolton (1990).

37 A similar approach is adopted by Green and Laffont (1991a and b). In their first paper, *ex post* bargaining costs are introduced. The aim is to ensure that the equilibrium outcome of the mechanism is efficient in each state – implying that, on the equilibrium path, there is no costly renegotiation *ex post*. Their second paper has efficient bargaining, but again the idea is to avoid renegotiation on the equilibrium path, so as to induce efficient (non-contractible) investment.

38 But, unlike in Hart and Moore (1988), the courts can impose trade. And there is no technological deadline.

39 The idea of controlling the renegotiation is borne from a simple observation: since the renegotiation process is itself a game form, in principle one ought to be able to incorporate it into the description of the mechanism. That is, why should renegotiation take place "outside" the mechanism?

I believe this view is mistaken. Aside from the obvious fact that a real-life renegotiation process may be extremely subtle and therefore impossible to describe in the mechanism, I see no compelling reason to believe that the outcomes of such a process (across states of nature) should be "implementable" in our formal sense. (Recall, for example, my earlier remarks about uniqueness at the end of section I. If a real-life renegotiation process is to be "implementable" in our formal sense, then we require that this process has a *unique* equilibrium outcome in each state of nature. But why should it necessarily? It is one thing to argue that the process has a *predictable* outcome, in the sense that, at the time the parties draw up their original mechanism, they have rational expectations about how they will renegotiate it. It is quite another to insist that the process only has one possible equilibrium outcome.) In fact, it may even be that we can utilize some exogenously given renegotiation process to our advantage, to implement a choice function that cannot be implemented otherwise. That is, we exploit the renegotiation despite the fact that the process itself may not be amenable to formal modeling, or even be understood.

40 "Real time" play is essential to Rubinstein and Wolinsky's analysis; that is how the formal renegotiation process specified in their mechanism comes to dominate the informal one.

41 In the good state, surplus at date T_3 equals:

$$\underset{q}{\text{Max}}\ \{35(1+\beta)q-14(1+\frac{1}{\sigma})q^2\}=\frac{175\sigma(1+\beta)^2}{8(1+\sigma)}.$$

And in the bad state, surplus at date T_3 equals:

$$\underset{q}{\text{Max}}\ \{28(1+\beta)q-32(1+\frac{1}{\sigma})q^2\}=\frac{49\sigma(1+\beta)^2}{8(1+\sigma)}.$$

Hence expected social surplus (net of investment costs), measured in T_3 dollars, equals:

$$\frac{1}{2}\times\frac{175\sigma(1+\beta)^2}{8(1+\sigma)}+\frac{1}{2}\times\frac{49\sigma(1+\beta)^2}{8(1+\sigma)}-14\beta^2-\frac{7\sigma^2}{144}$$

$$=\frac{14\sigma(1+\beta)^2}{(1+\sigma)}-14\beta^2-\frac{7\sigma^2}{144}\equiv \text{E}(\beta,\sigma),\text{ say.}$$

The first-order conditions for maximizing $\text{E}(\beta,\sigma)$ with respect to β and σ reduce to

$$\frac{\sigma(1+\beta)}{(1+\sigma)}-\beta=0 \text{ and } \frac{(1+\beta)^2}{(1+\sigma)^2}-\frac{\sigma}{144}=0,$$

which solve to give $\beta=\sigma=144$. (The second-order conditions for a global maximum are satisfied, since $\text{E}(\beta,\sigma)$ is strictly concave – the Hessian of $\text{E}(\beta,\sigma)$ is negative definite for $\beta,\sigma\geq 0$.)

42 In fact, this form of contract would also achieve first-best in the presence of a direct externality. Specifically, if the buyer's investment β affected the seller's costs directly, it would make no essential difference to the argument, because the contractually agreed quantity can be chosen to induce the buyer to invest at the first-best level anyway (irrespective of the externality); and, being the residual claimant, the seller's incentives are aligned with the social objective.

43 These papers further consider whether risk can be efficiently shared when there is scope to allocate all the *ex post* bargaining power to one or other of the agents. On this, see also Green and Laffont (forthcoming).

44 q might represent quality, not quantity; once the seller or buyer have settled the quality of the good, the decision cannot be reversed.

To my mind, a more natural assumption than (ii) might be the following. If the court imposes $q=128$ in the *bad* state then, given that production costs are sunk, there is no scope for renegotiation; but if the court imposes $q=128$ in the *good* state then the parties can always negotiate a supplementary trade. In short, the parties can increase but not decrease q. I do not know whether the first-best investment levels can be implemented under this alternative assumption.

45 One way to view implementation theory is that it is a theory for characterizing equilibrium outcome correspondences under different solution concepts. In this endeavor, the theory has been quite successful.

46 This rather quick-and-easy way of finessing bounded rationality – which,

surely, is the deeper reason for contractual incompleteness – has nonetheless delivered some important insights. For example: the theory of property rights in Grossman and Hart (1986) – and its implications for the nature of the firm (Hart and Moore, 1990); financial contracting (Aghion and Bolton, forthcoming and Hart and Moore, 1989, 1991); and industrial structure (Bolton and Whinston, forthcoming and Hart and Tirole, 1990). Hart and Holmström (1987) provide an excellent overview of the theory of contracts; in particular, section 3 discusses contractual incompleteness.

47 Another explanation is that, for the purpose of *practical* application, the Revelation Principle has been somewhat misleading. Direct revelation schemes presuppose that the θ's can be both described in advance and reported *ex post*. Indirect mechanisms (e.g., simple price/quantity schedules) have the virtue that agents' choice sets are relatively simple – but there can be some loss of generality in moving away from direct revelation schemes.

48 By "situation," I mean such things as: Can the agents communicate outside the mechanism? Can they collude? Can they affect the realization of θ?

49 Simplicity is of course a difficult notion to pin down. One should take into consideration not just simplicity of the mechanism itself, but also simplicity of the strategic calculations that we are presuming our agents to make. This brings us back to (i) – the bounded rationality of agents.

50 Cf. the work of Holmström and Milgrom (1987) on linear incentive schemes. They argue that knife-edge schemes may provide agents with poor intertemporal incentives.

51 Arguably, the classic impossibility result of Gibbard (1973) and Satterthwaite (1975) held back the search for more positive results – although that is no longer the case. It will be noticed that I have hardly touched upon dominant strategy implementation in part one, which is a serious omission. To compensate, section 1 of part two deals with the topic at some length.

52 This is currently being investigated by Barberà and Jackson (1991b), and Barberà, Gul, and Stachetti (1991), among others.

53 Srivastava and Trick (1991) have made interesting progress in this direction. An important starting point was the earlier work by Moulin (1979, 1983) on dominance solvability; his mechanisms can all be made into "trees."

54 In particular, I shall not refer much to the large literature on implementation in "general equilibrium" environments. (See the opening remarks of part one.) Fortunately, there are a number of surveys available: Groves (1982), Groves and Ledyard (1987), Hurwicz (1985, 1986), Laffont and Maskin (1982a), Ledyard (1987), T. Marshak (1987), Maskin (1985), Moulin (1982), Muller and Sattherthwaite (1985), Postlewaite (1985), Radner (1987), Reiter (1987), and Sattherthwaite (1987). Also the earlier research paper by Dasgupta, Hammond, and Maskin (1979) is remarkable in its scope.

Space restrictions prevent me from discussing implementation using a number of interesting alternative equilibrium concepts – for example *maximin* equilibrium (see, e.g., Green and Laffont, 1979, chapter 7, Dasgupta, Hammond, and Maskin, 1979, section 6, and Thomson, 1979a); *protective* equilibrium (see, e.g., Barberà-Dutta, 1982 and Barberà-Jackson, 1988);

strong equilibrium, which is related to the notion of implementing by means of the Core (see, e.g., Peleg, 1978, Maskin, 1979a, Moulin and Peleg, 1982, Moulin, 1983, Peleg, 1984a, Maskin, 1985, sections 5,8,9, Holzman, 1987, Corchon, 1989, Dutta and Sen, 1991a, and Abdou and Keiding, 1991); and *coalition-proof Nash* equilibrium (see, e.g., Peleg, 1984b and Bernheim and Whinston, 1987, section 4).

55 That is, Θ comprises a cross-product of the I agents' sets of possible preference orderings over A. Clearly, this would be implied by (but not imply) statistical independence of the I agents' preferences. Also, if Θ is universal, preferences obviously have independent domains.

56 A may comprise all lotteries over a set of deterministic outcomes – in which case each $\theta \in \Theta$ will index agents' risk preferences, and, in principle, f may be sensitive to these preferences. This would be consistent with the statement in the text.

57 For the most part, I shall not include the bracketed word "full," unless it be to distinguish (full) implementation from the weaker notion of truthful implementation.

58 I shall not complicate the exposition by including formal definitions of what are now standard equilibrium concepts.

59 That is, for all agents i and in all states θ, $a\ I_i(\theta)\ b$ implies $a=b$. Also assume here that preferences in Θ have independent domains.

60 See Dasguptga, Hammond, and Maskin (1979, sections 4.1 and 4.3).

61 A choice rule f is *dictatorial* if there is some agent i such that, for every $\theta \in \Theta, f(\theta)$ picks one of i's most preferred outcomes in the range of f.

62 See, for example, Schmeidler and Sonnenschein (1978) and Barberà (1983). Barberà and Peleg (1990) use the pivotal-voter technique developed in Barberà (1983) to prove the result for the case where Θ includes all continuous preferences on a metric space A.

63 See also theorem 3 in Satterthwaite and Sonnenshein (1981). Note that the early papers by Samuelson (1954, 1955) first pointed out that individuals would want to misrepresent their preferences in the provision of public goods.

64 A choice rule f is *Pareto efficient* if, for all θ and for all $a \in f(\theta)$, there does not exist some outcome $\hat{a} \in A$ such that $\hat{a}\ P_i(\theta)\ a$ for all i.

65 Thus Hurwicz formalized an intuition first expressed by Vickrey (1961). For a clear exposition of Hurwicz's result, see section 2.1 of Postlewaite (1985).

66 See theorem 1 of Zhou (forthcoming), which also allows for many goods. See also theorem 4.4.1 of Dasgupta, Hammond and Maskin (1979) – but note that for three or more agents there *do* exist efficient and strategy-proof mechanisms that are not dictatorial (footnote 2 of Satterthwaite and Sonnenschein, 1981). However, Zhou (forthcoming) conjectures that if non-dictatorial is replaced by a stronger condition, viz. "non-inversely dictatorial," then an impossibility result applies in the many-agent case.

67 In a private good economy, a choice rule f is *Walrasian* if, for all θ, $f(\theta)$ comprises a competitive outcome. There may be consumption externalities in the Satterthwaite–Sonnenschein framework, so competitive outcomes need not be Pareto efficient.

It should be noted that Satterthwaite and Sonnenschein confine their attention to choice rules that are "regular" at all points in Θ (or some open subset of Θ): regularity means that the allocation changes smoothly with small changes in preferences. It is not known how important regularity is to their conclusions.

It should also be pointed out that Satterthwaite and Sonnenshein's notion of "serial dictatorship" is a *local* condition, and their terminology may have a misleadingly pessimistic connotation. The notion in fact means that there is a hierarchical structure of influence: agent i can (locally) affect agent j, but not vice versa. Zhou (1991) points out that in a median voter mechanism, the median voter is a local dictator at any regular point. Moulin and Shenker's (1991) cost-sharing mechanism is a serial dictatorship which, they argue, is nonetheless "normatively impeccable." In a sense, then, Satterthwaite and Sonnenshein (1981) can be seen as contributing to the development of *positive* characterization results for dominant strategy implementation. See section 1.2 below.

68 Generically with respect to the Euclidean metric on the space of vectors of the agents' valuations u_i over D.

69 It is interesting to note that the second-price auction of Vickrey (1961) is the private good analogue of this rule.

70 This need not be true for a sufficiently restricted domain, however. See, for example, Holmström (1979).

71 However, as the number of agents I grows, the size of the imbalance shrinks, at the rate $(1/I)$. Note that if $k_i = 0$ for some agent i then he could absorb any surplus/deficit.

72 Sjöström (1991a) makes an interesting connection between the Groves–Clarke mechanism and the Shapley value. He considers the possibility that coalitions may form, and the members of any coalition (including the grand coalition) allocate surplus among themselves by means of an efficient strategy-proof mechanism. It turns out that the Shapley value of the induced cooperative game coincides with the actual payoff vector for the grand coalition if and only if *all* coalitions use the Groves–Clarke mechanism.

73 In another paper (1982b), Laffont and Maskin take D to be an interval, and Θ to comprise all quasi-linear preferences that are concave and differentiable over D. With other minor assumptions, they show that there exists some continuous, semi-strictly increasing function h defined on $\mathbb{R}^I \to \mathbb{R}$ such that, for each θ, $d(\theta)$ solves:

$$h[u_1'(d,\theta), \ldots, u_I'(d,\theta)] = 0,$$

where $u_i'(d,\theta)$ denotes the marginal utility $\partial u_i(d,\theta)/\partial d$. Compare this with theorem 1.2 above.

74 See also Thomson (1991).

75 With more agents, payments are determined serially ($\cong$inductively) on the number of agents, I. Supposing that q_1 is again the smallest amount demanded, then all agents pay $\frac{1}{I}C(Iq_1)$. In addition, agents $2, \ldots, I$ share the incremental cost $C(q_1 + \ldots + q_I) - C(Iq_1)$ according to the same serial procedure. That is, take the next-smallest demand, say q_2, and, hypothetically supposing that

these $I-1$ agents *all* demanded q_2, divide the incremental cost $C(q_1 + (I-1)q_2) - C(Iq_1)$ among them equally; etc.

76 In fact, the mechanism can be made even simpler than a revelation mechanism; see, for example, Reichelstein (1984b).

77 See theorem 7.1.1 of Dasgupta, Hammond, and Maskin (1979). Note that the reverse implication is obviously true too, since any dominant strategy equilibrium is a Nash equilibrium.

78 See, for example, Repullo (1986).

79 The quotation marks around "truthful implementation" and "revelation mechanism" denote the fact that we have enlarged agent i's strategy set from the set of his own preference orderings, $R_i(\theta)$, to the set of all states, θ. This is different from our earlier definitions.

80 This argument does rely on the existence of a bad outcome, though.

81 There were some issues left unresolved from Maskin's original work, which have since been resolved; see Williams (1986) and Saijo (1988).

82 For more on augmenting "revelation mechanisms," see Mookherjee and Reichelstein (1990).

83 For an important discussion of these issues, see Jackson (forthcoming).

84 For excellent surveys, see sections 2.2 – 2.4 of Postlewaite (1985), and section 4.1.2 of Groves and Ledyard (1987). Mention should be made of three early papers which use Nash equilibrium to implement Walrasian outcomes (for private goods environments) and Lindahl outcomes (for public goods): Schmeidler (1980), Hurwicz (1979a), and Walker (1981).

Another paper that should be highlighted in this context is Hurwicz (1979b); he proves the surprising result that, under certain continuity and convexity assumptions, and for a rich enough domain, the *only* Pareto efficient and individually rational choice rule f that can be Nash implemented in a classical private goods environment is Walrasian. (To show that f must contain the Walrasian choice rule, Hurwicz assumes that f is upper semi-continuous, which is a reasonable enough assumption. However, for the reverse inclusion he requires agents' choice sets to be convex, which is an unpalatable assumption because it relates to the mechanism itself (a design variable). Schmeidler (1982) relaxes the requirement of convexity; but his weaker condition still applies to the mechanism. Reichelstein (1984a) shows that some such assumption is essential to obtain this reverse inclusion.) See also Thomson (1979b).

85 On this, see, for example, Hurwicz, Maskin, and Postlewaite (1984), Reichelstein (1987), Postlewaite and Wettstein (1989), and Tian (1989).

86 For recent results and further references, see, for example, Williams (1986), Reichelstein and Reiter (1988), Saijo (1988), and McKelvey (1989). The seminal paper in this general area is Mount and Reiter (1974).

87 For two recent papers and further references, see Postlewaite and Wettstein (1989) and Tian (1989).

88 For references, see, for example, Shubik (1981).

89 See, for example, Thomson (1987), and Thomson and Varian (1985, especially section 5), and references therein. For a more recent paper, see Thomson (1991).

90 Maskin (1977) also proved another general sufficiency result, concerning

neutral choice rules. f is *neutral* if the labeling of outcomes is irrelevant. That is, if for all permutations π: $A \to A$ and $\theta \in \Theta$ we have $\theta_\pi \in \Theta$ and $\pi.f(\theta) = f(\theta_\pi)$ – where the profile θ_π is such that for all agents i, $a\ R_i(\theta_\pi)\ b$ if and only if $\pi^{-1}(a)\ R_i(\theta)\ \pi^{-1}(b)$. Maskin proved that, given three or more agents, a choice rule is Nash implementable if it is monotonic and neutral. Note that neutrality is an independent condition from no veto power, even in the presence of monotonicity; see footnote 13 of Moore and Repullo (1990) for counterexamples.

91 It must be noted that, although I have adopted Danilov's terminology, my definitions of essential and strong monotonicity are stronger than those given in Danilov (1992). Thus theorem 2.2 is a variant on his result. In particular, the necessity part of theorem 2.2 is stronger than his. And, although the sufficiency part of theorem 2.2 looks weaker than his, it is easier to check since fewer outcomes will be essential under my definition.

A universal domain is important to these results. The following is a counterexample: a choice rule f that is Nash implementable even though it does not satisfy my definition of strong monotonicity. The example has been constructed so that it does not satisfy Danilov's (weaker) definition of strong monotonicity either.

Consider a three-state, four-outcome environment, $\Theta = \{\theta, \phi, \gamma\}$, $A = \{a,b,c,d\}$, in which agents 1 and 2 have preferences:

Agent 1			*Agent 2*	
θ	ϕ	γ	θ and ϕ	γ
a	d	c	b	b
d	a	a	a	c
c	b	d	d	a
b	c	b	c	d

Suppose other agents are always indifferent across $\{a,b,c,d\}$.

Consider a choice rule satisfying:

$$f(\theta) = a,\ f(\phi) = b, \text{ and } f(\gamma) = c.$$

This can be Nash implemented using the following simple mechanism:

	Agent 2	
Agent 1	a	c
	d	b

(Top left is the unique Nash equilibrium in state θ, bottom right in state ϕ, and top right in state γ.) However, this f is not strongly monotonic, since, even though $a \notin f(\phi)$, there are no outcomes $\{y\}$ that are essential for any agent $i \neq 2$ in $L_i(a,\theta)$, and the only outcomes $\{y\}$ that are essential for agent 2 in $L_2(a,\theta)$ are a and c (for neither of which is it the case that $y\ P_2(\phi)\ a$).

92 In the case of fines, if the predesignated third party were to be included as a party to an *ex ante* contract, then he would of course have the right to veto any renegotiation.

93 At the opposite extreme, if the range of f equals the whole of A, then restricted veto power coincides with no veto power – which, as we have seen, would be a hopelessly strong condition in the two-agent case.

94 A closed ball is defined as a set of outcomes lying at most ε away from some fixed point, for some $\varepsilon > 0$.

95 Sjöström (1991c) shows that, given assumption B, non-empty lower intersection is also very close to being a *necessary* condition for Nash implementability.

96 However it should be noted that, with a *finite* Θ (a condition which Dutta and Sen need if their construction is not to have open sets), then all three of the mechanisms in Maskin (1979b), Roberts (1984, appendix), and Moore and Repullo (1990, corollary 4) could easily have avoided using open sets.

97 See Dasgupta, Hammond, and Maskin (1979), example 3.1.2. Refer to section 3.1 of their paper for a fuller discussion of monotonically closed domains – which they term simply "rich" domains.

98 See also Dasgupta, Hammond, and Maskin (1979), corollary 7.2.5.

99 In an interesting recent paper, Jackson and Srivastava (1991a) classify, and offer simple proofs of, a number of "impossibility" results for single-valued choice rules, using different equilibrium concepts. Their work sheds light on why certain equilibrium concepts lead to impossibility, and others do not. Note that theorem 2.6 is also true for two agents and *two* distinct outcomes; for a simple proof, see Jackson and Srivastava (1991b).

100 See example 3.1.4 of Dasgupta, Hammond, and Maskin (1979).

101 It should be stressed that this equivalence only applies to the set of implementable *decisions* $(d(\theta)|\theta \in \Theta)$ – it ignores the transfers $t_1, \ldots, t_I$. There are many choice rules $f = (d, t_1, \ldots, t_I)$ which are not strategy-proof but which are Nash implementable.

102 However, for the purposes of implementation, the equivalence turns out not to be exact. Gourvitch (1984) shows that there exist choice rules which can be implemented using dominance solvability applied to the normal form, but cannot be subgame perfect implemented using a tree mechanism.

103 See also McKelvey and Niemi (1978).

104 See also Mueller (1978) and Dutta (1983).

105 There is another niggling condition, namely: if, in state ϕ, outcome a_{T+1} is maximal in B for all agents except $j(T)$, then either $T=0$ or $j(T-1) \neq j(T)$. In the interests of understanding what is already quite a complicated-looking condition, I relegate this to a footnote. However, as can be seen from the necessity proof in Abreu and Sen (1990), it is this additional condition which causes most trouble – albeit that, in practice, for a large enough choice of B, it is highly unlikely that, in state ϕ, any outcome a_{T+1} will be maximal in B for $I-1$ agents (given $I \geq 3$). (Cf. the fact that no veto power is usually vacuously satisfied, since typically no outcome is top-ranked in A by $I-1$ agents.)

106 There is a slight problem with the sufficiency result in Abreu and Sen (1990): for their construction to work, it is important that, off the equilibrium path, agents

have *maximal* choices in the set B. A variety of innocuous assumptions could fix this problem.

107 Section 3 of Moore and Repullo (1988) gives an intuition for the necessity condition in theorem 3.1.

108 See also McKelvey and Niemi (1978), and Golberg and Gourvitch (1986).

109 The agents need not be risk neutral *ex ante*. Recall the risk-sharing example in section VIII of part one, in which the first-best was implemented using a simple sequential mechanism, even though monotonicity was not satisfied.

110 That is, if $\theta=\theta^t$ in condition M then $\Theta^-=\{\theta^{t-s}|s>0\}$ and $\Theta^+=\{\theta^{t+s}|s>0\}$.

111 This is what drives the risk-sharing example in section VIII of part one. Note that a single-crossing property does not necessarily imply monotonicity for every ordered pair (θ,ϕ), since $d(\theta)$ may be a boundary point of D; the risk-sharing example is a case in point.

112 There is a caveat. It is important that agent 1 does not "maliciously" challenge a true report by agent 2; that is the role of the $\varepsilon>0$ at stage 2 in the above mechanism. However, in general agent 1's preferences need not be quasi-linear; all that is really needed is that agent 1's preference reversal is strict in both directions (which is a mild assumption).

113 In the interests of keeping the exposition uncluttered, I have included this very weak condition. But note that it can be weakened further. Palfrey and Srivastava introduce a "Property Q" which a choice rule *must* satisfy if it is to be implementable in undominated Nash equilibrium.

114 It is possible to construct examples of games which are bounded, but in which one agent has no best response to certain other strategies of the other agents.

115 Note that condition (ii) in the definition of a chained choice rule can in fact be weakened to: there must exist some pair of agents $\{i,j\}$ and set of outcomes $\{x,y,b,z\}$, with $b\neq z$, such that:

$$x\ P_i(\theta)\ y \text{ and } y\ R_i(\phi)\ x$$

and:

$$b\ R_i(\phi)\ z \text{ and } b\ P_j(\phi)\ a\ R_j(\theta)\ z.$$

(The special case $z=a$ is the one given in the text.) Note that theorem 4.2 appears in an earlier (1990) version of Jackson, Palfrey, and Srivastava; the sufficiency result in later versions of the paper is confined to domains of strict preferences.

116 This mechanism has some similarity to the stage mechanism given in section VI of part one. However, notice that the present mechanism requires Solomon to know v^m and v^n so that he can set the fine ν appropriately; that was not true for the stage mechanism.

117 "Nothing" is a bad outcome for agent i (cf. section 2.1). Notice that the other agents need not be punished. Thus there is parallel here with the notion of a separable environment in Jackson, Palfrey and Srivastava (1991).

118 See Guesnerie (1990), and section 3 of Sjöström (1991b).

119 Cf. Saijo (1988), and the mechanism in part one (section VII). See also Postlewaite and Schmeidler (1986).

120 If f is a correspondence, however, more can be implemented in undominated strategy equilibrium using a bounded mechanism – see the choice rule in Börgers (1991), which is both Pareto efficient and does not exclude "compromises" (this choice rule represents the outcomes associated with eliminating dominated strategies when using approval voting).

121 A drawback of theorem 5.3 is that Θ is assumed to be finite – which would be a serious restriction in many applications.

122 This is only a sketch. In places, I have taken the liberty of simplifying Abreu and Matsushima's mechanism, in order to try and convey the intuition better. Readers are urged to look at their paper for the details.

123 Mechanisms with random outcomes date back to the early work of Zeckhauser (1969). Gibbard (1977, 1978) uses lotteries for implementation in dominant strategies.

124 Preferences are assumed to have independent domains (cf. the start of part two above).

125 I am glossing over certain details. For example, even though F' is small, it is large relative to F''. Also, a third (even smaller) fine is levied on anyone who is *ever* the "odd-man-out": that is, if all agents i announce a common θ_k^i except for agent j, then agent j is fined (regardless of whether or not this k is the first deviation from ρ along the K-vector).

126 Abreu and Matsushima (1991) make a spirited response to Glazer and Rosenthal.

127 As we saw in section 2.2, the Nash implementation of single-valued choice rules poses particular difficulties. One of the strengths of virtual implementation is that single-valued choice rules can be readily implemented.

128 A very mild assumption on preferences over lotteries is being made: any shift of probability weight from a less preferred to a more preferred (deterministic) outcome yields a lottery which is preferred. Clearly, this will be true if, for example, preferences satisfy the expected utility hypothesis.

129 The equilibria will almost always be coalition-proof too. (See Bernheim, Peleg, and Whinston, 1987).

130 Hence the order of elimination cannot matter; and, *a fortiori*, this encompasses (virtual) implementation in *rationalizable* strategies (see Bernheim (1984) and Pearce (1984)).

131 There would of course be no hope of implementing any choice rule that was not efficient, given the assumption that agents always bargain to the Pareto frontier; see below.

132 Note that assumptions R0 and R3 together imply that if a were θ-efficient in the first place, then $h(a|\theta)$ would equal a.

133 An apparently weaker asumption might be to suppose that $h(a|\theta)$ is a probability distribution over outcomes in A; i.e., that the agents have common expectations over the possible outcomes of the renegotiation, and attach the same priors to these. However, if we formulate A to include all lotteries over deterministic outcomes, then this possibility is embraced. Moreover, if, as would be the case if the agents were risk averse and the outcome set were divisible, a stochastic outcome (to renegotiation) is inefficient, then assump-

tion R2 asserts that one agent could propose a welfare-improving deterministic outcome which the others would accept.

134 And so by assumption R0 it must in fact be the same outcome: $f(\theta)$.

135 When renegotiation occurs, only the trade price p_1 is adjusted; the no-trade price p_0 stays fixed. Note that for $v<c$, there is no renegotiation.

136 To be accurate, the pairs v,c and $\hat{v},\hat{c}$ were *not* chosen arbitrarily, since we assumed (for the sake of exposition) that $v \geq c$ and $\hat{v} \geq \hat{c}$. However, the other cases can be dealt with similarly.

References

Abbot, F. and A. Johnson (1926), *Municipal Administration in the Roman Empire*, Princeton: Princeton University Press.

Abdou, J. and H. Keiding (1991), *Effectivity Functions in Social Choice*, Dordrecht: Kluwer Academic Publishers.

Abreu, D. and H. Matsushima (1989), "Virtual Implementation in Iteratively Undominated Strategies: Complete Information," mimeo, Princeton University. To appear in *Econometrica*.

(1990), "Exact Implementation," mimeo, Princeton University. To appear in *Journal of Economic Theory*.

(1991), "A Response to Glazer and Rosenthal," mimeo, Princeton University. To appear in *Econometrica*.

Abreu, D. and A. Sen (1990), "Subgame Perfect Implementation: A Necessary and Almost Sufficient Condition," *Journal of Economic Theory*, 50: 285–99.

(1991), "Virtual Implementation in Nash Equilibrium," *Econometrica*, 59: 997–1021.

Aghion, P. and P. Bolton (forthcoming), "An Incomplete Contracts Approach to Financial Contracting," *Review of Economic Studies*.

Aghion, P., M. Dewatripont, and P. Rey (1990), "On Renegotiation Design," *European Economic Review*, 34: 322–9.

(forthcoming), "Renegotiation Design with Unverifiable Information," *Econometrica*.

Arrow, K. (1951), *Social Choice and Individual Values*, New York: John Wiley. (2nd Edition, 1963, New Haven: Yale University Press.)

Bagnoli, M. and B. Lipman (1989), "Provision of Public Goods: Fully Implementing the Core Through Private Contributions," *Review of Economic Studies*, 56: 583–602.

Barberà, S. (1983), "Strategy-Proofness and Pivotal Voters: A Direct Proof of the Gibbard-Satterthwaite Theorem," *International Economic Review*, 24: 413–17.

Barberà, S. and B. Dutta (1982), "Implementation via Protective Equilibria," *Journal of Mathematical Economics*, 4: 49–65.

Barberà, S., F. Gul, and E. Stachetti (1991), "Generalized Median Voter Schemes and Committees," mimeo, Universitat Autónoma de Barcelona.

Barberà, S. and M. Jackson (1988), "Maximin, Leximin, and the Protective Criterion: Characterizations and Comparisons," *Journal of Economic Theory*, 46: 34–44.

(1991a), "A Characterization of Strategy-Proof Social Choice Functions for

Economies with Pure Public Goods," mimeo, Universitat Autónoma de Barcelona.

(1991b), "Strategy-Proof Exchange," mimeo, Universitat Autónoma de Barcelona.

Barberà, S. and B. Peleg (1990), "Strategy-Proof Voting Schemes with Continuous Preferences," *Social Choice and Welfare*, 7: 31–8.

Barberà, S., H. Sonnenshein, and L. Zhou (1991), "Voting By Committees," *Econometrica*, 59: 595–609.

Benassy, J-P. (1982), *The Economics of Market Disequilibrium*, New York: Academic Press.

Bernheim, B. D. (1984), "Rationalizable Strategic Behavior," *Econometrica*, 52: 1007–28.

Bernheim, B. D., B. Peleg, and M. Whinston (1987), "Coalition-Proof Nash Equilibria I: Concepts," *Journal of Economic Theory*, 42: 1–12.

Bernheim, B. D. and M. Whinston (1987), "Coalition-Proof Nash Equilibria II: Applications," *Journal of Economic Theory*, 42: 13–29.

Bolton, P. (1990), "Renegotiation and the Dynamics of Contract Design," *European Economic Review*, 34: 303–10.

Bolton, P. and M. Whinston (forthcoming), "Incomplete Contracts, Vertical Integration, and Supply Assurance," *Review of Economic Studies*.

Borch, K. (1962), "Equilibrium in a Reinsurance Market," *Econometrica*, 30: 424–44.

Border, K. and J. Jordan (1983), "Straightforward Elections, Unanimity and Phantom Agents," *Review of Economic Studies*, 50: 153–70.

Börgers, T. (1991), "Undominated Strategies and Coordination in Normalform Games," *Social Choice and Welfare*, 8: 65–78.

Brus, W. (1987), "Market Socialism," in J. Eatwell, M. Milgate, and P. Newman (eds.), *The New Palgrave: A Dictionary of Economics*, London: Macmillan, pp. 337–42.

Chung, T-Y. (1991), "Risk-Sharing, Specific Investment, and Incomplete Contracts," *Review of Economic Studies*, 58: 1031–42.

Clarke, E. (1971), "Multi-Part Pricing of Public Goods," *Public Choice*, 11: 17–33.

Corchon, L. (1989), "A 'Natural' Mechanism for the Allocation of Public Goods," mimeo, Universidad de Alicante.

Crawford, V. (1977): "A Game of Fair Division," *Review of Economic Studies*, 44: 235–47.

(1979), "A Procedure for Generating Pareto-Efficient Egalitarian Equivalent Allocations," *Econometrica*, 47: 49–60.

Danilov, V. (1992), "Implementation via Nash Equilibrium," *Econometrica*, 60: 43–56.

Dasgupta, P., P. Hammond, and E. Maskin (1979), "The Implementation of Social Choice Rules: Some General Results on Incentive Compatability," *Review of Economic Studies*, 46: 185–216.

Demange, G. (1984), "Implementing Efficient Egalitarian Equivalent Allocations," *Econometrica*: 52, 1167–77.

Demski, J. and D. Sappington (1984), "Optimal Incentive Contracts with Multiple Agents," *Journal of Economic Theory*, 33: 152–71.

Dummett, M. and R. Farqhuarson (1961), "Stability in Voting," *Econometrica*, 29: 33–43.

Dutta, B. (1983), "Further Results on Voting with Veto," in P. Pattanaik and M. Salles (eds.), *Social Choice and Welfare*, Amsterdam: North-Holland, pp. 239–50.

Dutta, B. and A. Sen (1991a), "Implementation Under Strong Equilibrium: A Complete Characterization," *Journal of Mathematical Economics*, 20: 49–68.

(1991b), "A Necessary and Sufficient Condition for Two-Person Nash Implementation," *Review of Economic Studies*, 58: 121–8.

Farquharson, R. (1957/1969), *Theory of Voting*, New Haven: Yale University Press.

Finley, M. (1951), *Studies in Land and Credit in Ancient Athens, 500–200 B.C.: The Horos-Inscriptions*, New Brunswick: Rutgers University Press.

Gibbard, A. (1973), "Manipulation of Voting Schemes: A General Result," *Econometrica*, 41: 587–602.

(1977), "Manipulation of Schemes that Mix Voting with Chance," *Econometrica*, 45: 665–81.

(1978), "Straightforwardness of Game Forms with Lotteries as Outcomes," *Econometrica*, 46: 595–614.

Glazer, J. and C-T. Ma (1989), "Efficient Allocation of a 'Prize' – King Solomon's Dilemma," *Games and Economic Behavior*, 1: 222–33.

Glazer, J. and R. Rosenthal (1990), "A Note on the Abreu-Matsushima Mechanism," mimeo, Boston University. To appear in *Econometrica*.

Golberg, A. and V. Gourvitch (1986), "Secret and Extensive Dominance Solvable Veto Voting Schemes," mimeo, Moscow.

Goligher, W. (1907), "Studies in Attic Law. The Antidosis," *Hermathena*, 14: 481–515.

Gourvitch, V. (1984), private communication. (Available from Hervé Moulin on request.)

Green, J. and J-J. Laffont (1977), "Characterization of Satisfactory Mechanisms for the Revelation of Preferences for Public Goods," *Econometrica*, 45: 427–38.

(1979), *Incentives in Public Decision Making*, Amsterdam: North-Holland.

(1991a), "Non-Verifiability, Renegotiation and Efficiency," mimeo, Harvard University.

(1991b), "Contract Renegotiation and the Underinvestment Effect," mimeo, Harvard University.

(forthcoming), "Renegotiation and the Form of Efficient Contracts," *Annales de Economie et de Statistique*.

Grossman, S. and O. Hart (1986), "The Costs and Benefits of Ownership: A Theory of Vertical and Lateral Integration," *Journal of Political Economy*, 94: 691–719.

Groves, T. (1973), "Incentives in Teams," *Econometrica*, 41: 617–31.

(1982), "On Theories of Incentive Compatible Choice with Compensation," in W. Hildenbrand (ed.), *Advances in Economic Theory: Invited Papers for the Fourth World Congress of the Econometric Society*, Cambridge University Press, pp. 1–29.

Groves, T. and J. Ledyard (1977), "Optimal Allocation of Public Goods: A Solution to the 'Free Rider' Problem," *Econometrica*, 45: 783–809.

(1987), "Incentive Compatibility since 1972," in T. Groves, R. Radner, and S. Reiter (eds.), *Information, Incentives, and Economic Mechanisms: Essays in Honor of Leonid Hurwicz*, Minneapolis: University of Minnesota Press, pp. 48–111.

Groves, T., R. Radner, and S. Reiter (eds.) (1987), *Information, Incentives, and Economic Mechanisms: Essays in Honor of Leonid Hurwicz*, Minneapolis: University of Minnesota Press.

Guesnerie, R. (1990), "The Arrow-Debreu Paradigm Faced with Modern Theories of Contracting: A Discussion of Selected Issues Involving Information and Time" (Paper presented at the Nobel Symposium No. 77, Stockholm), mimeo, DELTA, Paris.

Hart, O. and B. Holmström (1987), "The Theory of Contracts," in T. Bewley (ed.), *Advances in Economic Theory: Invited Papers for the Fifth World Congress of the Econometric Society*, Cambridge University Press, pp. 71–155.

Hart, O. and J. Moore (1988), "Incomplete Contracts and Renegotiation," *Econometrica*, 56: 755–86.

(1989), "Default and Renegotiation: A Dynamic Model of Debt," revised August 1989, University of Edinburgh Discussion Paper.

(1990), "Property Rights and the Nature of the Firm," *Journal of Political Economy*, 98: 1119–58.

(1991), "A Theory of Debt Based on the Inalienability of Human Capital," mimeo, Massachusetts Institute of Technology.

Hart, O. and J. Tirole (1990), "Vertical Integration and Market Foreclosure," *Brookings Papers: Microeconomics*, pp. 205–86.

Hayek, F. von (1935), "The Present State of the Debate," in F. von Hayek (ed.), *Collectivist Economic Planning*, London: George Routledge and Sons, pp. 201–43.

(1945), "The Use of Knowledge in Society," *American Economic Review*, 35: 519–30.

Hererro, M. and S. Srivastava (forthcoming), "Implementation via Backward Induction," *Journal of Economic Theory*.

Holmström, B. (1979), "Groves Schemes on Restricted Domains," *Econometrica*, 47: 1137–44.

Holmström, B. and P. Milgrom (1987), "Aggregation and Linearity in the Provision of Intertemporal Incentives," *Econometrica*, 55: 303–28.

(1990), "Regulating Trade Among Agents," *Journal of Institutional and Theoretical Economics*, 146: 85–105.

(1991), "Multi-Task Principal-Agent Analyses: Incentive Contracts, Asset Ownership and Job Design," mimeo, Yale University.

Holzman, R. (1987), "Sub-Core Solutions of the Problem of Strong Implementation," *International Journal of Game Theory*, 16: 263–9.

Howard, J. (1990), "Implementing Alternative Voting in Kingmaker Trees," *Games and Economic Behavior*, 2: 325–36.

(forthcoming), "A Social Choice Rule and its Implementation in Perfect Equilibrium," *Journal of Economic Theory*.

Hurwicz, L. (1960), "Optimality and Information Efficiency in Resource Allocation Processes," in K. Arrow, S. Karlin, and P. Suppes (eds.), *Mathematical*

Methods in the Social Sciences, Stanford: Stanford University Press, pp. 27–46.
(1972), "On Informationally Decentralized Systems," in R. Radner and C. McGuire (eds.), *Decision and Organization*, Amsterdam: North Holland, pp. 297–336.
(1973), "The Design of Mechanisms for Resource Allocation," *American Economic Review*, 63: 1–30.
(1975), "On the Existence of Allocation Systems Whose Manipulative Nash Equilibria are Pareto Optimal," mimeo, University of Minnesota. (Presented at the Third World Congress of the Econometric Society, Toronto.)
(1979a), "Outcome Functions Yielding Walrasian and Lindahl Allocations at Nash Equilibrium Points," *Review of Economic Studies*, 46: 217–25.
(1979b), "On Allocations Attainable Through Nash Equilibria," *Journal of Economic Theory*, 21: 140–65. (Also in J-J. Laffont (ed.), *Aggregation and Revelation of Preferences* (1979), Amsterdam: North-Holland, pp. 397–419.)
(1985), "A Perspective," in L. Hurwicz, D. Schmeidler, and H. Sonnenschein (eds.), *Social Goals and Social Organization: Essays in Memory of Elisha Pazner*, Cambridge University Press, pp. 1–16.
(1986), "Incentive Aspects of Decentralization," in K. Arrow and M. Intriligator (eds.), *Handbook of Mathematical Economics*, vol. 3, Amsterdam: North-Holland, pp. 1441–82.
Hurwicz, L., E. Maskin, and A. Postlewaite (1984), "Feasible Implementation of Social Choice Correspondences by Nash Equilibria," mimeo, University of Minnesota.
Hurwicz, L. and D. Schmeidler (1978), "Outcome Functions which Guarantee the Existence and Pareto Optimality of Nash Equilibria," *Econometrica*, 46: 144–74.
Hurwicz, L. and M. Walker (1990), "On the Generic Nonoptimality of Dominant-Strategy Allocation Mechanisms: A General Theorem that Includes Pure Exchange Economies," *Econometrica*, 58: 683–704.
Jackson, M. (forthcoming), "Implementation in Undominated Strategies: A Look at Bounded Mechanisms," *Review of Economic Studies*.
Jackson, M. and H. Moulin (forthcoming), "Implementing a Public Project and Distributing Its Cost," *Journal of Economic Theory*.
Jackson, M., T. Palfrey, and S. Srivastava (1991), "Undominated Nash Implementation in Bounded Mechanisms," mimeo, Northwestern University. To appear in *Games and Economic Behavior*.
Jackson, M. and S. Srivastava (1991a), "Implementing Social Choice Functions: A New Look at some Impossibility Results," mimeo, Northwestern University.
(1991b), "On Two-Person Nash Implementable Choice Functions," mimeo, Northwestern University.
The Jerusalem Bible (1968). New York: Doubleday.
Jones, A. (1974), *The Roman Economy*, Totowa: Rowman and Littlefield.
Kowalik, T. (1987), "Lange-Lerner Mechanism," in J. Eatwell, M. Milgate, and P. Newman (eds.), *The New Palgrave: A Dictionary of Economics*, London: Macmillan, pp. 129–31.
Kreps, D. (1990), *A Course in Microeconomic Theory*, Princeton: Princeton University Press.

Laffont, J-J. and E. Maskin (1982a), "The Theory of Incentives: An Overview," in W. Hildenbrand (ed.), *Advances in Economic Theory: Invited Papers for the Fourth World Congress of the Econometric Society*, Cambridge University Press, pp. 31–94.

(1982b), "Nash and Dominant Strategy Implementation in Economic Environments," *Journal of Mathematical Economics*, 10: 17–47.

Lange, O. (1936), "On the Theory of Socialism, Part I," *Review of Economic Studies*, 4: 53–71.

(1937), "On the Theory of Socialism, Part II," *Review of Economic Studies*, 4: 123–42.

Lange, O. and F. Taylor (1938), *On the Economic Theory of Socialism*. Edited and with an introduction by B. Lippincott. Minneapolis: University of Minnesota Press.

Ledyard, J. (1987), "Incentive Compatibility," in J. Eatwell, M. Milgate, and P. Newman (eds.), *The New Palgrave: A Dictionary of Economics*, London: Macmillan, pp. 739–44.

Lerner, A. (1936), "A Note on Socialist Economies," *Review of Economic Studies*, 4: 72–6.

(1944), *Economics of Control: Principles of Welfare Economics*, New York: Macmillan.

Lewis, N. (1983), *Life in Egypt Under Roman Rule*, Oxford: Clarendon Press.

Littman, R. (1988), "Greek Taxation," in M. Grant and R. Kitzinger (eds.), *Civilization of the Ancient Mediterranean*, vol. II, New York: Charles Scribner's Sons, pp. 795–808.

Ma, C., J. Moore, and S. Turnbull (1988), "Stopping Agents from 'Cheating'," *Journal of Economic Theory*, 46: 355–72.

McKelvey, R. (1989), "Game Forms for Nash Implementation of General Social Choice Correspondences," *Social Choice and Welfare*, 6: 139–56.

McKelvey, R. and R. Niemi (1978), "A Multistage Game Representation of Sophisticated Voting for Binary Procedures," *Journal of Economic Theory*, 18: 1–22.

Marschak, J. (1954), "Towards an Economic Theory of Information and Organization," in R. Thrall *et al.* (eds.), *Decision Processes*, New York: Wiley, pp. 187–220.

(1955), "Elements for a Theory of Teams," *Management Science*, 1: 127–37.

Marschak, J. and R. Radner (1972), *Economic Theory of Teams*, New Haven: Yale University Press.

Marschak, T. (1987), "Organization Theory," in J. Eatwell, M. Milgate, and P. Newman (eds.), *The New Palgrave: A Dictionary of Economics*, London: Macmillan, pp. 757–61.

Maskin, E. (1977), "Nash Implementation and Welfare Optimality," mimeo, Massachusetts Institute of Technology.

(1979a), "Implementation and Strong Nash-Equilibrium," in J-J. Laffont (ed.), *Aggregation and Revelation of Preferences*, Amsterdam: North-Holland, pp. 432–9.

(1979b), "Implementation of Two-person SCR's: Pure Exchange, Known

Endowments, Unknown Preferences," mimeo, Massachusetts Institute of Technology.

(1985), "The Theory of Implementation in Nash Equilibrium: A Survey," in L. Hurwicz, D. Schmeidler, and H. Sonnenschein (eds.), *Social Goals and Social Organization: Essays in Memory of Elisha Pazner*, Cambridge University Press, pp. 173–204.

Maskin, E. and J. Moore (1987), "Implementation and Renegotiation," mimeo, Harvard University.

Matsushima, H. (1988), "A New Approach to the Implementation Problem," *Journal of Economic Theory*, 45: 128–44.

Matthews, S. and A. Postlewaite (1989), "Pre-Play Communication in a Two-Person Sealed-Bid Double Auction," *Journal of Economic Theory*, 48: 238–63.

Mises, L. von (1920), "Die Wirtschaftsrechnung im Sozialistischen Gemeinwesen," in F. von Hayek (ed.) (1935), *Collectivist Economic Planning*, London: George Routledge and Sons, pp. 87–103.

Mookherjee, D. and S. Reichelstein (1990), "The Revelation Approach to Nash Implementation," mimeo, Indian Statistical Institute.

Moore, J. and R. Repullo (1988), "Subgame Perfect Implementation," *Econometrica*, 46: 1191–220.

(1990), "Nash Implementation: A Full Characterization," *Econometrica*, 58: 1083–99.

Moulin, H. (1979), "Dominance-Solvable Voting Schemes," *Econometrica*, 47: 1337–51.

(1980a), "On Strategy-Proofness and Single-Peakedness," *Public Choice*, 35: 437–56.

(1980b), "Implementing Efficient, Anonymous and Neutral Social Choice Functions," *Journal of Mathematical Economics*, 7: 249–69.

(1981a), "Prudence versus Sophistication in Voting Strategy," *Journal of Economic Theory*, 24: 398–412.

(1981b), "Implementing Just and Efficient Decision Making," *Journal of Public Economics*, 16: 193–213.

(1982), "Non-Cooperative Implementation: A Survey of Recent Results," *Mathematical Social Sciences*, 3: 243–57.

(1983), *The Strategy of Social Choice*, Amsterdam: North-Holland.

(1984a), "The Conditional Auction Mechanism for Sharing a Surplus," *Review of Economic Studies*, 51: 157–70.

(1984b), "Implementing the Kalai-Smorodinsky Bargaining Solution," *Journal of Economic Theory*, 33: 32–45.

(1991), "Excludable Public Goods and the Free-Rider Problem," mimeo, Duke University.

Moulin, H. and B. Peleg (1982), "Cores of Effectivity Functions and Implementation Theory," *Journal of Mathematical Economics*, 10: 115–45.

Moulin, H. and S. Shenker (1991), "Serial Cost Sharing," mimeo, Duke University.

Mount, K. and S. Reiter (1974), "The Informational Size of Message Spaces," *Journal of Economic Theory*, 8: 161–92.

Mueller, D. (1978), "Voting by Veto," *Journal of Public Economics*, 10: 57–75. (Also in J-J. Laffont (ed.), *Aggregation and Revelation of Preferences* (1979), Amsterdam: North-Holland, pp. 225–41.)

Muller, E. and M. Satterthwaite (1977), "The Equivalence of Strong Positive Association and Strategy Proofness," *Journal of Economic Theory*, 14: 412–18.

(1985), "Strategy-Proofness: The Existence of Dominant Strategy Mechanisms," in L. Hurwicz, D. Schmeidler, and H. Sonnenschein (eds.), *Social Goals and Social Organization: Essays in Memory of Elisha Pazner*, Cambridge University Press, pp. 131–71.

Palfrey, T. (1992), "Implementation in Bayesian Equilibrium: The Multiple Equilibrium Problem in Mechanism Design," in J-J. Laffont (ed.), *Advances in Economic Theory: Invited Papers for the Sixth World Congress of the Econometric Society*, vol. I, Cambridge University Press.

Palfrey, T. and S. Srivastava (1991), "Nash Implementation Using Undominated Strategies," *Econometrica*, 59: 479–501.

Pattanaik, P. (1973), "On the Stability of Sincere Voting Situations," *Journal of Economic Theory*, 6: 558–74.

Pearce, D. (1984), "Rationalizable Strategic Behavior and the Problem of Perfection," *Econometrica*, 52: 1029–50.

Peleg, B. (1978), "Consistent Voting Schemes," *Econometrica*, 46: 153–61.

(1984a), *Game Theoretic Analysis of Voting in Committees*, Cambridge University Press.

(1984b), "Quasi-Coalition Equilibria, Part I. Definitions and Preliminary Results," mimeo, The Hebrew University, Jerusalem.

Postlewaite, A. (1985), "Implementation via Nash Equilibria in Economic Environments," in L. Hurwicz, D. Schmeidler, and H. Sonnenschein (eds.), *Social Goals and Social Organization: Essays in Memory of Elisha Pazner*, Cambridge University Press, pp. 205–28.

Postlewaite, A. and D. Schmeidler (1986), "Implementation in Differential Information Economies," *Journal of Economic Theory*, 39: 14–33.

Postlewaite, A. and D. Wettstein (1989), "Feasible and Continuous Implementation," *Review of Economic Studies*, 56: 603–11.

Radner, R. (1987), "Decentralization and Incentives," in T. Groves, R. Radner, and S. Reiter (eds.), *Information, Incentives, and Economic Mechanisms: Essays in Honor of Leonid Hurwicz*, Minneapolis: University of Minnesota Press, pp. 3–47.

Reichelstein, S. (1984a), "A Note on Allocations Attainable Through Nash Equilibria," *Journal of Economic Theory*, 32: 384–90.

(1984b), "Incentive Compatibility and Informational Requirements," *Journal of Economic Theory*, 34: 32–51.

(1987), "A Note on Feasible Implementations," *Economics Letters*, 25: 315–18.

Reichelstein, S. and S. Reiter (1988), "Game Forms with Minimal Strategy Spaces," *Econometrica*, 56: 661–92.

Reiter, S. (1977), "Information and Performance in the (New)^2 Welfare Economics," *American Economic Review*, 67: 226–34.

(1987), "Efficient Allocation," in J. Eatwell, M. Milgate, and P. Newman (eds.), *The New Palgrave: A Dictionary of Economics*, London: Macmillan, pp. 107–20.

Repullo, R. (1986), "The Revelation Principle under Complete and Incomplete Information," in K. Binmore and P. Dasgupta (eds.), *Economic Organizations as Games*, Oxford: Basil Blackwell, pp. 179–95.

(1987), "A Simple Proof of Maskin's Theorem on Nash Implementation," *Social Choice and Welfare*, 4: 39–41.

Roberts, J. (1987), "Incentives, Information, and Iterative Planning," in T. Groves, R. Radner, and S. Reiter (eds.), *Information, Incentives, and Economic Mechanisms: Essays in Honor of Leonid Hurwicz*, Minneapolis: University of Minnesota Press, pp. 349–74.

Roberts, K. (1979), "The Characterization of Implementable Choice Rules," in J-J. Laffont (ed.), *Aggregation and Revelation of Preferences*, Amsterdam: North-Holland, pp.321–48.

(1984), "The Theoretical Limits to Redistribution," *Review of Economic Studies*, 51: 177–95.

Rosenthal, R. (1981), "Games of Perfect Information, Predatory Pricing, and the Chain-Store Paradox," *Journal of Economic Theory*, 25: 92–100.

Rubinstein, A. (1991), "Comments on the Interpretation of Game Theory," *Econometrica*, 59: 909–24.

Rubinstein, A. and A. Wolinsky (forthcoming), "Renegotiation-Proof Implementation and Time Preferences," *American Economic Review*.

Saijo, T. (1988), "Strategy Space Reductions in Maskin's Theorem: Sufficient Conditions for Nash Implementation," *Econometrica*, 56: 693–700.

Samuelson, P. (1954), "The Pure Theory of Public Expenditures," *Review of Economics and Statistics*, 36: 387–9.

(1955), "Diagrammatic Exposition of a Theory of Public Expenditure," *The Review of Economics and Statistics*, 37: 350–6.

Satterthwaite, M. (1975), "Strategy-Proofness and Arrow's Conditions: Existence and Correspondence Theorems for Voting Procedures and Social Welfare Functions," *Journal of Economic Theory*, 10: 187–217.

(1987), "Strategy-Proof Allocation Mechanisms," in J. Eatwell, M. Milgate, and P. Newman (eds.), *The New Palgrave: A Dictionary of Economics*, London: Macmillan, pp. 518–20.

Satterthwaite, M. and H. Sonnenschein (1981), "Strategy-Proof Allocation Mechanisms at Differentiable Points," *Review of Economic Studies*, 48: 587–97.

Schmeidler, D. (1980), "Walrasian Analysis via Strategic Outcome Functions," *Econometrica*, 48: 1585–93.

(1982), "A Condition Guaranteeing that the Nash Allocation is Walrasian," *Journal of Economic Theory*, 28: 376–8.

Schmeidler, D. and H. Sonnenschein (1978), "Two Proofs of the Gibbard-Satterthwaite Theorem on the Possibility of a Strategy-Proof Social Choice Function," in H. Gottinger and W. Ensler (eds.), *Proceedings of a Conference on Decision Theory and Social Ethics at Schloss Reisenberg*, Dordrecht: Reidel, pp. 227–34.

Shubik, M. (1981), "Game Theory Models and Methods in Political Economy," in

K. Arrow and M. Intriligator (eds.), *Handbook of Mathematical Economics*, vol. 1, Amsterdam: North-Holland, pp. 285–330.

Sjöström, T. (1991a), "A New Characterization of the Groves-Clarke Mechanism," *Economics Letters*, 36: 263–7.

(1991b), "Implementation in Undominated Nash Equilibrium without Integer Games," mimeo, Harvard University. To appear in *Games and Economic Behavior*.

(1991c), "On the Necessary and Sufficient Conditions for Nash Implementation," *Social Choice and Welfare*, 8: 333–40.

(forthcoming), "Implementation in Perfect Equilibria," *Social Choice and Welfare*.

Sprumont, Y. (1991), "The Division Problem with Single-Peaked Preferences: A Characterization of the Uniform Allocation Rules," *Econometrica*, 59: 509–19.

Srivastava, S. and M. Trick (1991), "Sophisticated Voting Rules: The Case of Two Tournaments," mimeo, Carnegie-Mellon University.

Thomson, W. (1979a), "Maximin Strategies and Elicitation of Preferences," in J-J. Laffont (ed.), *Aggregation and Revelation of Preferences*, Amsterdam: North-Holland, pp. 245–68.

(1979b), "Comment" on L. Hurwicz, "On Allocations Attainable Through Nash Equilibria," in J-J. Laffont (ed.), *Aggregation and Revelation of Preferences*, Amsterdam: North-Holland, pp. 420–31.

(1987), "The Vulnerability to Manipulative Behavior of Resource Allocation Mechanisms Designed to Select Equitable and Efficient Outcomes," in T. Groves, R. Radner and S. Reiter (eds.), *Information, Incentives, and Economic Mechanisms: Essays in Honor of Leonid Hurwicz*, Minneapolis: University of Minnesota Press, pp. 375–96.

(1991), "Manipulation and Implementation of Solutions to the Problem of Fair Division When Preferences are Single-Peaked," mimeo, University of Rochester.

Thomson, W. and H. Varian (1985), "Theories of Justice Based on Symmetry," in L. Hurwicz, D. Schmeidler, and H. Sonnenschein (eds.), *Social Goals and Social Organization: Essays in Memory of Elisha Pazner*, Cambridge University Press, pp. 107–29.

Tian, G. (1989), "Implementation of the Lindahl Correspondence by a Single-Valued, Feasible, and Continuous Mechanism," *Review of Economic Studies*, 56: 613–21.

Tirole, J. (1992), "Collusion and the Theory of Organizations," in J-J. Laffont (ed.), *Advances in Economic Theory: Invited Papers for the Sixth World Congress of the Econometric Society*, vol. II, Cambridge University Press.

Varian, H. (1990a), "A Solution to the Problem of Externalities and Public Goods when Agents are Well-Informed," mimeo, University of Michigan.

(1990b), "Sequential Provision of Public Goods," mimeo, University of Michigan.

Vickrey, W. (1961), "Counterspeculation, Auctions, and Competitive Sealed Tenders," *Journal of Finance*, 16: 1–17.

Walker, M. (1978), "A Note on the Characterization of Mechanisms for the Revelation of Preferences," *Econometrica*, 46: 147–52.

(1980), "On the Nonexistence of a Dominant-Strategy Mechanism for Making Optimal Public Decisions," *Econometrica*, 48: 1521–40.
(1981), "A Simple Incentive Compatible Scheme for Attaining Lindahl Allocations," *Econometrica*, 49: 65–73.
Williams, S. (1986), "Realization and Nash Implementation: Two Aspects of Mechanism Design," *Econometrica*, 54: 139–51.
Yamato, T. (1991a), "On Nash Implementation of Social Choice Corrrespondences," mimeo, University of Rochester.
(1991b), "Double Implementation in Nash and Undominated Nash Equilibria," mimeo, University of Rochester.
Yang, C-L. (1991), "Robust Weak Dominance Implementation Solving the King Solomon Dilemma," mimeo, University of Dortmund.
Zeckhauser, R. (1969), "Majority Rule with Lotteries on Alternatives," *Review of Economic Studies*, 36: 696–703.
Zhou, L. (1991), "Impossibility of Strategy-Proof Mechanisms in Economies with Pure Public Goods," *Review of Economic Studies*, 58: 107–19.
Zhou, L. (forthcoming), "Inefficiency of Strategy-Proof Allocation Mechanisms in Pure Exchange Economies," *Social Choice and Welfare*.

CHAPTER 6

Implementation in Bayesian equilibrium: the multiple equilibrium problem in mechanism design*

Thomas R. Palfrey

1 INTRODUCTION

Implementation theory links together social choice theory and game theory. At a less abstract level, its application provides an approach to welfare economics based on individual incentives. The underlying motivation for implementation theory is most easily seen from the point of view of a relatively uninformed planner who wishes to optimize a social welfare function that depends on environmental parameters about which relevant information is scattered around in the economy. Thus, the planner wishes to both collect as much of this relevent information as possible, and, with this information, make a social decision (e.g., an allocation of resources). This is the classic problem identified by Hurwicz (1972). In the twenty years since, we find numerous research agendas falling into the general category of implementation problems: the study of planning procedures, contracts, optimal regulation and taxation, agency relationships, agendas and commitee decision-making, comparative electoral systems, non-cooperative foundations of general equilibrium theory, and even much of the recent theoretical work in accounting and the economics of law.

The dilemma such a planner faces is that the individuals from whom the information must be collected will not necessarily want to share their information, or worse, they may wish to misrepresent their information. Moreover, exactly how they choose to conceal and misrepresent their information (what we will call their *deception decision*) depends upon three things. First and foremost, it depends on expectations of how the planner intends to put to use the information that is being collected. Second, it depends upon their expectations about the deception decisions of the other agents. Third, it depends on their information, so it is convenient to think of a deception decision as a *plan* of what to reveal as a function of information.

The thoughtful planner, realizing this, takes account of the possibility that there may be deceptions when deciding how to translate the collected information into a social decision. But in order to do this the planner needs to have a basis for predicting how deception decisions vary as a function of the individuals' expectations about how he intends to translate the information into social decisions. Game theory provides a large family of such predictions, in the form of equilibrium concepts, and each of these provides an internally consistent theory of individuals' expectations about the deception decisions of the other individuals. In addition to a theory of behavior, the planner also needs to consider how he can manipulate the individuals' expectations of how he will translate the information into social decisions. The latter problem has, at least until very recently, been finessed in implementation theory by the *commitment assumption*:[1] the planner may commit to any feasible outcome function, which is a rule for translating collected information into social decisions. This assumption implies that the individuals' expectations exactly coincide with whatever outcome function the planner has announced he will use. Finally, the planner must have the ability to control the information collection process. To simplify this problem implementation theory usually imposes *the control assumption*: the planner may choose any message space and the individuals must communicate exactly one message from this message space, may not communicate any additional messages, and may not communicate with each other. The combination of a message space and an outcome function is called a *mechanism*.

Given an equilibrium concept and a class of environments, or domain, one can pose the incentive compatibility question: For what allocation rules does there exist a mechanism for which that allocation rule is an equilibrium outcome? If we can answer that question in the affirmative for some allocation rule, that allocation rule is incentive compatible. For many equilibrium concepts there is a well-known result called *the revelation principle*, which states that, if an allocation is incentive compatible, then it can be produced as the equilibrium outcome to a particularly simple kind of mechanism, called a direct mechanism. In a direct mechanism the message spaces are simply the individuals' information sets and the outcome function is the allocation rule itself. If an allocation rule is incentive compatible then it is the "truthful" equilibrium outcome to its associated direct mechanism.

However, incentive compatibility is only half of the implementation problem. The other half is the *multiple equilibrium problem.* While an allocation rule may be incentive compatible, it may have the problem that any mechanism for which that rule is an equilibrium outcome also produces other allocation rules as equilibrium outcomes. An unfortunate implication of the multiple equilibrium problem is that the revelation principle may be of only limited usefulness. In particular, it is concievable (and many plausible examples have been constructed, see section 2) that under some equilibrium concepts certain incentive compatible allocation rules are uniquely implementable, but the direct mechanism associated with that allocation rule is plagued by multiple equilibria. This suggests (correctly, as it turns out) that the guts of the mechanism design constructions to uniquely implement incentive compatible allocations are typically quite messy – in particular the individuals are asked to report messages that have additional components[2] beyond the direct announcements of their private information. Nevertheless, despite this greater complexity, it turns out that one can prove a simple characterization theorem establishing that the multiple equilibrium problem cannot be resolved unless a particular set of inequality conditions hold. These inequality conditions are referred to as *monotonicity conditions*. The problem of designing mechanisms to solve both the incentive compatibility problem and the multiple equilibrium problem is sometimes called *full implementation*. For brevity, I drop the word "full" and simply refer to it here as implementation.

To this point, the discussion has focused on implementing a specific allocation rule (or *social choice function*). More generally, one can talk about implementing collections of allocation rules, or *social choice sets*. For example, one might wish to implement the set of competitive equilibria rather than one particular selection from the competitive equilibrium correspondence. The theoretical issues of implementing correspondences are in many ways the same as the issues that arise in implementing specific allocation rules, so, for simplicity we will concentrate mainly on allocation rules.[3]

The first equilibrium concept to be applied to the implementation problem was *dominant strategy equilibrium*. This equilibrium concept has two important features. First, it circumvents the difficult problem of how to model players' expectations of other players' deceptions. If something is a dominant strategy equilibrium, then nobody cares how other individuals are behaving – or at least such expectations will not usually affect behavior. Second, and for more subtle reasons, it trivializes the second half of the implementation problem. Dominant strategy incentive compatibility very nearly implies any multiple equilibria can be avoided.[4] This is turn implies that little generality is lost in restricting attention to direct mechanisms if dominant strategy equilibrium is the solution concept.

Of course the cost of these simplifications is known to be steep. Specifically, the Gibbard–Satterthwaite theorem tells us that if we consider sufficiently broad domains then practically nothing is implementable in dominant strategies. The reason is the difficulty of satisfying incentive compatibility. In their terms, non-trivial *strategy-proof* allocation rules generally do not exist. Domain restrictions are needed before it becomes possible to implement interesting allocation rules.[5]

While it would have been convenient to have obtained more positive results with dominant strategy mechanisms, it is unfortunately not the case. The natural next step was to explore the implications of implementation in Nash equilibrium.[6] Using Nash equilibrium as the solution concept means that individual expectations about other individuals' deceptions are modeled explicitly and are important. In the Nash implementation approach, the assumption that players know nothing about their opponents' private information is replaced by the assumption that everyone's private information is common knowledge among the individuals.[7] For this reason, this line of research is appropriately viewed as "implementation with complete information."

The most promising applications of the complete information approach would probably be to contracting between two agents. In such situations, it may often be the case that the two contracting parties are relatively well-informed about each other's preferences and beliefs, but the planner (or the courts that will be enforcing the contract) is poorly informed about their preferences and beliefs. In this case, the mechanism may be thought of as a state-contingent contract that the players agree to *before* the state of the world (including their preferences) is realized. Such an interpretation might also apply to relatively small groups such as committees and legislatures, who interact frequently enough that they become relatively well-informed about each other's preferences. On the other hand, this raises the problem that these static models are probably *least* applicable where agents interact frequently enough to know each other's preferences, since reputation building and supergame considerations become important.

Another important difference with Nash implementation as compared with dominant strategy implementation is that the multiple equilibrium problem rears its ugly head. While the problem with dominant strategy implementation was incentive compatibility (strategy-proofness) the problem with Nash implementation is multiple equilibria. This is not surprising, as it is relatively difficult to construct game forms which have dominant strategies across a range of preference profiles, but it is easy to construct games with Nash equilibria. However, it is more difficult to construct games with unique Nash equilibrium.

The incentive compatibility issue becomes trivial for many domains because the redundancy of the individuals' information enables the planner to use the direct mechanism equivalent of "forcing contracts," where a universally bad outcome is enforced unless all the reports of private information agree.[8] For almost any allocation rule, it is possible to use such constructions to make truthful reporting a Nash equilibrium in a game where everyone reports the economy-wide profile of private information. Unfortunately, in some of these constructions almost any profile of mutually consistent deceptions is also a Nash equilibrium. Thus the move from dominant strategy implementation to Nash implementation turns the problem around completely so the focus is almost entirely on the multiple equilibrium problem rather than being almost entirely on the incentive compatibility problem.

Because of this multiple equilibrium problem, it is no longer sufficient to restrict attention to direct mechanisms.[9] The constructions required to "weed out" undesirable or extraneous Nash equilibria involve adding nuisance components to individual messages besides simply requesting individuals to submit an announcement of their information.

Finally, we reach the topic of this chapter: Bayesian Nash implementation, or simply Bayesian implementation. This approach combines features of the dominant strategy approach and the Nash approach. Not only is the planner incompletely informed, but now individuals have truly private information – they know things that the other individuals do not know. If this private information is sufficiently exclusive[10] then there is no role at all for forcing contracts. However, unlike the dominant strategy approach some additional structure is imposed on the priors players have about other players' private information. The incentive compatibility conditions of strategy-proofness are replaced by "Bayesian incentive compatibility" conditions in which individuals condition on private information and on specific expectations about the deceptions of the other individuals. Thus, like Nash equilibrium, optimal equilibrium behavior depends upon expectations about other individuals' behavior. For this reason, the potential difficulty of multiple equilibrium that arose in Nash equilibrium is still present.[11]

Thus, unlike either dominant strategy implementation or complete information Nash implementation, Bayesian implementation distinctly has two components to it – **incentive compatibility** and **multiple equilibrium**. As a result it should not be surprising that there are really two distinct literatures that have developed. One literature, easily the larger and more applied of the two, explores the implications of incentive compatibility. The other line of research, the more recent of the two, explores the implications of the multiple equilibrium problem, attempts to characterize exactly when it can be overcome, and provides some clue about the nature of the indirect mechanisms that need to be used to eliminate undesirable equilibria. The latter approach is also beginning to investigate implementation using refinements of Bayesian equilibrium, an approach that has been applied in complete information Nash implementation as well. Refinements mitigate the multiple equilibrium problem, and for some domains solve the problem entirely.

The remainder of this chapter focuses on the less well-known and more recent line of work on the multiple equilibrium problem, and for the most part ignores the now vast literature on Bayesian incentive compatibility.[12] Section 2 offers three simple examples to illustrate the multiple equilibrium problem that can arise and to illustrate how it can or cannot be avoided. Section 3 presents a simple and useful characterization theorem about unique implementation in Bayesian equilibrium, and gives a detailed proof of the result. Section 4 catalogs a variety of alternative characterizations, explains the role of different assumptions, and draws some comparisons with complete information Nash implementation. Section 5 investigates some extensions of the usual Bayesian mechanism design approach, where the assumptions of commitment and control are relaxed somewhat, and where refinements of Bayesian equilibrium are used. Section 6 raises and discusses without resolution some issues that need to be confronted more carefully and systematically in the near future.

2 SOME EXAMPLES

Example A

This is based on an early example to illustrate the multiple equilibrium problem in Bayesian implementation that appeared in Postlewaite and Schmeidler (1986). There are three agents and two equally likely states of the world, s,s'. Agent 1 is uninformed and believes the two states are equally likely. Agents 2 and 3 are perfectly informed.[13] There are three feasible alternatives, $A=\{a,b,c\}$. State-contingent preferences are strict, with the rankings given by:

P_1	P_1'	$P_2=P_3$	$P_2'=P_3'$
b	a	a	b
c	c	b	a
a	b	c	c

Thus, player 1's preference between a and b is always the opposite of the informed players' preferences between a and b. Everyone has a von Neumann–Morgenstern utility function at each state which assigns a utility index of 1 to the first choice, 0 to the last choice, and $v>\frac{1}{2}$ to the middle choice. The planner is player 1's twin brother and he wishes to implement x, given by $x(s)=b$, $x(s')=a$.

If a direct mechanism is used where truth is an equilibrium strategy, then only players 2 and 3 report messages, and the outcome function g must look like:

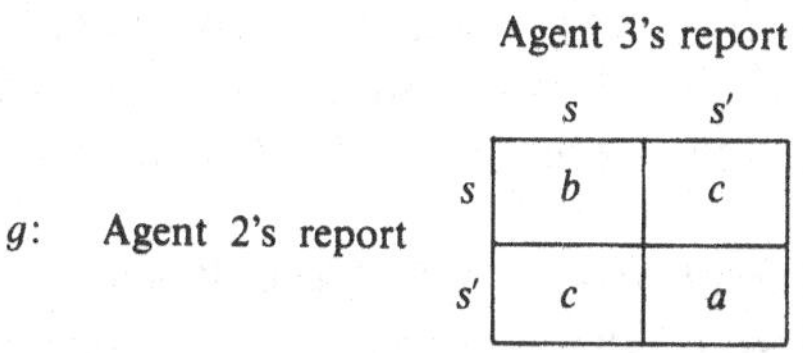

Figure 6.1 Direct game

If the direct game were not as in figure 6.1, then either truth would not be an equilibrium strategy or $g(s,s) \neq b$ or $g(s',s') \neq a$.

But this game also has a non-truthful equilibrium in which agents 2 and 3 always lie, as well as two pooling equilibria, where 2 and 3 either always reports s or always report s'. In fact, the lying equilibrium makes both informed agents better off and makes the planner (and agent 1) worse off.[14] Therefore, we see that some indirect reporting is necessary to avoid the bad equilibria.

The way to accomplish this is by giving player 1 some messages which change the outcome function $g(m_2,m_3)$. It has been observed by Mookherjee and Reichelstein (1990) that it may be possible to "selectively eliminate" the bad equilibria by giving player 1 exactly one message for each equilibrium (of course these new messages may add new equilibria, but that can be dealt with later). Matsushima (1990a) has observed that we may then label these new messages by the equilibrium strategies of the players in the direct game. In this example, it turns out that *all* of the non-truthful equilibria can be eliminated in the same way so that we only need to give agent 1 two strategies, which we call "truth" and "not truth." One may think of these strategies of player 1 as being an announcement of whether he believes the others players are using the good equilibrium (truth) or one of the bad equilibria (not truth). The expanded outcome function is:

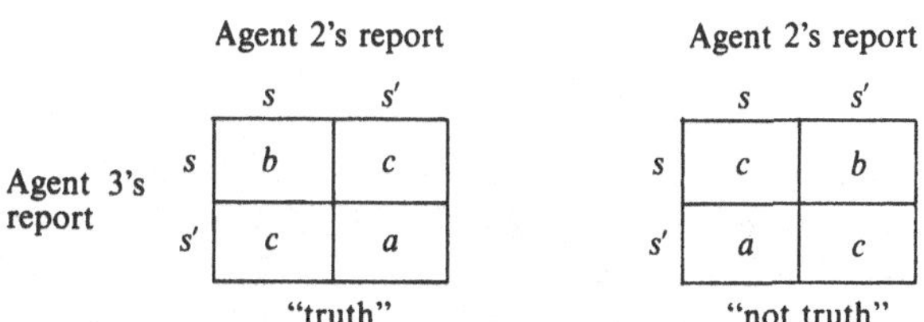

Figure 6.2 Indirect mechanism to implement $F(s)=bF(s')=a$ in example

It is easily verified that this indirect mechanism solves the implementation problem in this example. However, notice that there are still two equilibria.

One corresponds to the truthful strategy of the direct game (with agent 1 saying "truth"). The other has agent 1 saying "not truth," agent 2 always lying, and agent 3 always telling the truth. Both equilibria produce x as the equilibrium outcome.

It is critical in the above example that $v > 0.5$, that is, it is more valuable to player 1 to receive c in both states that it is for player 1 to receive either a in both states or b in both states. If this is not the case, then it may be impossible to implement the desired social choice function because only one of the pooling equilibria can be selectively eliminated. This problem is vividly illustrated in example C below. However, as we will see in section 3, the existence of a transfer good (money) with no income effects will usually solve the problem even if $v < 0.5$.

Example B: Double auctions

In simple two-agent bargaining problems where the use of double auctions has been explored, a single seller owns an indivisible object which he values at v_s. A single buyer values it at v_b. These values are each private information to the respective party. An interesting special case is when it is common knowledge that v_s and v_b are independently drawn from a uniform distribution on $[0,1]$. An allocation rule is a mapping which assigns a probability of a transfer $p(v_s,v_b)$ and a transfer payment $t(v_s,v_b)$ for any $(v_s,v_b) \in [0,1]^2$. It is well-known (Chatterjee and Samuelson, 1983; Myerson and Satterthwaite, 1983) that, of all incentive compatible allocation rules, the one that maximizes the expected sum of buyer surplus plus seller surplus is:

$$p(v_s,v_b)=\begin{cases}1 \text{ if } v_s \leq v_b-\frac{1}{4},\\ 0 \text{ otherwise}\end{cases}$$

$$y(v_s,v_b)=\begin{cases}\frac{1}{6}+\frac{1}{2}(v_b+v_s) \text{ if } v_s \leq v_b-\frac{1}{4}.\\ 0 \text{ otherwise}\end{cases}$$

This is equivalant in (interim) expected utility to the allocation rule resulting from a piecewise linear bidding equilibrium of the split-the-difference double auction, where a buyer submits bid b and a seller submits an offer s and the buyer gets the object if and only if $b \geq s$. If trade occurs, a transfer of $\frac{2b+s}{2}$ is made from the buyer to the seller. The equilibrium bidding functions are $B(v_b)=\min(v_b,\frac{2}{3}v_b+\frac{1}{12})$ $S(v_s)=\max(v_s,\frac{2}{3}v_s+\frac{1}{4})$.

Unfortunately, the double auction with these rules, or in fact *any* direct mechanism yielding an allocation rule which is interim equilivant to this one is plagued by multiple equilibria. Satterthwaite and Williams (1989) and Leininger, Linhart, and Radner (1989) show that there is a continuum of multiple equilibria.

In turns out that the efficiency properties of this allocation rule allow us to implement it, essentially uniquely. All of the extraneous, inefficient equilibria can be selectively eliminated. Details are given in Theorem 6.

Example C: Public goods

Consider the following simple public goods problem without side payments. There are two feasible public good decisions, $A=\{a,b\}$. There are three agents, each of whom either strictly prefers a to b (type t_a) or strictly prefers b to a (type t_b). Each knows his own type. It is common knowledge that each player's type was an independent draw with prob $(t_a)=q$, prob $(t_b)=1-q$. An allocation rule is a mapping from the set of eight possible type profiles to a probability p of deciding "a".

An optimal (by many criteria) allocation rule x, selects a with probability 1 if at least two players are type t_a and selects b with probability 1 if at least two players are type t_b. This is the majority rule solution, it maximizes *ex ante* welfare, it is anonymous, incentive compatible, and all sorts of other nice things. *It is even implementable in dominant strategies*! However, for some values of q, x is not Bayesian implementable. The reason is that if q is large, then the allocation rule "always a" is a Bayesian equilibrium outcome in any mechanism for which x is a Bayesian equilibrium outcome. If q is small, then "always b" is an equilibrium outcome in any mechanism where x is an equilibrium outcome. Therefore, x is implementable only if q is sufficiently close to $\frac{1}{2}$ – i.e., only if players have poor information about each other.

It is instructive to see exactly why this is true. Suppose we have a mechanism for which x is an equilibrium outcome. Then it must be that equilibrium strategies exist which produce outcomes as in figure 6.3. (Player 3 is the row player. Player 2 is the column player, and player 1 is the matrix player.)

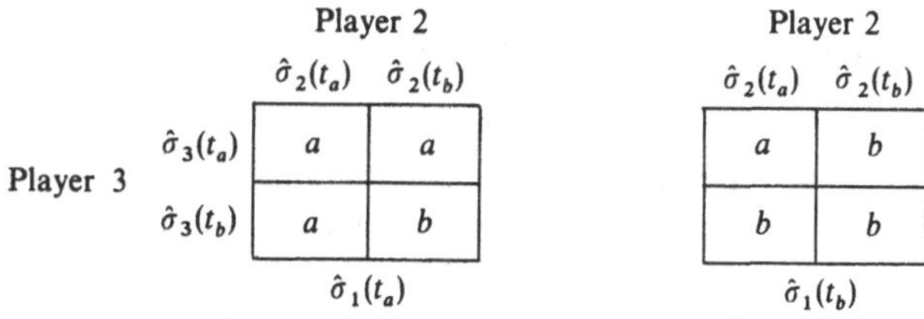

Figure 6.3 Equilibrium resulting in x with players using σ

Consider the strategy profile $\hat{\sigma}$, where $\hat{\sigma}_i(\cdot)=\sigma_i(t_a)$ is a constant strategy for all i. That is, each player acts as if his type were always t_a. This produces the outcomes given in figure 6.4.

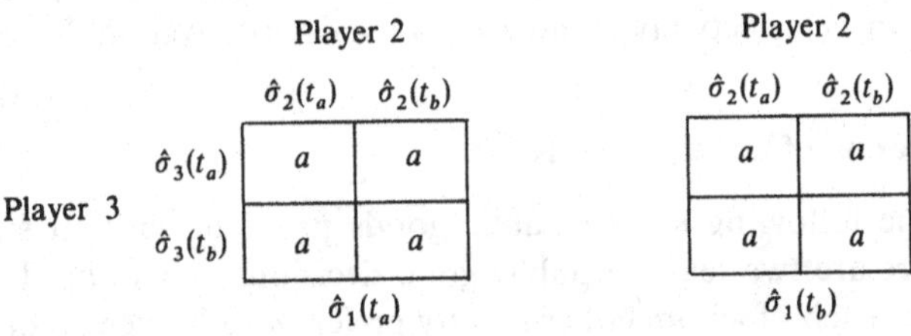

Figure 6.4 Equilibrium with players using $\hat{\sigma}$, yielding "always a"

We now can show that if $q>\sqrt{.5}$ then $\hat{\sigma}$ will be an equilibrium. Suppose not. Then some player, say player 1, must have a message available to him, m, so that $g(\hat{\sigma}_{-1},m)=b$. But this means that $g(\sigma_{-1},m)$ produces the allocation rule in figure 6.5.

Player 2

Player 3	$\sigma_2(t_a)$	$\sigma_2(t_b)$
$\sigma_3(t_a)$	b	?
$\sigma_3(t_b)$	?	?

Figure 6.5 Outcome if players 2 and 3 use σ and player 1 uses m

Now observe that no matter what the "?" entries are in figure 6.5, player 1 is better of using m instead of $\sigma_1(t_b)$ when he is type t_b, if everyone else uses σ and $q>\sqrt{.5}$. Therefore σ is not an equilibrium, a contradition. If $1-q>\sqrt{.5}$, a similar argument shows that the constant strategy $\hat{\sigma}(\cdot)=\sigma(t_b)$ is a Bayesian equilibrium.

3 A SIMPLE AND USEFUL CHARACTERIZATION THEOREM

As of the writing of this survey, there are quite a few different characterizations of social choice correspondences that are implementable by Bayesian equilibrium (Postlewaite and Schmeidler, 1986; Palfrey and Srivastava, 1989a, 1989b; Jackson, 1991; Mookherjee and Reichelstein, 1990; Matsushima, 1990a, 1990b; and others). These characterizations differ from each other in their assumptions about the number of individuals, the existence of money transfers, the finiteness of the space of individual private information, the amount of conflict between individual preferences, the amount of redundancy in the individuals' private information, and a number of other specifics. The next section will discuss differences between the various characterizations in more detail. In this section, a very simple one is presented in detail. This characterization is new. It is suggested by example A of the previous section in which the presence of an uninformed agent is exploited to "break" the mutual deceptions of the informed agents.

Consider an environment with a structure of private information of the following sort. There is a *set of feasible alternatives*, A, and a continuously transferable good that everyone values (call it money), that is in fixed supply, W. There are $N \geq 2$ individuals. Let $D = \{(w_1, \ldots, w_N) \in R^N | w_1 + \ldots + w_N = W\}$, be the set of feasible transfers, so arbitrarily negative transfer payments are feasible. Each individual i may be one of T_i possible types, where T_i is finite. A feasible allocation rule, $x(t) = (a(t), w(t))$, is a mapping from $T = T_1 \times \ldots \times T_N$ into $A \times D$. The set of feasible allocation rules is X. Each individual i has preferences over A that depend on T, and these preferences are represented by a von Neumann–Morgenstern utility index $V_i(a,t)$ for $a \in A$ and $t \in T$. Given an *allocation* (a,w,t), individual i's utility is $U_i(a,w,t) = V_i(a,t) + w_i$.

The structure of private information is that there is a common prior over profiles of types, denoted $q(t)$ and we assume $q(t) > 0$ for all $t \in T$. This latter assumption is called *diffuse information* (Palfrey and Srivastava, 1989a, 1989b). Individuals follow Bayes' rule, so that individual i, conditional on having observed t_i, updates his prior over T_{-i} by $q(t_{-i}|t_i) = q(t)/\Sigma_{\tau_{-i} \in T_{-i}} q(\tau_{-i}, t_i)$.

A *mechanism* consists of a Cartesian product of individual *message spaces*, $M = M_1 \times \ldots \times M_N$ and an *outcome function* g: $M \rightarrow A \times D$. A *strategy*[15] for player i, σ_i, is a function from T_i to M_i. Given a strategy profile $\sigma = (\sigma_1, \ldots, \sigma_N)$, denote $\sigma_{-i} = (\sigma_1, \ldots, \sigma_{i-1}, \sigma_{i+1}, \ldots, \sigma_N)$. The strategy σ is a *Bayesian equilibrium* to the mechanism (M,g) if, for all i, for all $t_i \in T_i$, and for all $m_i \in M_i$

$$\Sigma_{t_{-i} \in T_{-i}} q(t_{-i}|t_i) U_i(g(\sigma(t)),t) \geq \Sigma_{t_{-i} \in T_{-i}} q(t_{-i}|t_i) U_i(g(\sigma_{-i}(t_{-i}), m_i), t).$$

Given an environment, (A,q,T), an allocation rule x is *implementable* in Bayesian equilibrium if there exists a mechanism (M,g) with the following properties:

(1) There exists a Bayesian equilibrium to (M,g).
(2) *If* σ is an equilibrium to (M,g) then $g(\sigma(t)) = x(t)$ for all t.

Summarizing, we are maintaining the following assumptions throughout this section.

Assumption 1: $N \geq 2$
Assumption 2: $|T| < \infty$
Assumption 3: Unlimited balanced transfers without income effects
Assumption 4: Common prior on T
Assumption 5: Diffuse information

Finally, we make the following assumption.

Assumption 6: (An uninformed player) $|T_1| = 1$

This assumption, or anything resembling it, cannot be found in other implementation theorems. Nonetheless, it underlies a number of examples in the literature. The reason that uninformed individuals make the task of eliminating unwanted equilibria so much easier is quite subtle, but very powerful. First, note that the presence of this individual has no effect on the set of incentive compatible allocations. Second, the way a planner eliminates unwanted equilibria is by offering rewards to individuals for acting as stool pigeons and reporting undesirable strategizing by themselves and others to the planner. Of course the problem faced by the planner is how to design incentives for such behavior without encouraging stool pigeons to falsely report that deceptions are being employed. Thus it is quite difficult to design such selective incentives if the planner does not know an individual's preferences. However, if an individual does not have any private information, the planner knows exactly how to design the stool pigeon rewards for that individual.

In order to understand the statement of the theorem below, we need to introduce a bit more notation. Suppose we have a direct mechanism, so that $M_i = T_i$ for all i and the outcome function $g: M \to A \times D$ is therefore simply an allocation rule x. (Henceforth, we will write a direct mechanism (T,x).) Then a strategy for player i is simply any mapping from T_i into itself. We call the identity mapping from T_i to T_i the *truthful strategy* for i, and generally call any strategy for i in the direct mechanism a *deception by i*, denoted α_i. A profile of deceptions by the individuals is called a *joint deception* and is written $\alpha = (\alpha_1, \ldots, \alpha_N)$, and the profile of deceptions by everyone except for i is written α_{-i}. Any joint deception induces a probability distribution over the reported types of the informed individuals, denoted q_α, and also induces a new allocation rule, x_α defined by $x_\alpha(t) = x(\alpha(t))$ for all $t \in T$. Formally q_α is defined by:

$$q_\alpha(t) = \Sigma_{\tau \in \alpha_{-1}(t)} q(t)$$

where

$$\alpha_{-1}(t) = \{\tau \in T \mid \alpha(\tau) = t\}.$$

Following the terminology of Matsushima (1990), α is called a *consistent deception* if $q_\alpha = q$. That is, a joint deception is consistent if it generates the same distribution of reports by the informed individuals as if they had all used their truthful strategies.

Assumption 7 (no consistent deceptions): $q_\alpha \neq q$ for all non-truthful α.

It is well-known that a necessary condition for Bayesian implementation is that x is implementable only if it is *incentive compatible*. An allocation rule x is incentive compatible if the truthful strategy profile is a Bayesian equilibrium of the direct mechanism (T,x). That is:

DEFINITION 1 An allocation rule x is *incentive compatible* if for all i and for all t_i, $\tau_i \in T_i$

$$\Sigma_{t_{-i}\in T_{-i}}\, q(t_{-i}|t_i)U_i(x(t),t) \geq \Sigma_{t_{-i}\in T_{-i}}\, q(t_{-i}|t_i)U_i(x(t_{-i},\tau_i),t).$$

THEOREM 1 Under assumptions 1–7, x is incentive compatible if and only if x is implementable.

Proof "If" follows from standard results by Harris and Townsend (1981) Myerson (1979), and others. "Only if" is more complicated. As in all characterization proofs in implementation theory, a general mechanism is constructed. In this case the message spaces can be simply given by:

$$M_i = T_i \quad i=2,\ldots N,$$
$$M_1 = \{\hat{w}: T \rightarrow R^N : \Sigma_{t\in T}\hat{w}_1(t)q(t)<0 \text{ and } \Sigma_{i=1}^N \hat{w}_i(t)=0 \ \forall\ t\} \cup 0.$$

That is, all individuals with private information simply send reports of that private information. The uninformed individual requests a supplemental balanced transfer as a *function* of the reported types of the other individuals. This supplemental transfer rule must be either the **0** function or must have the property that the uninformed individual's expected transfer under the *true* type distribution is negative. The outcome function if agents $2,\ldots, N$ report t' and agent 1 reports $\hat{w}(\cdot)$ is:

$$g(m) = (a(t'),w(t') + \hat{w}(t')).$$

This mechanism uniquely implements x. That is, there is a unique Bayesian Nash equilibrium which produces x as the equilibrium allocation rule. Why does this mechanism work? First observe that since x is incentive compatible, it is a mutual best response for all the privately informed individuals to report truthfully if the uninformed agent requests **0**. It is strictly optimal for the uninformed individual to request **0**, given everyone else tells the truth. Hence x is an equilibrium outcome, and is the *only* equilibrium with truthful reporting by the informed individuals.

Can there exist an equilibrium with the informed individuals using a non-truthful joint deception α? No. If they use the deception α, then the probability distribution of reports is q_α. Since $q_\alpha \neq q$, there exists t such that $q_\alpha(t) > q(t)$. Therefore there exists $\hat{w}$ such that $K\hat{w}\cdot q < 0$ and $K\hat{w}\cdot q_\alpha > 0$ for all $K > 0$. Therefore, $\mathbf{0}$ is not a best response. By choosing K large, we can make $K\hat{w}\cdot q_\alpha$ arbitrarily large. But since $K\hat{w}\cdot q_\alpha$ can be made arbitrarily large the uninformed agent has no best response when the informed individuals use deception α. Therefore there is no equilibrium with the informed individuals using deception α.

This construction has several notable features. First, and most important, is the use of supplementary side payments by the uninformed agent. The planner (via a message space restriction) specifically disallows any supplemental request by the uninformed agent that would make him better off were the informed individuals adopting truthful reporting strategies. Since x is incentive compatible, this implies that x is still an equilibrium outcome in the expanded indirect mechanism (the uninformed player sends $\mathbf{0}$). On the other hand, suppose α were an equilibrium in the direct mechanism (T,x). Then α is no longer an equilibrium in the expanded mechanism because $q_\alpha \neq q$ implies that there exists a proposal $\hat{w} \in M_1$ where the uninformed individual prefers $(a_\alpha, w_\alpha + \hat{w}_\alpha)$ to $x_\alpha = (a_\alpha, w_\alpha)$. In the parlance of Mookherjee and Reichelstein (1990), x_α is "selectively eliminated" from being an equilibrium outcome by allowing the uninformed agent to propose $\hat{w}$. Finally, we have to make sure that the mechanism has been constructed to avoid the addition of any new equilibrium which involves $\hat{w} \neq 0$. No such equilibrium can arise for any proposal $\hat{w} \neq 0$ the uninformed agent might want to make, the proposal $2\hat{w}$ makes him even better off.

Thus we see that there are three goals to accomplish in the construction. One may make a loose, if somewhat morbid, analogy with the medical practice of surgically removing diseased tissue. Goal number one is to remove the diseased tissue (bad equilibrium). Goal number two is to *not* remove the healthy tissue (good equilibrium). Goal number three is to make this selective removal sanitary, without creating a "secondary infection" (creating *new* unwanted equilibrium). Implementation constructions generally have this structure, and the proofs consist of establishing that the constructed mechanism accomplishes these three goals.

Usually, the solution is not as simple as the one above, either because there does not exist a completely uninformed agent, or because there exist consistent deceptions (as for example would be the case with a continuum of types), or because side payments are infeasible or restricted. These lead to complications in several ways: by necessitating different individuals to play the role of breaking different undesirable equilibrium, depending on which equilibrium is to be excised; by needing to allow proposed allocations that differ in the "public decision" besides simply supplementing the money transfers; by restricting proposals to be ones that make *all possible types of the proposer* worse off if everyone is adopting truthful strategies; and by having some components of joint messages "incompatible"[16] with each other. These and other complications are dealt with in section 4. We next turn from sufficient conditions to necessary conditions.

Necessary condition: montonicity

It is fairly well-known now in the literature on implementation via Nash equilibrium with complete information that a social choice function must satisfy a monotonicity condition in order to be implementable. This condition, the importance of which relative to implementation theory was first recognized by Eric Maskin (1977), roughly states that if some alternative is the social choice for one profile of preferences, R, and we consider another profile in the domain, R', where that alternative does not go down in anyone's preference ranking relative to any other alternative, then it must also be the social choice for the new profile. This property was originally viewed as a desirable normative criterion without consideration of its implications for equilibrium of non-cooperative games.[17]

Formally, we have the following definition (for correspondences):[18]

DEFINITION 2 A *social choice correspondence* F is *monotonic* if, for all R, R'

If: $x \in F(R)$ (a)

$\forall\ i,y\ xR_iy \rightarrow xR_i'y.$ (b)

Then $x \in F(R')$.

What is the connection to non-cooperative game theory that Maskin noticed? It is most easily seen by considering a slightly rearranged statement of the definition.

DEFINITION 3 A social choice correspondence F is *monotonic* if for all R, R'

If: $x \in F(R)$ (a)

$x \notin F(R').$ (b)

Then $\exists i,y$ such that xR_iy and $yP_i'x$.

Henceforth we will call i a "test agent" and y a "test allocation," or (x,y) a "test pair."[19] Now it is almost trivial to see why monotonicity is necessary for Nash implementation. Suppose F is Nash implementable and let $x \in$

$F(R)$ and $x \notin F(R')$. Then there exists a mechanism in which $g(m)=x$ for some $m \in M$ and m is an equilibrium at R. But m is not an equilibrium at R', so there must be some $i,\hat{m}_i,y$ such that $y=g(m_{-i},\hat{m}_i)P_i'g(m)=x$. But, since m is an equilibrium at R, $x\,R_iy$. Therefore, we see that there exists a test agent i and a test allocation $y=g(m_{-i},\hat{m}_i)$ which makes x *not* an equilibrium at R'. This gives:

THEOREM 2 If F is Nash implementable then F is monotonic.

Turning to incomplete information, intuition suggests that, since Bayesian Nash equilibrium is simply a more general statement of Nash equilibrium there should exist an appropriate restatement of monotonicity that applies to Bayesian implementation. The first such extension was identified by Postlewaite and Schmeidler (1986), and it captures exactly the notion of a test agent and a test allocation. The critical diference is that the relevant notion of an *outcome* of a Bayesian game is now a function mapping type profiles into feasible allocations whereas one traditionally thinks of the equilibrium outcome of a complete information game as a single alternative. While one can of course build up such functions by concatenating all of the complete information outcomes for different profiles, this is not how monotonicity is usually stated with complete information.

This reinterpretation of outcomes of games as allocation rules means that "test allocations" are substituted with "test allocation rules." Since we look at allocation *rules*, we can no longer state monotonicity by simply comparing equilibrium outcomes at two specific type profiles (as we compared R and R' in the original definition of monotonicity), but must compare two strategy profiles, or alternatively, two deceptions. Thus, instead of comparing all pairs (R,R') we consider all **functions** $\alpha=(\alpha^1,\ldots,\alpha^N)$ with $\alpha^i: T^i \to T^i$. For a given α and a given t, the pair $(t,\alpha(t))$ is analogous to the pair (R,R') in the original definition of monotonicity. Similarly, the preferences, R_i, are replaced by interim preferences $\tilde{R}_i(t_i)$, where $x\,\tilde{R}_i(t_i)y$ iff $\Sigma_{t_{-i}\in T_{-i}}q(t_{-i}|t_i)U_i(x(t),t) \geq \Sigma_{t_{-i}\in T_i}q(t_{-i}|t_i)U_i(y(t),t)$. A social choice correspondence is then represented as a collection of social choice functions, and so is often called a *social choice set*. With this in mind we have (assuming diffuse information):

DEFINITION 4 F is *Bayesian Monotonic* if $\forall\ \alpha=(\alpha^1,\ldots,\alpha^N)$ with $\alpha^i: T^i \to T^i$, $\forall\ i$:

If: $x: T \to A \in F$ (1)

$\forall\ i,s_i,y: T^{-i} \to A \quad x\tilde{R}_i(t_i)y\ \forall\ t_i \in T_i$ (2)

$\Rightarrow x_\alpha \tilde{R}_i(s_i)y_\alpha.$

Then $x_\alpha \in F$.

Alternatively, we may write, instead of (2):

$$\forall\ i,s_i,y: T \rightarrow A \quad x\tilde{R}_i(t_i)y(\cdot\,|\alpha(s_i))\ \forall\ t_i \in T^i \qquad (2')$$
$$\Rightarrow x_\alpha \tilde{R}_i(s_i)y_\alpha,$$

where $x\tilde{R}^i(t_i)y(\cdot\,|\alpha(s_i))$ means:

$$\Sigma_{t-i \in T-i} q_i(t_{-i}|t_i)[U_i(x(t),t) - U_i(y(t_{-i},\alpha_i(s_i)),t)] \geq 0.$$

As was the case with the original monotonicity condition this can be rewritten in terms of the existence of a test agent i and a test allocation rule y.

DEFINITION 4′ F is *Bayesian monotonic* if for all α and for all $x \in F$, if $x_\alpha \notin F$ then $\exists\ i,s_i \in T_i,y: T \rightarrow A$ such that:

$$x\tilde{R}_i(t_i)y(\cdot\,|\alpha(s_i)) \quad \forall\ t_i \in T_i$$

but:

$$y_\alpha \tilde{P}_i(s_i)x_\alpha.$$

To prove that Bayesian monotonicity is necessary for implementation in Bayesian Nash equilibrium involves essentially the same argument used in Theorem 2. Suppose $x \in F$, $x_\alpha \notin F$, and F is Bayesian implementable. Then, since $x \in F$, there exists a profile of equilibrium strategies which produce x, call it σ. The joint strategy σ_α defined by $\sigma^i_\alpha(t_i) = \sigma^i(\alpha_i(t_i))$ for all i and t_i yields outcome x_α. Since this is not an equilibrium, some player i has some type s_i and some alternative message m_i such that $g(\sigma^{-i}_{\alpha_{-i}}(t_{-i}),m_i)\tilde{P}_i(s_i)x_\alpha$. Let y be the allocation rule defined by g when everyone else uses σ^{-i} and i always sends the message m_i, so $y(t) = g(\sigma^{-i}(t_{-i}),m_i)$. Then $x\tilde{R}_i(t_i)y\ \forall\ t_i$ since σ is an equilibrium, so y is a test allocation rule that satisfies the required inequality conditions. Observe that by the way y was constructed (with i) using a "constant" strategy m^i, this means that we may write $y_{-i}: T_{-i} \rightarrow A$ instead of $y: T \rightarrow A$ and this generates the definition of Bayesian monotonicity given in (2). Summarizing:

THEOREM 3 If F is Bayesian Nash implementable then F is Bayesian monotonic.

Returning to theorem 1 briefly, we can see exactly why Bayesian monotonicity is satisfied under assumptions 1–7. Since we assumed that every deception α generates a probability of reported types different from q (the "no consistent deceptions" assumption), this guarantees that for any α, the uninformed agent (agent 1) is one such test agent, and there will always exist a test allocation rule $y = \hat{w}$ simply involving a type contingent transfer scheme $(y: T^{-1} \rightarrow A)$ that satisfies $x\tilde{R}^1 y$ and $y_\alpha \tilde{P}^1 x_\alpha$. Notice that since 1 is uninformed – he has only one type – the dependence of R^1 on t_1 is suppressed.

Also observe that all players' utility functions are such that their preferences for lotteries over transfers do not depend on their type. Thus, if types are *independently* distributed, so we may write $q(t)=q_1(t_1)\cdots q_N(t_N)$ for any $t\in T$, a similar result holds, using a nearly identical construction.[20]

4 OTHER CHARACTERIZATIONS

The characterization in section 2 is special in a number of ways. The characterizations that have appeared in the literature are usually stated so that they apply to a broader class of environments than assumptions 1–7.

This section explores some of these alternative characterizations. First, we consider pure exchange environments where income effects and limited transfers do not permit the same kind of construction as the one used in the last section. Second we consider generalizations of pure enchange environments called "economic" environments. The basic ingredient in such environments is that there are always differences in preference between some individuals in the population. In particular, too much agreement on a most-preferred alternative is ruled out. Third, we explore the implications of relaxing the assumption of diffuse information. This provides results for the "gray area" between complete and incomplete information.

(A) Pure exchange environments

A feasible allocation of resources in a private goods economy with L commodities and N agents is a collection of individual allocations $a=(a_1,\ldots,a_N)\in R_+^{NL}$ such that $\sum_{i=1}^{N} a_{il}\leq\omega_l$ for all l, where ω_l is the aggregate endowment of commodity l. Observe that exact balancing of resources is not imposed, although the results below can also be proved when exact balancing is required.[21] Denote by A the set of all such feasible allocations. There are a set of states of the economy, S. Given a state $s\in S$, we denote individual i's utility of a_i is state s by $U^i(a_i,s)$ and assume it is strictly increasing in a_{il} for all l, and $s\in S$. The state also captures information players may have about each other. To maintain consistency with the notation introduced earlier, there is a finite set of types for each i, denoted T_i, so the set of states of the economy are the set of all vectors of types.[22] Let $X=\{x:T\rightarrow A\}$.

The definitions of incentive compatibility and Bayesian monotonicity are the same for pure exchange economies as for the environments discussed in the previous section. However, because (a) we are not guaranteed the existence of an uninformed agent, (b) there are limitations on transfers, and (c) there are income effects, it becomes very helpful to require at least three agents. While this is not a necessary condition for implementation, it simplifies the problem considerably, as will be apparent below.

For the case where information is diffuse, the set of Bayesian implementable allocations is characterized as a special case of a result in Palfrey and Srivastava (1989b).[23] One version of that result, adapted to our current notation and assumptions is:

THEOREM 4 If $N \geqslant 3$, T is finite, information is diffuse, and A consists of pure exchange allocations then x is Bayesian implementable if and only if x is incentive compatible and Bayesian monotonic.

Proof "Only if" follows from Theorem 2. "If" requires construction of a general mechanism. The following one works. For each i, let $M_i = X \times T^i \times \{0,1,\ldots,\}$, so each individual announces a social choice function (allocation rule), a type, and a non-negative integer, n_i. Let t' be the profile of reported types. If everyone reports x, and at least $N-1$ agents report 0, then the outcome is $x(t')$. If everyone except i reports x and 0 but agent i reports $y \neq x$ and any $n_i \in \{0,1,\ldots,\}$, then the outcome is:

$$x(t') \text{ if } y\ \tilde{P}^i(t_i)x \text{ some } t_i \in T^i$$
$$y(t') \text{ if } x\ \tilde{R}^i(t_i)y \quad \forall\ t_i \in T^i.$$

For any other profile of reports the outcome is determined by an "integer game." The individual who announces the highest[24] $n_i \in \{0,1,\ldots,\}$ receives ω and everyone else receives nothing.

This mechanism produces x as the unique equilibrium outcome. Clearly it is an equilibrium for everyone to send the message $(x,t_i,0)$ when type $t_i \in T$, since x is incentive compatible. There can be no equilibrium with some i announcing $y \neq x$, or $n_i \neq 0$ at some $t_i \in T_i$. First, note that because of the integer game no such equilibrium could arise with i announcing a y which gives *all* resources to some $j \neq i$. Therefore any $j \neq i$ is better off announcing an integer higher than any integers announced by anyone at any type (recall T is finite!).

Finally, if there were an equilibrium with individuals deceiving via α, so that each j reported $(x,\alpha_j(t_j),0)$ at t_j, then it must be that $x_\alpha = x$. Otherwise, since x is Bayesian monotonic there would be an agent i and a type $s_i \in T_i$ who could report y such that $x\tilde{R}^i(t_i)y(\cdot\,|\,\alpha(s_i))\ \forall\ t_i \in T_i$ but $y_\alpha \tilde{P}^i(s_i)x_\alpha$, so that an individual would be better off reporting y than reporting x when he is type $s_i \in T_i$.

Matsushima (1990a) has produced a proof that uses an alternative construction where undesirable (deceptive) equilibria are broken by a designated test agent $i(\hat{\alpha})$ who may report the joint deception $\hat{\alpha}$ being used, and which results in a pre-defined test allocation $y(\hat{\alpha})$. A related idea underlies the construction by Mookherjee and Reichelstein (1990). The point is that one may either allow agents to announce alternative allocations y and allow y if it passes the test in the Bayesian monotonicity definition, or the planner can simply define a function that maps reported joint deceptions into the appropriate test allocations.

(B) "Economic" environments

Many economies do not fit exactly into the pure exchange setting described above, such as environments with public goods, or production and consumption externalities. Nevertheless, in many of these problems of interest, there is always some minimal degree of conflicting preferences between the individuals in the environment.

For a broad class of these environments, virtually identical results to theorem 4 can be proved. The basic insight, originally due to Maskin's (1977) complete information results, is that implementation problems may arise if a social choice correspondence fails to select nearly unanimous "best alternatives." For complete information environments, we say an alternative is *nearly unanimous at state s* if at least $N-1$ agents rank it at the top of their preference ordering at s. A social choice correspondence satisfies *No Veto Power* (NVP) if $x \in F(s)$ whenever x is nearly unanimous at s. NVP is a very convenient sufficient condition for proving implementability of a monotonic SCC when $N \geq 3$.

In pure exchange environments with $N \geq 3$, there is nothing even close to a nearly unanimous outcome, and consequently no such auxiliary assumption is required. To generalize this beyond pure exchange environments, Jackson (1991) defines *economic environments*. This requires that "for any given choice function and state, there are at least two agents who prefer to alter the social choice function at that state" (p. 9). In other words, no outcome is nearly unanimous at any state.

For the case of diffuse information, we have, formally:

DEFINITION 6 The environment is *economic* if, for any $a \in A$ and $t \in T$, there exist $i \neq j$, and $b_1, b_2 \in A$ such that $b_1 P_i(t_i) a$ and $b_2 P_j(t_j) a$.

Assumption 8: The environment is economic.

This assumption is also made in Matsushima (1990b, p. 8) who additionally assumes that every type of every individual has a *most preferred alternative* that does not depend on the other players' types. This assumption is automatically guaranteed in pure exchange environments and also plays a role in the earlier work by Palfrey and Srivastava (1989a, 1991a) on implementation using undominated Nash equilibrium. Formally, this assumption is:

Assumption 9 (Matsushima, 1990b) (Existence of known best element). The environment is economic and for every i and every $t_i \in T_i$ there exists $b_i(t_i) \in A$ such that $U_i(b_i(t_i),t) \geq U_i(a,t)$ for all $t_{-i} \in T_{-i}$, and for all $a \in A$.

Notice that assumption 9 combines two features. First, it requires that everyone have a most preferred alternative that doesn't depend on the other players' private information. Second, the implementation problem must be "economic." These two components jointly require that $N \geq 3$.

THEOREM 5 If the implementation problem is economic, $N \geq 3$, $T < \infty$, and information is diffuse, then x is Bayesian implementable if and only if x is incentive compatible and Bayesian monotonic.

Remarks about theorem 5 Essentially the same proof as the one used to prove Theorem 4 works here. Jackson (1991) proves a more general version of Theorem 5 for correspondences in which he allows agents to have non-exclusive information. His proof also uses a different integer game, which he calls a matching game. It has the attractive feature that if A is finite then the message space is finite. Matsushima (1990b) proves a version of Theorem 5 using assumption 9.

(C) Non-exclusive information

The initial work on Bayesian implementation by Postlewaite and Schmeidler (1986, 1987) and Palfrey and Srivastava (1987) assumed non-exclusive information (NEI).[25] If states are represented by profiles of types, and players share a common prior q, then:

DEFINITION 7 There is *non-exclusive information* (NEI), if, for all i and for all t_{-i} there exists $\hat{t}_i(t_{-i})$ such that, for all $t_i \neq \hat{t}_i(t_{-i})$, $q(t_i,t_{-i})=0$.

Thus non-exclusive information changes the assumption that $q(t)>0$ for all $t \in T$, in a very special way. In particular, it implies that player i's type can be precisely inferred from knowledge of all the other players' types. That is, $q(\hat{t}_i(t_{-i}),t_{-i}|t_{-i})=1$ for all i and for all t_{-i}. The reason for the initial focus on these information structures was simple: with NEI incentive constraints are never binding in pure exchange economies. That is, for *any* allocation rule, x, one can always[26] design a forcing contract so that x is an equilibrium outcome. Therefore, essentially the only hurdle for implementation is the multiple equilibrium problem. In this way, there is a close resemblance to Nash implementation with complete information.

A useful insight gained from the case of non-exclusive information is that it encompasses complete information as a special case.[27] This means that Bayesian implementation is exactly the natural generalization of Nash implementation that one hoped it would be. What is perhaps a little surprising and unfortunate about NEI is that the simplicity gained by circumventing incentive compatibility is lost in the complexity of stating a more complicated Bayesian monotonicity condition, needing a more complicated constructive proof, and requiring an additional condition, called *closure*.

Closure is a property of a social choice correspondence. Any new allocation rule that is an appropriate mixture of some collection of allocation rules that are in the social choice set must also lie in the social choice set. These mixtures involve splicing[28] together a portion of one allocation rule for all type profiles in one common knowledge event of T with a portion of another allocation rule for all remaining type profiles in T. Therefore, closure only has bite if (a) the common knowledge partition of T consists of at least two non-empty events and (b) the social choice set F contains at least two allocation rules.[29]

Closure is most easily illustrated by an example with complete information and two type profiles, so $T=\{t,t'\}$. Suppose that $x,y \in F$ and $x(t)=a, x(t')=a'$, $y(t)=b$, $y(t')=b'$ and a,a',b,b' are all distinct elements of A. Then closure says $\hat{x}$ and $\hat{y}$ must also be in F, where $\hat{x}(t)=a, \hat{x}(t')=b'$, $\hat{y}(t)=b$, $\hat{y}(t')=a'$. Notice that closure implies, among other things, that with complete information a social choice set may be obtained as the Cartesian product of the images of a social choice correspondence. That is, with complete informtion, if F is a social choice set satisfying closure, then there exists a social choice correspondence $\hat{F}: T \rightarrow A$ such that $F = \times_{t \in T} \hat{F}(t)$.

In pure exchange environments, several results are known for the case of non-exclusive information. First, theorem 4 extends in a natural way, with the exception that incentive compatibility is not required and, accordingly, joint deceptions that are incompatible[30] can safely be ignored. Thus monotonicity can be stated by

DEFINITION 8 (NEI monotonicity) x is *Bayesian Monotonic* if, for all compatible α such that $x_\alpha \neq x$, there exists i,t_i and y such that $x\ R^i(\alpha_i(t_i))y$ and $y_\alpha P^i(t_i)x_\alpha$.

A second result is that if we restrict attention to pure exchange economies where preferences are strictly concave and satisfy a condition guaranteeing interior Walrasian equilibrium, then the rational expectations equilibrium correspondence is Bayesian monotonic and therefore implementable when information is non-exclusive.[31] Wettstein (1986) shows that, if the interiority condition is dropped, we may still implement the "constrained" rational expectations equilibrium, where demands are exogenously bounded by the aggregate endowment. Third, allocations which are interim envy-free are implementable with non-exclusive information. These and other applications of Bayesian monotonicity to pure exchange environments with non-exclusive information are found in Palfrey and Srivastava (1987).

Jackson (1991) extends these results with either exclusive or non-exclusive information in general economic environments (Assumption 8) and also provides a very general characterization for finite-type environments without the "economic" condition. He identifies a modification to Bayesian monotonicity which incorporates an interim version of the NVP condition used to prove sufficiency in Nash implementation. That combined condition is called *Monotonicity-No-Veto* (MNV). In fact MNV reduces to the separate conditions of monotonicity and NVP when information is complete. It is therefore not a necessary condition for implementation.

5 EXTENSIONS

In this section we will discuss extensions in three different directions:

(A) Refinements of Bayesian equilibrium
(B) Relaxing the commitment assumption (renegotiation and individual rationality)
(C) Relaxing the control assumption (message space constraints and preplay communication between the agents).

(A) Refinements of Bayesian equilibrium

The most obvious strengthening of Bayesian equilibrium, and the one that has received by far the greatest attention in mechanism design theory is dominant strategy equilibrium. However, as noted above, incentive compatibility in dominant strategies is generally very difficult to achieve, and when it can be achieved the multiple equilibrium problem does not arise.

Palfrey and Srivastava (1989a) investigate the equilibrium refinement of *Undominated Bayesian Equilibrium* (UBE), which is a Bayesian Nash equilibrium in which no player uses a weakly dominated strategy. Thus it combines the best response property of Bayesian Nash equilibrium with a dominance property. This refinement turns out to have a lot of clout.

The strength of this refinement is best seen by returning to the third example of section 2. In that example, we were trying to implement majority preferences over two alternatives. However, it turns out that, for most priors over types, the majority rule social choice function is not Bayesian monotonic. Nevertheless, we observed that it was implementable in dominated strategies. How do we resolve this apparent paradox? It would seem that if x is implementable in dominant strategies then x should also be implementable in Bayesian equilibrium, but that is unfortunately not true.

The resolution to this apparent paradox is simple: *all the extra equilibria that undermine the implementation of the majoritarian social choice rule involve the use of weakly dominated strategies.* The question then is: What other social choice functions are not Bayesian monotonic but can be implemented in UBE? The answer is that if individual preferences do not depend on other players' types ("private values") then virtually any incentive compatible social choice function is UBE-implementable.

The intuition behind this result borrows heavily from results about implementation with complete information using the undominated refinement of Nash equilibrium (Palfrey and Srivastava, 1991a). There it was shown that, if preferences are *value distinguished*, then with at least three agents any social choice function or correspondence satisfying no veto power is implementable in undominated Nash equilibrium.

Preferences are *strictly value distinguished* if, for each i, $t_i \neq t_i'$, there exists a test pair of outcomes, (a,b), such that $aP_i(t_i)b$ and $bP_i(t_i')a$. Weak value distinction allows for some weak preferences in the definition of the test pair. Thus value distinction is a condition that says two types are different if and only if their preferences are different.[32]

With incomplete information, it has been proved that, if $N \geq 3$, preferences are value distinguished and private, no one is ever completely indifferent over all outcomes, and best and worst elements exist for every type of every player, then a social choice function is incentive compatible if and only if it is implementable in UBE. If preferences are not value distinguished or depend on the entire profile of types, then a necessary condition must be satisfied that is weaker then Bayesian monotonicity, but is quite strong nonetheless.

The proof for "private values" is long but straightforward, at least for the case of strict preferences. The idea is to have players announce their type twice (plus some nuisance messages). In equilibrium, only the first announcement, t_i, matters. However, the mechanism is constructed so that the second announcement, t_i', may (out of equilibrium) trigger the use of a test pair $\{a(t_i,t_i'), b(t_i,t_i')\}$ with the property that $a(t_i,t_i')\ P^i(t_i)\ b(t_i,t_i')\ P^i(t_i')$ $a(t_i,t_i')$. If player i announces the pair (t_i,t_i'), for which his corresponding test pair is (a,b), then, when the test pair is triggered, the outcome is b, which is preferred to a in state t_i', but not in state t_i. The rest of the mechanism is set up so that, at state t_i', the report (t_i,t_i) is dominated by the report of (t_i,t_i'), which will effectively prevent any joint deception from being an equilibrium. To guarantee that there are no other equilibria, say with i reporting (t_i,t_i'), we introduce a new kind of integer game called "tailchasing." In addition to announcing (t_i,t_i'), each player also announces an integer. Whenever a player reports two *different* types then reporting the number M is weakly dominated by reporting any number larger than M. Details may be found in Palfrey and Srivastava (1989a). Constructions without resorting to tailchasing are considered in Jackson, Palfrey, and Srivastava (1992).

The restriction to private values and value-distinguished-types is quite important. For one thing it rules out some applications which might be important, including bargaining and auctions with common or affiliated values. The reason these assumptions produce such strong results is that, in order for a simple construction with test pairs, the choice of the test pair cannot depend on other players' types. And, if types were not value-distinguished (e.g., two types differ only in information about other players) then test pairs do not exist.

The following example illustrates how common values can create implementation problems even when using the UBE refinement. This example is a "common-value majoritarian" social choice function. There are three players and $A=\{a,b\}$. Everyone has identical strict preferences, but different information. Each player can be one of two types, $T_i=\{t_a,t_b\}$. Types are independently drawn with $q=\text{prob}\{t_a\}>\sqrt{.5}$. Each individual prefers a to b if and only if there are at least two type t_a players, otherwise everyone prefers b to a. The social choice function, x, we would like to implement is the obvious one: select a if everyone prefers a to b; select b if everyone prefers b to a.

Clearly x is incentive compatible, so that in a direct game everyone is better off honestly reporting his type than lying as long as everyone else is honestly reporting his type. However, one can show that there is also a pooling Bayesian equilibrium where everyone always claims to be type t_a, so a is always selected. This additional equilibrium outcome arises in any game for which x is an equilibrium outcome. Furthermore, one can never "refine" this bad outcome away by eliminating weakly dominated strategies and using tailchasing or other elaborate construction techniques. Therefore, x is not implementable in UBE.

The above example suggests that, in some seemingly innocuous cases, implementation may require resorting to stronger refinements such as those found in Kohlberg and Mertens (1986), or those based on sequential rationality such as sequential equilibrium or perfect Bayesian equilibrium. Little is known about implementability using these refinements in games of incomplete information. The work of Moore and Repullo (1988) and Abreu and Sen (1989) for subgame perfect equilibrium with complete information indicates that squential rationality refinements do expand the set of implementable social choice functions, but to a lesser degree than ruling out weakly dominated strategies. However, some of the "signaling" refinements of sequential equilibrium combine dominance-based refinements with sequential rationality, and so may permit the implementation of even more social choice functions.

Abreu and Matsushima (1990a) have taken a slightly different approach, examining implementation in iterative elimination of strictly dominated strategies. They obtain conclusive results with finite types and conflicting preferences. In order to obtain these strong results, they relax the implementability definition. According to this relaxed definition, a social choice function is *virtually implementable* if there exists an "exactly" implementable (possibly random) social choice function that approximates it arbitrarily closely.[33] This follows the earlier work of Matsushima (1988) and Abreu and Sen (1991). In addition to incentive compatibility, they identify a weak necessary condition for implementation called *measurability*. The details of their constructive proof are substantially different from the ones presented earlier in this survey. An interesting discussion (and criticism) of the construction appears in a subsequent note by Glazer and Rosenthal (1990).

(B) The commitment problem

In the standard mechanism design problem, an *uninformed planner* or perhaps a collection of uninformed players commit to a mechanism at the *ex ante* stage. In particular, they commit to an outcome function and to a message space. These completely determine the rules according to which they exchange information and decide on outcomes.

A large can of worms is opened when one attempts to relax the assumption that there are no constraints, other than feasibility, on the outcome function. Considerable attention has been focused on the implications of imposing various restrictions on the kinds of outcome functions that may be committed to. For convenience, we divide the "limited commitment" approaches into four broad categories:

(B1) Constraints on *ex post* allocations
(B2) Durability
(B3) Dynamic contracting
(B4) Information leakage

(*B1*) *Constraints on* ex post *allocations*

The two most common restrictions of the first type are *individual rationality* and *ex post efficiency*. In the Bayesian implementation literature, the analysis of Ma, Moore, and Turnbull (1988) carefully addresses issues of individual rationality. They construct a unique implementation of the Demski–Sappington optimal contract with two agents and two types. The individual rationality problem arises there because either agent may choose "non-participation" at the message sending stage. One may view the individual rationality constraint as reinterpreting the outcome function $g(m)$ as an "offer function," where the offer may be refused by any of the players, resulting in a status quo payoff, G_0^i, for some or all of the players. This is equivalent to adding an extra stage at the end of the mechanism in which each agent chooses between G_0^i and $g(m)$. In general, this may lead to feasibility problems, although not in the Ma, Moore, and Turnbull (1988) setting.

Individual rationality is frequently imposed in applications of the revelation principle to contracting problems. However, with the exception of the work by Ma, Moore, and Turnbull and related work by Rajan (1989), most of the work on the multiple equilibrium problems in Bayesian mechanism design has paid little attention to the problem of individual rationality.

The issue of *ex post* efficiency has been addressed in the complete information literature by Maskin and Moore (1989), in "renegotiation-proof" implementation.[34] Their work is motivated by the observation that, in many of the constructive proofs, multiple equilibria are selectively eliminated by allowing the planner to "enforce" relatively arbitrary outcomes. For example, the test allocations that are used to break unwanted equilibria may be very inefficient. They explore the implications of requiring the outcome function to always be efficient.

In order to impose this requirement, they assume that there is some sort of *ex post* bargaining process that follows the play of a mechanism and that *always* produces *ex post* efficient allocations. They represent this process in reduced form, with a function $E(g(m),s)$ which maps each state and each realization of the outcome function to another outcome[35] that is efficient when the true state is s. This E-function, or bargaining technology,[36] is then taken as a transformation on the final outcomes that will arise from any mechanism (M,g). It is important to observe that E incorporates information that is not in the planner's information set – in particular, E depends on s. This implies, among other things, that any efficient social choice function, f, is implementable with renegotiation relative to some E, namely $E(\cdot,s)=f(s)$. Thus it is not at all clear that we should view "renegotiation-proofness" of this sort as a constraint, since it may (almost by assumption) make some non-monotonic social choice functions implementable by embedding their implementability in the *technology*.

This approach is clearly intended to capture, in reduced form, the observation that the reporting of messages followed by a (temporary) outcome generated by the planner's outcome function is not the end of the game. Either the planner cannot reasonably commit to producing an outcome that he knows is inefficient, or the planner cannot prevent the players themselves from negotiating to a Pareto improvement. In either case, the implicit assumption is that there is a continuation game that follows the mechanism, and this continuation game always ends up selecting an efficient allocation. This raises some interesting new issues: What are examples of such continuation games that always lead to efficiency? What renegotiation functions $E(\cdot,s)$ can arise as unique equilibrium outcomes of such continuation games? The recent work by Rubenstein and Wolinsky (1989) offers one approach to this in a bargaining setting where a specific renegotiation process is proposed. Aghion, Dewatripont, and Rey (1989) also suggest an approach in which the renegotiation functions themselves are part of the designed mechanisms.

(*B2*) *Durability*

The problem of durability arises at the interim stage when one agent could propose to replace the mechanism with a new mechanism and all the other agents would agree to do so. There are many ways of formulating this problem,[37] which is very closely related to the problem of mechanism design by an informal principal.[38]

The fact that renegotiation takes place before any "official" messages have been sent distinguishes this class of variations on imperfect commitment from the others. As the problem was originally formulated in Holmstrom and Myerson (1983), the multiple equilibrium problem was not addressed. However, as Legros (1990, 1991) points out, the possibility of multiple equilibria suggests a reformulation, which he calls "strong durability."

Strong durability is a property of a mechanism-allocation rule *pair*, rather than being a property only of allocation rules, as in Holmstrom and Myerson. The idea is that such a pair is strongly durable if the allocation rule is implemented by the mechanism and there does not exist a mechanism that could be unanimously approved in a vote against the original mechanism that implements the allocation rule. An allocation rule is then called strongly durable[39] if there exists a mechanism such that the mechanism-allocation rule is strongly durable. Notice that an allocation may fail to be durable relative to its direct mechanism, but an indirect mechanism may exist that makes it strongly durable.

One can then show a close connection between strong durability and interim efficiency. For example, in independent private value models, an allocation rule is strongly durable if and only if it is interim efficient! This contrasts with the results of Holmstrom–Myerson, where the leading example of that paper demonstrates that interim efficient allocation rules may not be durable. The reason for the difference is that Holmstrom–Myerson restrict attention to direct mechanisms. One can generalize the result of Legros (1990) in an interesting way. He (and Holmstrom and Myerson, 1983) only considers *unanimous* voting procedures. In fact, one can reformulate much of the model to allow for arbitrary (finite) renegotiation processes, as extensive form games that are played prior to the mechanism, the continuation games of which are mechanisms. As long as side payments are possible, then one can show that in independent private value models any interim efficient allocation rule is strongly durable with this more general definition.[40]

(*B3*) *Renegotiation in dynamic environments and* (*B4*) *information leakage*

In many settings, it is optimal for the same mechanism to be applied over and over again in a multiperiod contracting problem (Stokey, 1979). However if player types are correlated across periods then *all* parties may wish to change the mechanism as time passes and the information structure evolves.[41]

At this point there has been very little work on the multiple equilibrium problem with renegotiation. The main reason for this is that sequential rationality is imposed in these models. The difficult issues of Bayesian implementation with sequential rationality are open questions. While characterization results for sequential rationality with complete information are highly developed,[42] there are no analogous results in Bayesian settings. Since dynamic contracting problems seem to be one major direction in which the mechanism design approach is headed, this is an unfortunate gap in the current state of Bayesian implementation theory.

For similar reasons, little is known about the problem of agents making inferences from the messages of other agents, and thus wishing to revise their message. This problem arises in the posterior implementation work of Green and Laffont (1987a). Chakravorti (1989) explores some of the multiple equilibrium problems with implementation, using a stronger posterior requirement.

(C) The control assumption

The standard approach to mechanism design assumes that the planner has complete control over the communication technology and complete control over the outcome function. Issues concerning renegotiation involve some limitations on the planner's ability to credibly commit to an outcome function, but other issues may arise quite independently of the commitment abilities of the planner. One possibility, collusion by preplay communication, is illustrated by the following example.

EXAMPLE: Collusion by preplay communication.

There are two agents, who work for a principal. The principal is trying to decide between two different projects to undertake. The agents have information about different aspects of the projects, say its cost and some other dimension that the agents care about a lot, but the principal cares about very little, such as whether it requires much effort on the part of the agents. For simplicity, agent 1 can be type t_1 or type t_2 and agent 2 can be type s_1 or s_2. If agent 1 is t_1 then the principal wants to undertake project A and if agent 1 is t_2 then the principal wants to undertake project B. Agent 2 only has information about the second dimension of the project that the principal doesn't care about. The agents' information is independent, and the distribution of types is common knowledge, with *prob* $(t_1)=0.5$ and *prob* $(s_1)= 0.4$. The agents have identical state contingent utility functions given below.

	s_1t_1	s_1t_2	s_2t_1	s_2t_2
A	0	1	1	0
B	1	0	0	1

Thus we see that the agents would prefer project B if the type profile were (t_1,s_1) or (t_2,s_2) and would prefer project A otherwise. One can easily see that the planners social preferred allocation rule, given in figure 6.6, is incentive compatible and is uniquely implemented in Bayesian equilibrium. However, the direct mechanism that implements it can be undermined if the agents are able to communicate prior to playing the mechanism. That is,

	s_1	s_2
t_1	*A*	*A*
t_2	*B*	*B*

Figure 6.6

there exists an extensive form game which consists of a "cheaptalk" stage followed by the play of the direct mechanism, which contains an equilibrium outcome different from the one intended by the planner.

Consider the following very simple form of preplay communication. Agent 2 tells agent 1 whether he is s_1 or s_2. Then the agents play the mechanism. One equilibrium of this two stage game is for agent 1 to ignore what agent 2 tells him and agent 2 always says he is type s_1, and then players act truthfully in the direct mechanisms. This produces the planner's choice. However, there is another equilibrium in which agent 2 tells agent 1 his true type, and agent 1 reports truthfully to the planner if and only if agent 2 tells him s_2 when 1 is type t, or agent 2 tells him s_1, when he is type 2. Thus, we see that some mechanisms may uniquely implement social choice functions but are not immune to preplay communication.

A number of recent papers have suggested that possibilities of cheaptalk may undermine the ability of a planner to implement some allocation rules, because of the multiplicity of equilibria that often arise in direct games with preplay communication.[43] This suggests a role for indirect mechanisms, and an application of the techniques developed for the existence/characterization theorems of section 4. Palfrey and Srivastava (1991b) investigate the use of indirect mechanisms for "cheaptalk-proof" implementations of interim efficient allocation rules in economic environments.

Given any mechanism (M,g), define a class of extensive form games, called the set of (finite) *communication extensions of* (M,g).[44] This consists of all games which begin with a finite number of communication stages where players transmit messages to each other, followed by a final stage in which the mechanism (M,g) is played out. Of course, there may be many new equilibrium outcomes in a communication extension of (M,g) because information may be transmitted between the agents, as in the example above.

Let $X(M,g)$ be the set of all Bayesian equilibrium allocation rules of the mechanism (M,g). Let $X^c(M,g)$ be the set of all Bayesian equilibrium allocation rules of all communication extensions of (M,g). We say that (M,g) is *cheaptalk-proof* if $X(M,g)=X^c(M,g)$. Unfortunately, it is hard to prove general theorems about cheaptalk-proof mechanism design, because it may be that $X(M,g)$ and $X^c(M,g)$ only differ in ways that are inconsequential in utility terms.

For this reason, we introduce the concept of *essential implementation*, as a slightly weaker implementation requirement.

DEFINITION 9 Let x be a social choice function. Then (M,g) *essentially implements* x if x is an equilibrium outcome of (M,g) and all other equilibrium alocation rules of (M,g) produce the same (interim) utility allocations to all types of all players.

We can define *essentially cheaptalk-proof* in a similar way. Let $\mathbf{U}(M,g)$ be the set of interim utility allocations associated with all allocation rules in $X(M,g)$, and let $\mathbf{U}^c(M,g)$ be the set of interim utility allocations associated with all allocation rules in $X^c(M,g)$.

DEFINITION 10 (M,g) is *essentially cheaptalk-proof* if $\mathbf{U}(M,g) = \mathbf{U}^c(M,g)$.

We may then show that there is a close connection between interim efficiency of an allocation and the possibility for it to be essentially implemented using an essentially cheaptalk-proof mechanism. Specifically, we restrict attention to environments of the following sort:

1 Sidepayments.
2 Private values: $U(x(t),t) = U(x(t),t_i)$ for all i,t,x.
3 Independent types: $q(t) = q_1(t_1) \cdots q_N(t_N)$ for all t.

THEOREM 6 If x is interim efficient and incentive compatible, then it is essentially implementable using an essentially cheaptalk-proof mechanism.

Proof (from Palfrey and Srivastava, 1991b) It is easiest to prove for the case of transferable utility, so that if we write $x(t) = (a(t),w(t))$ then for all i, t_i, and x we have $U_i(x(t),t_i) = V_i(a(t),t_i) + w_i(t)$. Given the allocation rule x, for each a, i, and t_i, let $P_i(a,t_i)$ be the (interim) probability of outcome a conditional on player i being type t_i and let $W_i(t_i)$ be the expected transfer to player i. The mechanism is defined as follows. The message space for each agent is $T_i \times [0,1]$. The outcome function is defined below:

(I) If $m_i = (t_i,0)$ for all i then $g(m) = x(t)$.
(II) If $m_j = (t_j,0)$ for all $j \neq i$ and $m_i = (t_i, \varepsilon)$ with $\varepsilon > 0$, then a is chosen randomly by the planner according to the distribution $P(\cdot,t_i)$ and i receives a transfer equal to $W_i(t_i) - \varepsilon$. All players $j \neq i$ divide the cost of this transfer equally.
(III) If more than one agent reports a positive number then the agent who reports the smallest positive number plays the role of i in (II). If there is a tie, then the agent with the lowest index plays that role.

It is easy to see that if x is incentive compatible then it is a Bayesian equilibrium for everyone to honestly report their type and for no type of any agent to report a positive number. Second, since x is interim efficient if any other type-reporting strategies coupled with always sending 0 is not interim utility equivalent to x then it cannot be an equilibrium, since some type of some agent would be better off reporting some small enough positive number. Third, there can be no equilibrium with any type of any agent reporting a positive number, since it is always better to report a smaller positive number.

This result, and the proof, extends to common value environments where the dependence of U_i on t_{-i} is additively separable from the dependence of U_i on t_i. This includes what Myerson (1981) calls "revision effects." The extent to which cheaptalk-proof implementation can be achieved with more general preferences or in environments with dependent types is an interesting open question. It is also not known when it is possible to implement inefficient allocations. However, it would seem to be the case that allocation rules such as the one in the example could not be implemented in a cheaptalk-proof way even with sidepayments,[45] mainly because it is inefficient from the point of view of the agents.

The construction in Theorem 6 exploits the fact that, in independent private values models, interim expected utilities depend only on the "reduced form" of an allocation rule, denoted above by $P_i(\cdot)$ and $W_i(\cdot)$, each of which depends only on player i's type. This is also true in common value models as long as the dependence of player i's utility on the other players' types enters separably.

If players' utilities only depend on the reduced form, the planner simply gives players the opportunity of unilaterally "buying out" of the mechanism in exchange for a small payment. If player i buys out of the mechanism, the planner ignores the other players' messages and simply imposes an (possibly random) allocation, depending only on i's reported type, t_i, that is equivalent in i's reduced form of the target allocation, x, that the planner was trying to implement. In exchange, the "buyer" of this option must pay a small price. Clearly, if all players other than i are behaving truthfully, then i will not want to buy out. However, as long as x is interim efficient, if players are not behaving truthfully, generating an allocation x_α, then either x_α is interim equivalent to x, or some type of some player would be better off "buying out" at some small enough price, $\varepsilon > 0$.

There are several applications of the above result, as a number of revelation principle applications involve models with independent private values, and/or revision efforts.[46] One such application would be the multiple equilibrium problem in the double auction of example B in section 2. For example, with a uniform distribution of types, the allocation rule corresponding to the linear bidding equilibrium of the split-the-difference double auction is interim efficient. Therefore, augmenting the double auction as in Theorem 6 will uniquely implement that allocation, despite the continuum of equilibrium in the direct game.

Notes

* Prepared for presentation at the invited symposium on Implementation Theory at the 6th World Congress of the Econometric Society, Barcelona, Spain, August 28, 1990. Support of the National Science Foundation is gratefully acknowledged. Mathias Dewatripont, Matthew Jackson, John Ledyard, and John Moore provided useful comments on an earlier draft. The author especially acknowledges many valuable discussions with Sanjay Srivastava, over a span of several years of collaboration on this subject.

1 The commitment assumption is being relaxed in the recent line of work on renegotiation in contracting. See, for example, Dewatripont (1989), Green and Laffont (1987b), Baron and Besanko (1987), Maskin and Tirole (1992), and Hart and Tirole (1987). Work on the durability of mechanisms is also relevant here. See Crawford (1985), Holmstrom and Myerson (1983), Legros (1990), and Cramton and Palfrey (1990b). Macroeconomists have also studied a closely related commitment problem for a planner ("time consistency"), albeit from a somewhat different perspective. (See, for example, Kydland and Prescott, 1977).

2 These are sometimes called "nuisance" messages. (Moore and Repullo, 1988).

3 That the basic issues are the same does not imply that all the theorems are the same. Where it is relevant we will discuss the differences.

4 This is true, for example, in domains with strict preferences. See Dasgupta, Hammond, and Maskin (1979).

5 For example, in public goods environments, we typically need an assumption of no income effects. This produces well-known positive results, summarized in Green and Laffont (1979) and Groves (1982). Under domain restrictions, we can get positive results with private goods as well, as in Vickrey (1961). More recently Mookherjee and Reichelstein (1989) have some further positive results.

6 Most of the early work on Nash implementation was formulated in general equilibrium settings. See for example Hurwicz (1979), Groves and Ledyard (1977), Schmeidler (1980), and the references cited in the Postlewaite (1985) survey. The solution concept of maximin equilibrium has also been explored (Thomson, 1978).

7 This nearly sounds like a contradiction. However, the planner is uninformed, so each individual has some private information that the planner does not know. The complete information assumption used in Nash equilibrium implementation means that players have redundant information. For example, if the planner does not know the individuals' preference, then by "complete information" we mean that the entire preference profile is common knowledge among the players. For alternative interpretations of Nash implementation, the reader is referred to Maskin's (1986) survey.

8 For characterizations of incentive compatibility in Nash equilibrium, see Mookherjee and Reichelstein (1990) and Moore and Repullo (1990). With more than two players, the incentive compatibility problem can be entirely avoided, without resorting to a universally bad outcome.

9 This point is clearly made in Repullo (1987).

10 Information is called "non-exclusive" (Postlewaite and Schmeidler, 1986) if the pooled information of any collection of $N-1$ of the agents refines the information of the Nth agent. In many applications, non-exclusive information and complete information structures produce essentially identical results (Palfrey and Srivastava, 1986; Blume and Easley, 1990).

11 The reason for this is pretty obvious, since Bayesian equilibrium is just a Nash equilibrium with a different information structure – or, alternatively, complete information Nash equilibrium is a special case of Bayesian Nash equilibrium. These connections are discussed at length in Harsanyi (1967–8). The distinction of the Bayesian implementation approach is most apparent when individuals have "exclusively private information" so that forcing contracts are not available to the planner.

12 As an historical note, the Laffont and Maskin (1982) survey for the Fourth World Congress ten years ago focused mainly on the incentive compatibility problem. They comment that "Bayesian incentive schemes are plagued by multiple equilibrium" (p. 77).

13 This is not critical. Agents 2 and 3 could have correlated information, and the same problem arises (see Palfrey and Srivastava, 1991c), but the analysis becomes messier.

14 A similar problem arises in the multiple-agent environment studied by Demski and Sappington (1984). Ma, Moore, and Turnbull (1988) construct an indirect mechanism to resolve the multiple equilibrium problem in that environment. They refer to it as the problem of "agents cheating." There may also be other *mixed* strategy equilibria, which would depend parametrically on the cardinal utilities. However, implementation theory usually considers implementation via *pure* strategies only. An exception is in a section of Matsushima (1990b).

15 These are *pure strategies*. Mixed strategies are, for the most part, ignored in implementation theory.

16 The possibility of incompatible messages arises when there is some degree of non-exclusivity of information.

17 Extensive analysis of related normative concepts may be found in May (1952) and Fishburn (1973).

18 In this section, we state the necessary conditions for social choice correspondence. The definitions for social choice functions are obtained directly.

19 This is Moore and Repullo's (1988) terminology.

20 Details of the construction with independent types are found in Palfrey and Srivastava (1991c).

21 The construction in Palfrey and Srivastava (1989b) allowed free disposal, in the sense that 0 was a feasible allocation. The free disposal assumption is not needed if information is diffuse.

22 Postlewaite and Schmeidler (1986, 1987) and Palfrey and Srivastava (1987, 1989b) use a different representation of information, in which player types are not explicitly mentioned. Instead, for each state $s \in S$, individual i observes an event, $E^i(s)$, which is the set of all states that he cannot distinguish from S. While these representations are essentially identical (see Mookherjee and Reichelstein (1990, p. 474) and Jackson (1991)), the "type" representation is less cumber-

some, especially when assuming a common prior $q(t)$ and diffuse information ($q(t)>0$ for all $t \in T$). We will stick with the type representation here.

23 They also provide a characterization of the set of Bayesian implementable allocations in exchange economies when information may be non-exclusive, and Jackson (1991) provides more general results for that case. See below. Finally, notice that theorem 4 does not require $N \geq 3$, in contrast to most other results.

24 Ties can be resolved in any number of ways. For example, they can be broken in favor of the agent with the lowest index.

25 The terminology "public information" and "publicly predictable information" was used in Palfrey and Srivastava (1986) and Blume and Easley (1983), respectively. Those concepts are equivalent to NEI.

26 This statement requires the caveat that there exists a universally bad outcome. The early results were for pure exchange economies, where the **0** outcome served that purpose.

27 In fact, it is equivalent to complete information when there are only two agents.

28 The term splicing comes from Jackson (1991).

29 Closure is not an issue with diffuse information, and does not play a role in the implementation of social choice functions.

30 A deception α is incompatible if $q(\alpha(t))=0$ for some t.

31 Generally, rational expectations equilibria are not incentive compatible. See, for example, Blume and Easley (1990). NEI environments are quite special in this respect.

32 With complete information, this assumption is very weak. With incomplete information, this assumption rules out a large class of interesting environments when a player's type indexes what he knows about the other players' types.

33 They obtain weaker results for exact implementation in Abreu and Matsushima (1990b).

34 There has been no analogous work in Bayesian implementation.

35 One could define $E(\cdot)$ arbitrarily. If E is efficient as s then we will have $E(g(m),s)=g(m)$ at s.

36 The outcomes determined by this bargaining technology may themselves not be attainable as Nash equilibrium to some mechanism.

37 See Crawford (1985), Holmstrom and Myerson (1983), Cramton and Palfrey (1990b), Legros (1990) and the references therein.

38 See Myerson (1983) and Maskin and Tirole (1990, 1992).

39 Perhaps *durably implementable* would be a better term.

40 This follows from the same logic as the proof of Theorem 2 in Legros (1990) or the proof of Theorem 3 in Palfrey and Srivastava (1991b). A general formulation of interim renegotiation-proofness in Palfrey and Srivastava (1991c).

41 See note 2. These problems can also arise with symmetrically informed agents if some state contingent contracts are not possible.

42 Abreu and Sen (1989), Herrero and Srivastava (1992), and Moore and Repullo (1988).

43 See for example, Matthews and Postlewaite (1989), Chakravorti (1989), and Zou (1990).

44 Farrell (1983) calls this a communication version of (M,g).

45 But, it may be possible with the addition of an uninformed player.
46 This would include, among others, Myerson (1981), Harris and Raviv (1981), Cramton and Palfrey (1990a) Ledyard and Palfrey (1990), Mailath and Postlewaite (1990), Myerson and Satterthwaite (1983), and others.

References

Abreu, D. and H. Matsushima (1990a), "Virtual Implementation in Iteratively Undominated Strategies: Incomplete Information," mimeo, Princeton University.

(1990b), "Exact Implementation," mimeo, Princeton University.

Abreu, D. and A. Sen (1989), "Subgame Perfect Implementation: A Necessary and Almost Sufficient Condition," *Journal of Economic Theory*, 50: 285–99.

(1991), "Virtual Implementation in Nash Equilibrium," *Econometrica*, 59: 910, 997–1021.

Aghion, P., M. Dewatripont, and P. Rey (1989), "Renegotiation Design Under Symmetric Information," mimeo.

Baron, D. and D. Besanko (1987), "Commitment and Fairness in a Continuing Relationship," *Review of Economic Studies*, 54: 413–36.

Blume, L. and D. Easley (1983), "Implementation of Rational Expectations Equilibrium with Strategic Behavior," manuscript, Cornell University.

(1990), "Implementation of Walsarian Expectations Equilibria," *Journal of Economic Theory*, 51: 207–27.

Chatterjee, K. and W. Samuelson (1983), "Bargaining under Incomplete Information," *Operations Research*, 31: 835–51.

Chavravorti, B. (1988), "Mechanisms with no Regret: Welfare Economics and Information Reconsidered," BEBR Faculty Working Paper No. 1438, University of Illinois.

(1989). "Sequential Rationality, Implementation, and Communication in Games," mimeo, University of Illinois.

Cramton, P. and T. Palfrey (1990a), "Cartel Enforcement with Uncertainty about Costs," *International Economic Review*, 31: 17–47.

(1990b), "Ratifiable Mechanisms: Learning from Disagreement," Working Paper No. 731, California Institute of Technology.

Crawford, V. (1985), "Efficient and Durable Decision Rules: A Reformulation," *Econometrica*, 53: 817–36.

Dasgupta, P., P. Hammond, and E. Maskin (1979), "The Implementation of Social Choice Rules: Some General Results on Incentive Compatibility," *Review of Economic Studies*, 46: 185–216.

d'Aspremont, C. and L. Gerard-Varet (1979), "Incentives and Incomplete Information," *Journal of Public Economics*, 11: 25–45.

Demski, J. and D. Sappington (1984), "Optimal Incentive Contracts with Multiple Agents," *Journal of Economic Theory*, 3: 152–71.

Dewatripont, M. (1989), "Renegotiation and Information Revelation Over Time:

The Case of Optimal Labor Contracts," *Quarterly Journal of Economics*, 104: 589–620.

Farrell, J. (1983), "Communication in Games, I: Mechanism Design Without a Mediator," mimeo, MIT.

Fishburn, P. (1973), *The Theory of Social Choice*, Princeton: Princeton University Press.

Fudenberg, D. and J. Tirole (1990), "Moral Hazard and Renegotiation in Agency Contracts," *Econometrica*, 58: 1279–319.

Gibbard, A. (1973), "Manipulation of Voting Schemes: A General Result," *Econometrica*, 41: 587–602.

Glazer, J. and R. Rosenthal (1990), "A Note on Abreu-Matsushima Mechanisms," mimeo, Boston University.

Green, J. and J. J. Laffont (1979), *Incentives in Public Decision Making*, Amsterdam: North Holland.

(1987a), "Posterior Implementation in a Two-Period Decision Problem," *Econometrica*, 55: 69–94.

(1987b), "Renegotiation and the Form of Efficient Contracts," HIER DP no. 1338.

Groves, T. (1982), "On Theories of Incentive Compatible Choice with Compensation," in W. Hildenbrand (ed.), *Advances in Economic Theory*, Cambridge University Press.

Groves, T. and J. Ledyard (1977), "Optimal Allocation of Public Goods: A Solution to the Free Rider Problem," *Econometrica*, 45: 783–810.

Harris, M. and A. Raviv (1981), "Allocation Mechanisms and the Design of Auctions," *Econometrica*, 49: 1477–99.

Harris, M. and R. Townsend (1981), "Resource Allocation with Asymmetric Information," *Econometrica*, 49: 33–64.

Harsanyi, J. (1967, 1968), "Games with Incomplete Information Played by Bayesian Players," *Management Science*, 14: 159–82, 320–34, 486–502.

Hart, O. and J. Tirole (1987), "Contract Renegotiation and Coasian Dynamics," *Review of Economic Studies*, 55: 509–40.

Herrero, M. and S. Srivastava (1992), "Implementation via Backward Induction," *Journal of Economic Theory*, 56: 70–88.

Holmstrom, B. and R. Myerson (1983), "Efficient and Durable Decision Rules with Incomplete Information," *Econometrica*, 51: 1799–819.

Hurwicz, L. (1972), "On Information Decentralized Systems," in R. Radner and C. B. McGuire (eds.), *Decision and Organization* (*Volume in Honor of J. Marschak*), Amsterdam: North Holland, pp. 297–336.

(1979), "On Allocations Attainable through Nash Equilibria," *Journal of Economic Theory*, 21: 140–65.

Jackson, M. (1991), "Bayesian Implementtion," *Econometrica*, 59: 461–77.

Johnson, S., J. Pratt, and R. Zeckhauser (1990), "Efficiency Despite Mutually Payoff-Relevant Information: The Finite Case," *Econometrica*, 58: 873–900.

Kohlberg, E. and J. F. Mertens (1986), "On the Strategic Stability of Equilibrium," *Econometrica*, 54: 1003–38.

Kydland, F. and E. Prescott (1977), "Rules Rather than Discretion: The Inconsistency of Optimal Plans," *Journal of Political Economy*, 85: 473–91.

Laffont, J. J. and E. Maskin (1982), "The Theory of Incentives: An Overview," in W. Hildenbrand (ed.), *Advances in Economic Theory: Invited Papers for the Fourth World Congress of the Econometric Society at Aix-en-Provence*, September 1980, Cambridge University Press, pp. 31–94.

Laffont, J. J. and J. Tirole (1987), "Comparative Statics of the Optimal Dynamic Incentive Contract," *European Economic Review*, 31: 901–26.

(1988), "The Dynamics of Incentive Contracts," *Econometrica*, 56: 1153–75.

(1990), "Adverse Selection and Renegotiation in Procurement," *Review of Economic Studies*, 57: 597–625.

Ledyard, J. and T. Palfrey (1990), "On the Optimality of Lottery Drafts: Characterization of Interim Efficiency in a Public Goods Problem," Social Science Working Paper No. 717, California Institute of Technology.

Legros, P. (1990), "Strongly Durable Allocations," CAE Working Paper No. 90–05, Cornell University.

Leininger, W., P. Linhart, and R. Radner (1989), "Equilibria of the Sealed-Bid Mechanism for Bargaining with Incomplete Information," *Journal of Economic Theory*, 48: 107–33.

Ma, C., J. Moore, and S. Turnbull (1988), "Stopping Agents from Cheating," *Journal of Economic Theory*, 46: 355–72.

Mailath, G. and A. Postlewaite (1990), "Asymmetric Information Bargaining Procedures with Many Agents," *Review of Economic Studies*, 57: 351–67.

Maskin, E. (1977), "Nash Equilibrium and Welfare Optimality," mimeo, MIT.

(1985), "The Theory of Implementation in Nash Equilibrium: A Survey," *Social Goals and Social Organization: Volume in Memory of Elisha Pazner*. Cambridge University Press.

Maskin, E. and J. Moore (1989), "Implementation with Renegotiation," mimeo.

Maskin, E. and J. Tirole (1992), "The Principal-Agent Relationship with an Informed Principal, II: Common Values," mimeo, MIT, *Econometrica*, 60: 1–42.

(1990), "The Principal-Agent Relationship with an Informed Principal, I: Private Values," *Econometrica*, 58: 379–410.

Matsushima, H. (1988), "A New Approach to the Implementation Problem," *Journal of Economic Theory*, 45: 128–44.

(1990a), "Unique Bayesian Implementation with Budget Balancing," manuscript, Stanford University.

(1990b). "Characterization of Full Bayesian Implementation," manuscript, Stanford University.

Matthews and Postlewaite (1989), "Pre-play Communication in Two-Person Sealed-bid Double Auctions," *Journal of Economic Theory*, 48: 238–63.

May, K. O. (1952), "A Set of Independent Necessary and Sufficient Conditions for Simple Majority Rule," *Econometrica*, 20: 680–84.

Mookherjee, D. and S. Reichelstein (1990), "Implementation Via Augmented Revelation Mechanisms," *Review of Economic Studies*, 57: 453–75.

(1989), "Dominant Strategy Implementation of Bayesian Incentive Compatible Allocation Rules," mimeo, Stanford University.

Moore, J. and R. Repullo (1988), "Subgame Perfect Implementation," *Econometrica*, 46: 1191–220.

Myerson, R. (1979), "Incentive Compatibility and the Bargaining Problem," *Econometrica*, 47: 61–74.

(1981), "Optimal Auction Design," *Mathematics of Operations Research*, 6: 58–73.

(1983), "Mechanism Design by an Informed Principal," *Econometrica*, 51: 1767–98.

Myerson, R. and M. Satterthwaite (1983), "Efficient Mechanisms for Bilateral Trading," *Journal of Economic Theory*, 29: 265–81.

Palfrey, T. and S. Srivastava (1986), "Private Information in Large Economies," *Journal of Economic Theory*, 39: 34–58.

(1987), "On Bayesian Implementable Allocations," *Review of Economic Studies*, 54: 193–208.

(1989a), "Mechanism Design with Incomplete Information: A Solution to the Implementation Problem," *Journal of Political Economy*, 97: 668–91.

(1989b), "Implementation with Incomplete Information in Exchange Economies," *Econometrica*, 57: 115–34.

(1991a), "Nash Implementation Using Undominated Strategies," *Econometrica*, 59: 479–501.

(1991b), "Efficient Trading Mechanisms with Preplay Communication," *Journal of Economic Theory* 55: 17–40.

(1991c). *Bayesian Implementation*, monograph, to appear in the series, *Fundamentals of Pure and Applied Economics*, Harwood Academic Publishers.

Postlewaite, A. (1985), "Implementation via Nash equilibria in economic environments," in L. Hurwicz, D. Schmeidler, and H. Sonnenschein (eds.), *Social Goals and Social Organization* (*Essays in memory of Elisha Pazner*), New York: Press Syndicate of the University of Cambridge.

Postlewaite, A. and D. Schmeidler (1986), "Implementation in Differential Information Economies," *Journal of Economic Theory*, 39: 14–33.

(1987), "Differential Information and Strategic Behavior in Economic Environments: A General Equilibrium Approach," in T. Groves, R. Radner, and S. Reiter, (eds.), *Information, Incentives and Economic Mechanisms – Essays in Honor of Leonid Hurwicz*, University of Minnesota Press.

Radner, R. (1979), "Rational Expectations Equilibrium: Generic Existence and the Information Revealed by Prices," *Econometrica*, 47: 655–78.

Rajan, M. (1989), "Cost Allocation in Multi-Agent Setting," mimeo, Carnegie-Mellon University.

Repullo, R. (1987). "On the Revelation Principle with Complete and Incomplete Information," in K. Binmore and P. Dasgupta (eds.), *Economic Organisations as Games*, Oxford: Basil Blackwell, pp. 177–95.

Rubinstein, A. and A. Wolinsky (1989), "Renegotiation-proof Implementation and Time Preferences," *American Economic Review*, in press.

Satterthwaite, M. (1975), "Strategy-Proofness and Arrow's Conditions: Existence and Correspondence Theorems for Voting Procedures and Social Welfare Functions," *Journal of Economic Theory*, 10: 187–217.

Satterthwaite, M. and S. Williams (1989), "Bilateral Trade with the Sealed Bid Double Auction: Existence and Efficiency," *Journal of Economic Theory*, 48: 107–33.

Schmeidler, D. (1980), "Walrasian Analysis via Strategic Outcome Functions," *Econometrica*, 48: 1585–94.

Stokey, N. (1979), "Intertemporal Price Discrimination," *Quarterly Journal of Economics*, 93: 355–71.

Thomson, W. (1978). "Maximin Strategies and the Elicitation of Preferences," in J.J. Laffont (ed.), *Aggregation and Revelation of Preferences*, Amsterdam: North Holland, pp. 245–68.

Vickrey, W. (1961). "Counterspeculation, Auctions, and Competitive Sealed Tenders" *Journal of Finance*, 16: 1–17.

Wettstein, D. (1986). "Implementation Theory in Economies with Incomplete Information," Working Paper No. 26–86, Foerder Institute for Economic Research, Tel Aviv University.

Zou, L. (1990), "The Revelation Principle, Multiple Equilibrium, and Communication Regimes," mimeo, Limburg University.

Implementation theory: discussion

Mathias Dewatripont*

Mechanism design may be considered as an esoteric topic by many. The two surveys by John Moore and Tom Palfrey will do much to change this perception, since they provide very clear, up-to-date and complete introductions to this field. The two authors are not content with simply exposing all the major contributions of the area, but they also provide a critical evaluation of its strengths and weaknesses. In this discussion, I will provide a view which is complementary to theirs, since I share many of their evaluations of implementation theory.

I will take as starting point of my discussion two recurring themes on the "state of economic theory as of 1990" as presented in this World Congress, which could be summarized as follows:

(A) our theories often lack predictive power (multiplicity of equilibria in repeated games, indeterminacy under incomplete markets, instability of perfect foresight equilibria);

(B) our results are often derived with unsatisfactory methods (shortcomings of rationality, Nash equilibrium, refinements).

While the various sessions have all mentioned promising work that attempts to address these two problems, it seems clear that the hardest issues are yet to be solved. I shall briefly evaluate how implementation theory has fared in those two respects.

With regard to problem (A), recent developments of implementation theory in fact yield a strong prediction: efficient outcomes can *most often* be implemented, that is achieved *uniquely*. Moreover, these positive results are derived with methods intensive in economic insights but with little mathematical complexity, so that the focus can really be on economic plausibility (which I will address below).

Specifically, under symmetric information between agents, Nash implementation requires monotonicity, not at all an innocuous assumption, since it basically rules out distribution concerns (see Moore, part two, section 2). Recent developments on complete information implementation allows a *dramatic* expansion of the set of implementable outcomes, basically doing away with this requirement. One way to achieve such a result is to appeal to *subgame perfection* (see Moore, theorem 3.1[1]), a now standard refinement of Nash equilibrium in game-theoretic applications. Another route is to appeal to the related refinement concept of *undominated Nash equilibrium* (see Moore, theorem 4.1). A third route is to use *iterated elimination of weakly dominated strategies* (see Moore, theorem 5.3). Finally, a fourth one is to weaken the requirement of Nash implementation itself to be only "*virtual*" (that is, with probability close to one; see Moore, part two, section 6).

One objection to implementation under complete information is the fact that agents cannot be realistically assumed to share exactly the same information: at best their information will only be approximately equivalent. Recent work on Bayesian implementation has however generalized the Nash implementation conditions to incomplete information (see Palfrey, theorem 3, on Bayesian monotonicity as a necessary condition for implementation, and theorems 1, 4, and 5 for sufficient conditions of implementation). These results are thus useful in showing how the complete information approach is *robust* to the introduction of a small amount of incomplete information.

A second set of results on Bayesian implementation weakening the Bayesian monotonicity requirements, in the same spirit as the complete information literature, is now emerging: by appealing to *undominated Bayesian* equilibrium, *iteratively undominated equilibrium or virtual* implementation (see Palfrey, subsection 5.1). The fourth route, Bayesian perfection, has not been investigated, being typically plagued by multiplicity of equilibria and a lack of agreement on further refinement of that equilibrium concept.

In short, implementation theory does have a lot of predictive power, in that almost any economically interesting outcome can be implemented using relatively innocuous definitions of either equilibrium or implementation.

The picture becomes less rosy however when it comes to problem (B), that is, to methods used to derive these positive results. Of course, as a field concerned with *applications* of game theory, implementation theory heavily relies on the foundations of game theory like rationality or Nash equilibrium. My discussion will however not address the shortcomings of these concepts, but will solely concentrate on the *excessive use* of game-theoretic tricks in comparison to "standard" game-theoretic applications.

Indeed, implementation theory is about designing optimal mechanisms or games, instead of analyzing economic problems approximated by "realistic" games. The search for positive implementation results has led to a series of excessively sophisticated games. While there is no reason for *a priori* restricting the set of acceptable mechanisms, it is of some concern that the presumed outcomes of these games rely on extremely subtle equilibrium behavior. If one were to actually apply these games in practice, one can doubt that the agents would play the equilibrium strategies. Optimal mechanisms have thus been questioned on two grounds:

(i) their excessive reliance on Nash equilibrium as a solution concept;
(ii) the fact that, from a purely positive point of view, we do not see these sophisticated message games used in reality.

The first point is addressed in detail in Moore's survey. Let me thus simply make a few remarks. One very common trick in the literature is the use of *unbounded* mechanisms (integer games, tail chasing,...) which are indeed unconvincing ways to eliminate unwanted equilibria. Another common trick concerns the *maintained assumption of rationality* in subgame-perfect implementation, even after one party has made a very big "mistake" (see Moore, part one, section VIII for example). Finally, a third trick concerns the use of *uninformed players* (see Palfrey, example A and theorem 1, which otherwise does not use integer games or any other of these tricks): there, a completely uninformed player is used to eliminate unwanted equilibria because, while he does not know the types of his opponents, he can *perfectly predict* their *strategies*, as always assumed in equilibrium analysis.

Note that these various tricks do not violate the rules of game theory. Instead, the uneasiness comes from the fact that these are played to their full extent, up to a point where their "plausibility" is in question. In short, the types of games constructed for these general implementation results may be of normative use, but are far remote from real-world games. The time has thus come to move away from the question: "how can we implement even more outcomes?" to the question: "which outcomes can be plausibly implemented?".

There are several ways to address this question. One route which has already been taken is to constrain from the start the set of possible games, for example by imposing *boundedness* (Moore, theorems 4.2 and 5.2; and theorem 1 of Palfrey, also satisfy this requirement). Another promising direction which has been taken is to restrict mechanisms to *perfect information* (Moore, theorems 3.2 and 3.3), and especially to games where players move only *once* (simple sequential mechanisms, in which subgame-perfect implementation is much more convincing, see Moore, theorem 3.3).

The above research strategy remedies the most glaring shortcomings of the game-theoretic methodology, even if it unavoidably ends up imposing somewhat arbitrary restrictions on the set of possible mechanisms. Another useful direction is to enquire about the robustness to *preplay communication* (theorem 6 of Palfrey) or about the *renegotiation proofness* of mechanisms (Moore, part one, section IX and part two, section 7). It is worth emphasizing that allowing for renegotiation simplifies efficient mechanisms when, without renegotiation, one would require much more complex mechanisms: in effect, renegotiation can sometimes replace message games altogether (see Moore, part one, section IX), certainly a worthwhile achievement in terms of realism!

These various approaches are in my view a good starting point in the search for plausible mechanisms. Achieving this objective would then amount to completing the two-step procedure which I see as the research program of implementation theory: first, determine the optimal implementable benchmark, using the methods surveyed by Moore and Palfrey; second, investigate how simple, incomplete, contracts can approximate this benchmark. The first step of the procedure, on which implementation theory has mostly focused until now, is a way to guide the incomplete contract analysis and to avoid starting *a priori* from specific and possibly arbitrary simplicity restrictions. In this sense, implementation theory could end up successfully meeting both problems A and B.

Notes

* Université Libre de Bruxelles, CEPR and CORE.

1 In this discussion of the two surveys, I refer directly to the results presented by Moore and Palfrey, not to the original material.

Printed in the United States
By Bookmasters